Paraprofessionals
in
Education

Paraprofessionals
in
Education

Kathryn Jane Skelton

Delmar Publishers

an International Thomson Publishing company I(T)P®

Albany · Bonn · Boston · Cincinnati · Detroit · London · Madrid
Melbourne · Mexico City · New York · Pacific Grove · Paris · San Francisco
Singapore · Tokyo · Toronto · Washington

NOTICE TO THE READER

Cover Design: The Drawing Board

Delmar Staff
Publisher: William Brottmiller
Senior Editor: Jay Whitney
Associate Editor: Erin O'Connor Traylor
Production Editor: Marah Bellegarde

COPYRIGHT © 1997
By Delmar Publishers
a division of International Thomson Publishing Inc.

The ITP logo is a trademark under license.

For more information, contact:

Delmar Publishers
3 Columbia Circle, Box 15015
Albany, New York 12212–5015

International Thomson Editores
Campos Eliseos 385, Piso 7
Col Polanco
11560 Mexico D F Mexico

International Thomson Publishing Europe
Berkshire House 168–173
High Holborn
London, WC1V 7AA
England

International Thomson Publishing GmbH
Königswinterer Strasse 418
53227 Bonn
Germany

Thomas Nelson Australia
102 Dodds Street
South Melbourne, 3205
Victoria, Australia

International Thomson Publishing Asia
221 Henderson Road
#05–10 Henderson Building
Singapore 0315

Nelson Canada
1120 Birchmont Road
Scarborough, Ontario
Canada M1K 5G4

International Thomson Publishing – Japan
Hirakawacho Kyowa Building, 3F
2–2–1 Hirakawacho
Chiyoda-ku, Tokyo 102
Japan

10 11 12 13 XXX 08 07 06 05

Library of Congress Cataloging-in-Publication Data

Skelton, Kathryn Jane.
    Paraprofessionals in education / Kathryn Jane Skelton.
        p.   cm.
    Includes bibliographical references (p.) and index.
    ISBN: 0–8273–8182–4
    1. Teachers' assistants—United States.   2. Teaching—Vocational guidance—United States.   I. Title.
LB2844.1.A8S54   1997
371.14'124—dc21   96–37460
                                                            CIP

Contents

Preface

Paraprofessionals in Education is a view into the worlds of paraeducators. The book is primarily geared toward potential paraeducators, it is designed to help individuals understand the paraeducator role and evaluate their own suitability for paraeducator positions. (For the purpose of this book, *paraprofessional* and *paraeducator* are used interchangeably.) The text guides individuals through the job search process, through the beginning days in an educational setting, and on to becoming more comfortable with an expanding paraprofessional role. *Paraprofessionals in Education* also provides insights for paraprofessionals who are already working in preschool, elementary school, middle school, and special education settings, and for teachers who work with paraprofessionals. The goal is that readers will learn the importance of being an effective member of a successful teaching team.

The text provides information about:

- the variety of roles and work settings for paraeducators;
- the need for working out a balance between the paraeducator and the lead teacher;
- legalities related to a job as a paraeducator;
- basics of child development;
- special education and how it affects paraeducators;
- daily procedures for paraeducators;
- using learning activities and educational games;
- classroom management and organization;
- resources for paraeducators;
- advancing status for paraeducators.

Some special features of the book include:

- tips on interviewing and getting a job as a paraeducator;
- tables and illustrations which will help a potential paraeducator become familiar with components of the job;
- ideas for learning activities, educational games, and organizational pointers that paraeducators can use immediately as they are or as starting points for new ideas of their own;
- appendices with additional forms and tables to aid paraeducators in several aspects of their jobs.

Acknowledgments

The author wishes to acknowledge and express gratitude to the following for their support, encouragement, and information.

The reviewers of my manuscript contributed more than they can possibly know:

    Diane Comer, Becker College
    Milton Miller, Professional Career Development Institute
    Nancy K. French, Colorado University — Denver
    Nancy G. Moseley, Halifax Community College

Thank you to:

My family for so many reasons, especially laundry, dinner, and careful respect for stacks of manuscript.

Family and friends for asking and not asking questions at just the right times.

My editor, Jay Whitney, for giving me this opportunity, and to many of the Delmar staff for their assistance.

Roberta Berns, Rosalind Charlesworth, Lynn Marotz, Eileen Allen, Donna Bennett, Charlotte Meyer and D. Eugene Meyer for their contributions.

Anna Lou Pickett and the National Resource Center for Paraprofessionals in Education and Related Services for permission to share information.

My teacher aunts for their dedication to education and for their encouragement.

Special thanks to Jo Hogan and Mary Wofford, one of the best teacher-paraeducator teams anywhere, for inspiring and sharing.

Also special thanks to Jan Holbrook, who made the trek from stay-at-home mom to substitute teacher, to special education paraprofessional, to college, to special education teacher.

Acknowledgment to Jean Jackson, for her enthusiastic training of paraprofessionals in Cherokee County, Georgia, as well as many other people in the Cherokee County School System, including district personnel, principals, teachers, and paraprofessionals, who have given assistance and served as examples.

CHAPTER 1

Overview for Paraprofessionals

Paraprofessionals or paraeducators are in paraprofessional positions and work under the direct supervision of the professional staff at a school or other educational facility. The prefix *"para"* means "beside, alongside of; associated in a subsidiary or accessory capacity" (Webster's, 1986). These positions are also described as preprofessional.

According to the American Federation of Teacher's Paraprofessional and School Related Personnel (AFT/PSRP), one half million paraeducators work under titles such as instructional aide or assistant, special education or handicapped aide, preschool or early childhood aide, classroom paraprofessional, bilingual aide, and library aide. The titles used vary from state to state and even from division to division within a specific school or center. The old term *teacher aide* brings to mind a military aide-de-camp; a teacher aide is similar in that the assistance given is varied and invaluable. However, in recent years, teacher aide has been associated with more negative, less respected connotations. Educator Tony DiPaolo told his listeners at a preschool convention that *aide* rhymes with *maid* and the term *assistant teacher* should be used instead. Paraprofessional is another term that is used widely, but it is lacking in that it does not indicate to which profession the reference is made, and must be accompanied by further description in order to be definitive. For the purposes of this book, the term *paraeducator* will be used to cover this broad spectrum of people who serve as assistants to teachers and other professionals in an educational setting. This term is used in Canada and is preferred by two American leaders in the field, Dr. Kent Gerlach of Pacific Lutheran University in Tacoma, Washington, and Anna Lou Pickett, Director of the National Resource Center For Paraprofessionals In Education and Related Services, in New York. Anna Lou Pickett states her view this way:

> *In today's schools and other educational provider agencies, they work alongside teachers or other professional practitioners as technicians who are more aptly described as* paraeducators, *just*

*as their counterparts in law and medicine are designated as
paralegals and paramedics.   (1989)*

Paraeducators work with teachers to provide high quality learning
programs. In fact, according to Pickett (1993), "While there are many
reasons for employing paraeducators, the primary and in essence the
only reason is to improve the quality of education and related services
for children, youth, and their parents." Having a paraeducator in the
classroom can benefit the teacher, the children, and the children's families. The teacher profits from help with a multitude of tasks and simply by having an extra set of adult hands (and eyes!) in the room. The
children gain from the extra attention, reinforced explanations, and expanded activities made possible by having a paraeducator. Families benefit from increased communication and additional adult support for
their children.

There are some commonly cited advantages to utilizing
paraeducators, according to Richard White, in an article for *Social Policy.*
These include:

- Increased individualized attention for the students, fewer students
  per adult

- Freedom to have more small groups and one-on-one instruction
  activities

- Additional adult strengths and talents

- Broader observations of the students

- Mutual support and feedback for the teacher

- Connection to other school programs, when the paraeducator ac-
  companies students to other classrooms for special services, such
  as speech therapy

- Help with "time-consuming noninstructional chores"

(1984)

Paraeducators fill many different roles. The duties and responsibilities vary with each job title and setting; they will be unique to specific
situations. In some schools, paraeducators serve as *floaters,* moving
among classrooms to help with special activities. For example, floater
paraeducators may help with reading groups in several classrooms before lunch; then they may help with math and science experiments in

other classrooms in the afternoon. Other paraeducators will be assigned to more permanent partnerships such as working under the direction of the same teacher all day, everyday.

Paraeducators may assist in the following ways:

- Instruction and supervision of individual students or small groups
- Monitoring and scoring tests and class assignments
- Preparation of experiments, projects, demonstrations, and visual displays
- Operation of audiovisual equipment and computers
- Clerical duties such as keeping attendance records
- Fee collection and general housekeeping duties
- Arrangement of the classroom environment, especially bulletin boards

The paraeducator may also share many of the teacher's responsibilities, such as leading children's activities, planning lessons, and interacting with parents. It is often up to the teacher to design the job description for his or her assigned paraeducator. Each teacher and teacher aide duo works out their own balance, establishing responsibilities, and determining boundaries. White wrote that specific job descriptions are helpful when they prevent advantage being taken of a paraeducator, but are a hindrance when they limit the extent with which both the teacher and the paraeducator feel comfortable. White argued that, "the paraprofessional role ought to be dynamic and constantly expanding as the paraprofessional develops professionally" and that the role "needs to be continually redefined and negotiated with the teacher." (1984)

Some recent moves do both: provide for more clarification of roles *and* give opportunity for growth opportunities. Anna Lou Pickett (1993) recommends three levels for paraeducators: an entry level paraeducator, an instructional paraeducator, and an early intervention/childhood teacher assistant and/or transition trainer/job coach. Pickett's model provides for increasingly complex responsibilities and decreases in restrictions for paraeducators passing from a level 1 position to level 2 and on to level 3 positions. In Kansas a statewide system for permits for paraprofessionals who work in special education was developed in the late 1970s. The Kansas system has three levels of special education paraprofessional positions and also allows paraeducators to advance past the entry level. Each level is characterized by differing extents of training and experience.

In the 1980s a three-level certification system was established in Maine for all paraprofessional personnel working in the local public school districts. In Maine, paraeducators are ranked according to their level of training and experience, and have opportunities for advancement (Pickett, 1993).

The roles of paraeducators differ across the United States and even within the same school, but some generalities can be made as to a desirable personality profile for a paraeducator. Most importantly, a paraeducator must show a genuine liking for children. (Essa, 1996) Other desirable traits include:

- Compassion
- Dependability
- Interest in improving skills (Essa, 1996)
- Energy (lots!)
- Flexibility
- Sense of humor
- Discretion
- People skills (ability to work well with children, parents, and co-workers)
- Good example
- Initiative combined with knowledge of boundaries

Many agree that teachers and paraeducators should sense a *calling* or driving motivation to their positions in order to effectively teach and encourage children. Many speak of an indefinable "knack," "being good with kids," or that inner something that delights in children as being the main ingredient for a good paraeducator.

Where do paraeducators work? The locations for employment vary just as the roles do. A paraeducator may work in an elementary school, a middle school, or in a high school. Other opportunities exist in vocational-technical centers, community colleges, adult education programs, preschools, child care centers, and private schools.

The AFT/PSRP states: "The demand for education paraprofessionals has increased steadily since the first teacher aides entered in public school classrooms during the 1950s. Today that demand is fueled by a nationwide education reform movement, which calls for more para-professionals to help teachers make classroom instruction more efficient, effective, and tailored to the individual needs of students." Initially, paraeducators were hired to free teachers from clerical tasks. The idea was that if the teacher did not have to spend time on noninstructional duties, then more time could be devoted to quality teaching. This help was considered beneficial, but not quite good enough. Many felt that paraeducators could make a greater contribution to the classroom (White, 1984). The role of paraeducators has changed since the beginning and continues to change.

One of the advantages to utilizing paraeducators is the improvement in teacher/pupil ratios. The public is rightly concerned with teacher/pupil ratios. There are constant desires and efforts to improve these numbers in most areas. With tight budget constraints, adding paraprofessional positions is a way to add extra help without paying a full professional salary. From 1964 to 1990 the student-to-employee ratio decreased from 13.3 to 6.4. The ratio dropped steadily with the exception of an increase during a recession. The increased numbers of paraeducators have significantly contributed to the improved ratios. ("Monthly Labor Review," 1994)

What are paraeducators paid? Paraeducators earn an average of $6 per hour. Rates may be as low as the federal minimum wage or as high as $15 per hour in areas where unemployment is low or demand for paraeducators is high. Information obtained by the Educational Research Service indicates that the average hourly wage for instructional assistants during the 1994–95 school year was $8.77, and $8.29 for noninstructional assistants. See Tables 1–1 and 1–2. Usually paraeducators are paid for the nine to ten months when school is actually in session. Some school systems break down the pay so that the employee receives a check every month of the year, even during the summer or other vacation times. Figure 1–1 is a copy of a monthly pay check sent to a paraeducator during summer vacation. Sometimes there are different pay scales for paraeducators within the same facility; these may be based on experience and educational levels. In some areas teacher aides with college experience are paid slightly more than those without college experience. The salary chart in Table 1–3 indicates just such a differentiation; Rank I employees have a high school education and Rank II employees have completed a certain level of college education.

TABLE 1–1   What Instructional Assistants Earn.   From "What We Earn: Instructional Assistants" by National Education Association, September 1995, *NEA Today Education Support Edition, 14, 1.* **Copyright 1995 by National Education Association. Used with permission.**

What We Earn — Instructional Assistants

National Average Hourly Wage, 1994-95 . . . . . .**$8.77**
National Average Hourly Wage, 1993-94 . . . . . .**$8.50**
Percent Salary Increase **3.2%**

1994-95 SALARIES BY SCHOOL DISTRICT

ALABAMA, Auburn
Enrollment 4,009
Number of persons in job 34
Low $7.50
High $12.75
Average **$9.50**

CALIFORNIA, Bakersfield
Enrollment 26,312
Number of persons in job 693
Low $7.58
High $11.19
Average **$8.00**

ILLINOIS, Peoria
Enrollment 16,256
Number of persons in job 147
Low $11.72
High $16.82
Average **$14.12**

MICHIGAN, Kalamazoo
Enrollment 12,000
Number of persons in job 101
Low $7.58
High $11.20
Average **$10.62**

NEW JERSEY, Gloucester
Enrollment 1,865
Number of persons in job 19
Low $7.88
High $8.47
Average **$8.35**

OHIO, Akron
Enrollment 32,157
Number of persons in job 160
Low $6.57
High $10.82
Average **$9.28**

TEXAS, Midland
Enrollment 23,100
Number of persons in job 260
Low $5.88
High $11.14
Average **$7.24**

WASHINGTON, Seattle
Enrollment 45,657
Number of persons in job 472
Low $10.46
High $19.48
Average **$14.38**

All figures taken from the *National Survey of Salaries and Wages in Public Schools: Part 3, Wages and Salaries in Paid Support Personnel, 1994-95* © 1995 by Educational Research Service. Hourly wage rates and salaries presented as national averages reflect non-weighted averages of the approximately 1,000 districts that provide data reported to ERS. Appreciation is expressed to ERS for use of these data.

TABLE 1–2 What Noninstructional Assistants Earn. From "What We Earn: Noninstructional Assistants" by National Education Association, September 1995, *NEA Today Education Support Edition, 14, 1.* Copyright 1995 by National Education Association. Used with permission.

What We Earn — Noninstructional Assistants

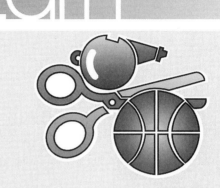

National Average Hourly Wage, 1994-95 ......$8.29
National Average Hourly Wage, 1993-94 ......$8.14
Percent Salary Increase 1.8%

1994-95 SALARIES BY SCHOOL DISTRICT

ALABAMA, Auburn
Enrollment 4,009
Number of persons in job 10
Low $7.50
High $12.75
Average $10.50

CALIFORNIA, Bakersfield
Enrollment 26,312
Number of persons in job 70
Low $7.58
High $11.19
Average $7.80

ILLINOIS, Peoria
Enrollment 16,256
Number of persons in job 35
Low $6.00
High $19.36
Average $10.20

MICHIGAN, Kalamazoo
Enrollment 12,000
Number of persons in job 21
Low $7.04
High $9.92
Average $8.82

NEW JERSEY, Gloucester
Enrollment 1,865
Number of persons in job 4
Low $7.88
High $8.47
Average $8.32

OHIO, Akron
Enrollment 32,157
Number of persons in job 53
Low $7.25
High $11.13
Average $8.81

TEXAS, Midland
Enrollment 23,100
Number of persons in job 15
Low $5.88
High $9.88
Average $6.81

WASHINGTON, Seattle
Enrollment 45,657
Number of persons in job 5
Low $11.11
High $11.55
Average $11.20

All figures taken from the *National Survey of Salaries and Wages in Public Schools: Part 3, Wages and Salaries in Paid Support Personnel, 1994-95* © 1995 by Educational Research Service. Hourly wage rates and salaries presented as national averages reflect non-weighted averages of the approximately 1,000 districts that provide data reported to ERS. Appreciation is expressed to ERS for use of these data.

TABLE 1–3 Sample Salary Schedule for Instructional Aides (1991).

	Rank I Aide		Rank II Aide	
Years of Experience	**Month**	**Year**	**Month**	**Year**
0	622.00	7,464.00		
1	630.09	7,561.00	699.00	8,388.00
2	637.92	7,655.00	706.92	8,483.00
3	645.92	7,751.00	715.00	8,580.00
4	653.84	7,846.00	722.92	8,675.00
5	661.84	7,942.00	730.92	8,771.00
6	669.75	8,037.00	738.84	8,866.00
7	677.67	8,132.00	746.92	8,963.00
8	685.67	8,228.00	754.75	9,057.00
9	693.50	8,322.00	762.67	9,152.00
10	701.50	8,418.00	770.59	9,247.00
11	709.42	8,513.00	778.59	9,343.00
12	717.42	8,609.00	786.50	9,438.00
13	725.50	8,706.00	794.50	9,534.00
14	733.34	8,800.00	802.42	9,629.00
15	743.67	8,924.00	810.34	9,724.00
16	749.17	8,990.00	818.25	9,819.00
17	757.25	9,087.00	826.17	9,914.00
18	765.09	9,181.00	834.17	10,010.00

The table header reads: **Salary Schedule for Instructional Aides FYE 1991**

County Board of Education

Date: 8/31/94   Ck# 228926   NAME   15124

REG. SALARY	ADT'L PAY	TIME LOST	RATE OF PAY	TIME WORKED	SICK BAL	VAC BAL	GROSS EARNINGS
762.59							762.59

DEDUCTIONS & NET PAY

RETIREMENT	FED. W/H	F.I.C.A.	STATE W/H	PAGE	LIFE	HEALTH	DENTAL	
38.13	18.37	52.77	20.77	4.17	1.15	17.10	55.72	
								NET PAY
								554.41

YEAR-TO-DATE

GROSS	FED. W/H	F.I.C.A.	STATE	ANNUITY
6,143.57	157.42	431.16	171.80	

FIGURE 1–1 Sample Paycheck

Jean Jackson, a kindergarten teacher who conducts training work-shops for paraprofessionals in Cherokee County, Georgia, warns paraeducators that "you're not going to be in it for the money" and that they "must get rewards in other ways." Shelby, a paraeducator who works in a child care center says the main disadvantage to her job is the low pay and the fact that she cannot support herself; her salary is secondary. It is true that salaries for paraeducators are, in general, notoriously low. Therefore, high economic rewards cannot be the reason to choose this type of work. A paraeducator receives other valuable rewards, though. One day of observation reveals numerous moments of joy and challenge. There are also moments of great aggravation, but that same child who tries to manipulate you to the point of inward screaming may light up in comprehension and give you a spontaneous hug. There is that definite satisfaction of being useful and leaving a mark.

The reasons for choosing this kind of position are as individual as the people involved in the choosing. There are many good reasons for this choice, including the desire for specific hours (possibly the same schedule as one's own children), working as a paraeducator while pur-

From Shelby, who works in a day care center:

- Advantages to her job
  — She likes the part-time hours.
  — She can instill good values.
  — She feels useful.

- Disadvantages to her job
  —Low pay.
  — Shelby cannot support herself on her wages; hers is definitely secondary income.

- Challenges in her job
  — High noise level.
  — Trying to deal with four children at the same time.
  — Being pulled in different directions.
  — Motivating children. Shelby says that kids "want to veg out," that they tell her, "I just want to sit here."

- Joys in her job
  — Hugs.
  — Affection from the children.

. . . .

An anonymous paraeducator who works in a public elementary school, warns potential paraeducators that paraprofessionals:

- Are the ones who get dumped on.

- Run errands.

- Do the yuck work.

- Have to be able to work with someone else.

- Do much or most of the work and get none of the credit.

suing a teaching degree, and earning a steady supplemental income, with health benefits, but with limited responsibility, and therefore lower stress. Sometimes landing a job as a paraeducator happens quite naturally with the progression from substitute teaching to joining the staff full time.

Children often view their paraeducator as another teacher, but not as the *boss* teacher. The paraeducator does **not** have the final responsibility or authority but paraeducator can make an immeasurable contribution to an educational team and the life of a child. A special education teacher in Kansas City feels that she and her paraeducator work as a team, communicate constantly, and have personalities that mesh well. Richard White (1984) tells of a teacher who shared at a session at the Second Annual Conference on the Utilization and Training of Paraprofessionals in Special Education that she and her paraprofessional partner taught as a team and that it was not always possible for outside observers to tell who was the teacher and who was the paraeducator.

PARAEDUCATOR TRAINING

People who work as paraeducators hold a high school diploma or equivalent G.E.D. Ideally, paraeducators have studied basic subjects (math, English, science, history, etc.) and have at least an introductory knowledge in many areas, including child development and organizational skills. Further training guidelines differ among school systems and child care learning centers. Training ranges from mandatory formal post-high school education to casual orientation and on-the-job training.

In a small school district in Kansas City, Missouri, there is no formal training for paraeducators, but there is a great deal of on-the-job training. Many of them are certified to teach, receive benefits, and a flat monthly salary. Parkhill, a neighboring Kansas city school district makes an interesting distinction between paraprofessionals and teacher aides. In this district, teacher aides have teaching degrees, receive benefits, attend in-service training, and are paid $9.15 per hour. Their paraprofessionals are not certified personnel, receive no training, are paid $6.99 per hour, and are given a "letter of employment" indicating that their jobs are secure only as long as the enrollment numbers remain up.

California state law requires that all paraeducators pass a proficiency test, which includes sections on math, reading, and writing. The

The National Resource Center (NRC) for Paraprofessionals recommends that the goals of all training for paraeducators should be to prepare paraeducators to:

- Understand the value of inclusive education for children and youth with disabilities;

- Understand the rights of children and youth with disabilities and their parents;

- Respect diversity in cultural heritages, life styles, and value systems among children, youth, and their families;

- Understand the distinctions in the roles and duties of professional personnel and paraeducators;

- Communicate effectively with team members, children and youth, parents, and other people they come into contact with on the job;

- Practice ethical and professional standards of conduct;

- Participate effectively in different phases of the instructional process;

- Assist children and youth with disabilities to build self-esteem and interpersonal skills that will help them avoid isolation in different education and living environments;

- Follow emergency, health, and safety procedures established by the agency.

(Pickett, 1993)

Martinez Unified School District in Martinez, California has several classifications of paraeducators:

Instructional Assistant–A
Instructional Assistant–B
Instructional Assistant–C
Instructional Assistant–Bilingual
Instructional Assistant–Health Attendant
Instructional Assistant–Indian Education
Instructional Assistant–Microcomputer
Library Media Assistant

These paraeducators are "trained to do their jobs by the individuals they work with each day." Before being hired they must have a high school diploma and pass the basic skills test required by state law (Correspondence from Director, Administrative Services).

Another California school district, Mt. Diablo, in Concord, offers periodic in-service training such as First Aid and CPR. The Special Education Assistants in that district must complete two of four free training classes. Otherwise, much of the training occurs on-the-job and through a handbook of pertinent information. In the Mt. Diablo District, requirements vary according to the position, ranging from experience with students to two years of college to sign language training (Correspondence with Personnel Specialist).

Paraeducators may be required to hold a diploma, a license, or certain credentials. Depending on the area, these may be required before actual involvement with the children is allowed or may be ordered within a certain time after employment has begun.

For example, in Cherokee County, Georgia, paraeducators are required to attend a four-hour orientation seminar within the first thirty days of employment. There is also a mandatory forty-hour workshop course for all paraeducators hired within the previous year. The course is for paraeducators from elementary school through high school and alternative school. The paraeducators work in all areas, including kindergarten, profoundly retarded special education, vision, and media centers. The course includes a wide gamut of helpful information and training, including theories about learning styles and the chain of command in the county school system. By attending the week of workshop classes the paraeducators earn a license entitling them to work as paraeducators in the county school system for five years, after which their licenses must be renewed.

Day care centers often require their employees to go through Red Cross certification for CPR and First Aid. They allow a certain amount of time for completion. A paraeducator who works in a public school media center may have a deadline for watching training videos and turning in written worksheets and tests pertaining to library science. Again, the training requirements for paraeducators depends on the district standards and the type of work involved.

The *Guidelines for Early Childhood Programs in Associate Degree Granting Institutions* (1985) suggests and recommends that training programs provide opportunities to apply knowledge and skills of working with children in a variety of field experiences with increasing levels of interaction with children. Skills, knowledge, and attitudes gained from this type of training program prepare paraeducators to demonstrate the competencies needed to meet the varying requirements of their employers.

Paraprofessionals in Education is designed to help those who are considering a career as a paraeducator and provides a general orientation for those who have already made this choice. Paraeducators serve all ages, but the primary focus of these materials in on children from birth to grade eight and on special education students of all ages.

PROFESSIONAL CONDUCT

A general consensus is that paraeducators should conduct themselves in a professional manner; they should exemplify professionalism. Professionalism is defined by Webster's as "the conduct, aims, or qualities that characterize or mark a profession or a professional person." Two definitions of professional are:

- Characterized by or conforming to the technical or ethical standards of a profession or an occupation

- Reflecting the results of education, training, and experience (Webster's)

Note some key words: conduct, aims, ethical standards, reflecting results of training. The standards and aims of the teaching profession have traditionally been very high. Paraeducators work alongside teaching professionals and should strive to meet the same high standards of conduct and goals of quality as well. A paraeducator should aim for excellence, optimism about each child's learning abilities, and constant compassion. Desirable traits for paraeducators have been mentioned already. Some aspects of professional behavior are mentioned here and will be considered throughout this book since they are such central components to being a top-rated paraeducator.

Attitude

Creating a positive learning environment in today's highly unpredictable world is a great challenge. As a paraeducator, if you project genuine enthusiasm into the day, you are more likely to be successful in plugging children into learning. By positively reinforcing both students and coworkers, and by demonstrating a willingness to do extra work that benefits the children, a paraeducator exhibits the type of supportive encouraging attitude that is expected and needed. More about attitude will be discussed later in the book as it applies to specific tasks.

Initiative

An important ingredient that blends with attitude is taking initiative. When you are new and unsure, the tendency is to hold back and wait to be told exactly what to do. It *is* essential to respect limits; some actions should be reserved for the teacher or director. However, you should be willing to take the first step if you see a need. A paraeducator needs to move to communicate where appropriate, be available to respond to a child's concern, assist in distributing materials, and so on. Even though the teacher is the certified person, you, too, know the children and have common sense. You should speak up or intervene in suitable ways if you see something wrong. If you step in and your help is not wanted at that point, you may be told so, but, in general, you would be more faulted for lack of initiative than for taking reasonable initiative. One special education teacher says that she would "go crazy" if she had to tell her paraeducator everything. Fortunately she does not have to; she appreciates that the paraeducator who works with her "takes initiative, is perceptive, and is a real child advocate."

Confidentiality

A paraeducator is privy to a great deal of information, some of it personal, about coworkers and children and their parents. It is of utmost importance that teachers, paraeducators, and other school staff members exercise discernment in their communications inside and outside the classroom. Any time privileged information is shared inappropriately, there is a chance of hurting someone. Gossip originating from within a school or center can damage the integrity and reputation of the facility. There is also the possibility of legal action. You never know what might be construed as offensive or the amazing way words can spread. Be careful about sharing personal data about the students or their families; it is really best to confine such discussions to the teacher with whom you work and with the administration. More will be said about this crucial issue.

Dress

What you are expected to wear will depend on where you work and what you are doing. The dress for working in a day care center is often more casual than the dress for working in a private middle school. There are valid reasons for this; physical play and on-the-floor activities make up a large portion of the day in a preschool learning center. In some places and in some situations, the priority concerning dress is to be accessible to the children and make them comfortable. Some day care centers may have employees wear matching, easily identifiable shirts.

Many educational facilities have dress codes for staff members. Even if a dress code is not explicitly stated, you still need to pay attention to what you wear. Use good common sense; do not wear a dress and pantyhose or a dress shirt and tie when your class is going on a nature scavenger hunt. On the whole, though, teaching is a conservative profession. One safe method is to imagine what a teacher should ideally wear, then dress a notch above that.

Decent-length dresses and skirts, dress slacks, blouses, and sweaters are appropriate for women. Dress shirts, with optional tie, and twill or dress pants are fine for men. Neither men nor women should wear sneakers unless approved.

Children (and adults) seem to respond differently to educators in different clothes. You may find that it is easier to gain the children's respect the nicer you are dressed. Think about your own responses. Sometimes it seems that we all snap to attention a little more quickly when confronted with someone who is dressed in a business suit than with someone who is dressed in jeans and a t-shirt. How you dress also reflects on your school or center.

Respect

As a new person in the classroom you must earn the respect of both the students and the lead teacher. *Don't try to be the students' pal.* They will have greater respect and will like you much more if you display fairness and firmness in a warm manner with all the children.

You must make the best decisions you can and then stand by them. You must show that you can accept constructive criticism graciously. Remember that for optimal growth you must be given feedback and suggestions for growth. Be willing to openly discuss both your weaknesses and your strengths with your lead teacher; that helps you become a better paraeducator. Keep in mind that a good paraeducator learns something new every day (Bennett, Meyer & Meyer, 1994).

The flip side of respect involves giving respect. Professional behavior includes showing respect for all you work with—from the children to the janitorial staff to the administration.

Responsibility

As a reliable paraeducator, you are expected to demonstrate responsibility in your attendance and in your task performance. Find out ahead of time who to notify if you are unable to be there; go through proper channels for your school or center. Prioritize tasks constantly. Showing responsibility in daily tasks, getting the most crucial things done, is a big part of professional conduct. Be dependable!

Compassion

One of the best things a paraeducator can give to the children is compassion. That does not mean leniency or accepting less than someone's best. It does mean knowing that children have needs. Compassion is following through to meet those needs with caring and kindness. This may be one of the most important ways a paraeducator can demonstrate true professional conduct.

ETHICAL RESPONSIBILITIES

The National Resource Center for Paraprofessionals lists some ethical responsibilities for paraeducators. If you make fulfilling these responsibilities your goal, you will make great strides in exhibiting the highest standards of conduct as a paraeducator:

- Maintain confidentiality about all personal information and educational records concerning children, youth, and their families.

- Respect the legal and human rights of children, youth, and their families.

- Follow district or agency policies for protecting the health, safety, and well-being of children and youth.

- Demonstrate an understanding of the distinctions in the roles of various education personnel.

- Follow the directions of teachers and other supervisors.

- Maintain a record of regular attendance, arrive and depart at specified times and notify appropriate personnel when [you] must be absent.

- Demonstrate loyalty, dependability, integrity, and other standards of ethical conduct.

- Demonstrate respect for cultural diversity and individuality of the children and youth [with whom you work].

- Follow the chain of command for various administrative procedures.

- Demonstrate a willingness to participate in opportunities for continuing education provided by [your] district or agency.

(Pickett, 1993)

On the subject of ethical conduct for paraeducators, extra attention is required because of the age and vulnerability of young children, and the influence a paraeducator may have with students and with parents. Katz reminds us:

> *In any profession, the more powerless the client is in relation to the practitioner, the more important the practitioner's ethics become. That is to say, the greater the necessity for internalized restraints against abusing that power.*
>
> *Early childhood practitioners have great power over young children, especially in day care centers. Practitioners' superior physical power over young children is obvious. In addition, practitioners have virtually total power over the psychological goods and resources of value to the young in their care. (1987)*

It is an awesome responsibility and privilege to work with children and with older students. The importance of adhering to high standards of conduct and strong ethics cannot be overstated. Again, the imperative for patterns of professional conduct will be threaded throughout this book.

When you work as a paraeducator you have the opportunity to share in the lives of others. The whole paraeducator experience can be viewed as a miniature world, a slice of life, a human laboratory, which will be full of memorable events. As you experience these slices of life, you will grow. You will find your place in relation to people and situations aiming to provide quality care and educationally sound environments for children. Some basics concerning child development will be discussed in the next chapter. The general information in Chapter 2 about how children learn and grow will help you to understand and bring you closer to the children with whom you will work. The children are after all the most important component of your job. After a look at child development there will be further investigation into other aspects of a paraeducator's role.

2 Phases and Stages: Learning About the Children

Imagine a long trip in the car with a four-month-old baby. Most likely everyone in the car is tuned in to signals from that baby. Adults respond to the baby's cries for attention, for food, for soothing, and so on, and they breathe a collective sigh of relief when the baby succumbs to sleep. The baby doesn't notice the beautiful scenery outside the car, the baby doesn't fight with his sister, and the baby doesn't ask how much longer until we get there. The baby simply wants his basic needs to be met.

Now imagine the same trip with a three-year-old. Questions, questions, and more questions! "What is that?" "Why is the road painted black?" "How come cars don't have potties?" A lot of squirming and changing from one activity to another. She sulks when the adults refuse to let her get out of her car seat to change places.

With an eight-year-old, the car scenario is much different. Unlike the four-month-old, he does fight with his sister—CONSTANTLY. He sticks out an entire game of Alphabet, despite a couple of flare-ups: "nobody" helped him find a "J" and there weren't any "Qs" and "who made up this dumb game anyway?"

The car is pretty quiet with a thirteen-year-old. She sleeps, nods her head to the music in her headphones, and asks when they can stop for lunch. For a long time, she scribbles out a plan for spending her babysitting money and another plan for how to earn more. When any adults attempt to engage her in conversation, the responses come in monosyllables.

The car scenarios are certainly dependent on ages and stages, aren't they? Children at different ages and stages are able to do different things, they communicate differently, they respond differently; they are just different!

The phases and stages you see in the children with whom you work will have their own particular delights and challenges. Child development experts differ on theories behind the different phases and stages, but there are some areas of general agreement about what children need and what constitutes *normal development.*

N E E D S   O F   C H I L D R E N

Every child on this planet has certain *basic needs.* These needs must be met in order for individuals to grow and thrive to their fullest possible extent. Needs are separated into categories, physical and psychological, but in actuality are related and dependent on each other. If a child's physical needs are met but his psychological needs are ignored, then that child will be at risk, and vice versa.

Basic physical needs are summed up all our lives in the quick phrase, "food, clothing, and shelter." Think about these a little more deeply, though, and include the following additions:

- Shelter, including safety, protection from harm.
- Food; nutritious food, right for the child's age or immediate health needs.
- Clothing; adequate and appropriate for the climate.
- Medical and dental care; treatment when necessary, and preventive care when possible.
- Cleanliness; sanitary, healthful environment.
- Balance of rest and activity.

(Allen, 1994)

A child's psychological needs include love or affection and consistency, security, and appropriate adult expectations. Children need nurturing; they need to know that they can depend on their parents and caregivers to be there for them. They need "familiar surroundings with parents and caregivers who respond reliably and appropriately to [their needs]" (Allen, 1994). Some other important needs are:

- Acceptance
- The need to learn
- Opportunities to explore and ask questions

- The need for respect

- Opportunities to make and learn from mistakes

- The need to interact with others

- Acceptance of and recognition for accomplishments

> (Allen, 1994, and information from Cherokee County
> Department of Family and Children Services)

Although it is clear to the experts that children do not develop normally if their needs are not attended to, it is difficult to define what constitutes normal development. Allen and Marotz say that, "it implies that a child is growing, changing, and acquiring a broad range of skills according to some unobservable inner pattern or timetable," but also involves "a cumulative or 'building block' process" and "a continuous process of give and take between the child and the environment." They caution that there is no exactly *normal* child, that there is a wide range of normal development for different ages (1994).

Investigators have found that specific developmental events, markers called *developmental milestones* do occur in a standard order and generally occur with certain age ranges. Developmental milestones incorporate skills in several areas—motor, social, cognitive, and language, and include such events as smiling, sitting, walking, and putting two words together. Child development experts have seen that children learn new skills in a sequence of predictable steps, such as rolling over before learning to sit up, and that there are *norms,* typical patterns and typical ages at which babies learn new skills, such as crawling at around eight months old (Allen & Marotz, 1994; Berns, 1994). So we have expectations, called *age-level expectations,* about when and in what order little ones will acquire new skills. Therefore, babies are described as being within the norm, ahead of the norm, or behind the norm (Allen & Marotz, 1994). Roberta Berns says that, "Norms are useful because they provide a reference point for the normal course of development. Some children reach a developmental milestone earlier and some later. However, great deviance indicates a child has a problem" (1994). Some children, because of prenatal or environmental factors, are more likely to have developmental problems; these babies and young children are described as being *at-risk.*

PRENATAL DEVELOPMENT

What happens to a child before birth is vital. Much of the quality of a child's growth and development is related to prenatal beginnings. Factors that promote optimal fetal development include:

- *Prenatal care.* With regular medical supervision, problems and potential complications can often be detected, treated, or prevented.

- *Good nutrition.* Vitamin supplements are frequently given.

- *Healthy weight gain.* Although the numbers have been debated for many years, the current recommendation is that expectant mothers should gain between 22 to 25 pounds during their pregnancies.

- *Balance of sufficient rest and regular exercise.* Pregnancy is a huge physical stressor and fatigue producer; pregnant women need extra sleep and rest. Exercise helps lower stress levels.

- *Positive emotional state, low stress level.* "Prolonged or excessive stress can have negative effects on the fetus by reducing breathing rate, heart beat, and all activity level" (Allen & Marotz, 1994). Of course, it is not possible to get rid of all stress, but rest, a good balanced diet, and exercise do help.

- *Mother's age and health in general.* Studies have shown that the twenties are the best years to have a baby. Prematurity and low birth weight are more common with teenage mothers. Down syndrome and other problems occur more often with older mothers (Allen & Marotz, 1994).

Just as some factors increase the chances for having a healthy baby, there are other factors that have been shown to decrease the chances. Factors that affect a growing fetus in a negative way are called *teratogens*. Depending on when during a pregnancy a teratogen is introduced, different aspects of fetal development are affected. A developing fetus is especially vulnerable during the first weeks of gestation. The following are well-documented teratogens:

- Alcohol consumption: may lead to problems ranging from decreased physical size, smaller brain size, physical abnormalities, to death. The very serious consequences that may result from an expectant mother's alcohol intake are now diagnosed as Fetal Alcohol Syndrome (FAS) or Fetal Alcohol Effect (FAE).

- Smoking: tendency toward prematurity and lower birth weights, learning problems; decreases the amount of oxygen to the fetus.

- Addictive drugs, such as cocaine, heroin, and amphetamines: may cause profound defects or even death.

- Exposure to hazardous chemicals, such as mercury, lead, carbon monoxide, PCBs.

- Radiation.

- Some prescription medications, including tranquilizers, hormones, and antihistamines.

- Some maternal infections, among them, rubella (German measles), AIDS, cytomegalovirus, herpes, syphilis, toxoplasmosis.

(Charlesworth, 1996; Allen & Marotz, 1994)

Other factors are being studied presently. The following teratogen possibilities are controversial, but may be linked to birth defects (Allen & Marotz, 1994):

- Prolonged exposure to high temperatures, such as staying in a sauna or hot tub

- Pesticides

- Secondary smoke

- Some over-the-counter medications

- Electromagnetic fields (created by heating pads, electric blankets, and proximity to high voltage lines)

The timing of prenatal exposure is critical in determining the effects from teratogens. For example, if a woman contracts rubella during the first four to eight weeks of pregnancy when the heart, eyes, and ears are in extremely vulnerable stages of development, then the risk for that woman's baby to be born with heart problems or to be deaf or blind is higher (Allen & Marotz, 1994).

The average weight of a newborn is about 7 1/2 pounds and the average length is about 20 inches. Babies who weigh less than 5 1/2 pounds, low birth-weight babies, are more likely to experience developmental problems. So are premature babies. There are also complications that happen at the time of birth, such as lack of or decreased oxygen to the baby and very difficult deliveries, which increase the possibility for future problems (Berns, 1994).

NORMAL GROWTH AND ACTIVITY PATTERNS

Babies' actions are primarily reflexive at first. As they grow, they become more responsive. There are three main principles that pertain to the way babies develop; these are 1) cephalocaudal, 2) proximodistal, and 3) differentiation and integration. The term **cephalocaudal** refers to the way human development progresses from the head to the feet; cephalocaudal means from head to tail. Babies' heads are their biggest parts when they arrive and they develop before trunks and extremities. Babies gain control over their bodies from the top down. For example, babies hold their heads up, and then they sit up before they stand up (Berns, 1994).

Proximodistal means *near to far* and refers to the way development proceeds from the middle out. Before birth, the heart and other internal organs form before the arms, hands, fingers, legs, feet, and toes. Babies use their arms to reach toward objects long before they are able to use a thumb and forefinger grasp (a pincer grasp) to pick up small objects (Berns, 1994).

Differentiation and integration refer to the way babies become able to perform more "distinct and specific" actions and they are able to "combine and coordinate" simple actions into more complex actions with time. Berns gives the example that if an infant gets a finger caught in a zipper, she will probably cry and thrash her body. Later when the baby is older, actions become more specific, so if the baby gets her finger caught in a zipper again, she will probably still cry, but will probably only move the part that got caught. Even later, the child will be able to verbalize what happened. As the child grows and learns several distinct actions, these actions can be put together to form more complex actions such as rolling over or walking (Berns, 1994).

Chapter Appendix 1 gives a good summary of normal childhood development. This chart, from Roberta Berns' book, *Topical Child Development,* gives information about children from birth through 16 years, and includes skills and growth in six different areas of development: physical, motor, language, cognitive, social, and self.

Chapter Appendix 2, from Allen and Marotz's book, *Developmental Profiles: Pre-birth through Eight,* supplies information about daily routines for children from birth through eight years old. It also includes information about eating, sleeping, playing, and personal care/hygiene patterns at the different levels.

SIGNS OF DEVELOPMENTAL PROBLEMS

It follows that if there is a recognized range in which normal development takes place, that there is also a time when there should be some concern if a little one is way behind the "normal schedule." There are many sources that can tell you what to look for and when to be concerned. The National Easter Seal Society, Berns, and Allen and Marotz (1994) give warning signs or alerts to developmental problems. Chapter Appendix 3, from the National Easter Seal Society, tells many observable indicators of trouble. The chart from Berns (Table 2–1) shows things to look out for in babies. Allen and Marotz advise readers on some developmental alerts. For example, if no one outside the family can understand a child over three years of age, or if a six-year-old is unable to follow simple instructions and complete simple tasks, then there needs to be some follow-up with a professional. Following are some additional things to consider:

- A four-year-old should be able to:
    state his own full name.
    distinguish and name simple shapes.
    hop on one foot.
    dress herself with only a little bit of assistance.
    take care of his own toileting needs.

- A five-year-old should be able to:
    alternate feet when walking down steps.
    follow a series of three simple directions, such as "Go upstairs, get your dinosaur book, and bring it here."
    make appropriate four to five word sentences.
    use scissors to cut along a line.
    listen attentively to a short story.
    play with other children.

- A six-year-old should be able to:
    jump, run, and balance.
    at least try to read and write.
    show some self-control when she wants her way rather than only using unacceptable behavior to try to manipulate.

TABLE 2–1 Watch your baby for these signs *(Source:* R.M. Berns. (1994). *Topical Child Development.* Albany, NY: Delmar Publishers)

Watch your baby for these signs:		
NORMAL DEVELOPMENT	DEVELOPMENTAL PROBLEMS	
– pushes up on arms – holds head up **By 3 Months***	– unable to lift head or push up on arms – stiff legs	– pushing back with head – constantly fisted hand and stiff leg on one side – difficult to move out of this position
– sits with support – holds head up – straight back **By 6 Months***	– unable to lift head – round back – stiff arms	– arms held back – stiff, crossed legs
– sits without support – arms free to reach and grasp **By 8 Months***	– rounded back – poor use of arms for play – stiff legs, pointed toes	– poor head control – difficult to get arms forward – arches back, stiff legs – poor ability to lift head and back – will not take weight on legs
– pulls to stand **By 12 Months***	– difficulty getting to stand – stiff legs, pointed toes	–cannot crawl on hands and knees –uses only one side of body to move
– independent standing or walking **By 15 Months***	– walks on toes on one side of body – holds arm stiffly and bent – excessive tip-toeing when walking	– sits with weight to one side – uses predominately one hand for play – one leg may be stiff

- A seven- or eight-year-old should be able to:
    throw, catch, and climb.
    take care of his own personal needs; dress himself, brush his
        teeth, take a bath or shower.
    make friends.
    demonstrate a longer attention span than younger children.
                                            (Allen & Marotz, 1994)

EVALUATION OF CHILDREN'S DEVELOPMENT AND METHODS OF STUDYING CHILDREN

Newborns are evaluated according to the Apgar Scale one minute after they are born and again five minutes later. This scale was developed by Virginia Apgar in the early 1950s to assess a newborn's heart rate, breathing, muscle tone, circulation, and reflexes. Scores of 0, 1, or 2 are given in each of these five areas, so possible scores are between 1 and 10. Newborns scoring 7 or above are considered to be in good shape, newborns scoring from 4 to 6 need assistance, and newborns who score 3 or less are in critical condition (Berns, 1994).

Another tool used to assess newborns is the Neonatal Behavioral Assessment Scale (NBAS). Whereas the Apgar evaluates a baby's physical condition, the NBAS evaluates behavioral reflexes and responses. The scale was designed by pediatrician T. Berry Brazelton and his colleagues, and tests four categories of behavior: interactive behaviors, motor behaviors, control of physiological state, and response to stress. The NBAS is usually performed when babies are three days old and then again a few days later, and helps to detect when infants are at risk for developmental problems and to identify the best ways to aid at-risk infants (Berns, 1994).

The Denver Developmental Screening Test (DDST) is a standard assessment tool that is widely used by nurses, pediatricians, and educators in the United States to determine the developmental status of children from infancy through six years of age. The test detects developmental *lags* and *delays* in four areas of development: personal/social, fine motor/adaptive, language, and gross motor. A large Atlanta pediatric group screens one-year-old patients with this screening test at their check-ups. Nurses and pediatric assistants spend extra time with the babies determining whether the little ones can perform such tasks as stacking two cubes, picking up a raisin with a pincer grasp, scribbling spontaneously, and rolling a ball back and forth. Some schools use this screening test to assess children before they enter kindergarten. The DDST has been shown to determine developmental problems fairly accurately. Berns reports that, "Follow-up research shows that the abnormal category on the DDST accurately identifies over 85 percent of infants and preschoolers who continue to be developmentally delayed into the middle childhood years, most of whom experience serious learning problems after they enter school" (Berns, 1994; Frankenberg, et al., 1975).

You may also hear about the Gesell tests. These readiness tests focus a lot on fine motor skills such as copying shapes or designs, and printing names. Claims have been made that the Gesell tests do a good job of predicting whether children are ready for school (Carll & Richard), but there have been some criticism and controversy over the tests, especially "regarding using the Gesell as a gatekeeping instrument" (Meisels, 1987). For example, some feel that a child's performance on the Gesell should not be the sole evidence used to deny entrance into kindergarten, that no one should be able to point to the Gesell results and say that a particular child should wait a year before entrance.

There are many ways investigators study child development in general and individual children in particular. Some of these are:

- Naturalistic observation
- Case studies
- Surveys
- Laboratory experiments and field experiments
- Standardized tests, such as the Minnesota Multiphasic Personality Inventory
- Physiological tests, such as galvanic skin response tests (measure anxiety levels through perspiration and electrical conductance), and electromyographs (measure muscle tension)
- Cross-cultural research
- Longitudinal studies
- Cross-sectional studies
- Sequential studies (Table 2-2)
- Diaries
- Parent and child interviews

(Berns, 1994; Charlesworth, 1996)

MAJOR CONTRIBUTORS TO THE FIELD OF CHILD DEVELOPMENT

Just as there is a long list of methods used to learn more about child development, there is also a long list of people who have made significant contributions to the field of child development. The following is certainly an abridged list of people who have had an impact on the understanding of how children develop and learn:

TABLE 2–2 Summary of Ways to Analyze Developmental Change *(Source: R.M. Berns. (1994). Topical Child Development.* Albany, NY: Delmar Publishers)

Study Method	Procedure	Advantages	Disadvantages
Longitudinal Study	Same individuals are observed repeatedly over time	Provides data on changes in aspects of development of individuals over a long period; can analyze relations between early and later behaviors	Time consuming, expensive, dropout rate can lead to biased sample; repeated testing can lead to inaccurate results because of effects of practice; subject to cohort effect
Cross-Sectional Study	Individuals of different ages are observed and compared at one point in time	Provides quick result; inexpensive; provides information on comparing aspects of development of different ages or cultures	Subject to cohort effect, does not provide information on individual developmental change over time
Sequential Study	Individuals of different ages are observed sequentially and repeatedly over time	Provides means by which to study both cohort and developmental effects	More costly and time consuming than cross-sectional study; results cannot be generalized beyond groups studied

Jean Piaget
Erik Erikson
B. F. Skinner
Robert Sears
Albert Bandura
Carl Rogers

Lev Vygotsky
Sigmund Freud
Abraham Maslow
Arnold Gesell
Maria Montessori

The major theorists have approached the study of child development from different perspectives. The *developmental* theories are based on the view that as children physically grow (undergo biological influences or from forces *within)* and learn, then changes in development result. The *behaviorist* theories enter the field from the approach that developmental changes result primarily from forces *outside* children, that change comes about from an interaction between the environment and learning (contextual influences). Then there are yet other theorists who believe that developmental changes are the result of interactional influences, from both outside *and* within children (Berns, 1994; Charlesworth, 1996). See Tables 2–3 and 2–4.

TABLE 2–3 Major Theories of Development *(Source: R.M. Berns. (1994). Topical Child Development.* Albany, NY: Delmar Publishers)

Some Developmental Perspectives	Focus	Sample Theories	Key Theorists
Forces within the child (biological influences)	Biology	Maturation Ethology	Gesell Lorenz, Bowlby
Forces outside the child (contextual influences)	Learning Culture	Behaviorism Social Cognitive Sociocultural Historical	Watson, Skinner Bandura Vygotsky Elder
Interaction between forces within and outside the child (interactional influences)	Psycho-analysis Cognition Systems	Psychosexual Psychosocial Cognitive-Developmental Information-Processing Ecological	Freud Erikson Piaget No major theorist Bronfenbrenner

Sigmund Freud

A theorist whose name is quickly recognized is Sigmund Freud. Freud (1856–1939) was a doctor who specialized in neurology. He based his theory on his work with troubled patients. He used the psychoanalysis technique, whereby a person's troubles could be diagnosed and helped by bringing the contents of the unconscious mind up and out into the conscious mind. Believing that all the activities of the mind were "fueled by energy from the basic instincts" (Berns, 1994), Freud focused on parts of the personality called the id, the ego, and the conscience or super-ego. Freud's theory was comprised of the following stages and beliefs:

- Oral Stage: birth through 1 year—the mouth the focus of activity; normal development dependent on the optimal amount of oral stimulation; child "stuck" or fixated at this stage if experiences too much or too little oral stimulation; cigarette smoking, for example, could be result of oral fixation.

- Anal Stage: 1 to 3 years—toilet training the focus of activity.

TABLE 2–4 Major Theories of Development *(Source: R. Charlesworth. (1996). Understanding Child Development,* 4th ed. Albany, NY: Delmar Publishers)

Tries to Explain Changes in:	Type of Theory	
	Developmental: Growth and Learning Interact	**Behaviorist: Learning is the Main Determiner of Behavior**
Cognitive Area • language • concepts • problem solving • intellectual needs	Cognitive-Developmental (Jean Piaget; Lev Vygotsky) Normative/Maturational (Arnold Gesell) Self-Actualization (Abraham Maslow) Example: A supportive adult and a rich environment with freedom for exploration will allow for learning and intellectual growth.	Behaviorist (B.F. Skinner) Examples: Learning to speak. Learning red, blue, and yellow are colors. Social Cognitive Theory (Albert Bandura) Example: The child observes the language users of his culture and imitates what he sees and hears.
Affective Area • aggression • dependency • cooperation • fears • self-concept • affective needs • motivation	Psychosexual (Sigmund Freud) Psychosocial (Erik Erikson) Self-Concept (Carl Rogers) Self-Actualization (Abraham Maslow) Examples: Through play the young child learns the benefits of cooperation. Dependency must develop first in order for the child to become independent later.	Behaviorist (B. F. Skinner; Robert R. Sears) Examples: Learning to hug and not to hit. Learning to help others. Social Cognitive Theory (Albert Bandura) Example: The child observes another child being praised for helping set the table. The child imitates what he has seen and heard.
Physical and Motor Areas • body size and growth rate • motor skills (creeping, walking, grasping, etc.)	Normative/Maturational (Arnold Gesell) Example: The head and thus the brain has the fastest growth rate during early childhood, therefore neurological growth is rapid and determines cognitive and motor growth.	Behaviorist (B. F. Skinner) Examples: Complex skills such as riding a bicycle or skating, and physically related behavior, such as eating nutritious food. Social Cognitive Theory (Albert Bandura) Example: The child is told to watch while the coach kicks the soccer ball and then is asked to try to kick it the same way.

- Phallic Stage: 3 to 5 years—sex role identification and love and desire for opposite sex parent the focus of activity; conscience developed.

- Latency Stage: 5 to 12 years—an "incubation period;" involvement with school and friends the focus; defense mechanisms developed; (Table 2–5 provides definitions of some common defense mechanisms.) no fixations from this stage.

TABLE 2–5 Some Common Defense Mechanisms *(Source: R.M. Berns. (1994). Topical Child Development.* Albany, NY: Delmar Publishers)

Defense Mechanism	Definition
Repression	Tendency of the ego to push anxiety-producing situations into the unconscious. Thus a person nondeliberately forgets. For example, incidents of sexual abuse are commonly repressed so the conscious mind does not have to deal with them.
Reaction formation	Repressed thoughts from the unconscious appear in the conscious part as opposites. For example, a woman who did not want to get pregnant has a child and becomes overprotective.
Regression	Under stress, a person may revert to using a tactic that was useful in reducing stress at an earlier age. For example, children will often suck their thumbs when faced with a situation they cannot accept.
Denial	The ego shuts itself off from certain realities that cause stress. For example, if a friend is killed in a car accident, a first reaction is "No, it couldn't have happened."
Projection	The tendency to see a disliked or guilt- and shame-producing aspect of oneself in another person. For example, the child who arrives at a hospital might say, "I have to hold my teddy bear tight because he's scared." The child wanted to be held by the parents but consciously knew bravery was required. Thus the child's unconscious desire was projected to the stuffed animal.
Rationalization	Presenting an excuse or justification for an action or behavior in which guilt or shame was felt. It occurs when the real motive for behavior is not accepted by the ego so an altered, less anxiety-producing motive is offered. For example, a student explained why he did not go to class for two days. One day he was ill. On the next day, the student was allowed by a parent to continue sleeping because the parent thought the student was still ill. When the student finally woke up it was late and the class would have been disrupted by a late arrival.
Displacement	A feeling, often anger, is transferred from its original threatening source to a safer, less powerful person or object. For example, one can be angry at a boss but fail to exhibit the feeling. Then the person goes home and yells at her spouse.

- Genital Stage: 12 to 18 or older—enter stage at puberty; opposite sex the focus; mature heterosexual love the normal outcome.

(Berns, 1994; Charlesworth, 1996)

Freud's theory has been criticized, mainly because of his emphasis on the sex drive, and also because his ideas about the structures of personality—the id, the ego, and the super-ego cannot be scientifically demonstrated. Another objection is that his focus was on unhealthy patients and that it may not be fair to generalize his theory to normal, healthy people (Berns, 1994).

Erik Erikson

Erik Erikson, on the other hand, did focus more on healthy development. Whereas Freud's theory is referred to as psychosexual, Erikson's theory is referred to as psychosocial. Contrary to Freud's view that personalities are developed within the first five years of life, Erikson (born in 1902) believed that personalities continue to develop throughout life. Erikson's view is that personalities result from the outcomes of eight different crises that occur at different stages over lifetimes. Successful resolution of the following conflicts, or crises, yield a healthy personality:

- Basic Trust vs. Basic Mistrust: Birth to 1 year—depends on quality and consistency of care; sets groundwork for future relationships.

- Autonomy vs. Shame and Doubt: 2 to 3 years—related to control of bodily functions and behavior.

- Initiative vs. Guilt: 4 to 5 years—child needs to overcome feelings of powerlessness and identify with the same-sex parent.

- Industry vs. Inferiority: 6 to 12 years—children need to develop a "sense of productivity and competence;" affects future ideas toward work and achievement (Berns, 1994).

- Identity vs. Role Confusion: 13 to 18 years and older—return of previous conflicts but at different level: trust vs. mistrust of friends, control reestablished over body and emotions, initiative of getting a job vs. guilt, performance at school, discovering identity and establishing goals the big objectives at this stage, although these continue all through life.

- Intimacy vs. Isolation: young adulthood—conflict between committing to a relationship and giving of oneself without losing one's own identity and not giving of oneself and remaining uncommitted and being lonely.

- Generativity vs. Stagnation: middle adulthood—involves concern over the next generation, making a contribution that will benefit others; negative aspect is self-absorption.

- Ego Integrity vs. Despair: late adulthood to death—reflection of whole life; wisdom the positive goal in this stage; negative outcome "feeling of futility in existence" (Berns, 1994; and Charlesworth, 1996).

Positive and negative happenings during some of Erikson's stages are shown in Table 2–6. Table 2–7 gives a comparison between Freud's and Erikson's theories (Berns, 1994).

Jean Piaget

Jean Piaget (1896–1980) is another name you hear often concerning advances in the study of child development. Piaget believed that "development occurs in an ordered sequence of qualitatively distinct stages and is characterized by an increase in complexity of thought, such as the progression from intuition to logic" (Berns, 1994). This cognitive theorist assumed that people have a "biological basis for acquiring knowledge" (Piaget, 1950), and that "thinking is a behavior that involves adaptation to an environment and results in organization of the mind" (Berns, 1994). Piaget said that humans constantly *assimilate* "schemes," organized patterns of thinking, as they develop. The four stages of cognitive development that Piaget proposed—sensorimotor, preoperational, concrete operations, and formal operations are all different and subsequent stages are more advanced than previous ones (Berns, 1994; Charlesworth, 1996). Piaget's stages of cognitive development are listed and described in Table 2–8.

During the **sensorimotor period,** babies' learning and development are predominantly influenced by what they can feel and do with their bodies. The biggest task for babies during this time is to learn to walk and run. During the **preoperational period,** the focus of development changes to language and speech. Charlesworth says that a child in this stage "develops almost all the speech skills he will use the rest of his life" (1996). Children learn new skills from imitating others during this period. Piaget found that a child in the preoperational stage would be egocentric, "meaning that he centers his perception on the most obvious and is bound by what he sees" (Charlesworth, 1996). Piaget also identified a **transition period,** which takes place between five and seven. During the transition period, a little one's thinking changes; a child becomes able to see things from other people's point of view and he isn't quite as apt to be fooled by appearances either (Table 2–9) When a child hits the **concrete operations period** she is able to look at more than the obvious and consider more than one variable at a time. Her thinking

TABLE 2–6 Healthy and Unhealthy Psychosocial Behavior *(Source: R.M. Berns. (1994).* Topical Child Development. *Albany, NY: Delmar Publishers)*

Infant **Trust:** relates well to caregivers; knows parent will return	**Mistrust:** cries at being left with caregivers; distances self from caregivers or is clingy
Toddler **Autonomy:** begins to control bodily reactions and emotions; takes pride in doing things for self; is assertive	**Shame/Doubt:** difficulty in controlling self; exhibits helplessness; is withdrawn
Preschooler **Initiative:** asks questions; exhibits imagination	**Guilt:** exhibits passive behavior; is conforming
School-ager **Industry:** enjoys achieving and producing; meets challenges confidently	**Inferiority:** is discouraged; avoids challenges
Adolescent **Identity:** exhibits self-confidence; is cooperative; can confront problems and ask for help	**Role-Confusion:** exhibits self-doubt, excessive conformity, or rebelliousness; avoids confronting problems (e.g., substance abuse, delinquency, running away, suicide)

TABLE 2–7 A Comparison of Psychosexual and Psychosocial Theories *(Source: R.M. Berns. (1994).* Topical Child Development. *Albany, NY: Delmar Publishers)*

Approximate Age	Freud's Psychosexual Theory	Erikson's Psychosocial Theory
Infant: 0–18 months	*Oral:* psychic energy concentrated on need of hunger	*Trust vs. Mistrust:* develop sufficient trust in others to explore the world
Toddler: 18 months–3 years	*Anal:* psychic energy concentrated on need for elimination	*Autonomy vs. Doubt:* develop control over behavior; carry out intentions
Preschooler: 3–6 years	*Phallic:* psychic energy concentrated in genital organs	*Initiative vs. Guilt:* develop sense of responsibility for own actions
Schoolage: 6–12 years	*Latency:* sexual energy channeled into other behavior	*Industry vs. Inferiority:* develop sense of self-esteem through interaction with peers
Adolescence: 12–20 years	*Genital:* earlier resolution of conflicts return for reconsideration	*Identity vs. Role Confusion:* develop sense of identity
Young Adult: 20–40 years		*Intimacy vs. Isolation:* develop relationship with another person
Middle Adult: 40–65 years		*Generativity vs. Stagnation:* develop sense of productivity in work and raising families
Old Adult: >65 years		*Integrity vs. Self-Despair:* develop sense of satisfaction with one's life

TABLE 2–8 Piaget's Stages of Cognitive Development *(Source: R.M. Berns. (1994).* Topical Child Development. *Albany, NY: Delmar Publishers)*

Approximate Age	Stage	Activity
0–2 years	Sensorimotor	Action on environment through motor activity (e.g., touching) and perceptual activity (e.g., seeing)
2–7 years	Preoperational	Development of language (use of symbols to represent actions)
7–11 years	Concrete Operations	Development of reasoning ability on real objects or experiences
11–15 (+) years	Formal Operations	Development of reasoning on abstract and hypothetical problems

grows closer to that of an adult, but it is still pretty literal, or *concrete.* Some important skills acquired during this period include:

- Classification—ability to categorize objects.

- Conservation—"ability to understand the transformation of materials without being fooled by appearances" (Charlesworth, 1996). (Look at Table 2–9 again.)

- Seriation, or ordering—putting things into correct sequence.

- Spatial concepts—understanding prepositions such as in, on, over, under, etc.

- Causality—figuring out "why."

LANGUAGE DEVELOPMENT

If you work with young children, it is likely that you will be charmed by the words they say and how they put them together. Language acquisition is an amazing phenomenon; investigators have determined that "language development proceeds through the same stages in every culture" (Charlesworth, 1996). There are three types of rules used with language. The first set of rules deals with which sounds to use and how to put the appropriate sounds in order. These first rules involve phonemes,

TABLE 2–9 Change in Thinking

Change in Thinking				
Stage	First Position		Transformation	
Preoperational View	Ten		More Now More than Ten	
Concrete Operational View	Ten		Same Number, Still Ten	

the basic units of sound, and morphemes, the smallest meaningful units of speech. The second set of rules, syntax, concern placing words in correct sequences to form acceptable sentences and phrases. The last language rules, semantic and pragmatic, concern the meanings of words and phrases and choosing the most appropriate language for specific situations (Berns, 1994; Charlesworth, 1996).

Babies generally come forth with their much heralded first words at about one year of age. Usually their first words refer to objects or people that are important to them or to familiar parts of their lives. Some common characteristics of beginning speech are:

- Overextension—when one single word is used for many different meanings. An example is a little one's use of *milk* to mean other liquids as well, and *doggie* to include cats, rabbits, and even horses.

- Underextension—when a word's meaning is incorrectly restricted, such as limiting *car* to only those vehicles that look like the family minivan.

- Holophase—when a single word is used to convey an entire thought.

(Berns, 1994)

Observations have shown that children put two words together about seven months after they say their first words (Reich, 1986). Children usually put two words together between 18 and 24 months of age. The beginning sentences of toddlers are called *telegraphic speech,* because only the most meaningful words are included. Then, usually between two and three years old, children's language develops to the point of using more than two words in a sentence, and they're on their way to speaking in paragraphs. Sentence lengths at the beginning stages are often measured in terms of *mean length utterances*, the average of the number of morphemes rather than actual words used. For example, "The kitty is purring" has more morphemes than "The cat makes noise," (5, because the suffix *ing* has meaning, compared to 4), even though the number of words is the same (Berns, 1994).

The rate at which children progress through the steps from simple language to complex language depends upon "inborn capacity and the response from the environment" (Charlesworth, 1996). As a para-educator, there are ways you can enhance that response from the environment and promote normal language development. Some good things for you to do include:

- Provide infants with a great amount of exposure to language, through talking and singing, describing actions and things in the environment.

- Respond to babies' communication efforts, including their gestures and facial expressions. Label things they point to and ask them questions about what they want.

- Read to little ones from very young ages on. Read, read, and read some more. Encourage them to read by giving opportunities, incentives, and choices. Limit television and electronic games.

- Encourage children's communications by listening attentively and being responsive.

- Encourage children to write with introductions to many forms, such as letters, journals, diaries, and descriptions of happenings or pictures.

(Berns, 1994)

Research has provided some interesting insights about the way adults commonly speak to babies. All over the world, adults, especially mothers and caregivers, have a special way of talking to babies, often called *baby talk*. Generally, baby talk is composed of short simple sentences, and slow, high-pitched speech. Some experts call this type of speech *motherese;* others call it *child-directed speech*. Language development researchers have found that this child-directed speech serves several big functions, that it actually helps babies to acquire language (Charlesworth, 1996; Berns, 1994; and Ferguson, 1977).

OTHER ASPECTS OF DEVELOPMENT

Emotional Development

During the early years, children learn about emotions, how to label them, and how to handle their emotions in appropriate ways. Selma Fraiberg is one who believes that adults are too quick to try to stifle the feelings of children and says that a little person has "the right to feel" (1959). Young children often deal with fear, of both real and imaginary parts of life. Hyson and others advise that the normal fears of young children are best handled by "facing them and not pretending they do not exist" (Charlesworth, 1996). Hyson (1979) makes some suggestions about dealing with children's fears:

- Talk to children about their fears. Help them to describe their fears through words or word pictures, or by showing pictures.

- Let children act things out with role plays or other drama opportunities.

- Use a desensitization, or gradual process, to build up tolerance or acceptance of a feared object. Expose a fearful child to "little bits at a time." For example, if a little one is scared to get in a large swimming pool, let the child play in a tub of water, then a small wading pool, and so on.

- Help children learn coping skills for dealing with their fears. Prepare for fearful situations whenever possible. For example, read books or use puppets to help a child get ready for a hospital visit.

- Be honest. Don't ever tell a child something is "no big deal" if it is big to him, or that it "won't hurt" if it might very well hurt.

Humor

There are even recognized stages of developing a sense of humor. Honig (1988) reports that the first actions of smiling and laughing build a foundation for later humor. Toddlers think it is funny when they or others mislabel objects; preschoolers find humor in absurdity and like plays on words. Children between five and seven are big on riddle jokes (and often find humor going through all the riddles in a book over and over and over for days and days!). As children become adept at concrete operations, their humor becomes more sophisticated (Charlesworth, 1996).

Moral Development

Moral values go through changes as children grow and develop. Kohlberg (1968) and Piaget (1965) have proposed that as people become less egocentric their moral judgments become more mature. Piaget's theory is that children go from a stage of *moral realism* through a transition stage and then to a final stage of *moral autonomy.* In the moral realism stage, children focus on their own desires, are controlled by outside forces such as fear of punishment or loss of approval, and key in to amounts of damage rather than intentions when they evaluate wrong-doing. Later, hopefully, people arrive at a stage where morals are internalized and they do the right thing just because it is the right thing and not out of fear of punishment or censure (Charlesworth, 1996). Lickona (1983) suggests that moral development takes place according to the following briefly summarized six stages:

- Stage 0: Egocentric Reasoning—preschool years through about 4; characterized by seeing things from their own point of view, and testing the limits.

- Stage 1: Unquestioning Obedience—about kindergarten age; characterized by respect for authority and tattletaling.

- Stage 2: What's-In-It-For-Me Pairness—early elementary grades; characterized by less belief that the adult's viewpoint is *the* right one, many comparisons with others, and demands for equal treatment.

- Stage 3: Interpersonal Conformity—middle to upper elementary grades on through possibly to mid-teens; characterized by search for social approval and self-esteem.

- Stage 4: Responsibility to "The System"—high school years or late teen years; characterized by cooperation and desire to be a "responsible person."

- Stage 5: Principle and Conscience—young adulthood; characterized by respect for others and actions being motivated more by moral principles and conscience than outside forces.

(Charlesworth, 1996)

Kohlberg and Lickona (1990) suggest that having a "just community" atmosphere in classrooms enhances moral development. Some techniques you can use to encourage good moral development in the children you teach are:

- Let students help make rules.

- Provide clear moral objectives for the classroom. Have well-stated, clear rules, make sure children know policies of fairness, such as taking turns, etc.

- Allow groups to make decisions together.

- Foster a moral community.

- Develop and encourage caring, respectful relations.

- Give opportunities for children to learn and play cooperatively.

(Charlesworth, 1996)

HELPING CHILDREN TO DEAL WITH THEMSELVES AND WITH OTHERS

Any time you work with people, you will see those who are more and those who are less accepted by the group. As a paraeducator you will see some children who are not popular, who just do not seem to fit in. Roopnarine and Honig (1985) pointed out that some unpopular children are *socially isolated,* withdrawn from others, and possibly very shy, while other unpopular children, possibly very aggressive, who try to interact with their peers, but are rejected. Charlesworth says that:

> *This has become an important area for study since it has been discovered that peer rejection during the elementary school years is predictive of school dropout, antisocial behavior, delinquency, sexual disorder, and psychopathology in adolescence and early adulthood. (1996)*

The hope is that these children can be identified early and then be helped. When helping less accepted children with social skills, be especially careful with shy children. Bullock (1993) reports that approximately 15 percent of all children are born with a tendency toward shyness and warns that shy children are likely to pull away even more if they are pushed (Charlesworth, 1996). Roopnarine and Honig found out from research into the subject of unpopularity that popular children usually stick with popular children and unpopular children generally hang around unpopular children (1985). Therefore, children who are not popular do not get as much opportunity to see how popular children interact with each other and to learn social skills from them. Charlesworth gives insight into a big difference between the two types of interactions, saying that, "Popular children give and receive more positive reinforcement than unpopular children" (1996). Rubin (1982) reports that the play among less accepted children is "less cognitively mature." This becomes a real vicious cycle because social play has been shown to enhance cognitive development (Charlesworth, 1996).

Berns (1993) offers some suggestions for educators and parents and others who work with children. These are listed below, with some added suggestions, especially concerning kindness, which often seems to be lost in this world.

- Be an example by demonstrating helpfulness, cooperation, and sharing.

- Discuss, teach, and *preach prosocial behavior.* Use everyday circumstances and happenings to teach children about sharing, helping, and being kind.

- Be warm and accepting.

- Set firm standards of behavior with clearly stated consequences for disobedience. Make sure children understand the reasons for rules.

- Provide drama opportunities (play writing and role plays) for children to learn about how actions affect others.

- Provide activities that enhance and require cooperation, such as group projects and learning games.

- Give specific suggestions about how children can be kind, cooperative, and helpful.

- Praise good interactions; *prosocial behavior.*

- Do not tolerate aggressive or unkind behavior. Help children figure out other ways to solve problems.

- Anticipate possible situations where unkind or aggressive behavior is more likely to occur and try to ward it off through redirection or preparation.

A concept that often goes hand in hand with popularity is self-esteem, because a person's self-esteem "emerges from interactions with others" (Berns, 1994). Self-esteem refers to the "value that an individual places on her identity." Self-esteem is usually described as falling on a range from high to low. Berns says that, "One's level of self-esteem has been shown to influence such things as one's general satisfaction with life, one's relationships with others, and one's achievement" (Table 2–10) (1994). Coopersmith (1967) believes that self-esteem is composed of the following four parts:

1. Competence—a person's success in meeting demands for achievement.

2. Power—a person's ability to control and influence others.

3. Virtue—a person's adherence to moral and ethical standards.

4. Significance—the acceptance, attention, and affection a person receives from others.

Harter (1983, 1989) has developed scales, Self-Perception Profiles, for measuring the self-esteem of middle grade children and adolescents. Her scales evaluate responses to statements about self-worth, such as "I have a lot of friends" and "I am good at school work." In addition to the five areas measured in her scales for children-scholastic competence, athletic competence, social acceptance, physical appearance, and behavioral conduct, Harter includes the categories of job competence, romantic appeal, and close friendship in the scales for adolescents (Berns, 1994).

TABLE 2–10 Terms Relating to Self (Source: R.M. Berns. (1994). *Topical Child Development.* Albany, NY: Delmar Publishers)

Term	Definition	Influences	Measure
Self-concept	Perception of one's identity as distinct from others	maturation, cognitive development, culture	observation of mirror-image interviews
Self-esteem	value one places on her identity	parenting, peer-interaction, achievement (history of success or failure) cultural ideal type	Piers-Harris Scale Self-Perception Profile
Self-control	control of one's actions, emotions, thoughts	interactions with environment, interactions with others	Locus of Control Scale (internal or external)

Berns offers some suggestions for aiding the way children feel about themselves. As a paraeducator, these may be some of the most important gifts you can give to the children with whom you work:

- Enable children to feel loved through warmth and affection, acceptance, talking and listening.

- Enable children to be autonomous by letting them do things by and for themselves, giving them choices, allowing them to explore, giving them challenges, and encouraging pride in achievement.

- Enable children to be successful. Set a good example, set clear limits and explain consequences for behavior, praise accomplishments, and help children learn from their mistakes.

- Enable children to interact with others by giving them opportunities to work things out with others, helping them understand the points of view of others, allowing them time to work and play together, and helping them to understand and deal with feelings.

- Enable children to be responsible by expecting them and providing them opportunities to take care of their own and community things, encouraging them to help others, and helping or giving them a chance to correct their mistakes.

(Berns, 1994)

DEVELOPMENTALLY APPROPRIATE CLASSROOMS AND PRACTICES

Many of those who have studied child development have ideas about good and bad places for children to learn and good and bad ways to teach and deal with children. A term heard often in reference to facilities and methods is *developmentally appropriate* (Charlesworth, 1996). The National Association for the Education of Young Children (NAEYC) defined developmentally appropriate practice as "a safe and nurturing environment that promotes the physical, social, emotional and cognitive development of children birth to eight while responding to the needs of families. Appropriate environments provide children challenges, support and success based on individual needs, interests and learning abilities" (from a brochure from the Quality Early Education Coalition). For you and the teacher with whom you work to use good developmentally appropriate practices, you must consider how children grow and develop and apply these considerations to your plans and your interactions with children.

A major concept that you need to be aware of in your work as a paraeducator is that of *self-fulfilling prophecy,* "the process by which one's initial belief, prediction, or impression elicits behavior that confirms the belief, prediction, or impression" (Berns, 1994). Good and Brophy (1984) have explained that educators contribute to self-fulfilling prophecies when they see standardized test scores or past records, for example, from students and then they tend to treat students according to the expectations they have formed based on what they have seen or been told. Good and Brophy say that teachers treat students differently based on their expectations, giving them different levels of attention and approval. That, in turn, affects how children perform and how they feel about themselves (Berns, 1994). The idea behind this is that if a child is treated as if he were capable, he will believe that he is capable. If a child is treated as if she can do math well, she will believe that she can do math well. If a child gets the message that he is stupid, he will believe he is stupid, and will likely act in such a way as to fulfill the initial message.

Bearing in mind what you have learned about child development, developmentally appropriate practices, and self-fulfilling prophecy, you can see that as a paraeducator it is so important for you to have realistic and compassionate expectations about what children can and will do, to communicate in ways they can best understand, and provide them with the strong message that you believe they are wonderful people with their own unique capabilities and with the potential to do great things.

Appendix 1 Normal Child Development

Age birth–8 months

Physical Development

Birth:	*Average size:* 7 1/2 lbs. 20 in. long.
1 month:	*Average size:* 10 lbs., 21 in. long. *Sleep:* needs 16 hrs. per day. *Hearing:* can perceive differences among various sounds
2 months:	*Perception:* preference for fixation on faces and for red and blue colors rather than greens and yellows.
3 months:	*Sleep:* needs 14 hrs. per day.
4 months:	*Hearing:* can locate source of a sound.
6 months:	*Average size:* 16 1/2 lbs., 26 in. long. *Teeth:* lower central incisors appear, total of 2 teeth. *Perception:* depth perception begins to develop.
7 months:	*Teeth:* lower lateral incisors appear, followed by the central incisors, total of 6 teeth.

Motor Development

Birth:	moves around a lot, kicks, lifts and turns head, waves arms, head sags when not supported.
1 month:	lifts chin when lying on stomach.
2 months:	holds head erect when held
3 months:	steps when held erect, turns from side to back, reaches for objects but misses them, hands mostly open; no grasp.
4 months:	sits with support, hands open and close, stares at and shakes objects held in hands.
5 months:	sits on another's lap, rolls from back to side, grasps objects without using thumbs.
6 months:	sits in high chair, uses hands for support when sitting alone, reaches with one hand, grasps dangling objects, moves objects from one hand to the other.
7 months:	sits without support, attempts to crawl, rolls from back to stomach.
8 months:	stands with help, crawls (arms pulling body and legs), uses thumb in grasping, picks up small objects with thumb and fingers.

Language Development

1 month:	cries, makes small throaty noises.
2 months:	crying markedly decreased at 8 weeks, begins producing vowel-like cooing noises; sound, however, not like adults.
3 months:	cries less, coos, gurgles at the back of the throat, squeals, and occasionally chuckles.
4 months:	eyes seem to search for speaker, cooing becomes pitch-modulated; vowel-like sounds begin to be interspersed with consonantal sounds, smiles and coos when talked to.
5 months:	vowel sounds are interspersed with more consonantal sounds (*f, v, th, s, sh, z, sz,* and *n* common) which produces one-syllable babbling. Displays pleasure with squeals, gurgles, and giggles and displeasure with growls and grunts.
8 months:	displays adult intonation in babbling; often uses two-syllable utterances such as *baba, didi, mama,* imitates sounds. Reduplication or more continuous repetition becomes frequent. Utterances can signal emphasis and emotions.

Cognitive/Piagetian Development

Birth–1 month: *Sensorimotor development—substage 1: Reflexes:* activating reflexes, sucking, grasping, staring, listening are actions that trigger reactions or responses. *Object permanence:* objects have no independent existence. *Space:* no single organized space exists, rather a collection of separate spaces related to specific sensorimotor schemes (e.g., visual space, tactile space). *Causalty:* no sense of cause and effect, at most events are related to needs and tensions. *Times:* it is "practical" and linked to feelings of need and effort.

1–4 months: *Sensorimotor—substage 2: Primary circular reactions:* first acquired adaptations, assimilation becomes separated from accommodation and there is a coordination of reflexes, sucking a pacifier differently from a nipple or grabbing a bottle to suck it. *Object permanence:* no interest in vanishing objects, they exist only as part of an action.

4–8 months: *Sensorimotor—substage 3: Secondary circular reactions:* tries to preserve interesting sights, responds to people and objects, actions are repeated because of their consequences. *Object permanence:* objects just seen are searched for, if thrown there is an anticipation where they may fall, if objects are partially hidden they are reached for, objects are also associated with others' actions. *Space:* initial awareness of spatial relations between objects but still defines all space in terms of actions. *Causality:* perceives own actions as having effect. Magical sense of causality, feeling of efficacy, of relating to acts. *Time:* elementary sense of before and after as part of action, recollects the immediate past but own acts remain central to sense of time.

Social Development

Attachment: 0–3 months; reacts to other people and environmental events indiscriminately; uses sucking, rooting, grasping, smiling, gazing, cuddling, and visual tracking to maintain closeness to primary caretaker; at 6 months seeks out mother and reacts to her especially (Bowlby).

Period of trust vs. mistrust: will last until age 2. Mother is main human relationship; successful outcomes of a dilemma at this stage produce hope and trust in the environment and the future knowing that others will care for the basic needs of nourishment, sucking, warmth, cleanliness, and physical contact (Erikson).

Play: 1 1/2 months, smiles responsively; 3 months, smiles spontaneously; 7 months, plays peek-a-boo. *Oral stage:* the mouth is the focus of pleasurable sensation and feeding is the most stimulating activity (Freud). *Emotions:* distress to 6 months expressed by cries because of hunger, fatigue, pain, cold, loud noises, or sudden loss of support. Pleasure and contentment occur when securely wrapped or cuddled, rocked, or well fed. Enjoys hearing soothing sounds and looking at interesting sights. Smiles a half smile at pleasant sounds or full stomach at 6 weeks; social smile or grins at another's face at 4 months; laughs and smiles broadly at something particularly exciting at 6 months. *Fear:* at 1 month, often looks scared when placed in a warm bath or held high up; at 6 months, intrigued rather than intimidated; at 7 months, wariness sets in.

Self-Development

0–1 month: shows no awareness of body.

2 months: "discovers" hands when catches of sight of them, becomes fascinated by their movement, but "loses" them when they move out of line of vision.

4 months: smiles at self in mirror.

7 months: pats own mirror image.

8 months: still has no concept of where own body ends and someone else's body begins.

Age 9–17 months

Physical Development

9 months: *Teeth:* upper lateral incisors appear, total of 8 teeth.

10 months: *Sleep:* needs 13 1/2 hrs. per day.

12 months: *Average size:* 22 lbs., 30 in. long. *Teeth:* lower 1st molars appear, total of 10 teeth. *Body changes:* child has average body temperature of 99.7°F.

14 months: *Teeth:* upper 1st molar appears, total of 12 teeth.
16 months: *Teeth:* lower cuspids appear, total of 14 teeth.

Motor Development
9 months: stands holding on to furniture.
10 months: sits up easily, pulls up to stand, creeps (arms and legs alternate, body free).
11 months: creeps on hands and feet, walks when led.
12 months: seats self on floor, walks a few steps without help, holds and releases a ball.
13 months: crawls up stairs.
14 months: stands alone, will take a few steps unaided.
15 months: walks alone.

Language Development
10 months: understands some words and associated gestures (e.g., "no" and shakes head); may pronounce *dada* or *mama* and uses holophrases (single words with many different meanings).
12 months: employs more holophrases such as *baby, bye-bye,* and *hi;* may imitate sounds of objects, such as *bow-bow;* has greater control over intonation patterns, gives signs of understanding some words and simple commands (e.g., "show me your eye"). Has produced the sounds of many languages and mastered the sounds of his own.

Cognitive/Piagetian Development
9 months: *Sensorimotor—substage 4: Coordination of secondary circular reactions:* adaptation and anticipation occur; becoming more deliberate and purposeful in responding to people and objects; schemes now have goals. *Object permanence:* pursues hidden objects presumed to be at a previous site. *Space:* comprehends relation between object in front of and behind a barrier; interested in displacement of objects seen from different perspectives. *Causality:* understands means-ends relationships; uses others to achieve effects. *Time:* emergence of ability to remember events when own acts are not central; continued confusion of time and space.
12–18 months: *Sensorimotor—substage 5:* exploration and experimentation by varying behavior to achieve goals. *Object permanence:* monitors all visible displacements. *Space:* understands body as occupying space, moves objects all around and studies relations among them. *Causality:* understands that cause is external to self, takes into account spatial factors in cause-effect relationships. *Time:* can retain more events and an event series for a longer interval: more differentiation of time from own reactions occurs.

Social Development
Attachment: at 9–12 months, maintains attachment link over some distance with eyes, increasingly takes initiative in contacts; begins to fear strangers. Mother is central figure to whom infant seeks physical proximity and contact (Bowlby). *Play:* spends most time in solitary play but will increasingly spend more time in play with mother; at 9 months, plays pat-a-cake; at 13 months, plays ball with another older person; at 16 months, imitates housework. *Social skills:* at 14 months, drinks from a cup. *Anal stage:* at 1 year the anus is the focus of pleasurable sensations (Freud). *Emotions:* at 12 months, cries of frustration when forced to do something against will; cries when can't reach toy on a table; at 13 1/2 months, indicates wants without crying. *Pleasure:* smiles and laughs for same reasons most young children do; great joy is expressed for actions performed and at play with others. *Fear:* from 11–18 months, frightened by height and depth, a strange adult, a jack-in-the-box, a toy dog that moves, a mask, a loud noise.

Self-Development
10 months: responds to own name.
12 months: with development of object permanence, begins to realize that other people exist; can name family members (e.g., "dada, mama, baby").
16 months: teases and plays with parent.

Age 18–24 months

Physical Development
18 months: *Average size:* 24 lbs., 32 in. tall. *Teeth:* upper cuspids appear, total of 16 teeth.
20 months: *Teeth:* lower 2nd molars appear, total of 20 teeth.
23 months: *Sleep:* needs 13 hrs. per day.
24 months: *Average size:* 27 1/2 lbs., 34 in. tall. *Body changes:* brain development at 75% its full adult weight.

Motor Development
18 months: runs awkwardly and falls a lot, pulls and pushes toys, throws a ball, fills a spoon but spills it when inserting it into mouth.
24 months: walks smoothly, runs well and with legs apart, walks alone up and down stairs, jumps, kicks large ball, builds tower of 6 or 7 blocks, turns book pages singly, holds glass in one hand, places marks on paper, uses scribbles (vertical and circular) to cover all or part of a page.

Language Development
18 months: vocabulary of about 30 words, increasing rapidly. Some words begin to have a general meaning (e.g., *dog* means any dog; *black* or *white, live* or *toy, big* or *small*). Words that are easily produced (*beep-beep, tu-tu*) said one at a time. Sounds heard are easily imitated. Babbling is reflective of adult speech, more intricate intonation patterns used.
20 months: begins to use 2- or 3-word sentences.
24 months: begins to use 4- or 5-word sentences. Vocabulary has 50–400 or more words. Easily repeats words and simple sentences produced by adults. Speech becoming a mechanism to communicate a request, a wish, an impression. During play, speaks a lot about own actions and speech is more emotionally expressive. All phrases appear to be own creation.

Cognitive/Piagetian Development
18–24 months: *Sensorimotor—substage 6: Beginning of thought:* new schemes or meanings devised through mental combinations before acting, thinking before doing and creating in new ways. *Object permanence:* can now take invisible displacements into account. *Space:* understands that goals may be reached by many different paths. *Causality:* infers causes from effects and effects from causes by mental representation. *Time:* can recall remote events; represents past and future; time exists apart from individual experiences.
24 months: *Beginning of preoperational or symbolic stage;* becomes able to represent something with something else; uses representation and mental imagery in speech, play, gestures and with mental pictures.

Social Development
Attachment: at 20 months, long-term separation from mother will lead to protest, then despair, followed by relative detachment (Bowlby). *Period of autonomy vs. shame and doubt:* will last until age 4. Parents are main human relationship; child learns to be self-sufficient in many activities, and opportunities to try out these skills will lead to a sense of self-control, self-esteem, and autonomy; overprotection or a lack of support will lead to doubt (Erikson). *Play:* by 2 years, involved in parallel play with peers; decrease in time spent playing with mother. *Social skills:* at 18 months, uses a spoon; at 22 months, helps with simple tasks in the house. *Emotions:* has developed empathy, shame, embarrassment, and pride. *Fear:* decline begins to occur again. Aggression: begins to appear at 2 years.

Self-Development
18 months: self-consciousness emerges.
24 months: labels self using own name. Able to recognize mirror image.

Age 3–4 years

Physical Development
3 years: *Average size:* 32 lbs., 38 in. tall. *Sleep:* needs 12 hrs. per day. *Perception:* still slightly farsighted—easier to see distances.
4 years: *Average size:* 37 lbs., 40 in. tall.

Motor Development
3 years: rides tricycle, can walk on tiptoe, hops with both feet, runs smoothly, walks up and down stairs one foot on each step, buttons and unbuttons, pours from a pitcher, builds tower of 9 blocks and makes bridge with 3 blocks, tries to make the basic shapes (triangles, circles, and squares), catches ball, arms straight.
3 1/2 years: uses basic shapes, scribbles to make designs, uses circles within circles, etc.
4 years: balances on 1 foot for 5 seconds, hops on 1 foot, can walk forward heel to toe, throws ball overhand, dresses self, catches small ball, elbows in front of body, does stunts on tricycle, descends short steps, alternating feet, hand preference nearly established.

Language Development
3 years: sentences contain many words with plural endings. Uses the declarative in a raised tone to ask questions. Sometimes uses nouns or other substantives with a negative word to express negation. A greater variety of emotions is now reflected in speech. Vocabulary is about 850 words. Can understand meaning of adult speech about events that have not personally been experienced. Easily repeats songs. Begins to use subordinate sentences. Most pronunciation correct except *r, l,* and the hissing sounds.
4 years: vocabulary of about 1500 words; most grammatical endings now known; deviation from adult speech more style than grammar. Begins to use future tense; two or more ideas are regularly expressed in complex sentences. Comprehends feelings (e.g., cold, tired) and prepositions; recognizes color names.

Cognitive/Piagetian Development
3 years: *Symbolic phase of preoperational stage* still in effect. *Imagination:* ability to pretend during play develops; engages in dramatic play. *Conservation:* beginning development of the conservation of amount. *Egocentrism:* reduction in the amount of egocentrism; more able to take other people's perspectives into account. *Classification:* objects are included in a particular class for personal reasons (e.g., "this makes a house"). *Time:* talks almost as much about the past and future as about the present; often pretends to tell time and talks about time a great deal; tells how old he is, what he will do tomorrow or on his birthday.
4 years: *Intuitive phase of preoperational stage* begins to operate; the thought processes begin to involve such things as a new understanding of relationships. *Motivation:* rewards continue to need to be fairly immediate and sensual; still very sensitive to praise and attention. *Time:* past and future tenses very accurately used; refinement in the use of time words; broader concepts expressed by use of month, "next winter," "last summer" a much clearer understanding of daily sequence of events emerges.

Social Development
Attachment: by age 4, will accept temporary absence of mother without protest and will accept substitute attachment figures (Bowlby). *Play:* at 3 years, most children involve themselves in peer play; by 4 years, most involved in cooperative play.
Social skills: at 3 years, washes and dries hands and face; at 4 years, dresses with or without supervision. *Phallic stage:* both sexes have sexual fantasies about their parents for which they feel guilty; stage will last until age 6 (Freud). *Sex role and identity;* knows own sex but does not realize maleness and femaleness are permanent characteristics. *Moral development:* rules of a game are sacred and unchangeable but they tend to be applied in an egocentric manner.

Self-Development

3 years: period of acute possessiveness and egocentrism. Capable of scanning and responding to inner states (e.g., identifying mood states and changes in one's own moods).

4 years: beginning to understand "mineness" and "ourness" and to see self as reflected in others. If told he is cute or devilish will include these characteristics in own self-concept. Adult responses to that image give him a positive or negative image about himself.

Age 5–7 years

Physical Development

5 years: *Average size:* 41 1/2 lbs., 43 in. tall. *Sleep:* needs 11 hrs. per day. *Perception:* development has advanced so that child can scan and focus reasonably well. *Body changes:* brain development at 90% full adult weight; average body temperature at normal 98.6°F; fewer stomachaches, digestive system more regular, fewer ear infections, distance from outer ear greater, respiratory infections lessened due to a longer trachea.

6 years: *Average size:* 45 1/2 lbs., 46 in. tall. *Teeth:* at 6 1/2 permanent upper and lower 1st molars and lower central incisors appear.

7 years: *Average size:* 53 lbs., 47 in. tall. *Teeth:* at 7 1/2 permanent upper central incisors and lower lateral incisors replace baby teeth.

Motor Development

5 years: catches bouncing ball with elbows at sides, balances on 1 foot for 10 seconds, skips, descends large ladder, alternating feet easily, throws well, copies designs, letters, numbers, triangles, and squares, folds paper into double triangle, tries to form pictures of animals, people, and buildings.

6 years: can walk backwards heel to toe, running speed increases, jumping forms basis of many games and improves.

7 years: balance improves, more details are added to art work.

Language Development

5 years: language increasingly resembles adult models.

6 years: average vocabulary now 2500 words.

7 years: can recall grammatical sentences rather than strings of words and can make grammatically consistent word associations.

Cognitive/Piagetian Development

5 years: *Conservation:* beginning to understand the conservation of number. *Classification:* done largely on the basis of color.

6 years: *Classification:* done largely on the basis of shape discrimination using visual perception rather than touch. *Memory:* capacity is well developed and labeling aids greatly in recalling pictures.

7 years: beginning of *concrete operational period:* capable of certain logic so long as manipulation of objects is involved. *Classification:* uses definitions for grouping centering on one dimension, but still unable to use class inclusion. *Creativity:* drawings of the human are quite well defined and designs are very representative of reality.

7 1/2 years: *Conservation:* understanding of conservation of length, seriation, and number. *Motivation:* rewards come from correct information; begins to adopt internal standards of performance. *Humor:* ability to understand riddles.

Social Development

Period of initiative vs. guilt: the family is the main human relationship; children freely engage in many adultlike activities, and parents' patient answering of questions leads to initiative; a restriction of activities and treatment of questions as nuisance leads to guilt (Erikson). *Latency period:* not a stage but rather an interlude when sexual needs are relatively quiet and energy is put into learning skills—will continue until age 11 (Freud). *Aggression:* physical fighting often used as a means of solving problems or defending one's image. *Sex role and identity:* at 6 years, realizes that sex is a permanent characteristic. *Moral development:* rules in games are important as codes that must be respected, but they can be changed; children are more able to cooperate and share because they are less egocentric and develop a characteristic way of responding to others.

Self-Development

Understands that self is part of interrelated group of others (e.g., family, friends, kinships). Develops understanding that self is a sexual person and forms preferences for own sex. Perceives self as a moral person with goals for an ideal self. Understands self as initiator of novel and creative interactions.

Age 9–10 years

Physical Development

9 years: *Average size:* 68 lbs., 53 in. tall. *Sleep:* needs 10 hrs. per day. *Teeth:* permanent upper lateral incisors and lower cuspids. *Perception:* well-developed ability to read fine print.

10 years: *Average size:* males, 78 lbs., 58.7 in. tall; females, 77.5 lbs. 59.2 in. tall. *Teeth:* at 10 upper and lower 1st bicuspids and upper 2nd bicuspids appear, total now 26 teeth. *Body changes:* females begin to have rounding of hips, breasts and nipples are elevated to form bud stage, no true pubic hair yet.

Motor Development

Increased gains in vigor and balance in motor control and coordination; manual dexterity increases; greater muscular strength develops; improvement in accuracy, agility, and endurance; girls continue to run faster than boys; throwing and catching are better; jumping and climbing are done with ease and assurance; eye-hand coordination is good.

Language Development

Acquires an average of 5000 new words in this age range. Knowledge of syntax fully developed. Has the ability to understand comparatives (longer, deeper), the subjunctive (*if I were a. . .*), and metaphors (*rotten egg, dirty rat*). Language has become a tool and not just words that refer only to objects. Specialized vocabularies develop for different situations (e.g., games).

Cognitive/Piagetian Development

9 years: *Concrete operation period* still in effect: logic and objectivity increase; deductive thinking begins to appear. *Conservation:* understands conservation of area. *Causality:* has a firm grasp of cause-effect relationships. *Humor:* begins to appreciate use of certain metaphors in joking because of an understanding of the incongruous elements.

10 years: *Conservation:* understanding of the conservation of substances acquired. *Classification:* elements classified using a hierarchical construct. *Space:* able to make or interpret simple maps and distances. *Memory:* memory tasks involve use of mnemonic devices.

Social Development

Period of industry vs. inferiority: has been ongoing since age 7; the neighborhood and school are now the main source of human relationships. Children are busy learning to be competent and productive using skills and tools, exercising dexterity and intelligence to gain praise for their accomplishments leading to industry. Limitation of activities, feeling inferior, criticism, and inability to do well lead to inferiority (Erikson). *Aggression:* reduction in physical fighting to defend self-image; verbal duels now become the tool. *Sex role and identity:* at 10 years, emphasizes social roles more than physical development, believing that "men should act like men and women like ladies."

Self-Development
Develops a great variety of new skills and activities that lead to a sense of effectiveness.

Age 13–14 years

Physical Development
13 years: *Average size:* females, 99 lbs., 62 in. tall; males, 93 lbs., 60 in. tall. *Sleep:* needs 9 hrs. per day. *Teeth:* upper cuspids, upper and lower 2nd molars, and lower 2nd bicuspids appear, total number now 28. *Body changes:* average girl has had 1st menarche, pubic hair has appeared, hips have widened and shoulders narrowed, uterus becomes enlarged, vaginal lining thickens and secretion becomes acid, areola and nipples elevate to form primary breast; males, testes increase in size, scrotum grows, penis grows in length and circumference.

14 years: *Average size:* females, 108 lbs., 63 in. tall; males, 107 1/2 lbs., 64 in. tall. *Body changes:* average male has had 1st ejaculation; penis, testes, and scrotum continue to grow and become larger, prostate and seminal vesicles mature, voice lowers with growth of the larynx, peak period for height spurt occurs.

Motor Development
Boys are now able to run faster than girls, grip strength continues to increase, with boys showing greater strength. Motor awareness becomes somewhat uneven due to growth in muscles and bones, responses are now often quick, jerky motions. Balance is now quite mature. Girls tend to be better than boys in accuracy, agility, and rhythmic activities.

Language Development
Vocabulary increases to about 50,000 words. Increased use of specialized vocabularies (lingo) for additional new situations.

Cognitive/Piagetian Development
13 years: *Formal operational period* has begun and will continue throughout adulthood. *Conservation:* understanding of the conservation of weight now well established. *Logical reasoning:* has firm grasp of the general laws of inverse relationship; ability to reason during a discussion becoming more highly developed; persuasion is used rather than threats.

14 years: *Conservation:* ability to understand the conservation of volume develops. *Logical reasoning:* solutions to problems of logical thinking involve imaginative answers and often evoke the possibility of extenuating circumstances.

Social Development
Period of identity vs. role confusion: will last through adolescence: peer group and leadership models are the main source of human relationships. Individual sees self as unique and integrated person and tries to establish sexual, ethnic, and career identities; inability to establish leads to confusion (Erikson). *Genital stage:* the genitals are the focus of pleasurable sensation and satisfaction is reached through sexual stimulation. This stage will last into and throughout adulthood and its goal is a healthy life of love and work (Freud). *Sex role and identity:* at 14 adolescents emphasize psychological differences rather than physical

or social differences (e.g., women cry more easily than men and are not as aggressive as men). *Moral development:* understanding of social rules (good behavior is considered behavior that pleases other people) and law and order (right behavior means obeying laws set down by those in power) established.

Self-Development

Development of the concept of one's physical appearance, evaluation of that appearance is based on the culture's "body ideal."

Age 16 years

Physical Development

Average size: Females, 117 lbs., 63 1/2 in. tall; males, 129 lbs., 67 1/2 in. tall. *Sleep:* need 8 hrs. per day. *Teeth:* upper and lower 3rd molars appear, full set of teeth present for a total of 32. *Body changes:* in females, pubic hair fully developed, breasts filled out to adult form; in males, facial and body pubic hair nearly fully developed.

Motor Development

Slowdown in increases in height and weight allow for stabilization and reorganization of motor and muscle patterns. Boys' physical strength has doubled that found at age 12. Agility, control, and balance are greatly improved. Boys' throwing, catching, striking, and kicking have improved over girls. Endurance is greatly improved for both sexes.

Language Development

Increase in vocabulary continues and average number of words understood is 80,300. When defining words fuller and more abstract concepts are used.

Cognitive/Piagetian Development

Classification: is able to flexibly shift category criteria and can use abstract as well as perceptual categories. *Logical reasoning:* ability to use verbal transitive inference develops. *Memory:* "metamemory" improves; ability to assess own memory develops; mnemonic strategies greatly improved and used more often. *Egocentrism:* an "adolescent egocentrism" develops and adolescent will create an imaginary audience where he fantasizes how others will react to his appearance and behavior.

Social Development

Attachment: bonds become basic in the development of a self-reliant, mature adult able to form stable relationships. *Moral development:* beginning to understand social contracts (rules in society exist for the benefit of all and are established by mutual agreement) and universal ethical principles (general principles that determine right and wrong, e.g., do unto others, life is sacred) are established.

Self-Development

Development of the characteristics of adolescent egocentrism—the psychological rather than the physical world is primary. Period of search for identity, the self now the object of multiple role expectations

(Berns, 1994)

Appendix 2
Daily Routines

BIRTH TO 28 DAYS

Eating

- Takes 6 to 10 feedings, a total of approximately 22 oz. or 660 ml per 24 hours at the beginning of this period; later the number will be reduced to 5 or 6.
- Drinks 2 to 4 ounces of breast milk or formula per feeding.
- Takes from 25 to 30 minutes to complete a feeding.
- Expresses the need for food by crying.

Bathing, Dressing, Toileting Needs

- Signals the need for diaper change by crying (if crying does not stop when diaper has been changed another cause should be sought).
- Enjoys bath; keeps eyes open and gives other indications of pleasure when placed in warm water.
- Expresses displeasure when clothes are pulled over head (best to avoid over-the-head clothes).
- Enjoys being wrapped firmly (swaddled) in a blanket; swaddling seems to foster feelings of security and comfort.

- Has 1 to 4 bowel movements per day.

Sleeping

- After the first few days, has 4 to 6 sleep periods per 24 hours; one of these may be 5 to 7 hours in length.
- Falls asleep toward the end of feeding.
- Cries before falling asleep (usually stops if held and rocked briefly).

Play and Social Activities

- Enjoys light and brightness; may fuss if turned away from the light.
- Stares at faces in close visual range (10–12 inches; 25.4–30.5 cm).
- Signals the need for social stimulation by crying; stops when picked up or put in infant seat close to voices and movement.
- Content to lie on back much of time.
- Before being picked up, need to be forewarned by first being touched and talked to.
- Enjoys lots of touching, fondling, and holding; may become fussy with over-stimulation.
- Enjoys "en face" (face to face) position.

1 TO 4 MONTHS

Eating

- Takes 5 to 8 feedings, each 5 to 6 ounces, per day.
- Begins fussing before anticipated feeding times; does not always cry to signal the need to eat.
- Needs only a little assistance in getting nipple to mouth; beginning to help by using

own hands to guide nipple.
- Sucks vigorously; may choke on occasion with the vigor and enthusiasm of sucking.
- Becomes impatient if bottle or breast continues to be offered once hunger is satisfied.
- Not ready to eat solid foods.

Source: K.E. Allen, & L. Marotz. (1994). *Developmental Profiles: Pre-birth through Eight,* 2nd ed. Albany, NY: Delmar Publishers)

Daily Routines (Continued)

---

1 TO 4 MONTHS *(continued)*

Bathing, Dressing, Toileting Needs

- May enjoy bath; kicks, laughs and splashes.
- Has one or two bowel movements per day; frequently skips a day.
- Establishes a regular time for bowel movements according to infant's own pattern.

Sleeping

- Often falls asleep for the night soon after the evening feeding.
- Begins to sleep through the night; many babies do not sleep more than 6 hours at a stretch for several more months.
- Averages 14 1/2 to 17 hours of sleep per day; often awake for 2 or 3 periods during the daytime.
- Thumbsucking may begin during this period.
- Entertains self before falling asleep: "talks," plays with hands, jiggles crib.

Play and Social Activity

- Spends waking periods in physical activity; kicking, turning head from side to side, clasping hands together, grasping objects.
- Becoming "talkative;" vocalizes with delight.
- Likes being talked to and sung to; may cry when the social interaction ends.
- Appears happy when awake and alone (for short periods of time).

---

4 TO 8 MONTHS

Eating

- Adjusts feeding times to the family's schedule; usually takes 3 or 4 feedings per day, each 6 to 8 ounces, depending upon sleep schedule.
- Shows interest in feeding activities; reaches for cup and spoon while being fed.
- Able to wait half hour or more after awakening for first morning feeding.
- Has less need for sucking.
- Begins to accept small amount of solid foods, such as banana and cereal, when placed well back on tongue (if placed on tip, infant will push it back out).
- Closes mouth firmly or turns head away when hunger is satisfied.

Bathing, Dressing, Toileting Needs

- Enjoys being free of clothes.
- Splashes vigorously with both hands and sometimes feet during bathtime.
- Hands moving constantly; nothing within reach is safe from being spilled or dashed to floor.
- Pulls off own socks; plays with strings and buttons and velcro closures on clothing.
- Has one bowel movement per day as a general rule.
- Urinates often and in quantity; female infants tend to have longer intervals between wetting.

Sleeping

- Awakens between 6 and 8 a.m.; usually falls asleep soon after evening meal.
- No longer wakens for a late-night feeding.
- Sleeps 11 to 13 hours through the night.
- Takes 2 or 3 naps per day, (however, there is great variability among infants).

Play and Social Activity

- Enjoys lying on back; arches back, kicks, stretches legs upwards, grasps feet and brings them to mouth.
- Looks at own hands with interest and delight; may squeal or gaze at them intently.
- Enjoys playing with soft, squeaky toys and rattles; puts them in mouth, bites, and chews on them.
- "Talks" happily to self; gurgles, growls, makes high squealing sounds.
- Differentiates between people: lively with those who are familiar, anxious about or ignores others (this is sometimes referred to as a period of "stranger anxiety").
- Likes rhythmic activities: being bounced, jiggled, swung about gently.

Daily Routines (Continued)

8 TO 12 MONTHS

Eating

- Eats three meals a day plus midmorning or midafternoon snacks, such as juice and crackers.
- Begins to refuse bottle (if this has not already occurred).
- Has good appetite.
- Enjoys drinking from a cup; holds own cup; will even tilt head backward to get the last bit.
- Begins to eat finger foods; may remove food from mouth, look at it, put it back in.
- Develops certain likes and dislikes for foods.
- Very active; infant's hands may be so busy that a toy is needed for each hand in order to prevent cup or dish from being turned over or food grabbed and tossed about.

Bathing, Dressing, Toileting Needs

- Enjoys bath time; plays with washcloth, soap and water toys.
- Loves to let water drip from sponge or washcloth.
- Shows great interest in pulling off hats, taking shoes and socks off.
- Fusses when diaper needs changing; may pull off soiled or wet diaper.
- Cooperates to some degree in being dressed; helps put arm in arm holes, may even extend leg to have pants put on.
- Has one or two bowel movements per day.
- Occasionally dry after a nap.

Sleeping

- Willing to go to bed; may not go to sleep immediately, but will play or walk about in crib, then fall asleep on top of covers.
- Sleeps until 6 or 8 o'clock in the morning.
- Plays alone and quietly for 15 to 30 minutes after awakening; then begins to make demanding noises signaling the need to be up and about.
- Plays actively in crib when awake; crib sides must be up and securely fastened.
- Takes one afternoon nap most days.

Play and Social Activities

- Enjoys large motor activities: pulling to stand, cruising, standing alone, creeping. Some babies are walking at this point.
- Enjoys putting things on head: basket, bowl, cup; finds this very funny and expects people to notice and laugh.
- Puts objects in and out of each other: pans that nest, pegs in and out of a box.
- Enjoys hiding behind chairs to play "Where's baby?"
- Throws things on floor and expects them to be returned.
- Shows interest in opening and closing doors and cupboards.
- Gives an object to adult on request; expect to have it returned immediately.
- Responds to "no-no" by stopping; on the other hand, the infant may smile, laugh, and continue inappropriate behavior, thus making a game out of it.

Daily Routines (Continued)

THE TODDLER (12–24 MONTHS)

Eating

- Has a decreased appetite; lunch is often the preferred meal of the day.

- Sometimes described as a finicky or fussy eater; may go on food jags; neither requires, nor wants, a large amount of food.

- Occasionally holds food in mouth without swallowing it; usually indicates child does not need or want any more to eat.

- Uses spoon with some degree of skill (if hungry and interested in eating).

- Has good control of cup: lifts it up, drinks from it, sets it down, holds with one hand.

- Helps feed self; some two-year-olds can feed self independently; others need help.

Bathing, Dressing, Toileting Needs

- Tries to wash self; plays with washcloth and soap.

- Takes off own shoes, stockings, some pants; attempts to dress self, often with little success: tries to put both feet into one pant leg, puts shirt on backwards or upside down.

- Helps when being dressed; puts arm in armhole, lifts feet to have socks put on.

- Lets parent or caregiver know when diaper or pants are soiled or wet.

- Begins to gain some control of bowels and bladder; complete control often not achieved until around age three. Bowel training can begin around twelve months; control is often achieved by eighteen months. Begins some bladder control after eighteen months.

Sleeping

- Falls asleep around 8 or 9 p.m.; however, will often fall asleep at dinner if nap has been missed.

- Makes many requests at bedtime for stuffed toys, a book or two, a special blanket.

- Has some problems going to sleep; overflow of energy shows itself in bouncing and jumping, calling for mother, demanding a drink, insisting on being taken to the bathroom, singing, making and remaking bed, all of which seems to be ways of "winding down."

Play and Social Activities

- Developing a strong sense of property rights; "mine" is heard frequently. Sharing is difficult, hoards toys and other items.

- Enjoys helping, but gets into "trouble" when let alone: smears toothpaste, tries on lipstick, empties dresser drawers.

- Enjoys talking about pictures; likes repetition, as in *Drummer Hoff, Mr. Bear, Dr. Seuss.*

- Enjoys walks; stops frequently to look at things (rocks, gum wrappers, insects); squats to examine them; much dawdling with no real interest in getting any place in particular.

- Still plays alone (solitary play) most of the time, though showing interest in other children, lots of watching; parallel play once in awhile but no cooperative play as yet (exception may be children who have spent considerable time in group care).

- At bedtime needs door left slightly ajar with light on in another room; seem to feel more secure, better able to settle down.

- Continues naps; naps too long or too late will interfere with bedtime.

- Wakes up slowly from nap; cannot be hurried or rushed into any activity at this time.

Daily Routines (Continued)

TWO-YEAR-OLDS

Eating

- Appetite is fair; fluctuates with periods of growth; lunch is often the preferred meal.

- Sometimes described as a picky or fussy eater; often has strong likes and dislikes (which should be respected); may go on food jags (only eating certain foods such as peanut butter/jelly sandwiches, macaroni and cheese).

- Likes simple "recognizable" foods; dislikes mixtures; wans foods served in familiar ways.

- May need between-meal snack; should be of good nutritive value, with "junk" foods unavailable.

- Increasingly able to feed self, but may be "too tired" to do so at times.

- Has good control of cup or glass, though spills happen often.

- Learns table manners by imitating adults and older children.

Sleeping

- Amount of nighttime sleep varies between 9 and 12 hours.

- Still requires afternoon nap; needs time to wake up slowly.

- May resist going to bed; usually complies if given ample warning and can depend on familiar bedtime routine (story, talk time, special toy).

- Takes awhile to fall asleep, especially if overly tired; may sing, talk to self, bounce on bed, call for parents, make and remake the bed (these seem to be ways of "winding down").

Bathing, Dressing, Toileting Needs

- Enjoys bath if allowed ample playtime *(must never be left alone);* may object to being washed; tries to wash self.

- Usually dislikes, even resists, having hair washed.

- Tries to help when being dressed; needs simple, manageable clothing; can usually undress self.

- Shows signs of readiness for bowel training (some children may have already mastered bowel control).

- Stays dry for longer periods of time (one sign of readiness for toilet training); other signs may include interest in watching others use toilet, holding a doll or stuffed animal over toilet, clutching self, willingness to sit on potty for a few moments, expressing discomfort about being wet or soiled.

Play and Social Activities

- Enjoys dressing up and imitating family activities: wearing father's hat makes child a "daddy."

- Likes to be around other children, but does not play well with them: observes them intently, imitating their actions (parallel play).

- Displays extreme negativism toward parents and caregivers—an early step toward establishing independence (autonomy).

- May have an imaginary friend as a constant companion.

- Explores everything in the environment, including other children; may shove or push other children as if to test their reaction.

Daily Routines (Continued)

THREE-YEAR-OLDS

Eating

- Appetite fairly good; prefers small servings. Likes only a few cooked vegetables; eats almost everything else.

- Feeds self independently if hungry. Uses spoon in semi-adult fashion; may even spear with fork.

- Dawdles over food when not hungry.

- Can pour milk and juice and serve individual portions from a serving dish with some prompts ("Fill it up to the line;" "Take only two spoonsful."); fewer spills.

- Begins to drink a great deal of milk. (Must be sure child does not fill up on milk to the exclusion of other needed foods.)

Bathing, Dressing, Toileting Needs

- Does a fair job of washing self in bath tub; still resists getting out of tub.

- Takes care of own toilet needs during the daytime (boys, especially, may continue to have pants-wetting accidents).

- Usually sleeps through the night without wetting the bed; some children are in transition—some days or even weeks they are dry, then may again experience night-wetting for a period.

- Child still more skilled at undressing than dressing self, though capable of putting on some articles of clothing.

- Becomes more skilled at manipulating buttons, large snaps, and zippers.

Sleeping

- Usually sleeps 10 to 12 hours at night, waking up about 7 or 8 a.m.; some children are awake much earlier.

- May no longer take an afternoon nap; continues to benefit from a quiet time on bed.

- Can get self ready for bed. Has given up many earlier bedtime rituals; may still need a bedtime story or song and tucking-in.

- May begin to have dreams that cause the child to awaken.

- Night wanderings may occur; quiet firmness is needed in returning child to his or her own bed.

Play and Social Activities

- The "me too" age; wants to be included in everything.

- Spontaneous group play for short periods of time; very social; beginning to play cooperatively.

- May engage in arguments with other children; adults should allow children to settle their own disagreements unless physical harm is threatened.

- Loves dress-up, dramatic play that involves every day work activities. Strong sex-role stereotypes: "Boys can't be nurses."

- Responds well to options rather than commands. "Do you want to put your nightgown on before or after the story?"

- Sharing still difficult, but seems to understand the concept.

Daily Routines (Continued)

FOUR-YEAR-OLDS

Eating

- Appetite fluctuates from very good to fair.

- May develop dislikes of certain foods and refuse them to the point of tears if pushed.

- Uses all eating utensils; becomes quite skilled at spreading jelly or peanut butter or cutting soft foods such as bread.

- Eating and talking get in each other's way; talking usually takes precedence over eating.

- Likes to help in the preparation of a meal; dumping premeasured ingredients, washing vegetables, setting the table.

Bathing, Dressing, Toileting Needs

- Takes care of own toileting needs; often demands privacy in the bathroom.

- Does an acceptable job of bathing and brushing teeth, but should receive assistance (or subtle inspection) from adults on a regular basis.

- Dresses self, can lace shoes, button buttons, buckle belts. Gets frustrated if problems arise in getting dressed and may stubbornly refuse much-needed adult help.

- Can sort and fold own clean clothes, put clothes away, hang up towels, straighten room.

Sleeping

- Averages 10 to 12 hours of sleep at night; may still take an afternoon nap or quiet time.

- Bedtime usually not a problem if cues, rather than parents' orders, signal the command: when the story is finished, when the clock hands are in a certain position.

- Some children fear the dark, but usually a light left on in the hall is all that is needed.

- Getting up to use a toilet may require helping the child settle down for sleep again.

Play and Social Activities

- Playmates are important; plays cooperatively most of the time; may be bossy.

- Takes turns; shares (most of the time); wants to be with children every waking moment.

- Needs (and seeks out) adult approval and attention; may comment, "Look what I did."

- Understands and needs limits (but not too constraining); will abide by rules most of the time.

- Brags about possessions; shows off; boasts about family members.

Daily Routines (Continued)

FIVE-YEAR-OLDS

Eating

- Eats well, but not at every meal.

- Likes familiar foods, prefers most vegetables raw.

- Often adopts food dislikes of family members and caregivers.

- Makes breakfast (pours cereal, gets out milk and juice) and lunch (spreads peanut butter and jam on bread).

Bathing, Dressing, Toileting Needs

- Takes full responsibility for own toileting; may put off going to the bathroom until an accident occurs or is barely avoided.

- Bathes fairly independently but needs some help getting started.

- Dresses self completely; learning to tie shoes, sometimes aware when clothing is on wrong side out or backwards.

- Careless with clothes; leaves them strewn about; needs many reminders to pick them up.

- Uses tissue for blowing nose, but often does a careless or incomplete job; forgets to throw it away.

Sleeping

- Independently manages all routines associated with getting ready for bed; can help with younger brother or sister's bedtime routine.

- Averages 10 or 11 hours of sleep per night. The occasional 5-year-old still naps.

- Dreams and nightmares are commonplace.

- Going to sleep is often delayed if the day has been especially exciting or exciting events are scheduled for the next day.

Play and Social Activities

- Helpful and cooperative in carrying out family chores and routines.

- Somewhat rigid about the "right" way to do something and the "right" answers to a question.

- Fearful that mother may not come back; very attached to home and family; willing to adventure to some degree but wants the adventure to begin and end at home.

- Plays well with other children, but three may be a crowd: two 5-year-olds will often exclude the third.

- Shows affection and protection toward younger sister or brother, may feel overburdened at times if younger child demands too much attention.

Daily Routines (Continued)

SIX-YEAR-OLDS

Eating

- Has a good appetite most of the time; often takes larger helpings than is able to finish. May skip an occasional meal, but usually makes up for it later.

- Willingness to try new foods is unpredictable; has strong food preferences and definite dislikes.

- Table manners often seem deplorable by adult standards; may revert to eating with fingers; stuff mouth; continues to spill milk or drop food in lap.

- Has difficulty using table knife for cutting and fork for anything but spearing food.

- Finds it difficult to sit through an entire meal; wiggles and squirms, gets off (or "falls" off) chair, drops utensils.

Bathing, Dressing, Toileting Needs

- Balks at having to take a bath; finds many excuses for delaying or avoiding a bath entirely.

- Manages toileting routines without much help; sometimes is in a hurry or waits too long so that "accidents" happen.

- May revert to soiling or wetting pants during the first few weeks of school.

- Usually sleeps through the night without having to get up to use the bathroom. NOTE: some children (especially boys) may not be able to maintain a dry bed for another year or so.

- Careless about handwashing, bathing, and other self-care routines; needs frequent supervision and demonstration of skills to make sure they are carried out properly.

- Interested in selecting own clothes; needs subtle guidance in determining combinations and seasonal appropriateness.

- Drops clothing on floor or bed, loses shoes around the house, flings jacket down and often forgets where it is.

Sleeping

- Continues to need 9–11 hours of uninterrupted sleep.

- Usually sleeps through the night; some children continue to have nightmares.

- May need night-light, special blanket, or favorite stuffed toy (sometimes all three).

- Finds numerous ways to avoid bedtime; when finally in bed, falls asleep quickly.

- If awake before parents, usually finds ways to amuse self with books, toys, or coloring.

Play and Social Activities

- Strong sense of self is evident in terms of preferences and dislikes; uncompromising about wants and needs (often these do not coincide with adult plans or desires).

- Possessive about toys and books, parents and friends, but is increasingly able to share.

- May have close, friendly relationship with one or two other children (often slightly older); play involves working together toward specific goals.

- Intolerant of being told what to do; may revert to tantrums.

- Eager for teacher's attention, praise, reassurance; now views teacher (rather than parent) as the ultimate source of "truth."

Daily Routines (Continued)

SEVEN- AND EIGHT-YEAR-OLDS

Eating

- Most have a hearty appetite; boys typically eat more than girls. Those who have been picky eaters often show improved appetites.

- Eats most foods; has fewer likes and dislikes.

- Interested in foods; likes to help shop for and prepare meals.

- Takes pride in using good table manners, especially when eating out or when company is present; at home manners may be less than acceptable.

- Uses eating utensils with relative ease; seldom eats with fingers; some children still have trouble cutting meat.

- Often gulps food in order to return to play or a project in progress.

Bathing, Dressing, Toileting Needs

- Has good control of bowel and bladder; can delay going to the bathroom without having an accident; may urinate more frequently when stressed.

- Establishes fairly regular pattern of elimination.

- Handwashing often hurried; dirt tends to go on towel rather than down the drain.

- May dillydally at bathtime; once in the tub seems to thoroughly enjoy the experience; can manage own bath without help.

- Takes greater interest in appearance, selecting and coordinating outfits, brushing hair, looking good.

- Dresses self; dawdling continues but child can speed up when time becomes critical.

- Beginning to take more interest in caring for own clothes; hangs clothes up (at least some of the time), helps with laundry, folds and returns items to dresser.

- Skilled at tying shoes, but often can't be bothered.

Sleeping

- Averages 10 hours of sleep at night; many children need less (may account for their efforts to delay bedtime).

- Begins to question established bedtime; wants to stay up later; dawdles, becomes sidetracked while getting ready for bed.

- Sleeps soundly, no longer bothered by bad dreams or nightmares.

- Often wakes up early, reads or occupies self in bed with toys or a simple activity: counting out savings in piggybank, looking at baseball card collection, reading.

Play and Social Activities

- Likes to join clubs and participate in organized group activities (Girl/Boy Scouts, Boys' and Girls' Clubs, swim teams).

- Group membership becomes more important than the need for personal achievement.

- Enjoys competitive sports (soccer, baseball, swimming, gymnastics); eager to join a team; just as eager to quit if too much forced competition.

- Eager for acceptance from peers; beginning to imitate clothing styles, hairstyles, behavior, and language of most admired peers.

- May begin to act like a know-it-all toward the end of the eighth year; becomes argumentative with peers (and adults).

- Does not want to miss school or scheduled events; wants to "keep up."

CHAPTER 2

Appendix 3 Early Warning Signs of Childhood Problems

Recognizing early warning signs of childhood problems can improve your child's chances for a happy future.

Your child is special to you.

Sometimes even the most concerned and loving parents are unaware of problems their child may be having. Problems a child is born with or that he may acquire could ultimately interfere with his normal growth and development.

This doesn't have to happen. Many conditions can be corrected if parents recognize the early warning signs and seek help.

Here are some very simple things to watch for as your young child develops. These are some of the more common indicators of problems in small children.

If you suspect that your child may have a problem, call for qualified help. Don't delay. Immediate attention can make all the difference in the world for your child and for you.

Seeing — If your child. . .

- does not follow objects with his eyes by age 6 months
- is often unable to locate and pick up small objects which have been dropped
- frequently rubs his eyes or complains that eyes hurt; or has reddened, watering or encrusted eyelids
- holds head in a strained or awkward position (tilts head to either side—thrusts head forward or backward) when trying to focus on someone or something
- sometimes, or always, crosses one or both eyes
- fails to notice objects, people or animals around him when other children do

Talking — If your child. . .

- cannot say "Mama" and "Dadda" by age 1

- cannot say the names of a few objects and people by age 1 1/2
- is not attempting nursery rhymes or short TV jingles by age 2 1/2
- is not talking in short sentences by age 3.
- is not understood by people outside the family by age 3

Playing — If your child. . .

- does not try to put toys in his mouth by age 7 months
- does not play games such as peek-a-boo, patty-cake, and wave good-bye by age 1
- does not imitate parents doing routine household chores by age 2 or 3
- does not play group games such as hide-and-seek or tag with other children by age 4
- does not share and take turns by age 5

Hearing — If your child. . .

- doesn't turn to face the source of strange sounds or voices by six months; or if he sleeps through most noises
- rubs or pulls at his ears repeatedly; has frequent ear aches or runny ears
- talks in a very loud or soft voice
- does not react when you call from another room.
- turns the same ear toward a sound he wishes to hear

Thinking — If your child. . .

- doesn't respond to her own name when called by age 1
- is unable to identify hair, eyes, ears, nose and mouth by pointing to them at age 2

Source: National Easter Seal Society, In R.M. Berns. (1994). *Topical Child Development*. Albany, NY: Delmar Publishers

- does not understand simple stories told or read by age 3
- doesn't give reasonable answers to such questions as "What do you do when you are sleepy?" or "What do you do when you are hungry?" by age 4
- does not seem to understand the meanings of the words "today," "tomorrow" and "yesterday" by age 5

Moving — If your child. . .
- is unable to sit up without help or support by age 9 months

- uses one hand predominantly before 18 months
- cannot walk by age 2
- does not walk down steps by age 3
- is unable to balance on one foot for a short time by age 4
- cannot throw and catch a large ball bounced to him by age 5

Living Skills — If your child. . .
- doesn't drink from a cup or use a spoon by age 2
- can't help with dressing by age 3
- can't dress without supervision by age 5

Source: National Easter Seal Society, In R.M. Berns. (1994). *Topical Child Development.* Albany, NY: Delmar Publishers

CHAPTER 3

Preparation for New Challenges: Get Ready!

The Girl Scout motto *Be prepared* definitely applies to life as a paraeducator. The time you spend preparing the classroom environment and planning daily procedures and methods will pay off.

Chapter 12 discusses how important it is to become well acquainted with procedures and people and places around your school or center. Make sure you fully understand behavior and discipline policies, playground rules, and cafeteria procedures. Make notations of special schedules for subjects like music and physical education. Make an effort to meet the school nurse and any support staff who may work with your students. A tour and any orientation you are given will help you to be more prepared for future events. Find out ahead of time where to go and who will help. Of course, there is no way to anticipate everything, but if you meet people and find out what *they* do, then you will be closer to getting off at the right stop when the time comes.

Once you are placed in a paraeducator position you will become acquainted with procedures and people and the space within your own room. You may be walking into a situation where the procedures are well established and you have very little input; you may work alone or with the teacher to develop ways of doing things like collecting lunch money, assigning learning centers, or selecting the line leader.

Two keys to a successful start will be 1) initial interactions and 2) information gathering, as you get to know both the teacher with whom you will work and the children on your class roll. Take your lead from the teacher. Listen first and then ask questions. Try to get an idea of the teacher's cooperative working style as soon as possible. Find out general preliminary data about the students, too. These keys will have a bearing on all the other preparedness steps you take. Your first days will be very full as you assimilate all of this input and get started in your work.

INITIAL INTERACTIONS

Cooperative Working Styles

Teachers and paraeducators work together kind of like musical duets. Sometimes the singers sing totally separate stanzas or lines of music and sometimes they sing the same words at the same time but with harmonizing different notes. Other times the lines of music flow in the same direction but at different tempos, with the sounds of the singers overlapping as they sing basically the same thing but with one singer leading off and the other singer chasing the melody. You and the lead teacher may never sing the same stanzas; the teacher may prefer that you always sing only the second and fourth stanzas, while he sings the first, third, and fifth stanzas. You may have your sets of tasks and he has his own set of responsibilities and the two sets never have any common members. Or you will sing your duets with lots of harmonizing notes. You and the lead teacher may work concurrently toward the same objectives with a few variations in your methods. Or you may sing together much like you would sing a "round," with the teacher beginning the song and then you singing what she sings after a short interval. The teacher may initiate everything and expect you to join right in and follow with the same. It is most likely that your working duet will involve all three of these styles. Sometimes you and the teacher will perform entirely separate tasks; other times you will both be responsible for working on the same objectives at the same time, and yet other times the teacher will expect you to follow her lead. One thing is sure. The work duet you perform with one teacher will be different from any work duet you could perform with anybody else. You and your teacher will find your own patterns and interactions. Some teachers have a real independent style with paraeducators; they expect you to develop your own routines. Other teachers have a real mutually supportive, teamwork style where they discuss and decide many of the aspects of the school day alongside their paraeducators. Still others, hopefully the minority, are more authoritarian, and give their paraeducators explicit instructions and expect them to do what and only what they are told. Of course there are blendings of these cooperative working styles along the continuum. Finding this balance may be one of the most difficult aspects of being a paraeducator. Give yourself time, though, if the adjustment (sight-reading) seems hard. It may take time to learn your part, but you will learn it, and then you will be able to carry your part with confidence.

Clarifying Roles

Your beginning tasks will largely depend on whether you are walking into an ongoing set-up or if you are beginning work during preplanning before the children start school. There is an enormous amount to do before the school year starts. However, irregardless of the timing of your beginning as a paraeducator, you will need to clarify your role.

Some places give you a job description. (Examples are shown in Chapter 13.) If you are not given a formal job description, you will have to work out your own informally. It does help to have an actual job description; but, as you can imagine, there will be many aspects and possible scenarios that will be left out. Right from the beginning you must find out what is expected of you. Then you must remember that this is an **ongoing process**. It may be that as you gain experience, prove yourself, and the needs of your school change, you will advance to another level even if there is no concrete recognition of this advancement. Often as paraeducators grow in their positions and demonstrate new capabilities, more is expected and roles and responsibilities broaden.

Anna Lou Pickett says this about the changing roles of paraeducators:

> *Like the roles and responsibilities of their professional colleagues, the roles and responsibilities of paraprofessionals have become more complex and demanding since they were introduced into classrooms as teacher aides almost forty years ago. (1989)*

Pickett definitely states the necessity of delineating the "distinctions in the roles of teachers and paraeducators in differentiated staffing arrangements." She says that the changes in education have changed the role of paraeducators from primarily clerical and monitoring duties to involvement in "all components of the instructional process" (1993).

Once you do know what your responsibilities are, perform them in a timely, conscientious manner. We will discuss some likely set-up responsibilities. Make it your goal to *be prepared.*

CLASSROOM ENVIRONMENT

Getting Materials Ready

You will want to go through any materials that you will be using in order to become familiar with them and to organize them. Use file cabinets, drawers, stand-up files and desk/counter tops in ways that make materials readily available as you need them. Items you will use on a daily basis need to be easily accessible whereas little-used-but-vital-when-you-need-them materials may be placed out of the way. Organize your work space so that it works for you.

There are certain materials you will need to start off with in order to achieve your maximum organization potential. Check this list, and add your own "necessities":

> pencils, plenty of them, for you and needy children
> pens (Find out whether your school administration has a preference for blue or black ink on permanent records. Some do.)
> colored markers
> highlighters
> *sticky* notes
> files for EVERYTHING
> colored folders
> record books
> file cabinet
> desk or counter space where you may put standing dividers and bins
> notepads
> scrap paper kept in a neat box or container
> paper clips (several sizes) and rubber bands
> correction fluid
> tape, rubber cement, and glue sticks
> stapler and hole punch
> index card file

Some of you may not stay in the same classroom, or even in a classroom at all, for the entire day. Even so, you will have a schedule and information that you will have to keep track of. If you do travel from room to room, at least carry a notebook and something to write with wherever you go, if only to keep notes that will help you keep up with yourself. Even if you do not have a classroom that you can call "home," you will still need to check out the materials wherever you are during the day. Make sure that the tools you need to do your job are in every place you go, so that you don't waste time scrounging for markers, pencils, or paper clips. If you cannot depend on materials being there for you, take things with you in something that you can easily carry, such as a portfolio. If you are not in a classroom, but in a different environment such as the media center, there will still be materials you need in order to do your job. Find out quickly what those are for you specifically, and put them in an order that makes sense for quick and easy use.

You may or may not have your own desk or table. If one has not been provided for you, then ask what you may use for your work and storage area. Ask for a bit of private counter space at least. You'll need to establish your own work area. Be careful not to disturb/violate someone else's "personal work space." If you do have a desk or a table, be sure to keep it as uncluttered as possible. You will want to be sure your desk remains conducive to spreading out your work.

It probably is a good idea to keep an extra sweater at school for those days when you have playground duty and the weather report is inaccurate or you missed it entirely. Also, school buildings are notorious for being inconsistently heated or cooled and you never know when you might be more comfortable with that sweater even inside. Another good thing to keep on hand is a pair of cheap tennis shoes. Playground gravel can be hard on your better shoes. If you keep a pair of "yucky," comfortable shoes under your desk, it's easy to quickly slip them on before you go outside with the children.

Decorating the Surroundings

The lead teacher may want your help in decorating the surroundings. Here's where knowing a little about your group will help. Bulletin boards and other room decorations should be age-appropriate and should appeal to the interests and needs of your class population. For example, if you have visually impaired children in the room, decorate the room with objects that can be explored by touch. Some examples of tactile bulletin boards are shown in Figures 3–1 and 3–2. Some multi-impaired students helped to make the bulletin board in Figure 3–3 for their classroom. If many of your students come from varied cultures, mix some ethnic flavor into the surroundings. Use your imagination!

Ideally, decorations should also correlate to the purpose of your room. You will have a different focus for bulletin boards in the media center than for bulletin boards in the computer lab (Figure 3–4).

Student Areas

You may be asked to help arrange student areas. Make tables and desks and reading corners as inviting and comfortable as possible. Consider

FIGURE 3–1 Tactile Bulletin Board.

FIGURE 3–2 Tactile Bulletin Board.

FIGURE 3–3 Simple bulletin board in classroom for children with mental and physical disabilities.

FIGURE 3–4 Bulletin board in elementary school media center.

finding a place for each child's favorite color somewhere on his individual space. For example, let the child color and decorate a name tag that can be laminated and attached to the desk.

As you design the surroundings, you and the teacher will think about the needs of your class. It may be best for your room decor to remain simple and somewhat plain because overstimulation hinders your students' learning. Extra labels such as those seen in Figures 3–5, 3–6, and 3–7 may benefit your students. In the special education classroom shown, picture labels and objects are used along with, and instead of, word labels in order to help the children. Picture labels are used on the drawers and cabinets in the living skills area. Actual coins are taped on a student's desk to help her associate the right coin with the word for the coin and the amount of money the coin represents.

The room arrangement should be appealing to anyone entering the room and should also be functional for the teaching style used in the room. Many teachers still adhere to the norm of putting desks in rows facing the board. This arrangement may occasionally have merit, but it

FIGURE 3–5 In special education classrooms, picture labels can help children locate items.

FIGURE 3–6 Picture labels can be used in conjunction with word labels.

FIGURE 3–7 Coins, words, and numbers attached to the desk of a child with Down's syndrome help her learn about money.

ignores the needs children have to work in social groupings. It also causes more disruption when you have to move desks in order to group students for special projects or peer tutoring. If the desks are already placed in groups of four, for example, you already have the semblance of a table, and it is easy to move children into various group combinations. This avoids total furniture rearrangement, which can cause disruption. Whether the teacher uses a lot of group interaction is certainly something to consider when the room is arranged.

Other Classroom Areas

In addition to desks or tables for the students, some other specific classroom areas include:

- Reading area: This should be a warm, inviting place with a wide variety of interesting books, including some written by the students themselves. Pillows or beanbag chairs make this area comfortable and cozy.
- Art area: Materials should be readily available to the children. The materials should also lend themselves to creativity and innovation from the students and not so much from the teacher and the paraeducator. Preferably the art area should be close to a source of water and should have surfaces that are easy to clean up.
- Science/Nature area: Children should be given opportunities to explore and investigate. Materials should be changed frequently. (You might be responsible for changing the area.)
- Written Expression area: This area may include spelling or grammar games or learning centers, suggestions for poetry or story completions, displays of student work, or new vocabulary activities.

(Oppenheim, 1989; Perrone, 1993)

In some respects, arranging the classroom is like decorating your own home. When you are the paraeducator, you have at least one roommate, and that roommate (the teacher) pays more of the rent than you do, so the roommate gets the final say on how the place should be fixed up. If you are artistically inclined, though, and the teacher is not, you may be given free reign with the room. Bare walls and furniture can be stark and unfriendly, but when you and the teacher add your own touches, you can transform your room into a cheerful, comfortable place in which students learn and grow. Some touches you may want to add include:

plants
an aquarium

balance around the room
interesting groupings
learning stations
science/nature displays
the children's work
a rocker in the reading corner

How you and the teacher decorate your room will make a statement about you and how the children are incorporated into this environment for learning. Whenever you have any input, aim to make your room warm and inviting and "user-friendly."

Filing System

After you check on your materials and help prepare the classroom environment, one of your next considerations concerns your classroom filing system. From day one it will be important for you to understand the teacher's filing system or to develop your own. What kind of papers will be filed? How much space will you need? Just think about finding a place for all of the following:

- Student information sheets
- Anecdotal information on children
- Emergency phone numbers for the students
- Copies of all the forms you'll need for the year
- Old staff meeting notes
- Bulletin board ideas
- Art project patterns and ideas
- Field trip information
- Parent note forms
- Storage box contents
- Seasonal work sheets and puzzles
- Lesson plans
- Emergency notes for a substitute in case the teacher can't explain everything that you do

Think about how the filing system is set up or how you would like it to be. Many seasonal items are most efficiently filed by the month. You and your teacher may find it helpful to have a file for each month of the school year. Then, in February, when you are beginning to plan for March and you or the teacher want to do something pertinent to that month, you can pull the March file only instead of wading through too many papers. You might include seasonal bulletin board ideas, work sheets, art projects, poetry, a list of good stories, and creative writing ideas relative to the month. You will also need files with content headings. Much of the basic content materials will be best filed under content headings since their use will be based on the readiness of the students, and you can't predict the timetable for that. The sooner you come up with an organizational system, the better off you will be.

Other Suggestions For Your Classroom

Some other tips about the classroom environment are:

- Keep the room attractive, neat, and orderly.

- Change bulletin boards often.

- Display the children's work.

- Put displays and centers at the child's level.

- Store materials that are not being used out of sight.

- Centers should be easy to supervise.

Keeping your classroom organized is a year-long process. There will be more information about classroom organization in Chapter 9.

PREPAREDNESS

Make preparedness your mainstay; it will save you many pitfalls. Preparedness involves thinking through situations, planning ahead, and being organized.

Before Using Equipment

Always have your plans complete and materials ready in advance. Children lose interest more easily if you are cutting art papers or mixing paints as the lesson begins. If you have the tape player or VCR plugged in and ready to go, it is less likely that you will lose the students' attention or unwittingly enhance discipline problems. Just picturing the converse is enough to make you want to be prepared! Also, if you are responsible for selecting tapes or films, be sure to preview them to make sure they correspond appropriately to the teaching unit.

Before Storytime

Preparation is also important when it comes to something as seemingly simple as reading stories. You should be acquainted with a book before reading it to children. Check out pronunciations for unusual names. Familiarity with your story will give you a greater sense of confidence, and allow you to make interesting changes in emphasizing certain situations and/or different characters. By knowing the story, you can change your voice and the timing to create anticipation in appropriate places. Children love to be read to and it is an important part of most school days. When done well it gives children an enjoyable experience and motivates their interest in learning to read. In his autobiography written in his sixth grade year, one boy made this reference to his third grade teacher:

> *My teacher in third grade was Mrs. Weber. She would read to us every afternoon if she could. I always enjoyed that time of the day. I think her reading brought me to like reading (Brent).*

Do not let it throw you when a child says, "I've already heard that story." Be ready with a positive response, such as "Good, I'm glad; it's a great story. You can be my helper when we are done." Or, "Come stand beside me and together we'll keep the secret about what happens to Little Brown Bear." In other words, accept the information and give the child a sense of approval and importance.

Also decide whether you will show the illustrations. Sometimes it is best not to detract from your reading or the mood by holding the book facing the class and trying to show pictures as you go. If you are not going to show the illustrations as you go, let the children know ahead of time that this time you want them to make pictures in their minds as you read, and that the book will be available for them to look at for a few days. On the other hand, if you plan to show the pictures, state the rules up front. For example, you could tell them not to call out, "I can't see, I can't see," but to raise their hands or use some other *silent* signal if they are not able to see the pictures. Seeing the illustrations can be quite a big deal. As with so many aspects of your job as a paraeducator, it helps to be prepared.

MAINTAINING ORDER

The suggestions for being prepared will also help you maintain order. When you are well-prepared you have a greater sense of well-being and calmness; the children sense this and flow with you. On the other hand, if you are agitated and disorganized, the children will definitely pick up on that as well.

There must be some control to maintain order. It is necessary to develop orderly methods for doing everyday tasks. If you are in charge of lunch counts, attendance records, and checking communications from home, then you need to find a good, smooth way to do these things. Talk to other paraeducators and compare notes. From the **first day** on, you will need to be prepared to both gather the necessary information for counts and records and to distribute information to students and their families. Make yourself a list of everything you will need for the first day. This list might include the following:

- Attendance record for that day

- Lunch count for that day

- Information sheets for parents to read and fill out such as school discipline policy; student information sheet; car pool and bus routines

- Method for collecting lunch and after-school program money

- Important health information on each student (allergies, diabetes, asthma)

- Afternoon transportation information for each student (See Table 3–1.)

- Suggested supply list

- Sign-up sheets for classroom volunteers, field trip chaperones, room chairperson, etc.

Go ahead and make up plenty of copies of all the papers that will be sent home in the first days of school. Assemble a packet for each student expected. Also go ahead and assemble packets for additional students. One paraeducator has "new student folders" ready throughout the year. Every few weeks, she removes entries that no longer apply and she updates the folders by adding current field trip information, recent newsletters, and so forth. Then when the school secretary escorts a new child to her kindergarten room, this paraeducator is ready to go over

TABLE 3–1 Information for Parents Whose Child Will Ride A Bus *Courtesy of Jo Hogan and Mary Wofford.*

INFORMATION FOR PARENTS WHOSE CHILD WILL RIDE A BUS

PLEASE COMPLETE FULLY AND RETURN TO TEACHER BEFORE YOU LEAVE TODAY!

Child's Name

Check the Appropriate Ones:

Morning Transportation to School: *Afternoon Transportation From School:*

☐ Car   ☐ Car (1:15 pick-up)

☐ Bus   ☐ Car (after regular school hours)

      Bus Number _____   ☐ School Bus   _____ 1st load

                                    Bus Number _____   _____ 2nd load

                             ☐ Will stay for After School Program

                             ☐ Day Care Bus

My aide and I personally walk each child to their bus. Since we do load the children ourselves, it will not be necessary for their brothers or sisters to come to the room to get them!

---

pertinent information with the parent and to give the parent all the necessary paperwork without having to scramble for everything.

You need to know ahead of time whenever possible what conditions the teacher, the children, and you will need in order to work comfortably in the classroom. For example, if grinding noises such as pencil sharpeners grate on your nerves, develop an alternate plan *before* the nerves begin to fray. If the teacher does not want to waste time lining the class up to use the restroom, but you both will likely be annoyed by twenty-five individual requests during teaching time, then come up with a plan that will work for everybody. It might work to hang a wooden pass on a peg near the door and set up rules about going one at a time. Advantages to this kind of system are that the children have responsibility to take care of their own needs and learning time can be relatively uninterrupted.

Time-saving Techniques

Time-saving techniques can help you in your campaign to be prepared and maintain order. One way to help yourself enormously is to develop an efficiency-expert mentality. Look at your responsibilities and think about the best use of time. As a paraeducator there will be many mundane tasks that require attention and threaten to gobble up your time. Decide constantly to stick to your main objectives and don't let distractions rule and become time-wasters.

Here are some "tried and true" time-saving ideas that may help you:

- As much as possible, never deal with a paper twice.
- Keep "stick-ons" on hand for simple reminders.
- Prioritize everything immediately.
  Assign new "stuff" to one of three stacks:
  1. Urgent (especially dated stuff). Review this 1–2 times a day.
  2. Pending (can do later). Review daily.
  3. OK to eliminate or procrastinate. Review weekly.
- Don't be afraid to go ahead and assign some items to the trashcan.
- Make lists. Star (*) the most important items.
- Do not do for the children what they can do themselves.
- Organize your trips out of the room. Make a circuit as you turn in the lunch count, pick up supplies, sign up for the all-purpose room, etc., rather than making multiple trips.
- Use a filing system. (Here it is again!) File accurately and faithfully. Keep records on everything.
- Color-code. Use different color folders or highlighters.
- Go ahead and get that most dreaded task over with. This saves a lot of worrying and procrastination time. (Operate by the Premack principle.)
- Laminate things you will want to use repeatedly.
- Thank anyone who does something that saves you time or who gives you a time-saving idea; they may be more likely to do it again.

(Ideas from Jean Jackson, Paraprofessional Workshop)

System For Everything

A terrific paraeducator may have a system for everything, from rotating centers to collecting library books to choosing helpers. Don't let the words "method" or "system" scare you and bring forth connotations of rigidity and no fun. You can inject games and fun into anything! For example, at the end of the day, start a "Mystery Trash" contest. Mentally select one piece of trash (some little jiblet on the floor), start a timer or record, and set the children to picking up trash. Whoever picks up the "prize" trash (or throws away the most trash, or is the quietest while picking up trash, and so on) gets a reward, a merit, a piece of fruit or candy, a sticker, or whatever. This kind of method can be lots of fun and can achieve a good purpose.

Remember to evaluate your methods every now and then. Children change; what works best may change, too. More attention will be given to methods and organization in Chapter 9 since they need to be reevaluated periodically.

SAFETY

Although you will not have ultimate responsibility for room safety, it should very much concern every paraeducator. Safety is probably the first physical element parents look for in a school or care situation. You can help to provide a safe, child-proof environment geared to the developmental levels of your students. According to Gerber (1971), this should be the goal. She advocates total noninterference with infants' exploration whenever possible, and says this is only possible with the right kind of safe environment. Providing the right kind of safe environment is important for all age groups.

General Safety Precautions

You should be aware of essential safety considerations. This is such an important issue that you and the teacher should both be diligent in safety observations and practices. Following are some precautionary suggestions:

- Dangerous objects should either not be present or should be locked up, including sharp or breakable items, chemicals (drugs, cleansers, cosmetics), and plastic bags, balloons, or other items that can cause suffocation. (According to the American Medical Association, latex balloons are the cause of more choking deaths than any other object ["Atlanta Parent," 2–96])

- Furniture should be sturdy, and bookcases should be fastened to the wall, so that children will not pull them down on themselves.

- Electrical sockets must be plugged with child-proof inserts and children should not be able to pull electrical appliances down or turn them on.

- Heaters must be safe to walk on or touch or they should be covered with a safety grate.

- Windows and doors should be latched appropriately.

- The facility should be clean and well maintained; rugs should be fastened down and regularly vacuumed.

- Staff members must not drink coffee or other hot liquids where they could spill on children or children could consume them.

- Staff members should be vigilant about the activities of the children, rather than conversing among themselves.

- Caregivers need to be aware of health hazards and infectious diseases and take routine steps to minimize the spread of illness. It is an undervalued health fact that merely washing hands each time a diaper is changed or a nose is wiped can cut illness (or exposure to illness) by over 75 percent. Regularly wiping door knobs and washing toys can help also.

- Awareness of contagious illnesses and their symptoms must also be exercised, with rigid guidelines for nonattendance by children with symptoms.

- Lists of toxic plants should be readily available, particularly if there are indoor or outdoor plants within children's reach.

- Lists of parent emergency numbers, paramedics, and poison control centers should be posted in very visible locations. Emergency treatment consent forms must be on file for each child, with guidelines about parental preferences. You might consider keeping this information in an easy-to-spot-and-grab red folder.

- Lists of child allergies and medical conditions should also be readily available and visible.

- Food safety should be considered in cases of potential spoilage of dairy products left unrefrigerated, etc.

- Playground safety should be routinely evaluated and reinforced.

Playground Safety

Playground safety is an important issue in that more than 200,000 children are treated in emergency rooms for playground injuries every year. (U.S. Consumer Product Safety Commission, 1996; ERIC, 1993) In their book, *The Everyday Guide to Owning and Operating a Child Care Center,* Kingsbury, Vogler, and Benero remind readers that playgrounds have been shown to present the greatest source of risk to young children, with 80 to 90 percent of injuries to children in child care happening on playgrounds (1990). Experts say that the majority of playground injuries are preventable and that they generally occur because of one of the following four conditions:

1. The playground equipment is too high.
2. The playground surface underneath the equipment is not resilient enough.
3. There are specific hazards, such as broken equipment, on the playground.
4. There is a lack of proper supervision on the playground. (Hendricks, 1993)

There are guidelines concerning playground equipment and surfaces but there are no mandatory federal requirements yet. The U.S. Consumer Product Safety Commission established voluntary playground guidelines in 1990 and 1991. Since there is no official regulation of these guidelines, it is up to parents, paraeducators and teachers, and other concerned people to learn about playground safety and push for compliance with the guidelines in their local communities and their workplaces (Hendricks, 1993).

What should you as a paraeducator be aware of concerning the area where your students play? When you look at the playground at your facility, check for the following:

- Equipment that is not too high; maximum for climbing for young children: 4 feet; older children: 5 feet.

- *Give* in the area underneath and surrounding playground equipment, adequate *fall zone,* including absence of any objects that could injure a falling child.

- Protective guard rails.

- Blunt and sanded ends and edges, rather than anything sharp, pointed, or protruding.

- Close spacing of rungs or posts to prevent heads getting stuck. There should not be anything, including pull-up rings, in which a child could get his head trapped.

- Soft, rather than hard, seats on the swings.

- Safe moving parts without any "pinch and crush points." Check the middles of merry-go-rounds, gates, and see-saws, especially, to make sure that they are safe for little hands and fingers.

- Closed hooks. Open *S* hooks can allow parts to slip off and children to fall.

(Hendricks, 1993)

In an ERIC Digest from the ERIC Clearinghouse on Teacher Education, Charlotte Hendricks reminds us about the impact of falling onto an unyielding surface, saying that "a fall from an eight-foot high structure (the height of many slides) onto concrete or asphalt is the equivalent of hitting a brick wall at 30 mph in a car" (Hendricks, 1993; Ward, 1987). She goes on to give a list of advantages and disadvantages of common resilient playground surface materials, based on information from the Consumer Product Safety Commission. Organic mulch, wood chips, sand, pea gravel, and shredded rubber tires are some of the playground surface materials used these days. Some playgrounds also have commercially prepared surfaces. Factors that are considered in this choice include drainage of the playground area, whether wheelchairs are able to ride over the surface, the cost, the age range of the children, and the possibility of decomposition (Hendricks, 1993). Kingsbury, Vogler, and Benero recommend using pea gravel because the "small, washed stone offers fairly secure footing and good drainage." They also recommend against using wood chips and bark because of possibilities for splinters, poor footing, and drainage problems (1990). Heather Paul, executive director of the National SAFE KIDS Campaign, recommends a ten-inch layer of shredded mulch or rubber pads (LHJ, 7–96). Be aware of how your children do on the playground surface chosen for your facility. If there is a need for, or opportunity for change, make your suggestions. Contact the Consumer Product Safety Commission for current information.

Note: There are recommendations about handling emergencies in Chapter 4. In cases of safety, do not ever hold back out of fear of over-stepping your boundaries. When it comes to the safety of a child, you have no boundaries, only obligations.

KNOWING THE CHILDREN

It takes time and effort, but getting to know each child is an important part of the first days and weeks of school. Go over the class list with the teacher and try to be aware of any special health needs, such as hearing or vision impairment, asthma concerns, frequent bathroom needs, seizure disorders, and diabetes. This will better prepare you to accommodate your students with sensitive understanding. Knowing these kinds of facts can help you to seat children appropriately, clue you in to the need for quick response, and prevent seemingly inattentive or disruptive behavior.

As the students grow and change, you will continue to learn more about them throughout the year. Children need to feel wanted and liked by you, so it is essential that you give them a warm accepting welcome each day, listen well to the various little tidbits they wish to relate to you, and be sensitive to special needs. In fact, listening and nurturing should be among your top priorities as a paraeducator.

As much as possible, maintain a fair and friendly demeanor with all the children. You might as well go ahead and face the fact that you will be drawn to some children more than others. If there is a child you have difficulty liking, try very hard to remember that that child may need attention and acceptance more than any other child in the room. Make a conscious effort to care about each one, even or especially the ones who make it hard.

Continually bear in mind that children are different; they grow and progress at different paces. Review material on child development (from Chapter 2 and other sources) occasionally. Remember that children go through stages of physical, language, cognitive, and social development. It is not fair for you to expect them to all be at the same level.

There is also a significant amount of research information which indicates that people have different brain preferences and learning styles. People can be either left-brain (tendencies toward math, sad emotions, and analytical thinking) or right-brain (with leanings toward art, music, happy emotions, and global thinking) oriented with variations in between. People learn in different ways as well; some may be visual learners, others may be auditory learners, and others may learn best through hands-on methods. The bottom line is that the children you work with will not all respond to learning interactions the same way and that is okay.

Furthermore, attending children may come from widely diverse home life situations, cultures, and countries. They may belong to newly arrived groups or well-established older ethnic populations. You might as well expect conflicts to occur in values, goals, and parental child-handling techniques. As a paraeducator, you may have to do some quick research to learn about the culture or situation of a particular child and family. Dealing with these diversities will require tact and patience. It takes time to develop both mutual understanding and trust. In addition to getting to know the children, you and the teacher need to know what parents want for their children, and what concerns they experience when leaving their children at your facility. You, the paraeducator, can help strengthen bridges of communication and harmony as you take time to really know the children and their families.

COMMUNICATION

Communication is a broad term, defined as giving and/or receiving information, signals, or messages. Communication is so much more than the actual words; it is composed of three parts: 1) tone of voice, 2) nonverbal communication, including body language and facial expression, and 3) words (Figure 3–8). Human interactions are full of nonverbal signals accounting for 60 to 80 percent of most human encounters. De Spelder and Prettyman (1980) have identified some of the more easily recognized nonverbal communications:

facial expression
body position
muscle tone
breathing tempo
voice tone

So, it is important to watch not only the words you say but how you say them.

A two-way process of sending and receiving (input and output) information occurs in true communication. Though it is not easy, communication skills can be learned (Sciarra & Dorsey, 1979). It is impor-

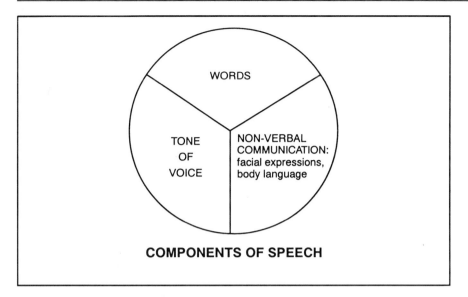

FIGURE 3–8 Components of Speech.

tant for paraeducators, and all others in the classroom, to have good communication skills and it is definitely worth the effort to learn them. This idea cannot be overemphasized. The whole climate of interpersonal relationships in an education center can be affected by an individual's ability to communicate. As Sciarra and Dorsey point out:

> *The director (principal) has the major responsibility for creating a climate of care, trust, and respect. This climate can best be achieved by demonstrating caring behaviors, by taking steps to build feelings of community, and by developing good communication skills among and between all members of the center (school) community. (1979)*

Success as a paraeducator can depend on communication skills, your own and those of others. According to Rogers, "It is through a mutually supporting, helping relationship that each individual can become better integrated and more able to function effectively" (1961). This is truly an important goal and communication is a key toward achieving it. Since every family encounters differences in opinion and values at times, a child center or school should expect disagreements between adults, between children, and between children and adults. This is why good, effective communication skills are essential.

No doubt your classroom may contain people with diverse opinions and backgrounds. As mentioned already, your school may also reflect our multiethnic and multicultural society. Communication between individuals is enhanced by feelings of trust and openness. In some discussions and verbal exchanges you are bound to gain insights into your beliefs and those of others. Jones (1986) believes:

> *I am unlikely to recognize the distinctive elements of my culture unless I have opportunities to compare it with other cultures— other ways of being human. Living in a multi-cultural society and world, I must learn to make the comparison—to become aware that any culture represents only one set of many possible choices, all of them valid ways of being human.*

Caring and sharing are foundational steps in communicating. Think about what makes a person interesting or easy to talk with. Why do you discuss problems with some people and not with others? Perhaps it is because that person with whom you can talk freely loves and accepts you as you are at that moment.

Conversely, when a message of nonacceptance is sent, communication is blocked. Gordon (1974) gives many examples of roadblocks to communication, including:

- Ordering, commanding
- Warning, threatening
- Moralizing, preaching, giving *shoulds* and *oughts*
- Judging, criticizing, blaming
- Name-calling, stereotyping, labeling
- Withdrawing, diverting
- Being sarcastic

If you want to be a good communicator with the children, the parents, and other staff members, be on the lookout for these obstacles and try to steer clear!

Love and acceptance can be demonstrated in a number of ways. Saying it may be the easiest way; showing it through actions may be the toughest. With children, giving attention and allowing them to make some choices help develop their feelings of self-worth and value. Touching also usually reinforces rapport; a pat, hug, or open lap for young children expresses love and acceptance. (Unfortunately, these days there is that strong need for caution even with totally innocent physical contact.) A wink, a notice of accomplishment, or a sincere recognition of a special quality helps feelings of caring and sharing grow, setting the stage for easy approaching and interacting. When you respect a child's (or an adult's!) needs, feelings, and desires and build a support system based on love and respect, you may, as Selye (1974) suggests, promote security and freedom from the distress that hinders the attainment of potential.

As a paraeducator you must plan ways to establish rapport with children. Communications depend on first contacts and interactions. Weir and Eggleston (1975) suggest there are definite skills, based on perseverance and know-how, that you can acquire to establish an easy flow of daily conversation with the children. Some of these have already been mentioned but are important enough to be restated.

- Offer a personal greeting to each child.

- Take time (within reason) to listen and respond to the child who is bursting to tell a story.

- Introduce new vocabulary; make sure they understand what the words you use mean.

- Help children plan for the day, building on prior experiences and introducing new ones.

- Permit children to solve their own problems through language.

- Find time to talk personally with each child during the day about important events or experiences in their lives.

- Avoid expressing shock or punishing children for asking questions about physical functions.

- Talk to the children more than to classroom adults.

- Give honest praise and state things in a positive way whenever possible.

In his series, *101 Educational Conversations With Your* _____, Vito Perrone has some excellent suggestions for talking with children of different ages. He proposes helping children find their own answers rather than spoon-feeding them, encouraging questions by asking questions, and asking open-ended questions. Find Perrone's book for your grade level and use the communication ideas.

Good communication skills are important in your relationship with the classroom teacher as well as with the children and their parents. Communication can be one of the biggest problems between a teacher and a paraeducator. Prepare yourself to ask questions in a helpful, non-critical manner. One good method for opening a discussion about a difficulty is, "I have this concern. What do you think?"

You, the paraeducator, may handle a lot of the interactions with parents. You may receive the notes from home, the permission slips and agreements to chaperone for field trips, and have the face-to-face meetings at carpool time. Make sure your communications with parents are clear and respectful. Sometimes a school climate can tend to set the staff and parents up as adversaries. You may, on occasion, come across the attitude that "the parents are not doing anything to help this child." The next step in this thinking is that "we know what would help this child." You need to constantly remember that though children are in your care for certain hours, the parents are the ones with final authority for their children. Do not fall into the trap of believing that just because there are some irresponsible parents out there that all parents fit into the same mold. Remember that you, the teacher, and the parents most likely want similar things for the children. Try to maintain a real spirit of cooperation in your interactions.

Becoming familiar with and helping to design your surroundings, clarifying your role, learning time-saving techniques and methods for maintaining order, and developing good communication and relationship skills are all ways you can be prepared to face the new challenges of a paraeducator. As stated repeatedly, many of these topics will be expanded later. As you go through preparation steps you should go ahead and implement many of the ideas in this chapter related to classroom management, time-saving, role clarification, and so on; however, these topics are not simply for the first days, but will be areas for continuing learning and practice. Find out what you need to do to help make your classroom a safe, happy environment for the children, the teacher, and you. Learn how to identify and fulfill the highest priorities, and what to do if the initial plans do not work. Many problems will be avoided with a preparedness mindset, but remember that there *are* solutions to problems when they occur. Just **be prepared** to see them through!

CHAPTER 4

Working and Playing with Infants, Toddlers, and Preschoolers

Special people spend their days with babies and other little people. Think back on the personality characteristics discussed in Chapter 1. Remember compassion and energy and flexibility and humor? There are times when you'll need these on a minute-by-minute basis as you work with little ones. An infant/toddler center is its own world, and when you work with infants and toddlers you will sometimes feel as though you are in another world. In this chapter, we will deal with places where hands-on care and play are the largest components of the day. Primarily such places are child care centers and will be the focus of this chapter. However, more and more, as legislation pertaining to children with special needs brings changes in the services provided through the public school system, the same kinds of activities and caregiving that you encounter in day care centers can be found in public schools. So even if you do not work in a child care center, read on because much of the information in this chapter (possibly even more than you would anticipate) may still pertain to you or can be adapted to your particular needs.

In 1986, there were over 40,000 child care centers operating across the United States. Since then the National Child Care Association estimates that there are now more than 50,000. A huge number of little people (more than two million) are served in these facilities (Kingsbury, et al., 1990). It takes another huge number of people to staff these facilities.

The definition of child care center varies from state to state. The number of children included in the definition differs. For example, in Texas a child care center is a facility that provides care for more than twelve children and in Florida a facility fits the definition of a child care center if it provides care for six or more children (Flating, 1991). The number of hours of operation vary also, though child care centers are usually specified to operate less than 24 hours a day. The range of activities varies in child care centers as well; however, the majority of states now require child care centers to have developmental programs with age-appropriate requirements and mandatory training for staff members (Kingsbury, et al., 1990). Sonja Flating gives a good general definition in her book, *Child Care: A Parent's Guide*, for an ideal child care center:

> *a public or private facility meeting the needs of the children it serves by providing quality care that promotes self-esteem, provides stimulating activities relative to the child's development, promotes social interaction, is safe and (is) emotionally secure. (1991)*

Kingsbury, Vogler, and Benero state their ideals for providers and classrooms for young children:

> *Teachers nurture, respect, and attend to children. Early childhood classrooms should be a place where children can make mistakes, then learn and grow from that experience. It should be a place where staff recognizes the inherent gifts of each child and uses that knowledge to challenge and encourage that youngster to reach his or her potential. (1990)*

Hopefully where you work is such a place.

Early child care is an increasingly important issue in our society. This is reflected in the fact that significant amounts of legislation related to our nation's youngest children are being passed. In their book, *The Everyday Guide to Opening and Operating a Child Care Center*, Kingsbury, Vogler, and Benero report that "32 states passed approximately 125 pieces of legislation related to child care and early childhood education" in response to facts related to increased numbers of children with mothers in the workforce (1990). In 1964, the federal government passed legislation that impacted the world of day care in a big way. Head Start, an early intervention program to help impoverished children and children with special needs, was established by the Economic Opportunity Act and has been shown to be effective. Currently there are moves toward more corporate involvement in child care, with increasing numbers of on-work-site child care centers (Flating, 1991).

Every infant/toddler center is operated a little differently. The importance of an employee handbook will be discussed. Make sure to request one if you are not given one at the start. Preferably, read it *before* your first day of work. Again, be prepared to ask questions about anything you do not understand. Babies need consistency, and it is important that you go along with center routines as quickly as possible.

The physical setting and philosophy of your center will determine how various routines are carried out. As previously stated, it is a good idea to familiarize yourself with both. Sometimes it is very helpful to understand the whys behind procedures.

Centers usually have specific rules and routines regarding health and safety, medications, emergencies, feeding, diapering, and naps. Although centers *are* different and will have some differences in their recommended procedures, there will be similarities as well. Most centers have similar regulations regarding issues such as children's health, caregivers' health, and diaper-changing procedures. The following are some generally accepted recommendations and rules.

GENERAL GUIDELINES

Health and Safety

- Smoking is not allowed in infant/toddler centers.
- Hot drinks should be consumed in staff areas only.
- **Never** leave a child unattended on a changing table or in a high chair.
- Do not leave little ones unattended inside or outside. Injuries happen more easily and quickly than you think they will.
- Sick babies should not be in the center. Infants who have bad colds, fevers, or contagious diseases should be cared for at home or away from other little ones.
- If you are ill, you should not be in the center. If you try to work when you are sick, you will not do as good a job and you may spread something to the children. You need to let the center know if you contract a contagious illness. For example, if you should come down with strep throat, others need to know so that if anyone else begins to show symptoms, parents and staff members will be alerted to the need for a throat culture.
- Wash your hands *constantly*. As mentioned previously, *the* most important health measure you can take is to wash your hands before and after diapering, cleaning noses, or feeding a child.
- Watch for signs that a child may not feel well. Some symptoms are digging at or pulling ears, listlessness, glassy eyes, diarrhea, loss of appetite, etc. Sometimes a little one just may not seem like herself. It is important to pay attention.

Medications

Normally, a specified person will be allowed to give medication. Even if that person is not you, you should be aware of medication schedules for your children. You may be able to help with reminders that it is time for the next dose. It is good to have back-up on the thinking part of giving medication, but it is also good to have only one person responsible for the hands-on part of giving medication so that no overdosing mistakes occur.

You also need to be aware of the effects medications may have on the children. This will help you understand and be patient with changes in behavior and also help you spot when the changes are out of the ordinary. Some side effects of medication include sleepiness, agitation or irritability, and allergic symptoms. You need to watch for any problem side effects so that the parents and pertinent staff can be alerted as appropriate.

Emergencies

- *Stay calm.* That is the best thing you can do for the children in your care and for yourself.
- Speak calmly and quietly to the child.
- Alert the teacher or director according to your center guidelines.
- Administer appropriate first aid measures until the child gets medical attention. Go through the center's chain of command, if there are guidelines about who is authorized to give aid; but *never* neglect to give help when you are the only one capable or present.
- Help calm the other children. They will respond to the situation the same way you do. If you are agitated and upset, they will react to your feelings; likewise, if you remain calm, they usually will also.

Note the key word about handling emergencies.

Feeding

- Wash your hands. (You might as well go ahead and engrave it on your brain.)

- Check the file or chart to see what kind of food and/or formula to give and how much. (Remember: Don't feed a baby from a baby food jar; use a dish. Saliva contains bacteria and can get into the jar and spoil any remaining food.)

- Gather everything you will need before you begin feeding, including a bib, washcloth, and spoons. It may be helpful to let the baby hold a spoon; the baby may feel like he's "helping" and he also may be distracted from trying to grab the one you're using.

- Tell the baby what you are going to do. Let the infant anticipate being fed.

- Settle the baby comfortably. (You may want to make sure the baby has a clean, dry diaper. It's got to be hard to pay attention to your food if you feel gross.)

- Make sure you feed babies exactly as requested by the parents. Laying an infant flat to drink a bottle can cause fluid back-up in the Eustachian tubes and set up the perfect breeding ground for germs to grow. Parents of babies with chronic ear infections will not be happy if they have requested that their baby be held in an upright position while being fed and their instructions are not followed.

- Tune in to the baby's clues about speed of feeding and when more food is desired. (The baby's eating rhythm is more important than your time clock even if you do have umpteen things that need to be done in the next thirty minutes!)

- Talk to the child. Eating is a time when we adults enjoy good conversation and socialization, and little ones can begin to enjoy these aspects, too. Young children like being talked to. For a start, you can talk about the food, its texture, color, temperature, taste, etc. (Yum.) Eye contact is important.

- Encourage the child to help feed himself solids. It is a little (!) messier, but it means more independence later.

- If the small child refuses to take that last ounce of a bottle or that last dab of solid food, do not push it. She knows better than you when she is hungry.

- Burp bottle-fed infants when necessary. Be sure to check any special instructions from the parents.

- When the baby is finished, wash the face and hands. (This is usually a fun challenge.) Again, tell the baby you are going to do this. Be gentle with the washcloth.

- Clean up as soon as possible to avoid the spread of germs.

- Record what and how the child ate. The parents may need to know this.

Diapering

- Just as in feeding, gather everything you'll need before you start to change the baby: diapers, wipes, washcloth, clean clothes, etc.

- Tell the baby what you are going to do.

- Clean the child thoroughly with either a warm, wet cloth or baby wipes, depending on the wishes of the parents or center guidelines. Apply powder or ointment only according to the parent's instructions.

- Keep one hand on the child at all times if you are changing the child on a changing table.

- Talk to the child about the whole process. Talk about being wet, dry, and clean. Talk about the baby's clothes and body parts. Involve the baby in helping you whenever possible. Ask the baby to lift his legs or help put his arm through the sleeve. (*Note:* How diapers are changed gives children early messages about sexuality. If you are relaxed and casual about changing and cleaning them, children get the message that they are "okay.")

- Put the child in a safe place while you dispose of the diaper and dirty clothes. Follow center directions for this.

- Clean the changing surface with germicidal solution.

- Yes, wash your hands again (Figure 4–1).

- Record the diaper change. Be sure to note bowel movements. Make note of anything unusual: loose, runny stools, hard stools or constipation, diaper rash, unusually strong urine odor, or anything else that seems out of the ordinary.

P.S. An interesting new tip for treating diaper rash appeared in the medical journal *Contemporary Pediatrics.* Maalox was suggested to soothe irritated outsides just as it soothes irritated insides. The rationale is that when Maalox is applied to the diaper area and then allowed to dry, it counteracts the acidity of urine ("Atlanta Parent," 1995). Keep your eyes and ears open for helpful tips from reliable sources.

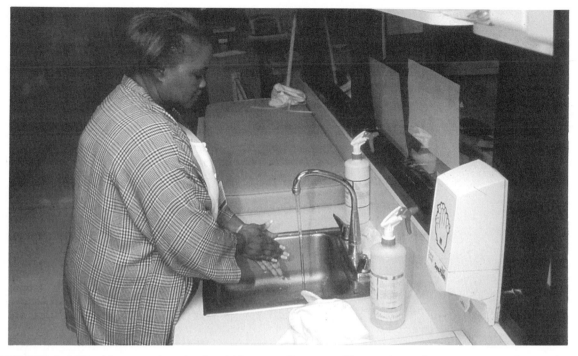

FIGURE 4–1 Washing your hands should be a routine, repetitive and very important part of your day.

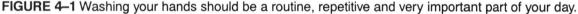

Nap time

Young children may vary considerably in their nap times. Ask any parent of more than one child! You need to key in to signs of sleepiness so you won't miss that opportune moment and also to prevent a little one from growing overtired. Watch for signs like yawning, rubbing eyes, pulling or twirling hair, thumb sucking, and disinterest in toys or people; these signs let you know that someone is "overdone."

When you see signs that a young child may be ready for a nap, quickly check his schedule before putting him down. Make sure the child is not due to be fed soon. You may want to feed a child a little ahead of schedule if he is sleepy. Make sure the diaper is dry and you have a clean crib and blanket. Also, see if the child has a special toy to sleep with.

Little children usually have definite preferences about sleep positions. Find out if the child prefers to sleep on her back, side, or stomach and help her get situated. Most children like to lie on their stomachs.

Parents may also have definite preferences about how their children sleep, especially if they are babies. Be sure to follow their instructions.

You and your center should also keep current on the latest information about infant sleep positions. Laying an infant on his side is considered a prime way to prevent choking should the baby spit up (Figure 4–2). Occasionally recommendations from the American Academy of Pediatrics change based on new information regarding Sudden Infant Death Syndrome (SIDS, or *crib death*) and other sleep findings. Periodically investigate new findings. Do not assume that just because you know something now that that knowledge will still be valid in two years. Research is being done all the time that may teach us new things about well baby care and prevention of tragedies.

You may find it helpful to sing softly, rub the back gently, or rock in order to help a little one settle down to sleep. Dimming the lights may have a calming effect. Sometimes the excitement of the center and the other children make it difficult for babies to sleep.

If you are helping a child who is new to the center, understand that the child may be reluctant to take a nap. This is because the child is in a strange place, full of strangers. You probably don't relax enough to sleep too easily under those conditions yourself! Be patient. Also be firm. Toddlers usually adjust very quickly to the nap schedule of a program. However, all ages and even the little ones who have been around for a while can get "off," so bear with them.

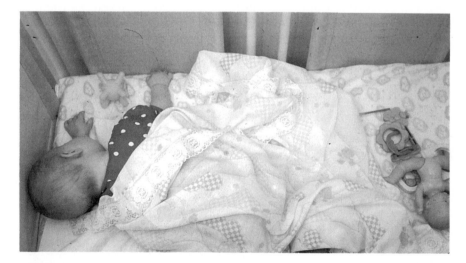

FIGURE 4–2 Laying an infant on his side is considered a prime way to prevent choking should the baby spit up.

Do not feel you have failed if you do not get instant success. Ask other staff members for suggestions. Infant center staff people are usually more than willing to answer questions, listen to concerns, or give advice. Do your part to foster a cooperative atmosphere in your center.

TOILET LEARNING

Toilet learning is too frequently treated with embarrassment in parenting books and research on the topic is meager. Many parents and caregivers do not understand that bladder and bowel control are skills that are *learned* when little ones are ready; they cannot be taught or trained.

Infants begin life with automatic emptying of the bladder and bowel. Bladder capacity is so small that wetting may occur every hour or so. Automatic emptying is triggered by the filling of the bladder or bowel that sets off rhythmic contractions; the infant has no control over these.

The nervous system has to mature before babies and toddlers are even capable of being aware of full bladder and bowel sensations. The development necessary for consistent awareness takes place during the first year or two. Of course, you will observe signs that alert you to the fact that a little one is becoming more aware of his bodily functions; you may see a look of concentration while all activity stops, crossing the legs, fidgeting, or holding the diaper area.

As the bladder capacity gradually increases, it becomes possible for little ones to consciously hold urine. By the second year, capacity has usually doubled and the frequency of wetting is about every two or three hours. Emptying is still automatic and dependent upon fullness.

By three years most children have learned a little about control; they usually go when it suits them. They are often capable of holding urine for a considerable time even when the bladder is full. This holding ability requires conscious control of some muscles (perineal muscles for urination and the bowel sphincter for bowel movements) and this control is only possible with physiological development. At this age, accidents still occur often since children do not have total control. This becomes so obvious when a little one who has just been taken to the toilet and did not urinate goes back to play and immediately wets all over the place.

When parents or caregivers boast that toddlers at 14, 18, or 21 months are toilet trained, be aware that it is much more likely that it is the parents or caregivers who are trained— trained to recognize the signs of impending need and trained to rush the child to the potty chair in time. Sonja Flating relates her experiences interviewing potential caregivers for her daughter. She tells how some interviewees informed her that they could have her baby trained by the time she was one year old. Fortunately, this mom had already discussed the physiological facts with her pediatrician, so she did not hire any of these. She did find out from references that these caregivers were "trained," adept at "catching" their charges at just the right time. The woman who *was* hired "responded that toilet training was something that would happen through imitation and intuition with no set time table" (1991).

During the fourth year most children have achieved good control over both their bowel and bladder muscles, but it is important to remember that full control is not fully accomplished until about six years old.

This information about development may help you to be understanding and compassionate with a little one who is going through the whole process of toilet learning. It may also help you to refrain from pressuring a child who is simply not ready and help parents with the same issue. It's good to remember that even though it involves some complex aptitudes, most children acquire toileting skills with a minimum of help *when they are ready.* Be patient!

How do you know a child is ready? Here are some things to look for:

- Clear signs of recognizing needs
- Ability to help with clothes, pants down or skirt up
- Ability to communicate
- Increasing dry periods

Toilet learning is far from simple. Think about what else a little one will have to learn in addition to the list above; she has to learn to flush the toilet (Most do not have any problem with this. It's the toilet overflow from overflushing that is the kicker!), use toilet tissue, and wash her hands afterwards. There is a lot to this!

How do you handle accidents? The number one rule is to remember that accidents will happen; they are inevitable. Treat accidents matter-of-factly. If you missed a cue from the child and did not move fast enough to help, acknowledge the child's attempt to get your attention. Recognize that some accidents may be your fault, not the child's.

People are generally free with criticism and/or advice about toilet learning. You and your lead teacher may disagree about how and when to help little ones learn toileting control. The lead teacher or another coworker may follow a routine of taking toddlers to a potty chair at regular intervals. Even if you know that complete control comes with physiological development, you can go along with the center's policy because regular toileting routines do help children acquire control at an earlier age than those with irregular routines. If a parent complains that her child was toilet *trained* before she placed him in your day care center and is angry because now she has been asked to bring in diapers, let the director or lead teacher handle the problem. Defer to the center policy if a parent tries to involve you in this kind of conflict. Also, be patient with parents who wait "too long" to begin toilet training, in your opinion. Perhaps, as busy, working parents, they find it easier to keep a child in diapers than to try to learn the child's subtle cues or to cope with accidents.

These stresses are simply not worth it. Try not to get caught up in the surprisingly high level of competition and emotion attached to the whole issue of toilet learning. Most children learn eventually with or without being taught! Relax and don't make a big deal out of it.

One thing you and the parents and anyone else involved need to consider is that if you begin toilet *training* too early, before the child is ready, you will likely encounter regression and will end up stringing the whole process out for a longer time. On the other hand, you can wait until the child is so ready that the child kind of does it on his own.

Most children learn by example. As one little one learns to use the toilet independently, he or she becomes a role model for other children. In a family-type center with a mixture of ages, the older ones are role models for the younger ones. Of course, parents are also role models for their children at home. Treat toilet learning like the natural process it is and do not put unfair or unkind pressure on the children. Above all, when a little one is successful, actually makes it to the potty and performs, praise him highly. Praise is a better motivator for continued success than fear of retribution after mistakes.

Occasionally there may be a problem such as constipation, diarrhea, or painful urination that contributes to accidents. You may be able to help parents check for any dietary-related factors (like a diet too low in fluid or fiber) that can be corrected.

APPROACHING AND WORKING WITH YOUNG CHILDREN

When working with infants and toddlers, remember that every child is an individual. Even tiny infants have preferences. They may like to be rocked instead of being walked when fussy; they may like to be burped with their heads at your shoulder rather than your knees. When you are caring for a child, take a minute to try and find out what some of her preferences may be.

When working with little children, remember:

- Your size may be frightening to a child.
- Keep confidential information to yourself. Medical, financial, personal, and family information are privileged information that help you understand the child more completely but do not need to be shared.

Working with Infants

Babies need to hear your voice, so talk to them. They need the social contact that only another person can provide. Hearing language is also the way babies learn to talk. Be sure you use clear, simple language. *Speak softly.* Voice tone and volume greatly affect children. If you speak in a loud, excited voice, the children are very likely to become loud and excited in response.

Encourage anticipation by telling the children what you are going to do. Say, "Now we are going to change your diaper" or "We are going to paint with our fingers, on the big white paper only." They will respond and cooperate when you let them know what to expect.

Try to be at eye level with the children as much as possible. Sitting or kneeling on the floor brings you closer to their line of vision. Make lots of *eye contact.* When bottle feeding, playing, diapering, and so on, look directly at babies. Meet and hold their gaze when talking to them. You like to have people look at you; babies undoubtedly feel the same way.

Move slowly around infants. They often get upset and overstimulated when adults run around them excitedly. Young infants need time to understand the changes that are happening. Be affectionate and warm but don't hover. Be ready to hug, hold, and comfort when they need it, but let them be free to explore. Young children need to be able to move around and experience their environment. They need to find their own solutions to problems whenever they can. Let the children experiment with toys and invent uses. Intervene only when they might get hurt, are obviously in distress, or are too frustrated to cope. Taking the first steps toward becoming independent, competent, and self-sufficient is hard work; little ones need love and security and safety to begin the process.

Encourage babies to help you in caregiving. You need to dress them, change them, and feed them. However, they will begin to help if you let them. Recognize their attempts to participate and encourage them. You may feel like it takes much longer, but it really doesn't take that much extra time and the rewards of independence are great.

Flating suggests that parents seeking care for their babies:

"look for someone who will hold your baby, talk to him, make lots of eye contact and possess a certain intuitiveness regarding your baby's temperament; someone who will allow your baby's individuality to develop into his own unique style." (1991)

Working with Toddlers

Toddlers are a very special group. They are just beginning to understand that they are people. They are seeing themselves as separate from their parents for the first time. They are compelled to explore and learn their environment. They must assert themselves as individuals. If you can recognize their need to be individuals without feeling personal affront, you will have made a giant step in dealing effectively with toddlers.

Toddlers, more so than infants, will challenge your authority (at every turn!) They will test you. Often they test until they can feel secure in your response. You will need to call on all your reserves of strength, firmness, patience, and love in order to deal with them. They are loving, affectionate, giving, sharing, joyful, spontaneous people who are capable of driving adults to distraction at times. Remember to take pleasure in them; they are a delight!

You may find some of the following ideas helpful when you are working with toddlers. Think about these suggestions and try to put them into practice.

Make *positive statements.* Say, "Feet belong on the floor" instead of, "Don't kick the chair." When children hear the words *don't* and *no* constantly, they begin to ignore them. Also be free with appropriate praise.

Choices are great and are important in facilitating independence in children, but be very cautious in giving them. Give choices only when you intend to honor them. If Drew's mom said that her son must wear his jacket outside, do not ask Drew, "Do you want to wear your jacket?" Instead, say "Your mom wants you to wear a jacket today." If you give a choice and the toddler says "no," you are already in a conflict you could have avoided. (And two-year-olds are tough in arguments!)

Avoid problems by _being alert._ Watch for signs that a child may be getting too frustrated to handle a situation or that a fight over a toy is about to break out. Use distraction whenever possible. If you see two children insisting on the same toy, see if the children can work it out themselves. If not, try to interest one of them in something else. You might point out another toy just like it or remind them of some other fun activity.

If an argument does erupt, _avoid taking sides._ Help both children understand how the other child feels. Encourage the use of words to handle situations. Encourage and teach the children to name things and express needs and emotions. Let the children talk. By all means, don't be concerned with correct grammar and pronunciation at this point. These will come later. Practicing verbal expression is the most important thing.

Act on your own suggestions. If you say, "Time to put your snacks away. Throw your garbage in the trashcan," the children are more likely to follow your suggestions if they are accompanied by actions. Let them see you throw your own napkin away. Facilitate the actions even if you want the children to do the actions themselves. For example, set the trashcan out for easy access or set the storage container out by the blocks.

Make alternative suggestions if a child continually ignores safety rules or disturbs others; suggest another activity the child likes; suggest taking turns; suggest cooperation; or remove the child from the activity. Be firm but calm.

Do not take a child's reaction personally. You may hear "I don't like you!" (or worse). Acknowledge the child's right to his feelings. You might say something like, "I know you are angry. It's okay to be angry." Even at such a young age, toddlers respect fairness. Yet they desperately want limits they can depend on even if this doesn't exactly come across through their communications.

Do not make promises you cannot keep. You will soon find out how important this is if you do not know it already, because toddlers remember everything! If you want to model and teach good values, then keeping promises is a vital component. When you keep your promises, you also show children that they can trust you. If there is something you are not sure about, do not promise anything; just say you will have to ask or find out. Toddlers understand that.

PRESCHOOL ACTIVITIES AND CURRICULUM AREAS

At prekindergarten levels you will help with abundant playing activities. Schickedanz (1990) notes "the preschool program pendulum once again swings back to play," and "children can learn a lot of academics while they play." She urges teachers to:

> *"be skillful, clever, and in tune with preschoolers' minds. They must take adult-oriented goals and fit them into a child's world. As one wise teacher once said to me, I know I must teach children, but I depend on them for ideas about how to do it." (1990)*

Play is often considered the most important work of a little person. Babies are capable of learning through play at very early ages. Bismarck said, "You can do anything with children if you only play with them."

There are two types of play: social play, in which the child interacts with *someone* else, and object play, in which the child interacts with *something*. Children of all ages engage in both types of play. Many of the following guidelines apply to all children but they are especially true for infants and toddlers.

- Activities for infants are not "geared down" preschool activities. Infants are a specific age group who need specific activities.
- Play *with* the children, not *to* them. Try to interact, not entertain. You can initiate the activity but should wait for the child to respond.
- Involve different ways of communicating in your interactions: looking, rocking, holding, laughing, talking, singing. Give babies a lot of different social responses to learn.
- Be sensitive to babies' signals. If they are interested, they will laugh, coo, look, smile, and reach. If they are tired or disinterested, they may fuss, turn away, or fall asleep.
- Again, talk to babies. Children learn to talk from the moment they are born. The more language they hear, the more they will learn. Name objects, actions, and people.
- Offer new ways of doing things. Demonstrate how something works. Do not insist the child use the toy the "right way," however. Encourage persistence. Let the child explore and experiment, but use judgment in matters of safety.
- Respond to the child.

A child can play with toys either alone or with an adult. Make sure you offer age- and developmentally appropriate toys. A toy that a two-month-old enjoys might not be appropriate for a nine-month-old. When offering playthings to children, remember:

- Toys should encourage action. Materials should not just entertain but elicit some action.

- Toys should respond to the child's action. When the child pushes or pulls a toy, the toy should react. The ability to control parts of one's world, to learn cause and effect, is an important part of learning at early ages.

- Playthings should be versatile. The more ways a toy can be used, the better it is.

- Whenever possible, toys should relate to more than one of the senses. For example, a clear rattle lets the baby see, as well as hear, the action.

Toys and playing are important for infants and toddlers. However, you should not be led to believe that constant stimulation is the aim. Even young infants need time to be alone and get away from it all. Be sensitive to the baby's cues to help avoid overstimulation and distress.

Activities for Infants

The following are some activity ideas especially geared toward infants from one to twelve months old. Some of these activities are appropriate for other ages as well.

- Change the baby's position for a different view, a change in scenery.
- Use bells, rattles, and spoons to make noise.
- Exercise the baby's arms and legs.
- Let the baby feel and play with different textured materials.
- Put large, clear pictures at eye level for the baby to look at.
- Imitate the sounds the infant makes.
- Record the children's sounds, and play them back.
- Put toys slightly out of reach to encourage rolling and reaching.
- Take babies outside on warm days. Let them feel the grass and see trees and plants. Warm sun exposure, though.
- Call little ones by name.
- Play peek-a-boo.

- Hide toys and encourage the children to look for them.
- Make puppets for the children to look at and hold and play with. Be careful about small parts.
- Let children play with mirrors. Babies love to look at themselves; so do older children.
- Play games and sing, using parts of the body. Make up songs about feet, hands, noses, etc.
- Play pat-a-cake and sing "row-row-row your boat." Begin songs and encourage the children to finish the songs for you.
- Listen for outside noises like airplanes, trucks, dogs, etc., and call the children's attention to them.
- Roll a ball to a baby and encourage the baby to roll it back.
- Play music for the children; encourage them to clap along or dance.
- Read to the children, even when they are little babies. Point out the pictures and encourage them to point to them.
- Play pretending games.
- Show little ones how to stack blocks.
- Make obstacle courses for the children to crawl over, around, and through.
- Let them play with measuring cups and spoons in water, sand, or cornmeal.
- Play "follow the leader."
- Make an incline for the children to roll objects down.
- Have the children set the table with plastic cups and dishes.
- Have purses and bags for the children to carry things in.
- Let the children finger-paint with nontoxic paint.
- Use old-fashioned clothespins for the children to put around the rim of a plastic container. (Make sure that any sharp edges are filed down.)
- Encourage the children to help put their toys away, even at young ages.
- Let them practice opening containers, e.g., plastic margarine bowls. Put a toy in the container to entice them to open it.
- Make toys for the children; be inventive. Let your imagination go, and remember toys do not have to be expensive. Also remember that toys should not have sharp edges and should be too large to fit in a little mouth.

Of course, as babies grow, their activities gradually become more and more complex. A child is usually walking and beginning to talk by twelve to fourteen months. A baby of this age is quite accomplished mentally. The infant understands that objects are separate and detached and will rotate, reverse, and stack things, and will put them in and out of containers in order to test and examine this separateness.

Because of their increased mental and physical abilities, you can try new projects and activities with toddlers. You can begin to use small group activities with some success. When planning activities for and working with toddlers, remember that they still need to be kept simple. In addition, plan ahead. Anything that can go wrong probably will. (Good old Murphy!) Bring everything you need to start and finish the project. Toddlers aren't always real patient!

Activities for Toddlers

Below are some ideas you might want to try with toddlers. The key word is *try* since toddlers are kind of unpredictable. If something doesn't work one day, don't be afraid to wait a while and try it again. Watch your children and you'll discover some things they might enjoy.

- Easel painting (with one color of paint mixed with soap to help it come out of clothes). Paint on cloth for a great gift for parents.
- Coloring. Use a limited number of large size crayons (because they will all want the same color) and a large sheet of paper. For a change, try covering the whole table with paper.
- Collage. Try using liquid starch and tissue paper with paint brushes.
- Finger-painting. For a change, try yogurt or pudding, but first clear it with parents who may not want their children to "play" with food.
- Music. Use drums, rhythm sticks, clapping games, and simple exercises to music.
- Flannel board stories. Keep them short and vivid and exciting.
- Bubble blowing. (Have the children sit down while blowing bubbles if they are using straws and remember to collect all straws afterwards. *Note:* A small slit cut near the top of the straw prevents a child from sucking up soapy water.)
- Gluing. Use torn paper, tissue, magazine pictures, etc. Avoid small beans or anything that could be swallowed or put up noses.

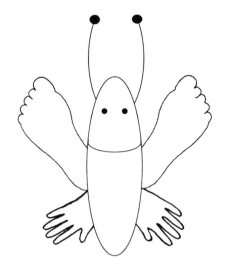

FIGURE 4–3 Butterfly made from hand and footprints. The antenna ends are finished with fingerprints.

- Play-dough. Made with salt, flour, and nontoxic ingredients. (Some recipes are given in Chapter 5.)
- Hand- and footprints. (You can use hand- and footprints to make art projects such as the butterfly in Figure 4–3.)
- Body tracings.
- Cardboard boxes. Cut shapes in the sides of a large one. Children can climb through the sides after they paint it.
- Simple shape rubbings (more suitable for older toddlers).
- Make simple roll-out cookies or use frozen dough for the children to roll out and cut with cookie cutters. They'll love eating them later. You might want to identify them because they could get a little gross. Names penciled on parchment paper does the trick.

Reading. Reading is an activity that bears mentioning repeatedly. It is never too early to read to children. Just the sound of the voice, the lilting quality of speech, and the caregiver's proximity ultimately aid in language acquisition. Initially, you may simply point to pictures and name objects for babies. Later, your explanations can be expanded and you may ask questions and ask for feedback from the children. Although it is never too early to read, it is important to match the level and length to how the children respond. Ability to concentrate varies dramatically among children. However, it is safe to say that young children generally have very short attention spans. The ability to focus on a given object or activity increases dramatically in the first years. Studies show, though, that even the "observing" child is participating and learning while not actively involved in the current activity. So, press on. Read, and continue reading. It is so important!

There are all kinds of books for little ones out on the market now. Heavy cardboard books are designed for small hands and are easily handled; these are a wonderful way for children to have their first experiences with *reading*. Today there are many fine examples of books designed to instill a love for books from early ages.

Remember to use music. It is usually a dependable interest catcher. There are hundreds of songs incorporating body parts and including movement components that bring forth peals of delight from children. In the context of music, even a shy child may be more readily drawn out and willing to participate. "With movement exploration activities children can find, as well, a wide range of body experiences through which they will naturally develop motor skills and knowledge of the operation of their own bodies" (Sullivan, 1982). Sullivan outlines a broad range of specific movement skills to explore and develop with young children. Music can be such an inspiring motivator for movement exploration and many other types of learning.

Preschool Curriculums

Most preschool curriculums include: arts and crafts; music and movement; language; science; large and small motor skill development; cooking and nutrition activities; numbers and measurement, perceptual motor activities; health and safety activities; social learnings; multicultural awareness activities; and plant and animal study. Kind of a lot for three-year-olds, don't you think? These subjects are incorporated in many normal play and daily activities, though.

New areas of study are springing up with different degrees of acceptance, including anti-bias, economics, and consumer awareness; ecology and energy study; moral and ethical values; the study of changing sex role responsibilities; the study of changing family patterns; introduction to photography; introduction to computers; and gardening. These sound even more intimidating for preschoolers than the basic set of subjects, but you might be surprised at how much of these complicated subjects can be taught on a very simple level. Some of these subjects can be fairly controversial; make sure you know the dictates of your center and your parent group.

TEACHING DURING ROUTINE ACTIVITIES

Your classroom will have planned activities and you will assist with these. Many times, though, you will teach without being conscious of it. Many areas of curriculum are encountered during routine caregiving activities. For example, think about what goes on even during a diaper change and ways a baby may be learning:

- You talk to the baby, and tell him what is going to happen. The baby is developing a sense of sequential events.
  language
  social
  mathematics

- You take off the baby's diaper and let him move his legs freely. The baby feels the air on his body.
  motor
  sensory

- You tell the child about the condition of his diaper.
  cognitive
  sensory

- You clean the baby. You may apply powder or diaper rash medication. You talk about how this feels.
  sensory
  language
  cognitive

- You put a new diaper on the baby and, possibly, new clothes. The new diaper is dry and feels more comfortable.
  sensory
  language
  cognitive

- You talk about what is happening and encourage the baby to help you by lifting his legs, putting out an arm, etc.
  language
  motor
  social

- The baby is now more comfortable and probably happier. You have had an opportunity for a special one-to-one experience with the child. For a few minutes of a busy morning, the baby has had your complete attention.
  self-esteem
  sensory
  social

Think about feeding.

- You know it is time to give a bottle or feed a baby. You tell the baby you are going to prepare the food. Again, you are helping a little one develop a sense of sequence of time.
  mathematics
  language
  social

- A little baby may just be starting to eat and learning to eat from a spoon; an older baby may be using fingers or learning to use a spoon. How special she'll feel when she succeeds!

  motor
  self-esteem

- You sit with the child or a small group of children while they eat lunch. You talk about what they are eating, about how it tastes, its texture, and color. A child who does not like peas may be encouraged to try three peas or two pieces of carrots.

  social
  language
  cognitive
  sensory
  mathematics

- A baby has your total attention when you are giving her a bottle. You talk to her, make eye contact, and hold her close and safe. The milk is warm.

  self-esteem
  language
  sensory

- After eating, you wash her face and hands with a warm, wet cloth. First, the right hand; then, the left. The child may be able to help you (but don't always count on it!).

  sensory
  language
  cognitive
  motor

Are you beginning to see what goes on "behind the scenes?" These are just two examples of the many routines that happen in an infant center. All through the day you will have opportunities for teachable moments. Carry with you a constant awareness that *you* are teaching little ones, so you can make the most of these natural opportunities.

HELP HOLD HIGH STANDARDS

Each state has rules and regulations regarding child care facilities, along with agencies to oversee them. In order for a child care center to be granted or maintain a license, it must comply with the rules and regulations in that state. Some of the regulations relate to the following areas:

- Developmental rather than custodial programs. Kingsbury, Vogler, and Benero report that "the concept of custodial care is now obsolete in most geographic areas (1990).

- Age-appropriate requirements for individual age groups.

- Separation of age groups.

- Regulations concerning group size.

- Physical space requirements.

- Staff-child ratios, ranging from one adult per three infants to one adult for every ten babies (Kingsbury, et al., 1990).

- Rights of the parents to visit the center. Kingsbury, Vogler, and Benero report a trend toward greater accommodation of parents' wishes to visit; in eighteen states parents have the legal right to visit anytime (1990).

- Staff training requirements. According to Kingsbury, Vogler, and Benero, the one factor that is most indicative of the quality of the staff of a child care center is their training and experience in the child care field (1990).

- Immunization requirements for attending children.

- Liability insurance requirements.

- Mandatory criminal records checks.

The agencies that regulate child care centers differ among the states. Table 4–1 lists the licensing agencies for all the states. Note that the agencies include health departments, human resources departments, social services departments, children's departments, and welfare agencies.

Of course it is in your and the children's best interest to help make your facility the very best it can be. Be supportive of efforts to hold high licensing standards. Think about what parents want in a child care center and the people who provide the care. Evaluate whether children are safe and happy at your center. Think through the answers to the following questions. Do what you can to make necessary positive changes at your facility.

- Are children's needs consistently met and are they given learning opportunities which are appropriate for their developmental levels?

- Is the communication with the parents satisfactory to all?

- Are parents invited to be as involved as they want to be?

- Is the staff consistent with the goals and policies of the center?

- Do the rooms look clean and welcoming and conducive to effective supervision?

- If any food is served, is it nutritious and supplied in adequate amounts?

- Are staff members kind and tuned in to children's needs?

TABLE 4–1 State Licensing Agencies

ALASKA
Department of Health and Social
  Services
Division of Family and Youth Services
P.O. Box H–05
Juneau, AK 99811–0630
(907) 465–3206

ALABAMA
Department of Human Resources
Division of Day Care and Child
  Development
Administrative Building
Ripley Street
Montgomery, AL 36130
(334) 242–1425

ARKANSAS
Department of Social Services
Child Development Unit
P.O. Box 1437
Little Rock, AR 72201
(501) 324–5827

ARIZONA
Arizona Department of Health
  Services
Child Day Care Facilities
1647 E. Morten, Ste. 240
Phoenix, AZ 85006
(602) 255–1221

CALIFORNIA
Department of Social Services
Community Care Facilities Division
744 P Street, Mail Section 17–17
Sacramento, CA 95814
(916) 324–4031

COLORADO
Licensing Administrator
Department of Social Services
1575 Sherman Street, Room 420
Denver, CO 80203–1714
(303) 866–5970

CONNECTICUT
Department of Public Health —
  Daycare
410 Capitol Ave.
MS #12 DAC
P.O. Box 340308
Hartford, CT 06134–0308
(860) 509–8045

DISTRICT OF COLUMBIA
Department of Consumer and
  Regulatory Affairs
614 H Street, NW, Room 910
Washington, DC 20001
(202) 727–7822

DELAWARE
Department of Services for Children,
  Youth and their Families
Division of Program Support
1825 Faulkland Road
Wilmington, DE 19805–1195
(302) 892–5800

FLORIDA
Department of Children and Family
  Safety and Preservation
Child Care Services
2811A Industrial Plaza Dr.
Tallahassee, FL 32301
(904) 488–4900

GEORGIA
Day Care Licensing Section
Office of Regulatory Services
2 Peachtree Street, NW Room 102
Atlanta, GA 30303
(404) 657–5562

HAWAII
Department of Social Services and
  Housing
Public Welfare Division
Program Development
P.O. Box 339
Honolulu, HI 96809
(808) 548–2302

IDAHO
Child Care Coordinator
Department of Health and Welfare
Bureau of Social Services
450 West State Street
Boise, ID 83720
(208) 384–3708

ILLINOIS
Department of Children and Family
  Services
406 Monroe Street
Springfield, IL 62006
(217) 785–2688

INDIANA
Department of Public Welfare
Child Welfare/Social Services Division
141 South Meridian Street, 6th Floor
Indianapolis, IN 46225
(317) 233–3376

IOWA
Bureau of Adult, Children and Family
  Services
Department of Human Services
5th Floor
Hoover State Office Building
Des Moines, IA 50319
(515) 281–5452

KANSAS
Kansas Department of Health and
  Environment
Bureau of Child Care Licensing
109 SW 9th St., Ste 410C
Topeka, KS 66612–2218
(913) 296–1270

KENTUCKY
Division for Licensing and
  Regulation
275 East Main Street
CHS Building, 4th Floor East
Frankfort, KY 40621
(502) 564–2800

LOUISIANA
Division of Licensing and
  Certification
Department of Health and Human
  Resource
P.O. Box 3767
Baton Rouge, LA 70821–3767
(504) 925–3796

MAINE
Licensing Unit for Day Care
Bureau of Social Services
221 State Street
State House, Station 11
Augusta, ME 04333
(207) 289–5060

MARYLAND
Department of Child Care Licensing
  and Regulation
Ste LL8, 409 Washington Ave.
Towson, MD 21204
(410) 321–2216

Department of Health and Mental
  Hygiene
Family Health
201 West Preston Street
Baltimore, MD 21201
(410) 225–6743

MASSACHUSETTS
Day Care Licensing
Office for Children
10 West Street
Boston, MA 02111
(617) 727–8900

MICHIGAN
Michigan Department of Social
  Services
Child Day Care Licensing Division
700 West Saginaw, 2nd Fl.
P.O. Box 30650
Lansing, MI 48909–8150
(517) 373–8300

TABLE 4–1 State Licensing Agencies (Continued)

MINNESOTA
Division of Licensing
Department of Human Services
444 Lafayette Road
Saint Paul, MN 55155–3842
(612) 296–3971

MISSISSIPPI
Child Care and Special Licensing
Department of Health Regulations
State Board of Health
P.O. Box 1700
Jackson, MS 39205
(601) 960–7740

MISSOURI
Missouri Department of Social
    Services
Division of Family Services
Broadway State Office Building
P.O. Box 570
Jefferson City, MO 65102
(573) 751–2450

MONTANA
Department of Family Services
P.O. Box 8005
Helena, MT 59604
(406) 444–5900

NEBRASKA
Department of Social Services
P.O. Box 95026
Lincoln, NE 68509–5026
(402) 471–3121

NEVADA
Nevada Bureau of Child Care
    Services
Department of Human Resources
711 E. Fifth Street, Suite 606
Carson City, NV 89701–5092
(702) 687–5911

NEW HAMPSHIRE
Bureau of Child Care Standards
    and Licensing
Division of Public Health Services
Health and Welfare Building, Hazen
    Drive
Concord, NH 03301
(603) 271–4624

NEW JERSEY
Division of Youth and Family Services
Bureau of Licensing
New Jersey Department of Social
    Services
50 E. State St. 5th Floor
Trenton, NJ 08625–0717
(609) 292–1018

NEW MEXICO
Public Health Division
Licensing Bureau and Certification
Health and Environment Department
525 Caminode Los Marquez Ste. 2
Santa Fe, NM 87501
(505) 827–4200

NEW YORK
New York State Department of Social
    Services
Day Care Unit
40 North Pearl Street
Albany, NY 12243
(518) 473–3170

NEW YORK CITY
Bureau of Day Care
New York City Department of Health
65 Worth Street, 4th Floor
New York, NY 10013
(212) 334–7712

NORTH CAROLINA
Division of Facility Services
Child Day Care Section
P.O. Box 29553
Raleigh, NC 27626–0553
(919) 733–4801

NORTH DAKOTA
North Dakota Department of Human
    Services
Children and Family Services
State Capitol – 600 E. Blvd. Ave.
Bismarck, ND 58505
(701) 328–2310

OHIO
Ohio Department of Human Services
Child Care Services
State Office Tower, 30th Floor,
    Sec. E & F
30 East Broad Street
Columbus, OH 43266–0423
(614) 644–9000

OKLAHOMA
Department of Human Services
P.O. Box 25352
Oklahoma City, OK 73125
(405) 521–3561

OREGON
Children's Services Division
Department of Employment
875 Union St., N.E.
Salem, OR 97311
(503) 378–3178

PENNSYLVANIA
Day Care Division
Department of Public Welfare
Office of Policy Planning and
    Evaluation
P.O. Box 2675
Harrisburg, PA 17105
(800) 692–7462

PUERTO RICO
Department of Social Services
Services to Families with Children
P.O. Box 11398
Santurce, PR 00910
(809) 724–7404

RHODE ISLAND
Rhode Island Department for
    Children and Their Families
Licensing Day Care Services
610 Mount Pleasant Avenue
Providence, RI 02908
(401) 457–4536

SOUTH CAROLINA
South Carolina Department of
    Social Services
DCD Regulatory Unit
P.O. Box 1520
Columbia, SC 29202–9988
(803) 734–5740

SOUTH DAKOTA
Department of Social Services
Office of Child Protection Services
Richard F. Kneip Building
700 Governor Drive
Pierre, SD 57501–2291
(605) 773–3227

TENNESSEE
Department of Human Services
Licensing Unit
400 Deaderick Street
Nashville, TN 37219
(615) 532–5132

TEXAS
Texas Department of Human
    Resources
Licensing Division
P.O. Box 15995
Austin, TX 78761
(512) 835–2350

UTAH
Department of Social Services
Day Care Licensing
120 North Temple "200 West"
Salt Lake City, UT 84103
(801) 538–4242

TABLE 4–1 State Licensing Agencies (Continued)

VERMONT
Department of Social and
   Rehabilitation Services
Division of Licensing and
   Regulation — Day Care
103 South Main Street, 2nd Floor
   Osgood Boulevard
Waterbury, VT 05676
(802) 241–2158
	WASHINGTON
	Department of Social and Health
	   Services
	Division of Children and Family
	   Services
	OB–41 D
	Olympia, WA 98504
	(360) 753–0614
		WISCONSIN
		Wisconsin Department of Health and
		   Social Services
		Office for Children, Youth and
		   Families
		Division of Community Services
		1 West Wilson Street
		P.O. Box 7851
		Madison, WI 53707
		(608) 266–8200

VIRGINIA Department of Social Services Division of Licensing Programs Blair Building 8007 Discovery Drive Richmond, VA 23229–8699 (804) 780–7441	*WEST VIRGINIA* Department of Human Services Division of Social Services 1900 Washington Street, East Charleston, WV 25305 (304) 558–4098	*WYOMING* Division of Public Assistance and Social Services Family Services Hathaway Building Cheyenne, WY 82002 (307) 777–6285
VIRGIN ISLANDS Bureau of Day Care Service Department of Social Welfare P.O. Box 550 Charlotte Amalie Saint Thomas, VI 00801 (809) 774–4570		

- Do staff members know enough about children and do they demonstrate appropriate humor?
- Are staff members open and informative with parents?

(Kingsbury, et al., 1990)

As a paraeducator, you will have many tasks in an infant/toddler center or preschool setting. Your primary function is to help the teacher achieve goals as effectively and efficiently as possible. Your understanding of the methods that the teacher and the center use to achieve these goals is essential to the success of the entire room. To be the best possible paraeducator you must operate in a way that is congruent to the lead teacher or director. Verify their goals and philosophies from time to time so that you can help balance the teaching team.

Remember to relax and enjoy the children. These young ages are a joy. There are also some trials. Focus more on the positive aspects rather than the negative ones and you and the children will be happier!

CHAPTER 5

Learning Activities: Hands-On Learning with All Systems Go

One definition for the word activity is simply *a learning situation* ("Facts on File Dictionary of Education," 1988). Facts on File defines *activity learning* as "any learning process in which a student must do something other than sit and listen, for example, conduct an experiment, make a model or research facts." That's the whole idea; a learning activity refers to doing, being involved in the learning process.

As a paraeducator, you will help prepare and present many types of learning activities. A day may contain both structured and unstructured activity times. Structured activities are planned by the teacher or paraeducator. During unstructured time, children are allowed choices and greater freedom. Schools, centers, and teachers differ in their preference for structured or unstructured activities. The balance between child-chosen and teacher-planned activities will be determined by the teacher's philosophy, the school's philosophy, the stated program goals, and the setting.

You may help arrange centers that encourage the children to discover and learn for themselves. According to Piaget, "Every time we teach a child something, we keep him from reinventing it. On the other hand, every time a child discovers it himself, it remains with him for the rest of his life."

Jones describes a classroom where children choose most of their activities:

> *Adults are responsible for structuring an environment full of developmentally appropriate choices, helping children choose among the possibilities, and enriching their experience by joining in it and building on it.*

> *and*

> *unique events keep happening....Good curriculum emerges out of those unique events. (1986)*

Your situation may be based on this open-classroom model. You may help create the appropriate activities and environment for this type of learning.

Talk to the lead teacher about his or her ideas and philosophies. Become familiar with school philosophies and goals. This information will be important to you because it will influence your day-to-day work. For example, does the lead teacher want all of the children to fingerpaint at the same time or for you to oversee several choices of artwork in a small group while the teacher conducts a reading group? Does the lead teacher want you to photocopy pages of math problems or does the teacher want you to set out math manipulatives for each child?

Neville Bennett identifies twelve styles of teaching, ranging from very informal (called progressive) with much student choice and less concern with conventional academic standards to very formal (called traditional) with less student choice and involvement and more concern with competition. He looked at characteristics such as active versus passive student roles and learning based on discovery techniques versus teaching based on memorization and rote learning. He and others have found that the majority of teachers use "what have been termed mixed styles, incorporating elements of both formal and informal practice" (Bennett, 1976).

Well, the teacher with whom you work is going to have his or her own style. You will probably develop your own style, too, but you will have to learn to complement and cooperate with each other. In thinking about the teaching styles in your classroom, consider the following characteristics:

- Teaching which incorporates several subjects, or treating each subject separately
- Degree of student involvement in the learning process and in classroom choices
- Reward and discipline system for the room
- Amount and regularity of testing
- Group versus individual student approach
- Value placed on creativity
- Teacher seen as a facilitator, or teacher seen as a disseminator of information

(Bennett, 1976)

If you just consider how these characteristics relate to your lead teacher, it may help you to understand her and the activity-teaching process for your classroom better. Hopefully through this type of consideration followed by communication you will gain some insights that will help you to be an effective assistant, who is an asset to the lead teacher and to the students.

IDENTIFYING CHILD INTERESTS

The activities you prepare will need to correlate with the classroom goals and philosophies. They should also correspond to the levels, interests, and needs of your children. Activities should appeal to and challenge the children. Watch them; listen to them for ideas. Write down (and save!) observations about their favorite activities, what captures their attention, or sparks their imaginations.

Holt (1964) emphasizes the need to be aware of children's interests:

> *We can begin by thinking of ourselves not as teachers, but as gardeners. A child's mind, like a flower, is a living thing. We can't make it grow by sticking things on it any more than we can make a flower grow by gluing on petals and leaves. All we can do is surround the growing mind with what it needs for growing and have faith that it will take what it needs and will grow. Our job as teachers is not to get the child to learn what we want but to help him learn what he wants.*

Classes have unique personalities, just as individual children do. Temperaments, learning levels, and interests will vary from group to group and year to year. You can help the lead teacher and the children enormously if you make a conscientious effort to find "the key" to your particular group of children.

Help children find and pursue their interests by asking them questions that make them dig deeper. Perrone suggests asking children thought-provoking questions as they learn and explore (1993). Develop your own repertoire of questions such as:

- What do you think is going on?
- Is there any other way to make that work?
- Do you have any idea why this is happening?
- Can you think of a reason they did that?

Perrone says that questions such as these keep learning conversations going and "also stimulate inquiry and discovery" (1993).

RESPONSIBILITY FOR PREPARING ACTIVITIES COVERS A RANGE

The responsibility level in preparing activities covers a large scale for paraeducators. The teacher may give you complete freedom; other times the teacher may have specific tightly defined tasks for you to do in activity preparation. The teacher may give you explicit instructions to copy this and cut out that. On the other hand, the teacher may ask you to prepare an activity on the weather, leaving decisions up to you. Where you fall on this responsibility scale may depend on the teacher's personality, the specific unit, and the school protocol. Also, in general, trust and interdependence grow over time as you work closely with someone. You will be given more leeway as you develop and prove your own capabilities.

ACTIVITY RESOURCES

Draw upon your own creative abilities in assisting the teacher. Too often teacher aides feel that tried and true activity ideas are superior to what they invent. You may feel more confident with old standbys or published ideas, but do not be afraid to try new things. The more you step out and implement your own ideas, the more confident you will feel. New activities and approaches add sparkle and originality to the classroom or center.

Look for ways to improve or modify old, good ideas. Revamp activities that have already been successful with your children. Sometimes adding a twist to an old favorite recharges the enthusiasm level.

Check out the supplies you have on hand. Some great activities have been designed because someone looked around at scraps or donated material and asked, "What can we do with this?" Visit storage closets to scrounge for forgotten treasures. Maybe you can be the one to reintroduce them in a clever, new way.

Volunteers can be wonderful with special and everyday activities. Invite parents and grandparents to volunteer in the classroom. If you and your lead teacher make volunteers feel welcome, you can tap a terrific source for help with an endless stream of beneficial activities. You might also consider asking teachers in older grades to send volunteer students to do one-on-one or small group activities with younger ones during off times like bus duty before or after the school bell rings.

Remember to use other teachers and paraeducators as resources for activities. The paraeducator from the room next door may have a brilliant plan she will be glad to share. If people you work with seem selfish with ideas, share first. Consider whether periodic meetings for exchanging ideas might be beneficial for paraeducators in your facility. Many areas have periodic workshops you may be eligible to attend.

FACTORS TO CONSIDER IN ACTIVITY PLANNING

Once your task has been defined and you have the foundation for an activity, there are still many aspects to examine before plunging into preparation. There are important factors you need to consider every time you plan and prepare any activity for children. Always evaluate safety issues; this cannot be overemphasized. Think through the goal or objective for the activity. Other factors include:

- Age appropriateness.
- Experience and skill levels. (Can our children handle this? Will it challenge or frustrate?)
- Suitable environment. (Do we have enough space?)
- Number of children and adults.
- Duration and time of day. (Would this activity hold their interest better in the morning?)
- Materials.
- Expense. (Will we ask for donations from parents? Will the classroom budget cover this?)

Considerations When You Plan Activities for Children

1. All of the aspects of a child (emotional, social, physical, and intellectual) are part of the learning process. A child learns as a whole person, not with just one facet of himself.

2. Children go through stages of development at their own rates, so remember that you will most likely have several levels of understanding within a group.

3. Children learn best when many senses are involved. Incorporate as many senses (hearing, seeing, touching, tasting, smelling) as possible in activities for children.

4. Children learn best when they are actively involved.

5. How information is given and how it is received may be as significant as the information itself (the atmosphere of the classroom, the attitudes of the teacher, and so forth).

6. Children learn in different ways, so provide diversity for your classroom. Vary your materials and approaches.

- Necessary clean-up.

- Transition to next activity.

- Appropriate language and values. (Is there anything about this activity that could offend anybody?)

Note the types of questions that should go through your mind. With experience, you will click through these factors rapidly and automatically. However, these considerations will never lessen in importance.

One of the most essential criterion of an activity's success is whether it captures and holds the children's attention. An activity for children should provide active involvement opportunities and minimal waiting time. It is generally agreed that activities for young children should also:

- Provide first hand sensory experiences.

- Have clearly stated directions and expectations.

- Allow for discovery and pursuit of interests.

- Build confidence.

- Build a bridge from previous learning toward future learning. Children need to be shown how this new information relates to what they already know and what they will learn in the future.

- Add to the quality of their lives.

- Be of a reasonable duration.

- Fit into the time of day (whether a quiet or active period) and into the location (noisy or quiet).

- Accommodate individual differences.

- Be flexible.

- Be intellectually stimulating.

You, the paraeducator, can influence the success of any learning activity you oversee. How you deal with the children will have a tremendous impact on how much is learned. Be sure to:

- Treat each child with respect

- Interact rather than entertain

- Demonstrate how something works but do not insist the child does everything "your way." (Of course, use your judgment in matters of safety.)
- Offer new ways of doing things. (Again, do not force.)
- Encourage persistence.
- Find something to praise.

The bottom line is to treat the children the way you would like to be treated during a learning activity. Children learn much easier if they are being treated with kindness and fairness.

WRITTEN ACTIVITY PLANS

As already stated, there may be a large deal of latitude in the area of activity planning responsibility. In matching with your level of responsibility, use written plans to as great an extent as you can. Written plans are helpful tools. When you write out plans, you can thoroughly think through the different parts of the activities. Written plans help teachers and paraeducators foresee possible problems and find solutions. You can approach each planned activity with a degree of confidence and security if you are adequately prepared. Children surely provide enough spontaneity without you multiplying the possibilities for uncertain moments because you have not planned well.

Successful implementation of a written activity plan by a competent paraeducator allows the teacher to make vital observations about the children. The teacher needs to identify who is having difficulty with what. The teacher should also check motivation and participation levels. The teacher must try to determine reasons for difficulties and uninvolvement; this takes time. When you carry out written plans, you free the teacher for a necessary part of his or her job.

When the teacher leads an activity, watch the children. Your observations are invaluable as well. You may notice persistent fatigue, boredom, or confusion in some children at times. A child may tell only you about a family problem. Since the teacher cannot see everything, the teacher will appreciate objective information about the students' responsiveness to learning activities.

Written plans can serve as important records once the activity is over (Table 5–1). This diary feature of written plans helps when students have been absent, when your supervisor questions something, or

TABLE 5–1 Shape Lesson

- Read *Circles, Triangles, and Squares* by Tana Hoban and the poem "Shapes" from *A Light in the Attic* by Shel Silverstein.

  (large group on the rug)

- Shape tracing guessing game (Allow no more than 10 minutes.) Have children pair off and take turns drawing shapes on each other's backs and guessing.

  (spread out)

- Group building of shapes. Have children draw a shape from container and then find others with the same shape to form their group. Each group will use the allotted materials to create a model of their assigned shape. Groups may rotate to other sets of material if there is time.

Ahead of time:

1. Cut out shapes for each group   5 ○ 's
                                      5 □ 's
                                      5 ▭ 's
                                      5 ◇ 's

2. Assemble shape building materials.
        yarn, blocks, playdough, etc.
3. Have book and poem ready.

- -

Comments:

---

simply to aid recollection. It is helpful to evaluate the success of an activity and make notations about what works and what does not.

ACTIVITIES

General Ideas

Now that some preliminaries have been covered, it is time to become creative and move on to the activities themselves. Here are some very general ideas to get you started. These ideas can be used with a wide

Activity Evaluation

Name of activity: _____

Description of activity: _____

Group activity: _____ Individual activity: _____

Best location for activity: Classroom _____

Outside _____

Stage _____

Multipurpose Room _____

Skills involved: _____

Success Rating: Student enjoyment _____

Amount of participation _____

Outcomes for Students:_____

Tips for Future Use of this Activity: _____

range of ages. They can be adapted or broadened to meet the needs of your specific group.

- *Painting.* • flat or on an easel
  - on paper or cloth or pavement
  - with brushes or fingers or sponges
  - small to gigantic
  Example: Paint a map of the United States or of your state on play area blacktop. Adults can paint the outline and color-code the states or regions for the students to fill in.

- *Music.* • singing, drums, rhythm sticks, etc.
  - raps or songs about current unit made up by the children or the teacher or paraeducator
  Example: Math facts put to music are enjoyed and absorbed by children.

One surefire activity of interest to children of any age is music. Simply singing can create lots of excitement. Music can provide many opportunities for learning. Children like the repetition in songs and learn words to songs easily; they respond well to the pattern of melody, rhythm, and rhyme. In this way music enhances language development.

Kurkjian (1990) uses a broad musical repertoire in her kindergarten class in order to facilitate English language learning. Most of her class is limited in their proficiency in English. According to Kurkjian, a daily ritual of children's songs helps her students.

- *Stories.*
  - picture book, chapter books, or flannel board written by the children or someone else
  - listening or active involvement
    (For example, groups can be assigned to make certain responses when key words or phrases are read.)
    Example: The beautiful young princess — "A-a-ahh."
  - open-ended stories or questions
    (Children may respond with a story, a poem, or a song.)

- *Play-dough/ Clay.*
  - may be homemade with nontoxic ingredients
  - art, social studies, math, or another subject
    Example: A child could be instructed to make an example of some form of transportation used in ancient Egypt.
  - individual or group projects

- *Writing.*
  - reaction to a picture
    What is happening?
      Answer Who, What, Where, How, and Why?
    Identification—Count and name the objects and people in the picture.
    Description—Encourage descriptions of the items or people.
    Inference—Ask leading questions that cause the students to consider clues—about temperature, the status of the people, etc.
  - newspaper activities
    Read an article, then summarize it into a "telegram," using no more than 25 words. Children could study the classified section (Certain sections only!), then write their own ad.

- calendars
  Students could write a poem for every month and add artwork then give as gifts.
- newsletters
  Once a year or once a week supervised by the teacher or paraeducator, or organized and written completely by students about routine activities or after special events like field trips sent home or kept as a class record.

- *Acting.*
  - scenes from stories to check comprehension
  - math word problems
  - charades of new vocabulary
  - puppet shows and pantomimes

- *Word puzzles.*
  - scrambles or codes or brain teasers
  - teacher or student designed

- *Research.*
  - riddles or current events
  - questions
    Students will need to use available reference material to find the answers.
  - scavenger hunts to find information

- *Opinion polls.*
  - used in any subject
  - range of ages
  Example: The simple question, "Which insect do you like best, the ladybug or the butterfly?" could lead to beginning graphs, art projects, reports, etc. (Figure 5–1).

- *Contrast/Comparison.*
  - useful for many subject areas
  Example: Lincoln vs. Washington
  urban vs. rural
  fall vs. spring
  What do these people, concepts, or things have in common? How do they differ? Place entries in the appropriate areas, in the separate areas for distinctions, and in the overlap area for similarities. Figure 5–2 shows a basic drawing to use with a contrast and comparison activity.

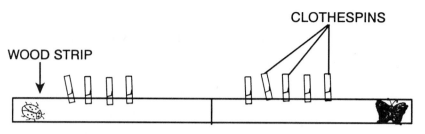

Stickers attached to show objects of opinion

FIGURE 5–1 Simple opinion polls may be used to initiate graphing. With the above materials, children can record their opinions by themselves.

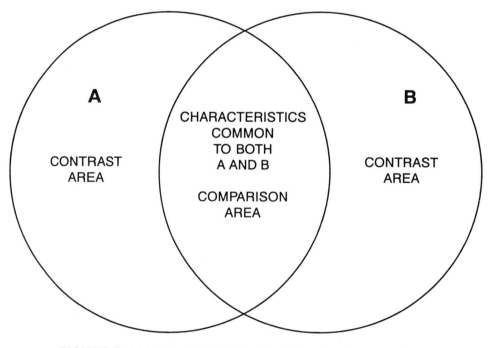

FIGURE 5–2 Venn diagram showing contrast and comparison.

- *Science experiments and observations.*
  - from elementary to complex
    Watch things grow.
    Weather observations.
    Take things apart, find out how things work.

Now that you have thought about some broad categories for activities, we will move on to specific activity ideas that may be appropriate for your group. Remember that even when an activity seems too simple or too advanced for your students' levels, you may be able to adapt it successfully. Some of the activities will work well for an entire class; others may be more suited to one-on-one work with a peer or an adult helper.

SUBJECT-RELATED ACTIVITIES

Art

Self-Portraits. There are many ways to do this. Children can draw or paint what they think they look like now, what they think they will look like when they grow up, or they can show something special about themselves.

Collages. Use different materials every time you do these. Relate the materials to subjects you are studying in other curriculum areas. Use leaves and twigs after a unit on trees or flour, rice, and cornmeal after a unit on grains. Other materials include lace, buttons, seeds, and toothpicks.

Mosaics. These may be done with tissue paper, colored napkins, old wrapping paper scraps, and construction paper. The papers may be cut or torn, glued down directly or painted over with watered down white glue or liquid starch.

Coffee Filter Art. Fold a coffee filter several times. Dip corners into water tinted with food coloring; use several colors. Open the folded paper and see a beautiful design.

Clouds. Tear free-form shapes from white construction paper. Paste these on blue paper. Read *It Looked Like Spilt Milk* by Charles Shaw or *Cloudy With a Chance of Meatballs* by Judi Barrett. You can also use cotton balls for clouds. Add rick-rack for lightning. Learn about weather.

Art activities are an important part of early childhood programs. Children not only enjoy art but expression through art is good for them as well. There are some strong valid reasons to include art in a preschool or early grade curriculum. A child is given the opportunity to express feelings and ideas through art. A child is given the chance to explore, experiment, observe, create, share, cooperate, and solve problems. It is important for you to remember that the process is more important than the finished product and only the child can show the art idea in his mind. Anne Rogovin's book includes a poem that makes a wonderful statement on behalf of the young artist:

> *"Please don't help me....*
> *Let me paint the way I want to....*
> *Even if you don't like it — it's all right with me.*
> *When you keep wanting to help me,*
> *I begin to think, 'I can't do anything right.'*
> *In a little while, I start to believe it....*
> *It makes me feel so bad inside,*
> *I just feel like giving up,*
> *AND THEN IT'LL BE TOO LATE TO BE ME ANY MORE."*

(1980)

Viktor Lowenfeld gives many suggestions in his book, *Your Child and His Art,* on how to deal with small artists. He recommends that you:

- give children space to work.
- appreciate their art work.
- encourage children to appreciate other's work.
- display children's art work (impartially!).
- refrain from demonstrating "how."
- avoid comparing children's art.
- realize that it is more important for the child to like her work than for you to.
- avoid dependence on coloring books and patterns.

(Lowenfeld, 1960)

There have been countless articles and writings concerning coloring books, patterns, and stencils. There is a concern that these items stifle children's creativity and lead to "cookie cutter" uniformity and inflexibility. Allow your children opportunities, even if it is not every time, to use their own personal artistic flair!

Caterpillars. Trace circles on different colors of paper. Cut the circles out, overlap them, and paste them together to make caterpillars. Read *The Very Hungry Caterpillar* by Eric Carle and do some library research about caterpillars.

Guidelines for Art Activities

1. Set up rules for the art center and make sure everyone understands them.

2. Provide art materials that are appropriate for the students' level.

3. Allow children as much freedom as possible; assist only when asked.

4. Show interest in what the children are doing.

5. Encourage children to try new things.

6. Avoid the use of demonstration models whenever there are free expression activities.

7. Accept every honest effort of the children.

8. Help the children see that the most important ones for them to please are themselves.

Color Jars. Experiment with water and food coloring in baby food jars. Mix primary colors in equal proportions to make secondary colors, and find different shades of favorite colors.

Painting.

White Glue: Squirt a design on heavy paper or cardboard. Let the glue dry. Paint over it with diluted tempera paint.

Deodorant bottle painting: Wash out a roll-on bottle and remove the roller ball. Fill the bottle with one-half liquid tempera paint and one-half liquid starch, or 8 teaspoons of powdered tempera, 5 teaspoons of liquid starch, and 3 teaspoons of water.

Water painting: Brush/paint the sidewalk, the desks, or playground equipment. Learn about evaporation.

Finger-painting: Use something different—icing, gelatin, pudding, shaving cream.

Straw painting: Put a few drops of tempera paint on paper and blow it with a straw to make crazy designs. You might want to do this outside! It could be made into a group project with a huge paper canvas and straws for everyone.

Crayon Activities.

> *Warming tray art:* Place aluminum foil over a warming tray. Draw a design or picture on the foil with crayons. The crayon will melt as the child draws. You can pick up the drawing by pressing manila paper over the foil.
>
> *Crayon transfer:* Color an entire paper with crayon, covering it thickly. Place this paper face down on another sheet and draw on it with a pencil. The design will transfer to the second sheet.
>
> *Crayon shaving:* Use scissors to shave different colors of old, broken crayons on to wax paper. Place another piece of wax paper on top of this. Then *an adult* may press over the set with a warm iron. These make pretty placemats.

Finger, Foot, Hand, and Thumb Prints. Use prints to make wreaths, animals, and many other objects. Hands make great suns, butterflies, and flowers. Fingerprints may be added to a winter mural to signify that just as snowflakes are unique, so are fingerprints.

Sculpture. In addition to play-dough and clay, use materials like styrofoam, small boxes, plastic film containers, and wood chips. These may be glued together and painted.

Year Round Art Activities. Match your art activities to a seasonal or monthly theme. There are several activity books on the market that will help you. One is *Just for Fun—Activities for Early Childhood,* by Dickherber, McMinn, and Stargel (1992). This book is filled with good arts and crafts ideas, enough to take you through a whole year with pre-kindergarten through second grade children.

Language Arts

Letters on Letter. Trace a large letter on to sturdy paper. Cut it out. Find words from magazines and newspapers that begin with the same letter, cut them out and glue them on to the big one.

Rhymes and Poems. These are not only fun, but they are important as well. Listening to rhymes and poems strengthens vocabulary, comprehension, and listening skills, and sets a foundation for reading. Gibson says it this way: "It is now known that children who find it hard to recognize which words rhyme with each other find it difficult to learn to read. This sheds new light on the importance of sharing rhymes and poems with young children" (1993). So, get out the Silverstein books and *The Random House Book of Poetry for Children* and Numeroff's *If You Give a Mouse a Cookie* and enjoy them with your children.

Participating Stories. Tell the class you are going to read them a story, but they are going to help. You may then assign parts either to an individual or to a group of students. You could also create your own story with repetitive phrases. An oldie is "The Three Little Pigs," where the children repeat "Little pig, little pig, let me come in," and "Not by the hair of my chinney chin chin." Children may also be assigned to stand or do some action whenever their phrase is mentioned.

Reading Out Loud. This is one of the best things you can do for your children or allow them to do. Even young children can begin to follow and enjoy the ongoing excitement of *chapter books.* Children also respond well to books whose chapters can stand alone, like Sachar's *Sideways Stories from Wayside School.* Some other short winners include the following authors and titles:

- Chris Van Allsburg
- Miss Nelson books by Harry Allard
- *Mr. Monkey and the Gotcha Bird* by Walter Dean Myer
- *Airmail to the Moon* by Tom Birdseye
- Arnold Lobel
- Curious George books by H. A. Rey
- Patricia Lee Gauch
- Robert McCloskey
- Judith Viorst

The following are interest-catching longer books and authors:

- Beverly Cleary
- C. S. Lewis' Chronicles of Narnia
- *The Indian in the Cupboard* by Lynne R. Banks
- *Island of the Blue Dolphin* by Scott O'Dell
- Jerry Spinelli

There are so many wonderful children's books. Your media specialist or your public librarian will probably be thrilled to help you find some great choices.

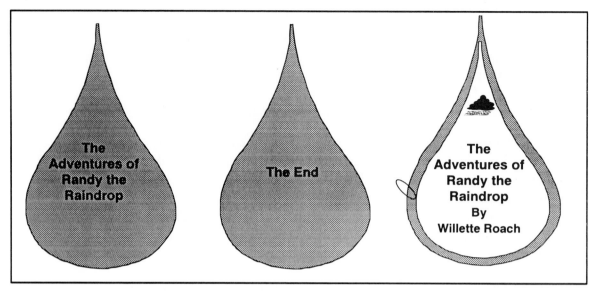

FIGURE 5–3 Simple book. *(Portions Copyright 1987–1990 by Micrografx, Inc. All Rights Reserved.)*

Making Your Own Books. Your students can make their own special books, using several different methods:

- Some schools have a binder machine that cuts slots into pages and combines the pages together with a plastic binder.

- For simple books, cut all the pages the same size and shape, laminate the pages, punch a hole in the same place on every page, and combine pages on a simple metal ring. (Figure 5–3 will give you the idea.) These make nice class books, where every student contributes one page about the same subject.

- *Step books* are easy to make, using as many sheets of paper as you want. The first step is to lay a stack of paper down and stagger the tops a uniform distance. Next, holding all the papers together, fold all the bottom portions of the papers up so that they create more *steps.* (Look at Figure 5–4 for help.) Staple near the fold. You'll have twice the number of *step* pages as you do sheets of paper.

Wonder What's Next! A child is invited to begin a discussion. This child may begin with a sentence or two about the subject of her choosing. Other children volunteer or are called on to add statements about the same subject. When no one can think of anything else to add, another "subject starter" can take a turn.

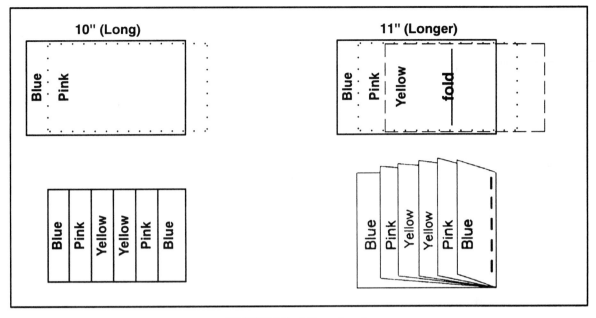

FIGURE 5–4 Step book.

First Things First. Cut up sentence strips from a reading story and scramble them. Have students put the story back together by putting the sentence strips in the correct order. Let other students double check, so everyone's understanding of sequence and the story's meaning are reinforced.

Journals and Individual Experience Stories. These can be fun and varied in subject and in complexity. Allow beginning readers and writers to write exactly as the words sound to them. It is more important for them to get some thoughts out than it is for them to spell correctly. This "writing as process" approach was inspired by Donald Graves, of the University of New Hampshire, and some others around the country. Children are given the freedom to simply write without being hampered by their immature spelling and handwriting (Oppenheim, 1989). A typical entry for a kindergartener might look like the ones in Figures 5–5 and 5–6.

Subjects may range from everybody's "yesterday" experience, to one student's "hot" topic, to current state, national, or world events. A weekly topic might be chosen and different aspects of that topic could be assigned daily. For example, have younger ones do a booklet about themselves and include drawings and sentences about the following:

- Who they live with
- Where they live

FIGURE 5–5 A typical kindergarten entry.

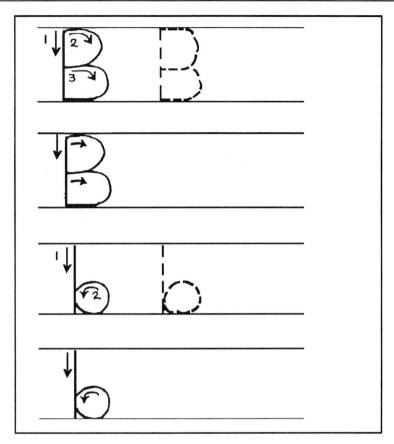

FIGURE 5–6 One of your tasks may be to prepare tabletsheets for handwriting practice.

- Their friends
- Favorite things to do at school
- Favorite things to do on the weekend

Life Skills

Phone Number Songs. Set telephone numbers to a familiar melody like "Mary Had a Little Lamb" (Rogovin). Many rote learning tasks can be aided by singing, including learning the days of the week and the months of the year.

Try to Remember. A picture is shown to the students. They are encouraged to look closely and carefully. The picture is removed from their sight and then the students see how many things they can recall from the picture. Of course, pictures may vary greatly in complexity for different age groups. A tray of small items may also be used.

Hit the Mall. Students are directed to go on a shopping spree, to "buy" items seen in newspaper or grocery store advertisements. An amount is stipulated. Item lists or product categories may be designated, too. For example, all the students might be instructed to stock certain staple kitchen items and they may look through the grocery store ads to find the best prices. When students find the items, they record the pertinent information (price, location, and total) in columns.

You can also post pictures or items that are already priced, "give" the students a certain amount to spend, and let them make their choices. Have them record their own itemized sales receipts.

Don't Take a Hike. Invite the students to go on a trip. Have them use maps, chamber of commerce information, the travel section from the newspaper, and brochures to gather information. Guide them to figure out how much it will cost, how to get there, what to take, and what to do once they're there. This is a good group activity that can incorporate math, reading, and social studies skills.

Math

Early Number Skills. Bring an awareness of numbers and early math skills to everyday activities. Number rhymes and songs are a fun way to familiarize children with what they need to know. Look for patterns in things around you and have the children make their own patterns; this is important foundation for math learning. Constantly sort things around you. Ray Gibson says, "Even such everyday activities as sorting things into groups, is an essential part of learning to count. By differentiating between various objects, children will start to think about sameness and difference and how things can be categorized. (*"You and Your Child Number Games,"* 1993).

Will You Please Hang Up and Dial Again? Write any phone number on the board. Challenge the students to make as many telephone numbers as they can using the numerals from that phone number.

Odd or Even. Beginning mathematicians can use newspapers or old magazines and crayons or markers to color code numbers, evens marked with one color and odds with another. More advanced mathematicians can mark multiples of numbers. Start off with tens and fives.

Cooking. Kids love to cook! In addition to helping with listening and following directions, cooking activities are a good way to reinforce teaching on measurements, fractions, temperature, time, and multiplication (as in doubling a recipe). There are many simple recipes that adapt well to the classroom. Some cooking resources will be included in Chapter 10.

Checks and Balances. Set up a mock budget scenario. Give students certain stipulations about jobs and salaries, help is allowed from parent and other sources. Have them keep an imaginary checkbook, balance it, and work out a workable budget. This activity can really become in-depth if you have students investigate pay, rents, and costs of groceries.

Science

Process Songs. Set natural events to music. A simple song like "The Farmer in the Dell" lends itself to teaching about processes. For example, plant growth, physiology, and evaporation go well with this song ("The sun dries the rain" and "Seeds begin to sprout" and "The heart pumps the blood").

Models. Children love models. Just look at the success of all the commercial construction toys. Use whatever seems best and let the students learn about structures and objects by doing. You might set up a "build a bridge with toothpicks" contest and award the student who builds the strongest bridge (Sixth Grade Teachers, Johnston Elementary, Woodstock, GA).

Social Studies

Be the Navigator. Give small groups maps. Direct the groups to find any symbols on the map and find their meanings. Also, have them use the mileage key to determine distances between several locations.

Let the students brainstorm and draw map symbols on the board (Figure 5–7). Then the class could be divided into groups to draw their own maps of imaginary islands, cities, etc. Students might pull pieces of cut-up maps (very simple and color-coded to complex) from a pretend glove compartment and reassemble them in order to find their groups.

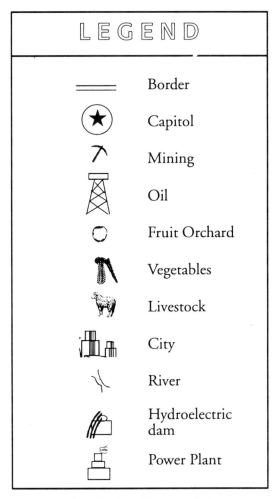

FIGURE 5–7 Map symbols.

Found a Town. Help students go through the thinking required to plan a town, set up city government, and go through mock campaigns and elections. A school in Georgia (Benteen Elementary) was featured on television news because students wrote their own constitution, voted on it, and adopted it for the school. They included statements such as, "We will be fair" and "We will always do our best." The students set up polling places in the school. After they completed the process, a superior court judge came to visit and commend them. Don't hesitate to use their example and invite local officials to visit your students.

Historical Cartoons. Instruct the children to write and draw cartoons from the historical period you are studying. In order to do this, students will learn about speech, dress, and customs of the time period.

TIPS ON MATERIALS

Chalk

- Soak chalk in sugar water before drawing on construction paper. The colors will be vivid.

- A great swirl art activity can be done with chalk. Begin with a shallow tray or dish of water. Scrape pieces of chalk (jumbo chalk is easiest) onto the surface of the water. A sheet of paper can then be slid underneath the water, pulling it from one side of the tray to the other.

Scissors

With small children, scissors should be sharp but blunt. Give little ones opportunities for free cutting as well as cutting on lines. Keep a scrap box available for practice. Help by holding a small child's hand still while you move the paper around. (A child between four and four-and-a-half years old should be able to cut along lines without too much frustration.)

Play-dough and Clay

Recipe #1:   1 cup flour
1 cup water
1 teaspoon to 1 tablespoon oil
1/2 cup salt
1 to 2 teaspoons cream of tartar
food coloring
a few drops of mint or lemon extract, if desired

Cook over medium heat (on stove or in electric fry pan) until mixture pulls away from the sides of the pan and becomes like play-dough in consistency. Knead it until it is cool. This will keep for up to three months unrefrigerated. Put it in a plastic storage bag or in an airtight container.

Recipe #2:   1 cup salt
1/2 cup flour
1/2 cup water

Heat over small flame and stir occasionally until it is rubbery. Knead when cool. If it is too sticky, add more flour and knead it again.

Recipe #3:   *Kool-aid Play-dough*
1 pkg. of Kool-aid (0.20 oz envelope)

1 tablespoon alum (You can find this in the spice section
    at the grocery store.)
3 cups of flour (may need more)
water, about two cups, boiling
about 1/2 cup of salt
3 tablespoons of oil

Stir all the ingredients together. Add more flour if you need to so that it won't be sticky. Store the play-dough in an airtight, resealable bag or a plastic container. This kind of play-dough smells great!

Recipe #4:   *Uncooked Play-dough*

2 to 3 cups flour
1 cup salt
3 tablespoons baby oil
1 cup water

Mix the dry ingredients together. Stir in the oil and water. Add more water, as needed, to form a soft, pliable dough. Food coloring may be added.

Edible Clay/Peanut Butter Clay:

peanut butter
dry milk

Mix dry milk and peanut butter until it is not sticky. Mold and play with it. Use more dry milk if you need to.

Baking Clay:

2 cups of flour
1 cup salt
water

Mix the two dry ingredients and add enough water to make dough stick together. Let students mold their creations and then lay them on parchment-lined baking sheets. (You can pencil their names by their creations.) Bake the dough objects at 300 degrees for about an hour, or longer if the creations are thick or bulky.

Other Recipes

Goop: 1 cup white glue
                 1/2 cup liquid starch
                 food coloring or paint, optional, added to the glue before
                     mixing with the starch

Mix these together very quickly, then knead the mixture until it is no longer sticky. Store in an airtight container. Be careful with clothing because though this stuff can be fun, it's a mess!

Soap Paint. Color detergent flakes with tempera paint to make pastel shades. Mix with water and beat until fluffy. A little liquid starch added to the stiff mixture makes it less fragile when dry.

Finger Paint:　　1/2 cup dry laundry starch
　　　　　　　　　　1 quart boiling water
　　　　　　　　　　1/2 cup cold water
　　　　　　　　　　2–4 tablespoons baby detergent flakes
　　　　　　　　　　Food coloring or tempera paint

Mix starch and cold water thoroughly. Pour boiling water into this mixture. Stir constantly and bring to a boil. Boil until thick and smooth. Cool, add detergent flakes and food coloring, then store in a jar. Add food coloring.

Self-Check for Activity Planning

Every now and then, check out your effectiveness in planning and helping with activities.

Think about the following:

1. Do I plan carefully for activities, or do I use the "wing it" method?
2. Do I prepare well enough that I have everything ready for activities so that no time is wasted?
3. Do I know the children? Do I watch them enough to know what they like and dislike, what works and what does not?
4. Do I focus on good behavior during activities or do I tune in to inappropriate behavior so much that I don't encourage the children who do a good job?
5. Do I listen to the children? Do I pay enough attention to their participation in activities?
6. Do I follow the teacher's instructions?
7. Do I make it so easy on the children that I stifle their thinking or creativity?

   Or do I make it so hard for the children that I discourage them?

8. Am I helping the children to learn responsibility or do I clean up after activities myself? Do I decide to "just do it myself" because it can be quicker and easier?

(Adapted from Cherokee Co. Substitute Materials)

Colored Glue: white glue
food coloring
water

Measure about one-half cup of glue. Add food coloring one drop at a time until the desired color is reached. Add water to thin if necessary and mix until smooth.

Some additional suggestions for paint:
- Use one part of liquid soap and one part of liquid starch to every two parts of dry tempera paint. First mix the paint and the soap, then add the starch. If the paint gets too thick, add more liquid soap; don't add any water. The soap helps make cleanup easier, and the starch makes painting without drips easier.
- Mix food coloring with light corn syrup. Students may paint different colors on paper plates and cut out designs after the paint dries. Give this paint five or six days to dry completely.

The possibilities for educational activities are endless, extending as far as your imagination and resources. If you still claim the creative element was deleted from your personality menu, there is a multitude of material waiting out there for you. Chapter 10 gives additional information about resources. More educational games and learning center ideas will be discussed in Chapter 6.

Planning and implementing learning activities is a top priority in a paraeducator's world. By assisting the teacher with learning activities, you can broaden the educational experience of a child. You can add to the interest and enthusiasm levels in your classroom or center. Fulfill your role to whatever level of responsibility you are given and know that a paraeducator is much more than an assistant; a paraeducator is an important part of an instructional team.

CHAPTER 6

Games and Learning Centers: Making It Fun and Making It Stick

As a paraeducator you will likely be required to prepare, create, and assist with educational games. Again, the extent of your involvement will depend on your particular workplace and your particular coworkers. Whatever your responsibility level, be prepared to enjoy this vital component of the teaching plan.

Educational games must be appropriate for the academic content of the grade level. It is good to constantly make yourself aware of the present skills and content being studied in your classroom. Then you can work to develop games and supplemental centers that reinforce this learning.

REASONS FOR GAMES

You may think of games as recreation or entertainment and question what place they have in an educational setting. Games encompass many values important to the developmental growth of children. Games are fun, for another thing. While having fun and engaging in learning (without being painfully aware of learning), the children are given constructive social interaction, as well.

According to author Rae Pica (1995), games may be viewed one of two ways:

1. **Appropriate Practice:** Games are selected, designed, sequenced, and modified by teachers and/or children to maximize the learning and enjoyment of the children.

2. **Inappropriate Practice:** Games are taught with no obvious purpose or goal, other than to keep children "busy, happy, and good." Emphasis is placed upon the structure, rules, and formations of the games.

Teacher, consultant, and teaching games author, Peggy Kaye, writes of the many skills children must master in the early grades. She says she has found "game-playing can be a perfect aid" in both tutoring and classroom teaching (1991). She goes on to say that:

> *Games can help a child learn and practice almost every skill that school requires. And games can do this in a wonderfully effective manner. For when a child sits down to play a well-designed and interesting game, the child relaxes and concentrates at the same time—relaxes because the game is entertaining, and concentrates because the game is challenging. A child who simultaneously relaxes and concentrates is in a perfect frame of mind for learning. (1991)*

In the introduction to his number game book, Ray Gibson speaks of the benefit games bring for children learning early number skills. He says that repeated practice is necessary for skill mastery and games provide fun, relaxed repetition, and that, "Children who have fun and enjoy their first encounters with numbers will be much more likely to develop a positive, confident attitude toward math" (1993).

Classroom teachers use games with children for motivation and to reinforce newly learned skills. In their selection of educational games, Bell and Wieckert say that the competition and cooperation aspects of games help to promote the learning of skills and the reinforcement of skills (1980). Games enhance the instructional program and provide an enjoyable way to review skills and subject content.

Providing learning through the use of games creates a legitimate vehicle for children to practice interaction skills and to work on social behavior objectives. When an insecure child grasps a new skill in a small group setting, there is both the positive reinforcement of "getting it" and the confidence building of peer support. Children need social contact

---

Play

Play serves a number of functions for the young child: it aids in developing problem-solving skills; promotes social and cognitive competence; aids in the development of the distinction between fantasy and reality; promotes curiosity and playfulness; helps communication, attention span, self-control, social, language, and literacy skills; provides a vehicle for the adult to learn how children view the world; and can be therapeutic. (Charlesworth, 1996)

aside from the limits of recess and the confines of highly structured classrooms. One of your tasks as a paraeducator will be to make this necessary social contact accessible and appropriate.

Utilizing games in the classroom develops greater independence,
better organization, and stronger work study skills in students. Students
learn to work well in their seats in order to earn the privilege of playing a game, and then must conduct themselves appropriately in order
to maintain the privilege.

G R O U P I N G   F O R   G A M E S

It takes thoughtful organization on your part or the teacher's part to
group the children and assign them to certain games or teams. You
quickly learn combinations of girls and boys who work well together,
who finish their assignments in about the same time, and those who
make good peer helpers. A chart with pockets labeled with names can
be used to assign games to those needing reinforcement of a specific
skill. Be sure if you and the teacher make the group or team assignments
that you change these at least occasionally in order to keep things lively.

When ability levels are not a consideration and you use random
group/team selection, change your methods every now and then. Try
something besides counting off or assigning by rows. You might want
to try or modify one of the following:

- Cut up frames from as many comic strips as you want groups.
  Have each child draw one from a paper bag and then direct the
  children to complete their comic strips in order to find their
  groups.

- Look around quickly to see if there is a predominance of one color
  of clothes. If half your class is wearing green, let all the kids wearing green be on one team and the nongreen wearers on the other
  team.

- Have a container ready with slips of paper naming different animal sounds. After drawing a sound, the children must quietly
  make that sound until the group is assembled.

- Divide your class list. Last names beginning with A through L can
  be on one team, and last names beginning with M through Z can
  be on another; children with first names that end with a consonant
  may be on one team, and children whose first names end with a

vowel sound may be on the other; have children count the letters in their first names and divide into groups with other children with the same numbers.

ORDER OF PLAY

Sometimes games call for individual responses and the order of play is best worked out ahead of time. Also even when teams function as a group, there has to be a fair way to decide which team goes first. Consider one of the following methods, and then think of others:

- Alphabetical order by last name of individuals or captains

- Drawing names

- Teams submit their own "line-ups"

- Throwing dice

- Best answer to a timed skill question (How many words can you or your team make from the letters in the word "keyboard"?)

- Any other impartial method

GAME PREPARATION

When teachers and paraeducators work well together to lead games, the children can benefit in many ways. The children can learn to cooperate, share, and be patient and supportive to those giving slower responses. They also learn to be responsible if it is their turn to be the group leader for the day or for the week, to be a good listener when it is not their time to be the leader, to win or lose with grace, and to accept all the classmates into their group.

Part of your job will be to help pattern the children and yourself into the daily routine and rules of the classroom. This takes time and patience, but once this happens games can be a real asset to you and the teacher and a benefit to the children. As they learn to organize their time, stay on task with assignments, and participate in appropriate independent learning activities, there will be fewer interruptions as you and the teacher work with small groups. You will both have the assurance that the children are using their time constructively. Games are excellent motivational rewards for satisfactory work time.

Making It Fun

What makes a game a game? Kaye says that, "*fun* is the operative word" (1991). What makes a game fun? Educational games author, Mulac says that "It is the method of approach that makes work into play" (1971). One factor is as simple as addressing students as *players*. The goal and hope for educational games is that children will think of learning as more pleasure than work. Keep these learning game writers' words in mind. As you play a part in the day-to-day learning process, watch your approach toward little tasks as well as games as such; make sure you invoke enthusiasm rather than drudgery.

Learning centers or stations, though not classified as games, are mentioned here since they have many of the same attributes as games and complement the use of games. They foster good independent movement around the classroom and good use of time within the learning situation. A learning center, like a game, focuses on one area of learning or a particular skill. For example, a station could be set up with activities that change every week and center on the use of a dictionary, on poetry, how to use a telephone book, letter writing, compound words, or contractions. Children could be assigned to these individually, either by a special interest, desire for challenge, or by the need for reinforcement. While most games involve two to four children, learning centers generally involve one person; though it is possible to develop project-type activities that would engage more than one child.

Are you wondering how on earth you can do all this? How do you find the right kind of games? How do you group the children? What about the noise level? Who creates all this material? Will planning games be part of your job? These are good questions. You will need to consult with the lead teacher to answer them. Then you charge up your enthusiasm and develop your strategy. Go ahead and dream. Some of your ideas might not be possible, but none of them will be unless you work on them. Start simple and keep it growing. No one will expect you to develop a career's worth of games and learning centers during your first month of employment. You do not need to walk in on Monday morning with fifteen learning centers and twenty new games. First of all, it would be very difficult to come up with that much all at once, and secondly, the children could never digest it all. Pace yourself and the kids. They need gradual immersion into the total process of the classroom, including having games and learning centers as an integral part of their learning. As you and the lead teacher see a need to develop a specific learning skill, you can create the tool—a new game or two, or maybe a learning center—that will enhance the teaching and the children's interest in learning. Gradually you can add to the repertoire as need and enthusiasm motivate. Interest breeds interest; you and the teacher will both develop a feel for when to expand a unit and when not to.

Game Environment

If noise and enthusiasm levels rise too high, you may be able to help the teacher find possible causes and remedies. Perhaps you need to look at the room arrangement. This is an important factor; it will be discussed in Chapter 9. Rules are another thing to check. Make sure game rules are clear, few, and direct. Then make sure the rules are followed. State clearly what is an acceptable noise level and what is not. You need to help the children understand from the beginning what constitutes a need to return to seats, and be prepared to act on what you say. Consistency with children is extremely important. Remember that there is a definite difference between noise and *constructive* noise. The latter is far better than a dull, quiet classroom. You and the teacher can help each other to find that just right, acceptable noise level. You can help each other with the question, "Is it me or are these kids too loud?" Sometimes it is *you* and you may need to pull up your sense of humor and pull out the aspirin. Sometimes it *is* that the children are inching the noise meter up and up. Silent signals help a great deal. For example, the children could know that when the teacher's or your arm goes up, the mouths go shut.

Sources for Games

Who creates the games and materials that you want for your students? Take a look around you. Share ideas with coworkers. Check out the resources available in your own community. College libraries and public libraries have books on educational games. Educational supply stores have books on games for any age group. Ray Gibson has a series of educational game books with good ideas for primary readers and numbers learners. *Games for Learning* by Peggy Kaye is a collection of games for parents to play with their children, but the games have all been successful in Kaye's classrooms and seem to be particularly conducive toward the kind of one-on-one help a paraeducator might have opportunity to

Noise Level

Game playing can increase the noise level in a classroom in one split second. What is an acceptable noise level? It is important for you and the lead teacher to discuss this and reach some agreement ahead of time. You must also bear in mind the philosophies of your school and your principal. Hopefully, you will all concur on the difference between disruptive noise and productive noise. In *Smart Start: The Elementary Education for the 21st Century,* Barth and Mitchell mention the noise level in a Brooklyn school:

> *The most immediate difference that strikes the observer between an energetic elementary classroom and one based on the factory model of education is the level of noise. This may disconcert those who remember classrooms where quiet was equated with academic study, as it did us on our first visit to a school in the Red Hook section of Brooklyn. However, it soon became clear to us that the noise was actually the refreshing sound of children in active engagement with math and science projects or eagerly expressing opinions in class discussions. . . . . . . qualified teachers can effectively manage the activity and accompanying noise, keeping all children on task. (1992)*

When the noise level does exceed acceptance and good constructive levels, silent signals can help caution the children. Anything to which the students have been alerted previously, especially something goofy that they will be sure to notice right away, can work. Some possibilities include putting purple earmuffs on or pulling a zipper out of a drawer or off of your shoulder and zipping it up while holding it up high for all to see. Sometimes these kinds of particular class signals are fun for the children and they will obey the implied directive quickly because it is so much more pleasant than some types of verbal notifications.

During learning center and small group game or project time, you may want to play some classical music softly in the background. It can be stated ahead of time that as long as the teacher or paraprofessional can still hear the music, then the noise level is acceptable (DiPaolo, 1990, GA Preschool Conf.).

give in kindergarten through third grade. Kaye also gives suggestions for teachers at the end of her book. Bell and Wieckert's book, *Basic Classroom Skills through Games,* has a great selection of games that promote many classroom and media center skills. The authors even give permission for teachers and media specialists to copy gameboards from the book for classroom or media center use. Be sure to check for permissions and restrictions on use. (More information about resources will be given in Chapter 10.)

Take a look at commercial games. Some are appropriate for classroom use. Some can be adapted to your classroom needs. For example,

Battleship (Milton Bradley) gives students a greater concept of coordinate geometry. You could put tape across the bottom row and down the left side of the game; then you could number each tape from zero to ten to represent the positive quadrant. Dominoes is another commercial game you may want to use because it can give children practice in addition. There are other commercial games that will be listed later in this chapter.

There is another area of commercial possibilities for educational games that has exploded in recent years. There are constant new arrivals to the educational game computer software market. Some favorites include Oregon Trail, (Mecce, SoftKey Multimedia, Inc.) Where in The World Is Carmen San Diego? (Bröderbund) , Math Blaster (Davidson), Factory (Sunburst), and Scholastic's Magic School Bus Series (Microsoft). Make certain you have practiced enough to help students when they hit a snag or have a question. (Computer proficiency will be discussed further in Chapter 11, since computer skills could be important to upgrading your professional status.)

You can also be the creator of learning games and materials for your students. As was said about learning activities in Chapter 5, don't be afraid to use your imagination and try your own ideas. Also, if you and the lead teacher brainstorm together, there's no end to the innovative games you can develop. Bell and Wieckert state, "In all, the potential uses of the games to teach and reinforce skills depend solely upon the needs and imagination of the teacher or specialist" (1980). Sometimes it is good to simply begin with a tried and true traditional game like tic-tac-toe or bingo and adapt it for your class needs.

Materials for Games

Once you have decided on some games you would like to have for your class, get the necessary materials. Summers are a good time to add to your activity and game materials supply. Soliciting parents for materials helps. A parent may have a throw-away item from his workplace that will be the perfect *free* material for games. You won't know unless you ask or at least make it clear to parents from the beginning that donations are appreciated.

The whole process of game-making can be made easier by accumulating materials and keeping them together for easy accessibility. A large basket, plastic storage container, or heavy cardboard box can be useful. You may also collect smaller containers such as round oatmeal boxes, juice cans, or baby food jars to use as compartments for organizing supplies and keeping them handy. There are some great commercial organizing systems available through stores, if you want to spend the money or if class parents or the PTA want to buy something for your room. Since you cannot depend on that luxury, keep your eyes open for sturdy boxes. (You can always cover them with inexpensive self-adhesive plastic-coated paper.)

> Some materials you might want to include in your supply box are:
> crayons
> water base markers—both fine and wide
> permanent markers—not to be used under lamination as they
>   bleed
> rubber cement
> white glue or glue sticks
> hot glue or cool melt glue gun and glue sticks
> scissors
> paper clips
> rubber bands
> scotch tape
> pencils
> paper hole punch
> decorative stickers—make good game board markers
> tissue paper
> zip lock bags—hold game pieces
> yarn—various colors
> fabric scraps
> index cards—white or colored
> brass paper fasteners
> dice
> plastic discs or buttons—game markers
> plastic scraps
> spinners
> wooden cubes—good for dice with large numbers on them for
>   math games
> clear contact—for use on items that will not go through a laminator.

Various colors of tagboard may be available to you in your school. Tagboard can be cemented onto heavier cardboard. Index board and railroad board are other types of board that can be purchased where art supplies are sold.

Old workbooks and some coloring books are good sources for pictures. Remember you can use an opaque projector to enlarge pictures. Opaque projectors are easy to operate and give you quick enlargements. Do not forget copyright law concerning trademark registered cartoon figures, though!

Constantly keep an eye out for new possibilities for useable materials. For example, take note of all the plastic yogurt or pudding cups your family goes through. You will find many uses for items that you would typically toss in the garbage or recycle bin.

Use local sources to obtain suitable items. Styrofoam trays from the local deli, pizza boards from the pizzeria, old wallpaper sample books from the decorator shop, or large ice cream tubs from the ice cream parlor are useful in many ways.

Be sure that you use durable materials to create your games and once they are created, laminate as much as possible. Hopefully, they will be used a lot. You want them to be used. You will also want them to survive that use! If your school does not have a laminating machine, see what can be done about it. Go through proper channels and check on PTA money or fund-raising possibilities. (You might even consider spearheading the action.)

Help with Game Preparation

In addition to asking parents for game materials, ask them for help with game preparation and playing as well. A table in your classroom or the hall can be stocked with supplies (that box or basket mentioned earlier) and directions for parents. If you and the teacher invite parents to participate, provide a place for them to work and socialize, you may reap a great harvest of game and center activities for the students. Don't forget to invite grandparents, too. Another thing to consider is that sometimes working parents, who are busy during the day but who still want to volunteer in their children's classroom, will be willing to cut out or partially assemble things at night if you send a "materials and directions" packet home with their children. Volunteers who are able to come in during the school day can be a tremendous help when small group games are first introduced. These classroom volunteers may be assigned to supervise small groups and guide them through learning the rules. Parent volunteers may also be willing to sew simple drawstring bags for game storage.

Whenever you are blessed enough to get volunteer help in the classroom, always make sure you show appreciation. Volunteers will be more willing to come back again. If your school does not do this already, you might be able to initiate some sort of volunteer appreciation tea or coffee. When volunteers are instrumental to the success of projects or events, give some publicity with a photograph and a little blurb to your local newspaper.

As you proceed, both your ideas and your enthusiasm will grow. Again, the possibilities are endless. As you gather ideas and useful materials you will find it stimulating and contagious. Remember to keep an idea file. Begin an ongoing practice of gathering ideas into some sort of system for easy future reference. One method is to take photos and write descriptions and rules onto index cards and file them in a small card file. Make notes about what works and what does not.

IDEAS FOR GAMES AND LEARNING CENTER ACTIVITIES

Following are a few suggestions for game and learning center activities. As they have not been designated for age appropriateness you should make that decision. Besides, some of the more complicated games can be simplified easily and vice versa. For example, Twenty Questions can be adapted to any level, depending on the object to identify. Older students find it a good activity especially when they get to play the role of the leader.

Some of the references in this chapter are primarily to games with one subject focus, such as language arts. It is certainly not intended to limit the use of ideas. Many game formats can be used in several subject areas. Sometimes this will be brought out and other times it will not be; do not confine your adaptation plans.

There are games for one person only, others for two, three, or four players, and some that are good to use with the entire class. Again, as with the subject area, freely modify the numbers to your classroom needs when appropriate.

Multiuse Games and Methods

Triangle Board—The triangle board is a base component for educational learning centers. It can be large or small and is made from three pieces of sturdy board. Railroad board is good for this. Cut three pieces the same size. One recommended size is approximately 10" × 24". The

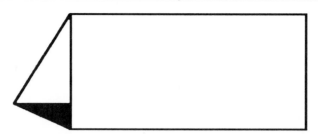

FIGURE 6–1 Source: D. Bennett, C.H. Meyer, & D.E. Meyer (1994). *Elementary Field Experiences.* Albany, NY: Delmar Publishers.

pieces may be covered with clear contact paper or laminated for durability. Tape them together with wide plastic tape (Figure 6–1).

Possible uses for triangle boards:

1. By using colored clips or clothespins, this triangle board can be used as a display stand for interesting items, challenging thoughts for the day, learning centers, and student work. By standing the triangle on end, all three sides can be used.
2. Set the triangle board on its side and place metal rings (key rings of various sizes work) into both pieces of board at the top of the triangle. Make cards, mark them as desired, and punch a hole in the top.
   a. Word Flip: write single letters or combinations on each card. Place on appropriate rings as in the example in Figure 6–2. Children then flip cards to make words.
   b. Sound Match: One set of cards will have initial consonant, blend, or diagraph cards. The other rings will have picture cards. Students will match appropriate pictures to correct beginning sounds. Figure 6–3 shows one variation of a sound match game using a triangle board.
3. Make the triangle into a board with adhesive-backed hangers attached to the surface. Make playing cards from index board, lami-

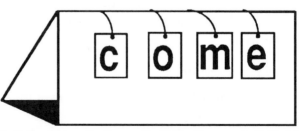

FIGURE 6–2 Source: D. Bennett, C.H. Meyer, & D.E. Meyer (1994). *Elementary Field Experiences.* Albany, NY: Delmar Publishers.

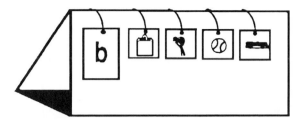

FIGURE 6–3 Source: D. Bennett, C.H. Meyer, & D.E. Meyer (1994). *Elementary Field Experiences.* Albany, NY: Delmar Publishers.

nate them, and punch them with holes for hanging. Words can be hung on appropriate hooks for matching and classifying in a variety of ways: beginning sounds, short vowels, long vowels, how many syllables, singular or plural, etc.

a. Picture-Word Match—Vocabulary Development: Picture cards are made for various parts of speech in specific categories: nouns, action words, adjectives, seasonal, transportation, etc. Corresponding word cards are made by writing the word with a Sharpie at the bottom of a clear plastic shape the same size as the picture cards or writing the word on a small piece of index board and covering it with two pieces of clear adhesive-backed plastic the same size as the picture cards. In this way, the picture will be seen after the word card is hung over the picture. The students hang up all the picture cards and then place the correct word card over each picture. The example in Figure 6–4 may get you started with ideas that will enhance learning for your particular group.

b. Build-a-Word Board: Six to eight hooks are attached to the board. Letter cards are made by consonants, blends, diagraphs, vowels, endings, etc. The cards are placed into containers by classification. The students find the correct letters for the desired word. This can be an alternate method of practicing spelling words (Figure 6–5).

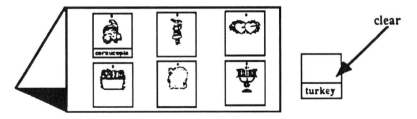

FIGURE 6–4 Source: D. Bennett, C.H. Meyer, & D.E. Meyer (1994). *Elementary Field Experiences.* Albany, NY: Delmar Publishers.

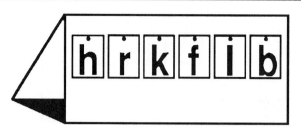

FIGURE 6–5 Source: D. Bennett, C.H. Meyer, & D.E. Meyer (1994). *Elementary Field Experiences.* Albany, NY: Delmar Publishers.

Bingo Games. You can make bingo cards for most any subject. First design one, make as many variations as you desire, then make copies enough for the whole group, and, finally, laminate them. Possible adaptations include:

- Language arts/vocabulary. The teacher would read an incomplete sentence, then the children would search for the correct word on their bingo cards.
- Math facts. The teacher would say a problem, then the children would compute the correct answer, then search for that answer on the card. Figure 6–6 shows an example.
- Pictures of landforms. The teacher calls the name of a landform and the children find the matching picture and mark it if it is on their card. Table 6–1 give indications of the ways bingo may be used to suit class levels and curriculum.

23	46	10	32	14
11	17	36	42	50
41	26	🏳	16	37
46	7	20	15	31
49	25	30	47	22

FIGURE 6–6 Bingo variation.

You can use most anything for markers—from buttons to shells to peanuts. Sometimes it adds a little spark to relate the markers to the subject, even if only in a remote and fun way. For example, just before Thanksgiving, play bingo with facts related to the holiday and use candy corn as markers.

Take advantage of every opportunity for reinforcement when playing bingo. Have the students verify the winner's card. That way they all hear it again, with the extra incentive of checking up on a classmate.

TABLE 6–1

The leader can hold up pictures of animals. Players find and cover the appropriate sound word.

MEOW	BARK	HISS
NEIGH	BAA	HEEHAW
MOO	CHIRP	OINK

A list of transportation methods may be written on the board. Players may write the entries on their own bingo sheets (in ink!) in the arrangement of their own choosing. The leader can then read about a transportation situation. The players find and cover the best mode of transportation for that scenario.

SNOWMOBILE	FEET	SHIP	CAR	JET
HORSE	SKATEBOARD	MONORAIL	MOTORCYCLE	SUBWAY
TRAM	CAMEL	FREE RIDE	BICYCLE	BLIMP
HOT AIR BALLOON	JEEP	BUS	HELICOPTER	MULE
SKYLIFT	AIRPLANE	TRAIN	ROWBOAT	SKIS

Tic-Tac-Toe Games. This game may be played by individuals or teams. Questions may come from any area of the curriculum. While it makes an excellent review game, it may also be used with current topics of the day. Here are a few variations:

- The traditional tic-tac-toe grid is used. This can be drawn on a chalkboard or whiteboard, on laminated poster board, on the sidewalk with jumbo chalk, in dirt or sand, and on and on. A player must answer a question correctly to earn the right to place a mark on any unoccupied spot on the grid. Marks can be the traditional Xs and Os, or any other two symbols.

  Example: In an astronomy review places may be marked with stars and moons.

- Human tic-tac-toe. Masking tape can line off the grid on the classroom floor or sidewalk chalk may be used to draw the grid on blacktop. When teams correctly answer questions, the team members mark the strategic places.

- A number grid is placed on the board. The student must answer the question corresponding with the number chosen. Correct answers get an X or an O depending on where it is on the grid. Several questions will be slated for each number so that if the first question is answered incorrectly, then there will be another opportunity to earn that grid space.

Simon Says. You or the teacher may begin the game and later choose a student to take the lead. It is a good choice of a game to use when students are getting restless and need to do some moving. This is also good for increasing listening skills. The traditional rules are that players only respond to the directions when they are preceded by the words, "Simon says." For example: "Simon says, stand up. Simon says, turn around. Simon says, shake your hands. Sit down." Those who sit down would be out, because the direction was not preceded by "Simon says." This simple game can be expanded to include directions related to subject content. Some variations follow:

  a. Counting variation—Simon could say to hold up different numbers of fingers on different hands.

  b. Language art variation—Simon could say to act out an action word with your mouth.

    c.   Curriculum review—Simon could say if such and such is true, then raise your right hand. For example, Simon says if the heart has four chambers, stomp your left foot, or Simon says if 9 × 9 = 81, wiggle your eyebrows.

Scavenger Hunts. These hunts may be for written material, pictures, or items themselves. Scavenger hunts can be used in many subject areas, and are especially good for teaching research skills. Searches may be carried out by individuals, pairs, or competing teams. Search areas and allotted time must be agreed upon before beginning. Lists of search items are handed out. At the signal, the teams have the agreed upon amount of time to find the listed items. The winners are the ones who find the most items from the list.

    a.   General observation skills:
Examples:
- someone with blue eyes
- someone with a barrette in her hair
- someone wearing stripes
- something that is at least 1 meter long
- a sphere
- a cylinder

    b.   Social studies or geography scavenger hunts, using reference materials:
Examples:
- three states beginning with the letter A
- countries along the equator
- longest river in Europe
- U.S. president who might have done the Charleston

    c.   Research of any type, including years of invention or patents for common household items, Nobel Prize winners, different categories of books, etc.

As you can see, the difficulty levels of scavenger hunts can vary according to your students' levels.

Alphabet Games. These may also be played by individuals or groups and may relate to any subject area. Players may be told to find an object in the room for every letter of the alphabet. The first one to complete the list is the winner. Then everybody checks the winner's list. Other possibilities include names of children's authors, space exploration words, action verbs, insects, and so on.

Alphabet games may also be played on a point basis. Five points may be awarded for every letter having a suitable entry. If a letter has more than one entry, then one point could be awarded for additional entries. Players would figure out that they rack up the most points by filling each letter slot first.

Baseball Games. Most children love and understand baseball and the format is conducive to reviewing subject content. Draw a baseball diamond on the board. (White boards, flannel boards, and lines in the sand work well.) Divide the group into two teams. The teams take turns getting "up to bat." Questions are asked and correct responses advance "the runner." An inning limit needs to be decided before play begins. Here are some additional applications:

a. Math facts or spelling—The player "at bat" is given a word to spell or a math problem to complete. The opposing team is "out in the field" and they must listen to see if the "batter" answers correctly. If the response is right, the "batter" scores a "hit" and a marker is put on first base. If the response is wrong, and the "fielders" catch it, then an out is scored. If the response is wrong, but the opposing team does not recognize it, then the runner advances on an "error," and the response is corrected. After three incorrect responses are recognized, the teams change sides. A cap for runs per inning may be decided before beginning (Mulac, 1971).

b. Arrange chairs in the classroom or set up bases outside. Allow the children to actually move themselves, rather than advance markers or draw.

c. Other subject material may be reviewed using a baseball format, too.

Password. Words to be guessed may be printed on index cards. One person from each team gives a teammate clues to try to get that teammate to guess the word. The points for guessing the right word decrease as the number of clues given increases. If the first team member to attempt a word guesses correctly after the first clue is given, then that team is awarded ten points. If that first guess is not right, the other team gets a chance; if they are successful, they are awarded nine points, and so on. Team members who are not on the clue-giving and guessing panel may help by listing clue possibilities to be passed to the clue giver for their team. The number of words allowed for one clue must be decided before play begins. This may range from only one word to a full phrase. For example, if the word to be guessed is Illinois, some of the clues might be: Prairie State, produces corn and soybeans, sometimes called the Land of Lincoln, etc.

One variation may be to allow the guessing team to earn extra points by naming additional facts. When they run out of facts, the other team may earn points if they can think of any more.

Pantomines. Give the player a card with an activity or word on it. He or she acts it out, and the class or the team tries to guess what the player is doing. Some ideas include:

   a. Pantomine making a bed, putting a puzzle together, or eating spaghetti.

   b. Act out different occupations after a unit on careers.

   c. Charades of spelling or vocabulary words. To earn bonus team points after the word is guessed, the word must be spelled or defined correctly. The team may go into a huddle to confirm their group response, and then have a spokesperson give their answer.

Picture This. This game is a great way to have fun with spelling lists and other subject material. Divide the class into two teams. Players take turns being the illustrator. Players may draw a card with a vocabulary word, a science concept, a geography or other term on it. They will attempt to draw something that will make fellow team members guess what it is. Points may be scored for correct guesses and also for additional facts given. It is probably best to allow only one team to draw and guess at a time in order to eliminate arguments about which team gave the right answer first.

Eagle Feathers. Make a large headband of sturdy cardboard. Attach twenty or thirty feathers to it with paper clips (this way the activities may be changed easily). The student selects a feather and performs the task that is written on it. For example: add three numbers, recite the months of the year, or write five short vowel words.

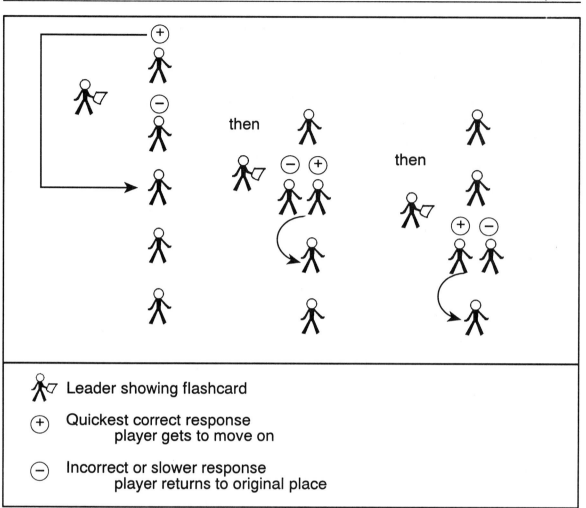

Leader showing flashcard

⊕ Quickest correct response
player gets to move on

⊖ Incorrect or slower response
player returns to original place

FIGURE 6–7 Around the World.

Around the World. This is a game that may be played with any skill you are working on, arithmetic facts, vocabulary recognition, etc. Flashcards are used. Two children compete to see who can get the sum of two numbers faster after the teacher shows the flashcard. The first two children stand up to compete. The winner then stands behind (or next to the third child) and waits to see the next flashcard. The game continues in this way around the class or circle. (If you are having a hard time visualizing this, Figure 6–7 may help.) The winner is the one who defeats all the others or goes "around the world."

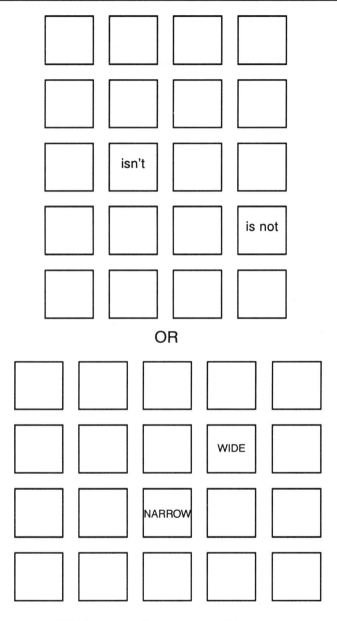

FIGURE 6–8 Concentration/Memory.

Concentration/Memory. This classic game uses pairs of information from any subject. Cards with either pictures or words are shuffled and arranged upside down in some sort of uniform pattern, usually a square with straight rows (Figure 6–8). Players take turns turning the cards over two at a time in an attempt to find matches. If a player turns a card over, then turns the matching card over, that player is allowed to take up the matched pair and take another turn. If the player is unsuccessful, the play passes to another player. The trick, of course, is for players to remember everything they see. The winner is the one with the most matches.

This game works best with small groups of two to four players. Some educational possibilities are:

- Math facts—one card with the problem, the other one with the solution.

- Punctuation—one with a sentence with incorrect punctuation, the other with the sentence written the right way; the player who makes the match must decide which one is correct in order to win the point.

- Animal pairs—the name and picture of a baby animal is written on one card, the name and picture of the adult animal on the other.

Category Games. These may be used with many subjects and may be played individually or with teams. The object is to fill in all the slots on the category chart before the opponents do. Subject areas or category headings are written across the top of the chart. Letters are listed down the left side of the chart. Players must write entries beginning with the particular letters for each category. An example is shown in Table 6–2.

Hangman. Use this old favorite to review vocabulary or spelling words from any subject. The object is for the players to figure out what word fits in the blanks before the leader's man can be "hung." Kaye offers a great variation called Eraser. In her game, the leader erases a portion of the crazy "Eraserman" whenever an incorrect letter is guessed. She also suggests letter frames instead of the traditional nondescript dashes in order to help young players with a visual reference for the mystery word (1991).

Specific Subject Games and Center Ideas

Language Arts. *Whirl for Words.* Put a spinner in the center of a circle of vocabulary words. Players take turns whirling the spinner. They must

CALIFORNIA

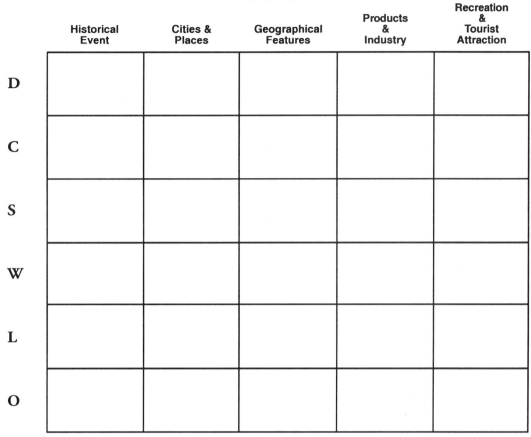

	Historical Event	Cities & Places	Geographical Features	Products & Industry	Recreation & Tourist Attraction
D					
C					
S					
W					
L					
O					

TABLE 6–2

read the word or give the correct definition for words the spinner points to. If players respond correctly, then they get to keep the card and spin again until they miss. Then play passes to the next player. Or the first player can see how many cards he can identify correctly before he misses, then the cards can be replaced, and the next player can take a turn.

Same Word, Different Meanings. Children can work on these at a learning center or by competing on teams. The object is to find as many things as possible to which a word may relate. For example, the word *ring* may relate to a "wedding band," "a circus ring," "ring around the collar," or a "token ring network." Mulac gives a list of other possibilities in the book, *Educational Games for Fun.* (1971), including match, shoe, and shell. If this is used for a learning center, the student may be asked to write a sentence for each use of the word. If used for a game, teams may brainstorm for uses, have team leaders read the list when time is called, and be awarded a point for each use.

Dictionary Skills. To practice dictionary skills, a letter and a topic may be written on the board. (For example: B—a kind of bird.) The students think of a suitable word and locate it in the dictionary. The first student to find the dictionary entry will read the meaning of the word. Correct responses might include bluebird and blackbird. A reward could be given to first finders; rewards could be anything from stickers to bonus points. Some other adaptations include:

   a. As above, but with the addition of telling the word above and below, and finding the guidewords for the dictionary page.

   b. Find newspaper headlines or magazine article titles with words having more that one meaning. Find the correct meaning for that context in the dictionary entry. Write a new sentence with the word, using that particular meaning (Bell and Wieckert, 1980).

   c. Bell and Wieckert have a clever game called *Capture,* which gives practice on finding guide words. In the game, animals are "captured" by putting the animal word in the cage with the correct guide words (1980).

Dingy Definitions. A difficult or obscure word is selected from the dictionary. Players are asked to make up their own definitions for the word. All the definitions are taken up and read, including the correct definition. The reader tries to bluff his or her way through even ridiculous definitions. The players have to guess which one is the right one. Players who choose the correct definition get to take turns selecting other words and reading the definitions. Points may also be awarded for correct choices. This is a forerunner or take-off on the commercial Balderdash, a bluffing definition discernment game; Mulac has a version called *Poker Face Definitions.*

Homonyms. Use a nonsense word such as "sassafrass" or "McGillecuddy" to take the place in a sentence of two words with the same sound but different meanings. An example is, "Those girls think they're so sassafrass that it's begun to sassafrass on my nerves." The answers are "great" and "grate."

Classified Expressions. We use many common expressions which initially meant something different from the way we use them now. We also have taken expressions that refer specifically to a category or action, and we have broadened the use. For example, we use many sports terms in different ways than originally intended (strike out, out of bounds, hit the showers). Give categories and have students find expressions. The students may play as individuals or be divided into teams in which they brainstorm to come up with more than opposing teams. Consider these:

- Birds (for the birds)
- Flowers (smelling like a rose)
- Food (toasted, doesn't know beans)
- Body parts (chip on his shoulder)

The students may have fun thinking of other categories (Mulac, 1971).

Relays. Children can get in some helpful review with relays. The teams can be the rows in the classroom. One piece of paper is used for all the team members' responses, and is passed along the row until everyone does his or her part. Some variations include:

a. Spelling relays—Instructions may be given to write a four-letter word beginning with *b* and ending with *d.* Each team member must take a turn to write one, without any repeats. The first team to go through the row wins. The whole class checks the validity of the winning list. Next time you may want to begin the relay with the last people in the row with different letter directions (five-letter words beginning with *d* and ending with *y*). Mulac gives a good resource list for these (1971).

   - Another spelling relay—This one uses letter tiles, cards, or blocks on separate tables or areas of the room. A word is called out and then the teams scramble to their areas and spell out the word with the tiles. The first team to correctly arrange the letters for the word wins. If large letter cards are used, the players may hold them and arrange themselves properly to spell the word.

- Or, a large letter may be taped to the front or the back of each team member, with all the teams having the same assortment of letters. Words that are spelled with those particular letters are called out. Players try to arrange themselves to spell the word correctly before the other teams do.

    b.   Parts of speech relay—This can be crazy but fun. Instructions are given for players to write certain parts of speech, then pass the paper on to the next player to write the next directed part of speech, until a sentence is completed. The first players in the relay row might be directed to write a word that is an "article." One suggested order is:

> First player—article
> Second player—adjective
> Third player—noun
> Fourth player—verb
> Fifth player—adverb

It is interesting to see how these hodgepodge sentences turn out. The class can then vote on the one they like the best.

    c.   Paragraph relay—The first player gets to write the topic sentence for a paragraph. The next players take turns adding sentences, until the paragraph makes it through the whole relay row. The first team to finish a paragraph that makes sense wins.

Math Games. Let's Go Shopping. This is a game form of the activity mentioned in Chapter 5. Teams can compete, pretending to be families. Each "family" is given a list of items that must be purchased to furnish their "home". All the families are given an equal amount of newspapers and advertisements. They may use newspaper advertisements to find prices and locations for their items. A reward may go to the family that furnishes their home first; another reward may go to the family that furnishes their home the most economically.

Bouncer. This game helps with both early counting skills and listening skills. A child is chosen to be the first bouncer. The bouncer will bounce the ball any number of times between 1 and 10 (or any other previously decided range). Then the bouncer may call on another player to clap his hands the same number of times as the ball was bounced. Players are told to listen carefully and count to themselves as the bouncer bounces. If the player who was called on claps the right number of times, then he becomes the bouncer.

Buzz Buzz. In this game, players count in sequence and signal certain kinds of numbers by saying "buzz." For example, the counting begins with each player saying one number and continues around the room. Whenever it is time to say an even number, players say "buzz." Players who mess up and say a number instead of "buzz" are out. To add variety and also to increase the skill level, the "buzz" numbers may be changed. Players may be asked to say "buzz" for multiples of five or other numbers. (Adapted from Cherokee County Substitute Survival Kit.)

Start Your Bidding. Pictures may be used to represent items or actual items may be demonstrated. Miniatures, like doll furniture or Matchbox cars, may also be used. Players are given an opportunity to examine and consider auction items for a few minutes before the auction begins. Each player is allotted a certain amount of money or given the same amount of play money. Players may be instructed in some good auction strategies, such as beginning the bidding lower than the expected price. (Real prices may be attached in order to help the players with reality.) Players may buy as much as they want as long as their money lasts. After the auction, players may do the addition to see how much they spent and the subtraction required to see how much they have left. Be creative concerning auction items. Consider these possibilities:

- Farm auction, with farm equipment and animals.

- Fine art auction at the end of a unit on art. Have fun seeing if players are able to distinguish between the "real stuff" and junk.

- Household items, including refrigerators, sofas, CD players, books, TV.

- Trip preparation, the items needed to travel abroad.

- Fun items for kids, like toys or cars.

Number Battle. You probably know this old card game. Two players split a deck of cards and turn over their top cards together. Whoever has the highest value card wins the "battle" and gets to take the other player's card "prisoner." This is a good quick way to drill "greater than, less than" concepts.

Social Studies Games. *The Name Game.* This game is useful for reviewing information about story characters, historical figures, or current newsmakers. One player starts the game. The teacher tapes a character's name to the player's back without her seeing it. The student shows the rest of the players her back, then tries to figure out the person's identity by asking questions. The player may only ask questions that may be answered with a *yes* or *no.* For example, "Am I a leader of a country?" or "Am I a villain?" The player may be given a certain number of questions (ten is good) to determine the secret identity. The class may also be divided into teams that compete to see which team discovers the right identity the quickest.

Pass the Globe. The players sit in a circle and the leader holds out the globe. The leader calls the name of a player and rolls the globe to that student. The leader asks a question such as, "Can you find both North and South America on the globe?" If the player locates correctly, he or she rolls the globe to another player and gets to ask the question. Here are some modifications:

- The same question is asked of all the players, especially with younger children.

- Players who locate correctly are allowed to change the question to one of their own choosing as long as it has been covered in class.

- The globe may be considered "hot" and players find the right place as quickly as possible.

Strange Names. This idea may be used for a game or a learning center to familiarize students with map reading. Students may use road maps, atlases, and zip code directories to find funny and strange names of places. After the individuals or groups find a certain number of places with unusual names for their lists, then they may pick one and figure out the map route to get from where they are to that place. For example, a group may chart the way to get to Broad Bottom, KY or Meddybumps, ME. Prizes might be given for the craziest lists or the longest distance traveled (Mulac, 1971). This project may be expanded in the following ways:

- Find landmarks or tourist attractions along the route.

- Research the population of the town or city.

- Younger ones might have to list the states you would travel through to get to this place.

- Write to the chamber of commerce to investigate how the place got its name.

Play on Places. In this game a player says the name of a place (city or town or body of water or whatever has been designated) and the next player names another place beginning with the last letter of the one just mentioned. This may be played individually or by teams. The play may proceed in a logical fashion around the room or through the rows. If played individually, and a player misses, then that player is eliminated. If played by teams, then the play can go back and forth between the teams, with points being scored for correct entries and points deducted for misses. If several misses occur in a row, then the first volunteer from either team may score a point and get the play resumed (Mulac, 1971). A possible chain of answers could be Atlanta, Albuquerque, El Paso, Oakland, Detroit, Trenton, and so forth. Answers may be limited to those in players' memory banks or may be helped by atlases but with time limits.

States and Capitals Show-down. This game may also be played by individuals or by teams. A player names a capital or a state and the next player must complete the pair. Individual players who miss may be eliminated from play and team players who miss may cause a penalty point for their team. The player left at the end or the team with the most points wins. Some variations are:

- Countries and capitals
- World rivers and countries

- Mountain ranges and countries

- First and last names of presidents

- Top export products and countries

- Events and dates

Science Games. *Oops!* This is a good way to review after studying areas of nature. It is patterned after the backyard basketball game of "Horse." The leader gives a category found in nature, such as things found in the ocean. Players take turns naming things. If a player is unable to name something, then the player earns the first letter in "Oops." When a player earns all four letters, he or she is out of the game. If all the players earn a letter or the leader determines that the players have exhausted the possibilities, then a new category is given. Mulac has a similar idea called *Nature Goofs* and she gives several good category suggestions as well as a reference list for the teacher to use (1971).

Natural Inquiry. Players use brainstorming and observation skills to list things in the room that were not made by man. Players or teams try to come up with the longest list. There are endless other topics for hunt, including things made with water, and things affected by the weather.

Commercial Games

As mentioned earlier, there are many commercial games that can actually be used quite legitimately in the classroom. Other commercial games may be adapted successfully. Be on the lookout in traditional toy stores and in new stores like Zany Brainy and Natural Wonders which have a decidedly fun educational bent. Some commercial possibilities not previously mentioned include:

- Sentence Scrabble (Milton Bradley)

- Brain Quest (grade level sets of general knowledge questions and answers, Workman)

- I Spy (memory, observation, and riddle game by Martine Redman and put out by Briarpatch)

- ASAP (a quick thinking card game put out by University Games)

- Slamwich (another quick card game, a memory builder/challenger, by Gamewright)

- Chess (Parker Brothers, Cardinal, and others)

- Uno (Mattel, Inc.)

- Cribbage (Cardinal Industries, Inc.)

- Tri-ominos

- Scrabble (Milton Bradley)

- Boggle (Parker Brothers)

- Spill and Spell

- UpWords (Milton Bradley)

- Speak and Spell (Texas Instruments)

- Speak and Math (Texas Instruments)

- Checkers (Parker Brothers)

- Yahtzee (Milton Bradley)

- Where in the USA is Carmen San Diego? (Geography board game put out by University Games)

- Hi-Ho Cherry-O (beginning counting game, Parker Brothers)

- Tri-Bond (game for finding commonalities, Patch Products, Inc.)

- Blurt (The Webster's Game of Word Racing put out by Patch Products, Inc.)

- Catch Phrase (Parker Brothers)

- Outburst (Hersch & Company). This is a great game for brainstorm and word association. The idea of this game has many adaptations for the classroom. For example, teams may come up with as many words as possible associated with smell or transportation or geology. You or the teacher may also write down one bonus word; if the team says this one word they get extra points.

Extra Games

Twenty Questions. This is an excellent activity for reinforcing listening skills. The game requires a box (a shoe box will work). The leader places an object in the box. The players then have to guess its identity. The players are allowed to ask *yes* or *no* questions only. They may ask, "Is it red?" They may not ask, "What color is it?" The leader tallies the *no* responses on the board. If twenty are recorded without the players guessing what is in the box, the leader is the winner.

Goofy Guessing. The first player sits down in a chair that faces away from the class. An object is placed on the floor behind the chair. The teacher points to a person to come up, take the object, and say "Merry Christmas" in a disguised voice. This person then returns to his or her seat before the guesser is allowed to turn around and tries to guess who took the object. If the guesser guesses correctly within three tries, then he or she gets to pick the next taker and the last taker becomes the next guesser. This game may be played year-round with different holiday or seasonal phrases and objects. It's a good way to promote listening and self-control on the day before a vacation.

I'm Thinking Of Something. The leader says, "I'm thinking of something in this room that begins with the letter C." Children are called on to give their answers—chalk, crayons, Craig, chalkboard, chair, carpet, computer, clock, ceiling—until the correct answer is given. The child with the correct answer is the next leader. When appropriate, children can be asked to explain the beginning sound: C sounds like K, C sounds like S, or to identify the vowel sound found in their answer.

Select games carefully for young children. The games described in Figure 6–9 are appropriate for most four-, five-, six-, and seven-year old children (Herr, 1995).

Whenever possible involve the children in all aspects of playing games. (Figure 6–10 is a gameboard made up by a sixth grader.) Encourage the children to keep score at their desks even if a scorekeeper has been assigned. Remind them that the score is not open to dispute, but that you want them to practice listening and recording for themselves. Even early math learners can keep track of the score by using symbols and the traditional stick and bundle (⊬⊦⊦⊦) method.

1. Get Acquainted Game	The children sit in a circle formation. The teacher begins the game by saying, "My name is ——— and I'm going to roll the ball to ———." Continue playing the game until every child has a turn. A variation of the game is have the children stand in a circle and bounce the ball to each other. This game is a fun way for the children to learn each other's names.
2. Hide the Ball	Choose several children and ask them to cover their eyes. Then hide a small ball, or other object, in an observable place. Ask the children to uncover their eyes and try to find the ball. The first child to find the ball hides it again.
3. Which Ball is Gone?"	In the center of the circle, place six colored balls, cubes, beads, shapes, etc., in a row. Ask a child to close his eyes. Then ask another child to remove one of the objects and hide it behind him. The first child uncovers his eyes and tells which colored object is missing from the row. The game continues until all the selections have been made. When using with older children, two objects may be removed at a time to further challenge their abilities.

4. "What Sound is That?"

The purpose of this game is to promote the development of listening skills. Begin by asking the children to close their eyes. Make a familiar sound. Then ask a child to identify it. Sources of sound may include:

tearing paper	blowing a pitch pipe	raising or lowering
sharpening a pencil	dropping an object	window shades
walking, running,	moving a desk or	leafing through
shuffling feet	chair	book pages
clapping hands	snapping fingers	cutting with
sneezing, coughing	blowing nose	scissors
tapping on glass,	opening or closing	snapping rubber
wood, or metal	drawer	bands
jingling money	stirring paint in	ringing a bell
opening a window	a jar	clicking the tongue
pouring water	clearing the throat	crumpling paper
shuffling cards	splashing water	opening a box
blowing a whistle	rubbing sandpaper	sighing
banging blocks	together	stamping feet
bouncing ball	chattering teeth	rubbing palms
shaking a rattle	sweeping sound,	together
turning the lights on	such as a brush or	rattling keys
knocking on a door	broom	

A variation of this game could be played by having a child make a sound. Then the other children and the teacher close their eyes and attempt to identify the sound. For older children this game can be varied with the production of two sounds. Begin by asking the children if the sounds are the same or different. Then have them identify the sounds.

© 1995, Delmar Publishers

FIGURE 6–9 Activity Games.

5. "Near or Far?"

The purpose of this game is to locate sound. First, tell the children to close their eyes. Then play a sound recorded on a cassette tape. Ask the children to identify the sound as being near or far away.

6. Descriptions

The purpose of this game is to encourage expressive language skills. Begin by asking each child to describe himself. Included with the description can be the color of his eyes, hair, and clothing. The teacher might prefer to use an imaginative introduction such as: "One by one, you may take turns sitting up here in Alfred's magic chair and describe yourself to Alfred." Another approach may be to say, "Pretend that you must meet somebody at a very crowded airport who has never seen you before. How would you describe yourself so that the person would be sure to know who you are?"

A variation for older children would be to have one of the children describe another child without revealing the name of the person he is describing. To illustrate, the teacher might say, "I'm thinking of someone with shiny red hair, blue eyes, many freckles, etc...." The child being described should stand up.

7. Mirrored Movements

The purpose of this game is to encourage awareness of body parts through mirrored movements. Begin the activity by making movements. Encourage the children to mirror your movements. After the children understand the game, they may individually take the leader role.

8. Little Red Wagon Painted Red

As a prop for the game, cut a red wagon with wheels out of construction paper. Then cut rectangles the same size as the box of the red wagon. Include purple, blue, yellow, green, orange, brown, black, and pink colors.

Sing the song to the tune of **"Skip to My Lou."**

*Little red wagon painted **red.***
*Little red wagon painted **red.***
*Little red wagon painted **red.***
What color would it be?

Give each child a turn to pick and name a color. As the song is sung, let the child change the wagon color.

FIGURE 6–9 Activity Games. (Continued)

9. Police Officer Game

Select one child to be the police officer. Ask him to find a lost child. Describe one of the children in the circle. The child who is the police officer will use the description as a clue to find the "missing child."

10. Mother Cat and Baby Kits

Choose one child to be the mother cat. Then ask the mother cat to go to sleep in the center of the circle, covering his eyes. Then choose several children to be kittens. The verse below is chanted as the baby kittens hide in different parts of the classroom. Following this, the mother cat hunts for them. When all of the kittens have been located, another mother cat may be selected. The number of times the game is repeated depends upon the children's interest and attention span.

Mother cat lies fast asleep.

To her side the kittens creep.

But the kittens like to play.

Softly now they creep away.

Mother cat wakes up to see.

No little kittens. Where can they be?

11. Memory Game

Collect common household items, a towel, and tray. Place the items on the tray. Show the tray containing the items. Cover with a towel. Then ask the children to recall the names of the items on the tray. To ensure success, begin the activity with only two or three objects for young children. Additional objects can be added depending upon the developmental maturity of the children.

12. Cobbler, Mend My Shoes

Sit the children in a circle formation. Then select one child to sit in the center. This child gives a shoe to a child in the circle, and then closes his eyes. The children in the circle pass the shoe around behind them while the rhyme is chanted. When the chant is finished, the shoe is no longer passed. The last child with the shoe in his hand holds the shoe behind his back. Then the child sitting in the center tries to guess who has the shoe.

Cobbler, cobbler, mend my shoe

Have it done by half past two

Stitch it up and stitch it down

Now see with whom the shoe is found.

FIGURE 6–9 Activity Games. (Continued)

13. Huckle Buckle Beanstalk

Ask the children to sit in a circle. Once seated, tell them to close their eyes. Then hide a small ball in an obvious place. Say, "Ready." Encourage all of the children to hunt for the object. Each child who spots it returns to a place in the circle and says, "Huckle buckle beanstalk." No one must tell where he has seen the ball until all the children have seen it.

14. What's Different?

Sit all of the children in a circle formation. Ask one child to sit in the center. The rest of the children are told to look closely at the child sitting in the center. Then the children are told to cover their eyes while you change some detail on the child in the center. For example, you may place a hat on the child, untie his shoe, remove a shoe, roll up one sleeve, etc. The children sitting in the circle act as detective to determine "what's different?"

15. Cookie Jar

Sit the children in a circle formation on the floor with their legs crossed. Together they repeat a rhythmic chant while using alternating leg-hand clap to emphasize the rhythm. The chant is as follows.

Someone took the cookies from the cookie jar.

Who took the cookies from the cookie jar?

Mary took the cookies from the cookie jar.

Mary took the cookies from the cookie jar?

Who, me? (Mary)

Yes, you. (all children)

Couldn't be. (Mary)

Then who? (all children)

———— took the cookies from the cookie jar. (Mary names another child.)

Use each child's name.

16. Hide and Seek Tonal Matching

Sit the children in a circle formation. Ask one child to hide in the room while the other children cover their eyes. The children in the circle sing, "Where is ———— hiding?" The child who is hiding responds by singing back, "Here I am." With their eyes remaining closed, the children point in the direction of the hiding child. All open eyes and the child emerges from his hiding place.

FIGURE 6–9 Activity Games. (Continued)

21. Duck Duck Goose	Ask the children to squat in a circle formation. Then ask one child to walk around the outside of circle, lightly touching each child's head and saying "Duck, Duck." When he touches another child and says "Goose," that child chases him around the circle. If the child who was "it" returns to the "goose's" place without being tagged, he remains. When this happens, the tapped child is "it." This game is appropriate for older four-, five-, six-, and seven-year-old children.
22. Fruit Basket Upset	Ask the children to sit in a circle formation on chairs or on carpet squares. Then ask one child to sit in the middle of the circle as the chef. Hand pictures of various fruits to the rest of the children. Then to continue the game, ask the chef to call out the name of a fruit. The children holding that particular fruit exchange places. If the chef calls out, "fruit basket upset," all of the children must exchange places, including the chef. The child who doesn't find a place is the new chef. A variation of this game would be bread basket upset. For this game use pictures of breads, rolls, bagels, muffins, breadsticks, etc. This game is appropriate for older children.
23. Bear Hunt	This is a rhythmic chant which may easily be varied. Start by chanting each line, encouraging the children to repeat the line. **Teacher:** *Let's go on a bear hunt.* **Children:** *(Repeat. Imitate walk by slapping knees alternately.)* **Teacher:** *I see a wheat field.* *Can't go over it;* *Can't go under it.* *Let's go through it.* (arms straight ahead like you're parting wheat) *I see a bridge.* *Can't go over it;* *Can't go under it.* *Let's swim.* (arms in swimming motion) *I see a tree.* *Can't go over it;* *Can't go under it.* *Let's go up it.* (climb and look) *I see a swamp.* *Can't go over it;* *Can't go under it.* *Let's go through it.* (pull hands up and down slowly) *I see a cave.* *Can't go over it;* *Can't go under it.* *Let's go in.* (walking motion) *I see two eyes. I see two ears.* *I see a nose. I see a mouth.* *It's a BEAR!!!* (Do all in reverse very fast)

© 1995, Delmar Publishers

FIGURE 6–9 Activity Games. (Continued)

17. Listening and Naming

This game is most successful with a small group of children. The children should take turns shutting their eyes and identifying sounds as you tap with a wooden dowel on an object such as glass, triangle, drum, wooden block, cardboard box, rubber ball, etc.

18. Funny Shapes

Ask each child to choose a partner. One partner must make a large shape with his body. The other partner must follow the directions of movement. Roles reverse for the second set of directions. Provide directions such as:

1. Make a big shape.

go *over*
go *under*
go *through*
go *around*

2. Make a small shape.

go *over*
go *under*
go *through*
go *around*

19. Drop the Handkerchief

Direct the children to stand in a circle formation. Ask one child to run around the outside of the circle, dropping a handkerchief behind another child. The child who has the handkerchief dropped behind him must pick it up and chase the child who dropped it. The first child tries to return to the vacated space by running before he is tagged.

20. "If You Please"

This game is a simple variation of "Simon Says." Ask the children to form a circle around a leader who gives directions, some of which are prefaced with "if you please." The children are to follow only the "if you please" directions, ignoring any that do not begin with "if you please." Directions to be used may include walking forward, hopping on one foot, bending forward, standing tall, etc. This game can be varied by having the children follow the directions when the leader says, "do this," and not when he says, "do that." Play only one version of this game on a single day. Too much variety will confuse the children.

FIGURE 6–9 Activity Games. (Continued)

24. "Guess Who?"

Individually tape the children's voices. Play the tape during group time, and let the children identify their classmates' voices.

25. Shadow Fun

Hang a bed sheet up in the classroom for use as a projection screen. Then place a light source such as a slide, filmstrip, or overhead projector a few feet behind the screen. Ask two of the children to stand behind the sheet. Then encourage one of the two children to walk in front of the projector light. When this happens, the children are to give the name of the person who is moving.

26. If This Is Red—Nod Your Head

Point to an object in the room and say, "If this is green, shake your hand. If this is yellow, touch your nose." If the object is not the color stated, children should not imitate the requested action.

27. Freeze

Encourage the children to imitate activities such as washing dishes, cleaning house, dancing, etc. Approximately every 10 to 20 seconds, call out "Freeze!" When this occurs, the children are to stop whatever they are doing and remain frozen until you say, "Thaw" or "Move." A variation of this activity would be to use music. When the music stops, the children freeze their movements.

28. Spy the Object

Designate a large area on the floor as home base. Then select an object and show it to the children. Ask the children to cover their eyes while you place the object in an observable place in the room. Then encourage the children to open their eyes and search for the object. As each child spies the object he quietly returns to the home base area without telling. The other children continue searching until all have found the object. After all the children are seated, they may share where the object is placed.

FIGURE 6–9 Activity Games. (Continued)

29. Who Is Gone?

This game is played in a circle format. Begin by asking a child to close his eyes. Then point to a child to leave the circle and go to a spot where he can't be seen. The child with his eyes closed opens them at your word, then looks around the circle and identifies the friend who is missing.

30. It's Me

Seat the children in a circle formation, and place a chair in the center. Choose one child to sit on a chair in the circle, closing his eyes. After this, ask another child to walk up softly behind the chair and tap the child on the shoulder. The seated child asks, "Who is tapping?" The other child replies, "It's me." By listening to the response, the seated child identifies the other child.

31. Feeling and Naming

Ask a child to stand with his back to you, placing his hands behind him. Then place an object in the child's hands for identification by feeling it. Nature materials can be used such as leaves, shells, fruit, etc. A ball, doll, block, Lego piece, puzzle piece, crayon, etc., may also be used.

32. Doggy, Doggy, Where's Your Bone?

Sit the children in a circle formation. Then place a chair in the center of the circle. Place a block under the chair. Select one child, the dog, to sit on the chair and close his eyes. Then point to another child. This child must try to get the dog's bone from under the chair without making a noise. After the child returns to his place in the circle, all the children place their hands behind them. Then in unison the children say, "Doggy, Doggy, where's your bone?" During the game, each dog has three guesses as to who has the bone.

FIGURE 6–9 Activity Games. (Continued)

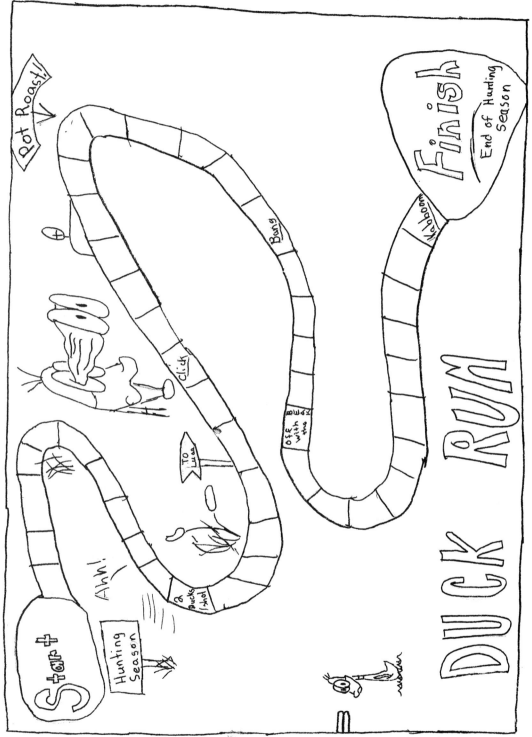

FIGURE 6–10 Student-designed generic game board.

Have fun with your students. Help them see how much fun learning can be. Educational games are a great tool for doing this. Bear in mind what Peggy Kaye said about her games, "Possibly the deepest lesson these games should teach is that concentration and intellectual challenge can be immensely enjoyable. The child who learns that will benefit forever" (1991). Educational games are kind of like vitamins in a fortified peanut butter and chocolate chip snack bar; kids get the nutritional value without even knowing it. The hope is that some day they will be hooked on just plain learning and that they will even grow to love vegetables! Help the lead teacher with new game ideas and help prepare and modify old game ideas to add new pizzazz to your classroom. You will all enjoy it!

CHAPTER 7

Working with Children with Special Needs

Most likely you already think that all children are special; and they are. We have already discussed that children grow and develop in stages and that children do not progress through developmental stages at exactly the same rate. So, one eight year old may read very well and have a fairly broad vocabulary and another may recognize fewer words and shy away from reading out loud. We cannot expect all children to be ready to understand and master the same skills at the same time. We do, however, recognize that there are certain ranges for normal development of skills and there are some children who do not fit within these ranges. It is important and necessary to recognize that some children have needs beyond those of the average. There are children who have mental or physical disabilities; some of these are present from birth and others are a result of illness or accidents. There are children whose differences are apparent to all from early ages and there are children whose disabilities are somewhat hidden and may not even be discovered until the school years. Some have needs that can be met only by a team of specialists working together for the welfare of these children. These children are frequently called *special* and are the recipients of *special education*.

The Council for Exceptional Children uses the term *exceptional* to refer to children who have disabilities or are gifted. In other words, *special children* are ones who have a need for something different than what the typical classroom provides. They may need alternative or individual classes or special assistance or tutoring. This is where you, the paraeducator, may come in to the picture. You may be the one to provide that extra bit of help that an "exceptional" or "special" child needs.

Manuel is a special child; he has been blessed with a sharp mind, but he has been blind from birth because of drugs his mother took while she was carrying him. On top of his blindness, he is tactilely defensive; that means he has a problem touching new things. Then there is Anya, who has cerebral palsy and some learning disabilities. Anya has had numerous surgeries in her young life to correct physical abnormalities in her skeletal system. Both of these children require special help at their public elementary school. Manuel must have someone to guide or keep tabs on him at all times. He also needs one-on-one help with the computer and Braille lessons. Anya must have someone to help her with bathroom needs as she is unable to lift herself out of her wheelchair. Years back neither of these children would have been in a public school. Now they have wonderful teachers and paraeducators who work toward the best education possible so that their futures can be as sparkling and hopeful as they are.

MEETING THE NEEDS THROUGH LEGISLATION

Public Law 94–142

To meet the needs of special children, the federal government passed into law the Education for All Handicapped Children Act, Public Law 94–142, in 1975. The Council for Exceptional Children was instrumental in the passage of this landmark legislation; there were also many individuals who were dedicated to this initiative. The goal was and is to make sure that children with disabilities and other special needs are given fair and quality educational opportunities. There are horror stories from the past where children were denied educational help because they were different from the rest. But now public schools are required to provide educational programs for each and every child, no matter what the differences or disabilities are.

In 1975, the states were given a deadline of Fall 1977 to implement Public Law 94–142 with legislation of their own. Legislation continues to be passed to this day that ensures educational intervention for more and more special children and at lower ages.

According to PL 94–142, handicapped children are defined as follows:

Sec 121a.5 Handicapped children.
(a) As used in this part, the term handicapped children *means those children evaluated in accordance with sections 121.a530–121.a.534 as being mentally retarded, hard of hearing, deaf, speech impaired, visually handicapped, seriously emotionally disturbed, orthopedically impaired, other health impaired, deaf-blind, multi-handicapped, or as having specific learning disabilities, who because of those impairments need special education and related services.*

Note: To obtain a copy of PL 94–142, write to your local congressman. More information on this law can be found in *Exceptional Children and Youth: An Introduction* by Edward L. Meyen.

Public Law 94–142 provides for a *free, public education* for all handicapped children between the ages of five and twenty-one. The law further guarantees the right of every citizen to have a full educational opportunity made available to them (Section 613). Hence, Manuel and Anya are in a public elementary school and are the recipients of many special and support services.

Mandates of PL 94-142.
- A free and appropriate public education (FAPE), including special education and related services, for all handicapped children ages five to twenty-one; programs for children ages three to five if mandated by state law.

  Special education is defined as instruction specially designed to meet the unique needs of handicapped children. It may include classroom instruction, physical education, home and hospital instruction, and institutional instruction. (Initially, physical education was often omitted from the curriculum for special children, especially those children [like Anya] with orthopedic handicaps, because it was felt that the physical and/or occupational therapy they received was equivalent to physical education. However, according to the intent of the law, physical therapy is not equivalent and may not serve as a substitution.)

  Related services are commonly referred to as support services, and include the following:

  > Speech therapy
  > Psychological counseling
  > Vocational counseling
  > Mobility education
  > Transportation

Note: Tables 7–1, 7–2, and 7–3 and Figure 7–1 give some breakdowns on where and how special children's educational needs are served and who does the serving.

- The law makes a distinction between *first priority* and *second priority* children. First priority children are those with severe handicaps within any disability category who are not receiving an adequate education. For example, the local public schools traditionally did not educate the severely emotionally disturbed, the severely mentally retarded, or even the deaf, blind, or deaf-blind. These children were normally educated in state or private institutions, if they were educated at all. So now, these children are considered first priority in order to change this tradition of nonservice.

- Parents must be informed about the evaluation and projections for the future of their children. This must be done in writing and in the parents' native language. By law the parents must be involved in the decision-making process and must give permission at every step, including identification, evaluation, educational placement, and evaluation of that placement. Parents have the right to see all the files, observations, tests, and so on pertaining to their children. Parents may question an evaluation and ask for a second opinion. In other words, the law mandates that parents are privy to anything the school has concerning their children and are the ultimate authority over their children's education. (When a second evaluation is requested, the law is not clear on who is responsible for ordering or paying for it—the school district or the parent.)

- Each child who has been deemed to need special education or related services must have an Individual Education Program (IEP). The IEP must be approved by the parents. The IEP includes:

  - Short-range objectives.
  - Long-range objectives.
  - Specific materials that will be used to accomplish these objectives.
  - The time given for objectives to be accomplished.
  - The name of the individual responsible for implementing the IEP.
  - The name of the individual responsible for evaluation of the IEP.

  The IEP is an on-going thing; it must be evaluated at least once a year. The IEP is usually developed by or at least influenced or checked by many different people; every certified person involved in the child's education, as well as representatives from the school or county administration take part in "staffing" meetings. All of these people are allowed input into the plan for the child; it is felt that the best interests of children are protected by this multidisciplinary approach.

- Each special child is to be placed in the *least restrictive environment.* The *Facts on File Dictionary of Education* defines least restrictive environment as "the principle that handicapped children who require special education services should, to the extent possible, receive those services in the same classroom and in the same school building that they would have attended if they were not handicapped" (Shafritz, 1988). What is least restrictive is unique to individuals; what is least restrictive for one child may not be the least restrictive for another child. For example, a child with severe athetoid type cerebral palsy (with limp, twitchy muscles) who is strapped into a wheelchair and is unable to communicate may not belong in a regular classroom until that child can communicate. At that point, when the child can at least communicate with peers, the child might properly be placed in the regular classroom and be supported with speech therapy, physical therapy, occupational therapy, and adaptive physical education. In a case like this, if there is no mental defect, the regular classroom teacher might not need any special materials in the class except a book holder and a raised desk that would fit over the child's wheelchair and some mechanism to hold the child's papers.

    In the 1983 case Roncker v. Walter, the definition of least restrictive environment was broadened to say that "to the maximum

TABLE 7–1 Number of Infants and Toddlers from Birth Through Age Two Receiving Services in Different Early Intervention Settings. December 1992. Source: U.S. Department of Education, Office of Special Education Programs, Data Analysis System (DANS).

Setting	U.S. and Outlying Areas	50 States, Washington, DC, and Puerto Rico
Early intervention classroom	36,541	36,483
Family day care	703	698
Home	40,896	40,826
Hospital (inpatient)	8,122	8,096
Outpatient service facility	37,409	37,390
Regular nursery school/day care	4,444	4,441
Residential facility	105	105
Other setting	10,987	10,982
All settings	139,207	139,021

Note: Data as of October 1, 1994.

TABLE 7–2 Early Intervention Services on IFSPs Provided to Infants, Toddlers, and Their Families in Accord with Part H. December 1, 1992. Source: Division of Innovation and Development "To Assure the Free Appropriate Public Education of all Children With Disabilities," *Seventeenth Annual Report to Congress on the Implementation of the Individuals with Disabilities Education Act,* Washington, DC: U.S. Department of Education, (1995).

	Assistive Technology Services/ Devices	Audiology	Family Training Counseling and Home Visits	Health Services	Medical Services	Nursing Services	Nutrition Services	Occupa- tional Therapy	Physical Therapy
U.S. and Outlying Areas	5,861	14,318	47,698	19,943	23,174	20,371	16,016	32,690	38,066
50 States Washington, DC and Puerto Rico	5,857	14,217	47,557	19,935	23,136	20,341	15,983	32,611	38,018

	Psycho- logical Services	Respite Care	Social Work	Special Instruction	Speech or Language Path- ology	Transpor- tation	Vision Services	Other Early Interven- tion Services
U.S. and Outlying Areas	12,639	11,189	32,760	47,144	41,976	20,203	5,417	32,383
50 States Washington, DC and Puerto Rico	12,538	11,177	32,673	47,081	41,933	20,148	5,402	32,383

extent appropriate, handicapped children must be educated with nonhandicapped children."

• Due process is guaranteed for every child and family. The parents have the right to sue the school district if they feel that the best interests of their child are not being served. For example, a mentally retarded child could be recommended for placement in a special day class. The parents might feel that the child can remain in the regular class for many activities such as art, music, physical education, lunch, and recess; the school district might not agree. Hopefully, the two parties would try to understand each other's positions and reach an agreement. However, if they are not able to

TABLE 7–3 Number and Type of Personnel Employed and Needed to Provide Early Intervention Services to Infants and Toddlers with Disabilities and Their Families. December, 1992. Source: Division of Innovation and Development "To Assure the Free Appropriate Public Education of all Children With Disabilities," *Seventeenth Annual Report to Congress on the Implementation of the Individuals with Disabilities Education Act,* Washington, DC: U.S. Department of Education, (1995).

State	All Staff		Paraprofessionals	
	Employed	Needed	Employed	Needed
ALABAMA	126	35	38	5
ALASKA	55	0	3	0
ARIZONA	157	53	37	8
ARKANSAS	228	47	93	24
CALIFORNIA*	351	15	.	.
COLORADO	73	10	12	2
CONNECTICUT	254	13	22	1
DELAWARE	102	18	11	5
DISTRICT OF COLUMBIA	125	29	28	1
FLORIDA	174	173	49	49
GEORGIA	525	234	118	29
HAWAII	300	81	143	34
IDAHO	109	463	10	241
ILLINOIS	294	44	36	4
INDIANA	450	126	88	12
IOWA	22	0	0	0
KANSAS	247	68	63	7
KENTUCKY	0	73	0	0
LOUISIANA	321	154	82	11
MAINE	376	0	26	0
MARYLAND	446	12	65	0
MASSACHUSETTS	571	718	60	75
MICHIGAN	441	0	29	0
MINNESOTA	1,122	0	570	0
MISSISSIPPI	61	20	6	4
MISSOURI	127	0	0	0
MONTANA	74	3	7	1
NEBRASKA	135	0	0	0
NEVADA	63	1	9	0
NEW HAMPSHIRE	73	1	6	0
NEW JERSEY	0	0	0	0
NEW MEXICO	167	0	43	0
NEW YORK	15,224	2,311	3,502	199
NORTH CAROLINA	.	.	.	.
NORTH DAKOTA	26	1	0	0
OHIO	2,390	283	0	0
OKLAHOMA	138	10	0	0
OREGON	0	0	0	0
PENNSYLVANIA	1,004	174	132	9
PUERTO RICO	225	0	26	0
RHODE ISLAND	50	18	7	4
SOUTH CAROLINA	119	0	27	0
SOUTH DAKOTA	189	53	35	2
TENNESSEE	561	78	132	16
TEXAS	1,073	47	264	6
UTAH	56	3	17	0
VERMONT	20	31	3	7
VIRGINIA	1,796	422	280	21
WASHINGTON	0	527	0	1
WEST VIRGINIA	138	11	31	4
WISCONSIN	366	0	0	0
WYOMING	95	83	6	5
AMERICAN SAMOA	31	0	1	0
GUAM	19	8	4	0
NORTHERN MARIANAS	13	0	4	0
PALAU	.	.	.	.
VIRGIN ISLANDS	.	.	.	.
BUR. OF INDIAN AFFAIRS	.	.	.	.
U.S. & OUTLYING AREAS	31,098	6,449	6,122	855
50 STATES, D.C., & P.R.	31,035	6,441	6,113	855

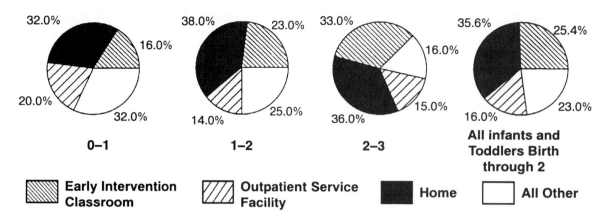

FIGURE 7–1 Settings in which Early Intervention Services Are Delivered by Age Group, 1992–1993. Source: U.S. Department of Education, Office of Special Education Programs, Data Analysis System (DANS).

reach an agreement, the parents might sue the school district for what they feel is an inappropriate placement for their child.

- Evaluation of special children must be done with instruments that are nondiscriminatory in terms of race and ethnicity. If a special child does not speak English well or at all, then testing must also be in the special child's dominant language.

- Provisions are included for the appointment of a *surrogate* or substitute in cases when a parent either refuses or is unable to participate in the process.

Implications of Public Law 94–142. It is clear that PL 94–142 includes early childhood education through upper grades. Because of this, it is likely that you have some "special" or handicapped children in your school or center. It is important for you to remember that your school must serve identified handicapped children if you have Head Start classes or any other type of publicly funded program.

Preschool, kindergarten, and early grade classrooms are especially appropriate for and conducive to meeting the needs of many "special children."

Children with orthopedic problems can fit in quite comfortably into regular education classrooms as long as the classrooms are accessible. (Accessibility is covered by PL 93–380, Section 504.) It may be important to note that not having wheelchair ramps is considered an invalid excuse for not admitting a child in a wheelchair. The child has the right to attend and it is up to the school to work things out for that child.

Visually impaired children, deaf or hard-of-hearing children, and children with mild retardation and emotional problems can be placed in so called "normal" preschool, kindergarten, or early grade classrooms. Such children can overcome their limitations and do well in the "mainstreamed" setting. Oppenheim offers a good explanation of the concept:

> *"In some instances a child's physical, emotional, or mental handicap may require a special program outside the scope of a regular classroom. In many instances, the school may design a schedule that combines instruction for part of the day with a specialist along with time in a regular mainstream classroom. Instead of isolating children in special classes, educators now believe that a great many handicapping conditions are better handled by enabling children to work alongside their agemates most of the day, while still providing individual instruction for short periods of time. Such pull-out programs give all children opportunities to learn about living in a world that includes people with and without handicaps." (1989)*

Both the *special* and *normal* child profit from interaction with each other. In fact, their association can provide wonderful life benefits for everybody. In one case involving a hearing-impaired child, all of the children in the class learned sign language in order to communicate better with that child. The children ended up learning sign language a lot faster than the teacher did! In another example, a child with behavior disorder (depressive) was placed in a regular preschool. The children quickly learned to tolerate temper tantrums and screaming fits. To visitors, they explained "Don't worry about Richie. He just needs to be alone now." In many ways the children were more accepting than some of the parents.

Mentally retarded children often integrate well into the preschool setting. They often have good social development, and their physical development may be almost normal. Their language may be simpler than that of their peers, but they often make their needs known through body language. They generally find very effective ways to communicate. Mentally retarded children may not be able to do some of the cognitive tasks well, but they can participate and derive as much pleasure from activities like painting, role playing, and playing with clay and blocks as any other child. Knowing that a child has some cognitive disabilities and is not on the academic level of the other children can spur you to look for and work with activities the child can do successfully. That may be a big part of your job; you can be an encourager, an advocate, for a special child, and also seek to protect that child from the stress of goals that are too high for that child.

One private preschool has a policy to integrate *special* and *normal* children. The director allowed four identified special children in a class of twenty-four. Over a period of ten years of having this policy, the school taught mentally retarded children, children with orthopedic problems, visually impaired, hearing impaired, emotionally disturbed, speech-impaired, and health-impaired children, as well as other children who had not yet been identified as having specific learning disabilities. With parental permission, other children even learned to help orthopedically challenged children with bathroom visits and other activities; both sets of children profited.

Look at the 1987 and the 1991–1992 statistics on numbers and categories of special children in Table 7–4 and Figure 7–2. Note that learning disabled, speech-impaired, and mentally retarded children comprised 84.5 percent of the total number of "special needs" students served. If behavior disorders are included, then 93.1 percent of all "special needs" children fall into these four categories. The implication is clear; you are more likely to have a student who is learning disabled, speech or language impaired, mentally retarded, or behavior disordered

TABLE 7–4 Numbers of Special Needs Children. Source: U.S. Department of Education, 1987.

Categories	Number of Students Served	Percentage of Total School Population
Learning disabilities	1,872,339	4.73%
Speech impaired	1,128,471	2.86%
Mental retardation	686,077	1.68%
Behavior disordered	376,943	0.95%
Multihandicapped	89,701	0.22%
Hard of hearing or deaf	68,413	0.17%
Orthopedically impaired	59,000	0.14%
Other health impaired	58,142	0.14%
Visually impaired	29,026	0.07%
Deaf-blind	2,132	0.01%
Total	4,370,244	10.97%

Students not receiving special education	89.98
Specific Learning Disabilities	5.02
Speech Impairments	2.34
Mental Retardation	1.14
Serious Emotional Disturbance	0.89
Other Disabilities	0.63

FIGURE 7–2 Disabilities of Students Ages 6–17 Receiving Special Education as Percentage of all Students Ages 6–17. Source: From *Teaching Exceptional Children by the Council for Exceptional Children,* Vol. 26. Copyright 1994 by The Council for Exceptional Children.

than one who is orthopedically impaired, hard of hearing, blind, or multihandicapped.

Public Law 99-457

This law, PL 99–457, Amendments to the Education for All Handicapped Children Act, was enacted in 1986. It reauthorized PL 94–142 and mandated programs for three- to five-year-olds for the 1990–1991 school year. (Under PL 94–142 these preschool programs were funded only if they were mandated by the states.) Now *all* states must provide programs for three- to five-year-olds in order to receive federal funding for this age group. Again, some of the same features found in PL 94–142 are also found in PL 99–457, including:

- Provision of a free, appropriate, public education (FAPE) for all identified three- to five-year-olds with disabilities.
- An individualized education plan (IEP) for each identified handicapped child, but with some modification for this age group.
- Placement in the "least restrictive environment."
- Due process protection.
- Nondiscriminatory testing.
- Confidentiality.

Differences Between PL 94–142 and 99–457

The principal difference between PL 94–142 and PL 99–457 is the recognition of increased need for family involvement with preschoolers.

FIGURE 7–3 Paraeducators are often called upon to offer one-on-one assistance for children with disabilities.

PL 99–457 stresses family participation in order to help these younger ones achieve their full developmental potential. Under PL 99–457 the IEP was changed to an Individual Family Service Plan (IFSP). It was recognized that for these very young children parental involvement is an equal or even more important component than the team of interested concerned educators.

A second difference between PL 94–142 and PL 99–457 is that PL 99–457 provides for state grant programs for infants and toddlers, and provides for assistance to be given "in planning, developing, and implementing a statewide system of comprehensive, coordinated, multidisciplinary, interagency programs" (Bauer and Shea, 1990).

A third difference is that although under PL 94–142 it is a requirement to apply a diagnosis to a special child's problems, under PL 99–457 a specific label or diagnosis is not required. The very real difficulty of pinpointing specific problems in the very young was recognized. Hence, there is a release from the requirement to fit the child in a category before the child is allowed to receive services.

These differences create significant ramifications for preschools and children's centers. Early diagnosis is encouraged and enhanced, and public school districts are directed to provide services to preschools and children's centers. One serious ramification is that school districts have found special education to be almost prohibitively expensive and the federal government has never completely funded these programs. States, however, do not want to risk losing what federal funds they do get, so, under the threat of losing all of their federal monies, they have had to make up the difference. Because of this problem, there has been *encroachment* into regular education money in order to fund special education. Directors and teachers of preschool and children's centers need to understand why a public school district might be reluctant to provide services for children who are less disabled or in need than the most severely handicapped. They also need to understand that school districts will only provide services for children who are residents of their own districts. Often children are placed in day care centers closer to a parent's workplace than their residence. Sometimes this happens with preschools, but not as often. In either case, though, if children are placed in facilities located in communities other than the ones where they live, the school district near the center may refuse to provide services and inform the center that they must contact the district where the child's family resides in order to get financial help for that child's educational services.

The preschool mentioned earlier in this chapter began to allow "special needs" students to enroll soon after the implementation of PL 94–142. The preschool itself was located in a school district that provided services to three- to five-year-old residents of the district. The parents of one of the four "special needs" children admitted one year mentioned something to the director that raised eyebrows. These parents informed the director that they had been paying for all of their mild cerebral palsied child's needs themselves. These needs included speech therapy, occupational therapy, and physical therapy. The director was surprised and let the parents know that the public school district should be responsible for helping with the needs of this four-year-old child. The director had already made arrangements for two children from the preschool to receive the services of a speech therapist from the local district, so she informed the district's Director of Special Services that there would now be three children to service from the preschool. However, when the child's address was checked, the preschool director was informed that the child lived one block over into another district. So then the second district was contacted, but the preschool director was told that the second district had no services for preschoolers. In the end, even though a speech therapist from the first school district was already servicing children at the preschool, the needs of this particular child could not be met. As you can see, trying to get the right help for special children could get pretty sticky. It still can and does, but under PL 99–457 what happened to this child with a mild case of cerebral palsy could not happen now as the child's home district would not be able to simply deny those services, but would have to find a way to provide them.

Other Legal Provisions for Special Children

If you work with special education, you also need to be familiar with the Individuals with Disabilities Act (IDEA). IDEA is what was formerly called the Education of the Handicapped Act (EHA); the name and some of the terminology were changed by the 1990 amendments. IDEA is the comprehensive law that incorporates 94–142, 99–457, the 1986 amendments, and the 1990 amendments, and sees to the educational provisions for people with disabilities. This act supports the efforts to provide educational services for children with disabilities from birth through age five and on through youth ages. As mentioned earlier, the provisions for special children have been extended even further over the years since the enactment of PL 94–142 and IDEA embodies these expanded provisions. IDEA is composed of eight parts, Part A through Part H.

Part B of IDEA (see Table 7–5) deals with the allocation of federal funds for helping with the costs of educating children with disabilities. Part B authorizes federal money to be given to the states based on a formula multiplying the number of children with disabilities by a percentage of the national average amount spent per pupil (ERIC Clearinghouse on Handicapped and Gifted Children, Legal Foundations, Winter 1992).

Under IDEA, there are two major programs serving the youngest populations, one for birth through age two (Part H), and the other for ages three through five (the Preschool Grants Program—Section 619 of Part B). There are other programs that provide assistance to these youngest ones with disabilities, including the Early Education Program for Children with Disabilities (EEPCD) (Section 623 of Part C).

The main provision for infants and toddlers with disabilities falls under Part H. The long name for this program is the Early Intervention Program for Infants and Toddlers with Disabilities (from birth through age 2). Since that is rather a mouthful, the program is generally referred to simply as Part H.

Section 504 of the Rehabilitation Act of 1973 is another important piece of legislation concerning people with disabilities. It prohib-

TABLE 7–5 Number of Children Served Under IDEA, Part B and Chapter 1 of ESEA (SOP) by Disability and Age Source: Division of Innovation and Development "To Assure the Free Appropriate Public Education of all Children With Disabilities," *Seventeenth Annual Report to Congress on the Implementation of the Individuals with Disabilities Education Act,* Washington, DC: U.S. Department of Education, (1995).

Disability	Under 1 Year Old	1 Year Old	2 Years Old	3 Years Old	4 Years Old	5 Years Old	6 Years Old	7 Years Old	8 Years Old
Specific Learning Disabilities	.	.	.	.	.	.	35,800	91,307	162,970
Speech or Language Impairments	.	.	.	.	.	.	198,304	203,777	183,378
Mental Retardation	.	.	.	.	.	.	22,256	31,099	38,111
Serious Emotional Disturbance	.	.	.	.	.	.	8,376	14,729	21,713
Multiple Disabilities	.	.	.	.	.	.	9,004	9,224	9,602
Hearing Impairments	.	.	.	.	.	.	4,452	4,847	5,273
Orthopedic Impairments	.	.	.	.	.	.	5,413	5,605	5,578
Other Health Impairments	.	.	.	.	.	.	5,353	6,940	8,031
Visual Impairments	.	.	.	.	.	.	1,556	1,800	1,927
Autism	.	.	.	.	.	.	2,084	2,024	2,040
Deaf-Blindness	.	.	.	.	.	.	100	99	105
Traumatic Brain Injury	.	.	.	.	.	.	253	296	338
All Disabilities	16,716	33,305	43,566	98,092	167,736	227,597	292,951	371,747	439,066

Disability	9 Years Old	10 Years Old	11 Years Old	12 Years Old	13 Years Old	14 Years Old	15 Years Old	16 Years Old	17 Years Old
Specific Learning Disabilities	219,045	250,419	261,412	258,475	253,283	237,473	212,950	189,323	149,898
Speech or Language Impairments	142,119	101,595	66,066	39,870	26,389	17,257	11,492	8,644	6,077
Mental Retardation	40,640	43,094	45,703	46,069	47,862	47,831	45,762	43,542	37,844
Serious Emotional Disturbance	27,234	32,157	36,710	40,411	44,956	46,995	46,412	41,727	30,182
Multiple Disabilities	9,309	9,056	8,887	8,177	7,757	7,270	6,828	6,474	5,580
Hearing Impairments	5,343	5,436	5,581	5,392	5,337	4,897	4,802	4,432	4,001
Orthopedic Impairments	5,197	4,932	4,657	4,174	3,901	3,734	3,477	3,237	2,824
Other Health Impairments	7,881	7,724	7,464	6,592	6,596	6,424	5,939	5,803	4,759
Visual Impairments	2,169	2,173	2,116	2,017	2,051	1,981	1,904	1,804	1,665
Autism	1,824	1,643	1,455	1,160	1,085	1,032	935	807	756
Deaf-Blindness	92	90	82	114	119	98	89	92	71
Traumatic Brain Injury	362	399	407	384	436	393	439	436	440
All Disabilities	461,215	458,718	440,540	412,835	399,772	375,385	341,029	306,357	244,097

its discrimination toward those with disabilities and also ensures that the educational provisions for those with disabilities be equal to the provisions for those without disabilities. Section 504 includes a different definition of handicapped than the definition found in IDEA. Under Section 504, a handicapped person is defined as: "any person who (i) has a physical or mental impairment which substantially limits one or more major life activities, (ii) has a record of such an impairment, or (iii) is regarded as having such an impairment.

This difference in definitions is crucial because some children who are not qualified for special education services under IDEA may be qualified for services under Section 504, and vice versa (ERIC, Legal Foundations, No. 1, Fall 1992).

You will also probably hear Chapter 1 mentioned. Chapter 1 of Public Law 95–581, the Education Consolidation Act of 1981, provides federal funds for compensatory education of children who come from low income families. Sometimes elementary schools will assign children whose families are "income eligible" to work with the Chapter 1 teacher to receive extra help.

SPECIAL CHILDREN: SOME SIGNS

One of the most wonderful things about children is how unique they are. Just as *normal* children are different from each other, so are *special* children. Not all special children are easily recognizable. There are some signs, though, that will help you identify children needing some special help or attention. We'll look at some characteristics that help clue adults to the need for further investigation. Store these in your memory bank for as long as you work with children and be alert to children who exhibit any of the following:

- Does a child hold his head to one side constantly? Does he squint? (The child may have a vision problem requiring glasses or something else.)

- Does a child ignore directions unless you are close to her and facing her? Is her speech unclear? Does a child have frequent bouts of otitis media (middle ear infections)? (The child may have a hearing problem.)

- Is there a child who does not seem to be learning to talk at the same rate as his peers? (He may have a language delay and it should be watched.)

- Is there a child who still uses baby talk after her peers have outgrown it? (She may actually have a speech problem.)

- Is a child frequently out of breath? Does he sneeze often? (He may have an allergy that should be diagnosed and helped by the doctor.)

Note: Most health problems are caught by the family and then diagnosed by the family doctor, but you do need to mention symptoms to parents in case they are not aware of them. Most often your role with any health problems will be to help monitor the child's medication and make sure that the school's medication policy and procedure are followed. Sometimes medication dosages must be adjusted to appropriate levels and you may be able to help by letting the parents and/or the doctor know if you observe any changes in the child's behavior, such as increased drowsiness or irritability.

- Is there a child who seems extremely aggressive or withdrawn? (She may be emotionally disturbed.)

- Does a child seem extremely active? With a short attention span? Is he easily distracted? Does he have trouble figuring out cause and effect relationships? Does he seem to have trouble putting his thoughts into words? (He may have a learning disability. More identifying factors for learning disabilities will be discussed later.)

- Is there a child who is much slower than her peers in talking and completing cognitive work like classifying objects? (She may be mildly mentally retarded.)

Note: These characteristics and other general identifying factors are only indications that there needs to be further, careful observation and investigation. They are not solid evidence that a problem exists and much sensitivity and discernment must be exercised when checking into the possibility of a problem. Always remember that only a qualified person can make an actual determination. As a paraeducator, though, you are someone who cares about the children and may be among the first to notice signs of problems for which children are entitled to get help. If and when you do notice bothersome characteristics, your responsibility is to tell the lead teacher first.

- Do you have a child in your facility who talks in sentences at just two and a half years old? Then do you notice that this same child began to speak in whole paragraphs pretty quickly? Is this child larger, taller, and heavier than other children of the same age? Does the child seem very healthy? Does he already know the names of the primary and secondary colors? Does he already know the letters in his name? Does he connect things when the relationships between the objects are not obvious? (He may be special in the sense that he may be a gifted or talented child.)

Identification Through Observation and Testing

When a child seems to have trouble in school, often parents and school personnel band together to try to find out why. Sometimes finding the answers requires time and much observation and testing. Although there is legitimate balking at "labeling" children, there are valid reasons for attaching labels to special children. In order to be eligible for federal and state funds, children must meet qualifications for these funds. Help from special programs and additional staff people cost money. The large amounts of money have to be justified. Funding is allotted for specified and defined categories. Look back at the categories listed in Table 7–5: learning disabilities, speech-impairment, mental retardation, behavior disorders, multihandicaps, hearing impairment, orthopedic impairment, visual impairment, deaf-blind, and other health impairments. It is obviously easier to discern some categories of disability than others. Let's look at a few types of special needs children and how they are identified.

CATEGORIES OF SPECIAL NEEDS

Mental Retardation

This category has several divisions, depending on the extent of the retardation, from mild to severe to profound. Retardation is easily measured by standard intelligence tests. In fact, one of the major advantages of the intelligence quotient (IQ) test is that it is so useful in diagnosing mental retardation. More will be said about tests and testing later. For now, though, look at the way the subcategories break down:

- Mildly Mentally Handicapped (MIMH)—functions below the average range of ability for age group.

- Moderately Mentally Handicapped (MOMH)—usually has intellectual ability of approximately one third to one half that of the average child of comparable age group.

- Severely Mentally Handicapped (SMH)—shows evidence of subaverage intellectual functioning that is far below average, falling in a range between 25 to 40, based on multiple measures of intelligence.

- Profoundly Mentally Handicapped (PMH)—shows evidence of intellectual functioning even further below average, below 25 based on multiple measures.

Slow Learners

You may have a great deal of interaction with children who fit into this category. You need to be so careful, though, not to say anything derogatory or stick children with labels that remain glued to them for life. Your job as a paraeducator will be to stay alert to a slow learner's needs, encourage him or her as much as possible, and *never* apply a label to one of these children yourself. You should concentrate on picturing the most hopeful future possible rather than ever leading a vulnerable child to believe a bleak forecast for his or her future even for a moment. Look for the following signs that a child may need some extra help:

- Low reading ability. (This characteristic shows a strong correlation with intelligence.)
- Lack of aggression or competition.
- Hands-on learning most effective.
- Inability to figure things out abstractly or theoretically.
- Difficulty with time, size, and spacial relationships.
- Lacks motivation and initiative, difficulty in overcoming obstacles.
- Gravitation toward younger playmates.
- Gullibility, naive acceptance of information and people.
- Relatively short attention span.
- Difficulty with concentration and organization.
- Impulsive behavior and focus.
- Lack of communication.
- Gravitation toward routines and manual type work.
- Emotional instability.
- High absenteeism.

Learning Disabilities

According to the U.S. Department of Education and PL 94–142, learning disability is defined this way:

> . . . . *"Specific learning disability". . . . means a disorder in one or more of the basic psychological processes involved in under-*

standing or in using language, spoken or written, which may manifest itself in an imperfect ability to listen, think, speak, read, write, spell, or do mathematical calculations. The term includes such conditions as perceptual handicaps, brain injury, minimal brain dysfunction, dyslexia, and developmental aphasia. The term does not include children who have learning problems which are primarily the result of visual, hearing, or motor handicaps, of mental retardation, of emotional disturbances, or of environmental, cultural, or economic disadvantage. (Federal Register 1977, 300.5)

This definition is pretty general and underscores the difficulties in deciding true learning disabilities. Learning disabilities are more difficult to distinguish than the other special needs areas, and this sometimes makes it even harder for the children who suffer from them. Often until someone puts a name to their problems, these children are accused of being lazy, stubborn, or unwilling to try. Then there needs to be caution against the opposite problem, that is, using the label of learning disability as an excuse.

School districts commonly define a learning disability in terms of a child's actual achievement in relation to what the achievement is of his or her same age peers. Sometimes this practice is unfortunate because it postpones the identification of a student until he or she is two or more years behind his or her peers. This can be heartbreaking because by the time identification is made, the child may have experienced three or even four years of failure, and the loss of self-esteem that goes with those years of failure. The damage done to the child's self-esteem can be almost irreparable.

Another commonly used definition is that a learning disability is reflected when there is a significant discrepancy between the child's potential ability and the actual achievement in learning to read, write, or compute math. Reading, language arts, and mathematics are areas in the curriculum most typically involved in this contradiction between predicted and actual achievement. The potential ability prediction is based on the child's scores on IQ and achievement tests, so, for example, a child who demonstrates an IQ of 110 but is having great difficulty learning how to read may need to be evaluated.

The broadness of the definition of learning disability also makes it difficult to calculate how many children actually have learning disabilities. Oppenheim says that the 15 percent number indicated by studies is considered to be a conservative estimate and that "part of the problem in counting heads is built into the definition of learning disabilities" (The Elementary School Handbook, 1989).

Another difficulty with the definitions of learning disability is that they seem to preclude preschoolers because of the reliance on school performance for determining the problem. Many preschool teachers, parents, educational psychologists, and capable diagnosticians disagree with preschoolers being left out of this category. There is the belief that learning disabilities can be manifested early and if early signs are ignored, then children are set up to fail when they enter school.

The Association for Children and Adults with Learning Disabilities (ACLD, 1985) has attempted to develop a definition that is not dependent upon school achievement:

> *Specific learning disabilities is a chronic condition of presumed neurological origin which selectively interferes with the development, integration, and/or demonstration of verbal and/or nonverbal abilities. Specific learning disabilities exists as a distinct handicapping condition in the presence of average to superior intelligence, adequate sensory and motor systems, and adequate learning opportunities. The condition varies in its manifestations and in degree of severity. Throughout life the condition can affect self-esteem, education, socialization, and/or daily living activities. (1985, p.2)*

Following are some characteristics that may even be seen in preschoolers that signal the possibility of a learning disability:

- Immaturity
- Difficulties with language, both in understanding and in expression
- Impulsive actions
- High energy level
- Poor coordination for age
- Difficulty following simple requests
- Dislike for change in routine
- Preference for interaction with younger children
- Difficulty transferring information
- Need for repeated reminders of the rules

Let's look at a child with some of these characteristics. Andre has trouble getting his words out. He frequently uses unreferenced pronouns because he cannot seem to remember the names for objects. Whenever the class plays with the "feelie" box, Andre can only think of one word to describe what he feels or he copies what a friend has just said instead of coming up with anything on his own. Andre seems clumsy and uncoordinated a lot of the time. He has a lot of trouble following directions, even when they are simple. Andre gets out of kilter when the regular routine is changed; change seems to really upset him. When the class goes out on the playground, there is about a fifteen minute overlap with a younger class. Andre has several buddies in that class. He enjoys playing with them and kind of mopes around a little while after they go in. One time when the class was playing a game where they would draw a number or a shape on each others' backs and then guess what it was, Andre could not seem to get the hang of it. He never guessed a triangle right even when the teacher herself did it with exaggerated size and clarity. All day long every day Andre was reminded of the rules in the class and out on the playground. He just seems to block them out of his memory.

Well, Andre might be a pretty extreme case. None of these characteristics acted out by Andre are enough by themselves to mean a possible learning disability, but taken all together and seen daily, these characteristics might hint strongly of the possibility of a learning disability. This kind of cluster of flag characteristics ought to suggest a more formal evaluation by a qualified expert in learning disabilities.

Both before and after a learning disability is determined, your role as a paraeducator may be to help the teacher with observations of the child, encourage the child, and help with more individualized teaching for the child.

There are investigators and researchers, notably Kirk (1972), Cruikshank (1977), and Kephart (1967) who, even in the early days of special education advocacy, believed that learning disabilities are a true category and did work to help clarify the definitions. Kirk even defined learning disabilities as a disturbance in the perceptual processes of the child; the child's vision is fine but what the child sees is distorted in relation to what others see. Likewise, another child might hear perfectly well but does not process or tune in to auditory stimuli. Still another child might not have good coordination; the child's kinesthetic sense seems off balance.

There is some evidence to suggest that the learning disabled child may have perceptual deficits. Some other possible culprits for learning disabilities include:

- Diet (Feingold, 1975)
- Disorders of input and/or output
- Disorders of verbal and nonverbal learning (Meyen, 1978)
- Brain functioning (Strauss, et.al., 1947)

Attention Deficit Disorder (ADHD)

One category in special education often seen in child care facilities and in schools today is Attention Deficit-Hyperactivity Disorder or ADHD. You will also see this category labeled ADD for Attention Deficit Disorder. Children with ADHD typically have difficulty concentrating for prolonged periods of time, some even for five or ten minutes. Identifying factors for ADHD include the following:

- Benefit from being kept busy
- Difficulty staying still
- Respond better to less stimulation than more, easily distracted
- Difficulty with too many choices
- Difficulty paying attention and listening
- Trouble staying on task
- Forgets often and loses things
- Disorganization

The American Psychiatric Association identifies two types of Attention Deficit-Hyperactivity Disorder. The first one is *Predominantly Inattentive Type* and the second one is *Predominantly Hyperactive-Impulsive Type.* The American Psychiatric Association differentiates between the characteristics of these two types in a clear cut manner (*Diagnostic and Statistical Manual of Mental Disorders,* 1994). The distinguishing characteristics are what you would expect from categories labelled *inattentive* and *hyperactive.*

Many children diagnosed with ADHD are treated with medications, such as Ritalin, Dexadrine, and Cylert. These stimulant drugs seem to help, although there has been a great deal of controversy concerning suspected overuse. Surprisingly, even the children who are hyperactive often respond well to these stimulants; the medications apparently have a paradoxical effect and calm the children down rather than rev them up.

Although the incidence of side effects from Ritalin and the other drugs varies and many children are able to take these medications without any side effects, the possibility of side effects exists with any medication. As a paraeducator in a day care center or in a school today, you need to be aware of the possibility of side effects for the drugs used for ADHD because chances are very good that you will have contact with children who are on one of these medications. Some of the most common side effects of Ritalin are loss of appetite, abdominal pain, weight loss, insomnia, and abnormally fast heartbeat (Physician's Desk Reference, 1994). Be supportive by communicating anything you see to the parents.

You are likely to see some ups and downs in children on Ritalin as it kicks in or wears off. Doses vary in how long they last (usually from 3 to 6 hours). You and others at school, the parents, and the doctor may all be involved in deciding the best dosing intervals (Thompson, Phi Delta Kappan, 1996).

The Food and Drug Administration (FDA) classifies Ritalin and Dexedrine as Class II drugs; this means there are special controls on how they are prescribed. Parents cannot just call the nurse and ask for these drugs to be phoned in to the pharmacy. Your facility will no doubt have some strict policies in regard to these medications; you need to do your part to see that caution is exercised.

Other methods, including using specially designed computer games, are used with children who are allergic to drug therapy or whose parents oppose the use of medication. New methods of organization and behavior changes are being tried successfully.

Dr. Sylvia Rimm feels that most children who demonstrate ADHD symptoms do not really need medication and that many can be helped with behavior programs. She recommends blind controlled tests (where the parents, teacher, and child do not know whether the child is taking real medication or placebos) to check the validity of drug therapy (1995).

Behavior Disorder

The area involving behavioral difficulties is a controversial one. At one point behavior disorders and emotional disturbances were confused and tended to be grouped together more. Now the term *behavior disorders* is more commonly used to indicate children who have problems with their behavior but who are not, in terms of psychiatric definition, *emotionally disturbed.*

The child with a behavior disorder may or may not present a problem in the classroom. There are several ways a behavior problem may be manifested, some are quieter and less attention-grabbing than others. A child with a behavior disorder may:

- "Act out", have outbursts
- Lack friends
- Daydream
- Fight and act aggressive
- Be withdrawn, depressed
- Need to be alone or away from the other children at times
- Need close supervision

Some techniques for dealing effectively with behavior disordered children will be discussed later.

Children Born to Mothers Who Were Substance Abusers

Unfortunately this is a serious enough problem to warrant a category of its own. A study by the National Association for Perinatal Addiction Research and Education found that an estimated 375,000 babies per year are born with problems caused by their mothers' prenatal drug use (ERIC Digest #E 505). Children born to mothers who were or are abusers are often born addicted to the drugs the mothers were abusing during pregnancy and are left with residual problems. The problems the mothers' drugs cause for the children are varied, dependent on the particular drugs used and the stage taken during pregnancy. Children whose mothers' drugs affected them may appear to be hyperactive, learning disabled, or to have an attention deficit. Some other common characteristics include:

- Premature births
- More susceptible to SIDS, dependent on monitors during infancy
- Overreactive to stimuli
- Difficult to console as babies
- Hard for them to adjust to change
- Unpredictable behavior
- Trouble establishing friendships

The problems associated with prenatal substance abuse have ramifications for our schools because the affected children have different and special educational needs.

COMMONLY USED TESTS

Intelligence Quotient Tests

As mentioned before, schools have to be accountable for the federal and state money they receive for special education. It is vital, then, that children be evaluated carefully and that standard methods of testing be used to make determinations. Intelligence testing is used frequently even though it has come under fire over the past fifteen to twenty years. Intelligence tests attempt to measure what a child knows, how the child processes information, the child's ability to solve problems, and the time it takes for the child to go through thinking exercises. Intelligence tests are used as a tool in understanding a child's intellectual development. They provide valuable information for predicting possible success in school when used with other measures of a child's development. Diagnosing mental retardation is considered to be one of the major advantages of intelligence tests.

Intelligence testing is often called IQ testing, for intelligence quotient. IQ test scores are compared to scores of children of the same age. Intelligence quotient is a figure that compares a child's mental age with his or her chronological age. IQ is used as the mean or average number so a child with an IQ score of 100 is considered to have average intelligence.

The Wechsler Intelligence Scale for Children (WISC), the Wechsler Preschool/Primary Intelligence Scale, the Otis-Lennon Test of Mental Abilities, and the Stanford-Binet Intelligence Scales are used with children. There is ongoing controversy over the use of intelligence tests but they are still being used because, even with their problems, they have proved to be good indicators of school performance. One major drawback to the Stanford-Binet is its verbal emphasis. The Wechsler scales attempt to provide both verbal and performance measures of intelligence. However, some believe that both of these tests may discriminate against a child from a racial and/or cultural minority. Even though both have been scrutinized and translated into other languages, there still remains a question of appropriateness.

Developmental Measures

Developmental checklists and instruments such as the Brigance Diagnostic Inventory of Early Development are used frequently with very young children. Developmental evaluations are preferred over IQ tests for little ones. IQ tests are not considered to be valid tools for predicting intellectual performance in preschoolers; it is recommended that IQ tests be used cautiously with little children" (Allen and Marotz, 1994).

Some other developmental screening tests you may see given to young children are:

- Social Skills Rating System (SSRS)—assesses social and problem-solving capabilities in children from 3 to 18.

- Denver Developmental Screening Test (DDST)—may be administered to newborns to six-year-olds, checks motor, language, cognitive, and personal-social development.

- Developmental Indicators of Learning (DIAL)—frequently used to screen for developmental delays before kindergarten entrance.

- Peabody Picture Vocabulary Test (PPVT)—used to evaluate the vocabularies of 2 1/2 to 18-year-olds, the words they comprehend and the words they use when talking.

- Gesell Institute's Developmental Examination—used widely to evaluate preschoolers before entrance into kindergarten.

Achievement Tests

Achievement tests are also used to evaluate children's progress. There are two major types of achievement tests: criterion-referenced tests and norm-referenced tests. Criterion-referenced tests check a student's comprehension and mastery of subject content against preset measures. Criterion-referenced tests give teachers an indication of subject areas that need to be strengthened. Norm-reference tests are divided into sections in order to test many different subject areas; these tests usually take several days to administer. The students' scores on norm-referenced tests are compared with scores from other students of the same grade level. The scores for achievement tests are complicated and include the following subscores:

percentile score
raw score
stanine
grade equivalents

Scores for achievement tests are often accompanied by an explanation sheet for parents so that they will be able to interpret their children's scores.

Some frequently used achievement tests include:

- Iowa Tests of Basic Skills
- California Achievement Tests
- Metropolitan Achievement Tests
- SRA (Science Research Associates) Achievements

Behavior Rating Scales

Behavior rating scales are used to evaluate children for ADHD; a disadvantage of these is that they are based on subjective rather than objective judgments. Children suspected of ADHD are also given tests known as CPTs (continuous performance tasks) in which they are instructed to perform some repetitive action, and their level of alertness is evaluated. The Gordon Diagnostic System (GDS) is a frequently used CPT tool (Armstrong, 1996).

Support and Encouragement During Tests

As a paraeducator, you can help children with test anxiety. If the adults around them act relaxed about testing, then it is a lot easier for the children to be relaxed. Remind students to get plenty of rest and to eat well before testing. Also remind them that the only thing they are expected to do is their best. There are many reasons that children do not score as highly as expected on tests, including:

- Not feeling well
- Being too tired or hungry to tune in
- Being uncooperative or irritable
- Losing their place between the test and the answer sheet
- Confusion over the directions

These are some of the same reasons that adults botch tests. Help children to understand that anyone can have a bad day, but encourage them to always do the best they can on any given day and at any given time.

ONGOING PROCESSES OF SPECIAL EDUCATION

Each special education student has to have a written educational plan, the IEP. As stated before, the IEP must be reevaluated every year. (A sample IEP is shown in Table 7–6). There are ongoing staffing meetings, where the involved parties get together to evaluate what has been decided about a child, what is being done for the child, how the child is progressing, and what needs to be done for the child in the future. The role of the paraeducator during staffing meetings is changing in some areas of the country. Whereas once paraeducators were more apt to be supervising "babysitters" during meetings and while teachers did the

TABLE 7–6 Example of an Individualized Program Source: K.E. Allen & I.S. Schwartz. (1996). *The Exceptional Child: Inclusion in Early Childhood Education.* Albany, NY: Delmar Publishers.

Child's Name: Tyrone S.   Age: 4 yrs, 2 mo
Center City Public School District
September 17, 1994

Present Level of Functioning
   Social development: Tyrone does not play with other children. He never approaches another child and runs away every time a child approaches him.

Annual Goals
   Tyrone will learn to play cooperatively with other children.

Short-Term Objectives
   Tyrone will play next to other children during highly preferred activities (for example, sandbox, sensory table, finger painting) for two 10 minute periods each day.

Special Services
   School district will provide transportation to and from community preschool placement and school district will pay Tyrone's tuition for a half day program at the Learning Center Community Preschool.
   Speech therapist will visit the preschool once a week to work with Tyrone and meet with the teacher.
   Behavior management program coordinated by classroom teacher and **itinerent special education teacher.**

Beginning and Duration of Services
   Tyrone will begin attending the Learning Center on October 5. Other services will be in place by October 12. Placement and services will be re-evaluated by April 5, 1995.

Evaluation
   Tyrone will be reassessed on the Preschool Profile in March. A graph will be kept showing the amount of time Tyrone spent playing next to children each day.

volumes of paperwork required in special education, now paraeducators are more likely to be asked for their input, and may even be invited to attend staffing meetings. For example, in Kent, Washington, *instructional assistants* now sit in on school inclusion committees (NEA Today, September, 1995).

There are also ongoing tasks of coordinating services for a special education child. Schedules have to be worked out between the resource or support personnel and between time in and out of the regular classroom. For example, let's look at the schedule for one visually impaired third grade boy. Every day he spends about half of his day in the regular classroom and the other half in the resource room for all the visually impaired children in the school. He does science, social studies, and health with his class, and he gets extra help with spelling, Braille, and computer skills in the vision room. During the week, he has three sessions with a visiting mobility specialist who helps him gain independence in navigating around the school and other places. He also spends a session with a visiting physical therapist every week. He has *adaptive physical education* three times per week. Then there is the paraeducator who is primarily assigned to this child; she has some other duties around the school, so when she can not be with Jeremy, then another paraeducator or the vision specialist must be ready to see to Jeremy's safety and special needs. There are then at least six people whose schedules must be coordinated. Multiply this for the other visually impaired children in the vision program at this school. Then throw in a change in the agency that sends the mobility specialist to the school. You can see that working out services is an ongoing challenge!

WORKING WITH SPECIAL CHILDREN

You must always remember that the "special child" is a child, and simply being a child makes that child special. Generally, working with *special* children is not much different than working with *normal* children. "Special" children just have some additional or some out-of-the-ordinary needs. They are no different from any other children, though, in that if you meet them with kindness and care, they will reciprocate.

The Council for Exceptional Children recommends thinking of a child with a disability as *a child first* and to consider the handicap as just one of the many other characteristics that make up that child (see Fig-

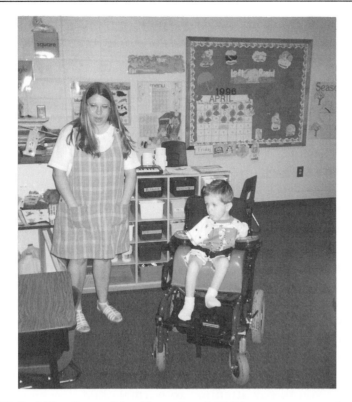

FIGURE 7–4 The Council for Exceptional Children recommends thinking of a child with a disability as "a child first."

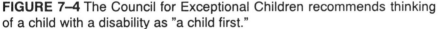

ure 7-4). They suggest that this thinking is less intimidating and will cut down your nervousness about a new student with disabilities (ERIC, 1990, Digest E366).

Also remember that a child with disabilities will have to live in our world and you will not do the child any favors by doing for him things he can and should learn to do for himself. In her book, *Why Bright Kids Get Poor Grades: and What You Can Do About It,* Rimm cited the quote from Eleanor Roosevelt: "The surest way to make it hard for children is to make it easy." Remember that if you and other adults give children the message that they "can't" or they "won't," they may incorporate that message into how they themselves feel about themselves and only live up to the expectations they perceive from others (ERIC E366, Rimm). When it comes to the messages that you personally send to any children with disabilities in your care, let the messages be ones of a future, a hope, and encouragement.

Your lead teacher will, in most instances, give you tips for teaching your students. If you and your lead teacher concentrate on what is best for the children in specific circumstances, you will do well. You can help each other with clues you pick up from the children themselves. Many times if you pay attention to the children, they will let you know the best ways to help them.

Combined with observations and information gleaned from developmental checklists or other evaluation tools, you and the lead teacher can develop a learning plan based on what you see. For example, if you note that three-year-old child Dara is able to walk upstairs alternating both feet without any trouble, but walks downstairs one foot at a time, you might want to have Dara hold your hand at first. Then you can have her hold onto the railing. Eventually, you can encourage Dara to try to walk down the stairs without any support. If you observe that a little one is still speaking only two-word sentences, you can try to provide more language experiences for that child on a one-to-one basis. In any and every case, we should not urge a child to accomplish tasks that are not appropriate to his or her developmental level. The child who cannot gallop will not be ready to learn to skip, but maybe the child *is* ready to learn to slide one foot after the other sideways. It is important for you to pay attention to normal child development and then look at each child individually in order to make evaluations and set fair expectations.

A child with speech or language impairment may need individualized tutoring. As mentioned before, lack of language skills or unclear speech are early indications of hearing problems. If you suspect that a child has a hearing problem, you should mention your observations to the lead teacher or director, who may then suggest a hearing test for the child. Sometimes when a child demonstrates a delay in language development, it may be because adults have not spent much time talking to the child. Unfortunately, some children speak more of what they hear on television than what they learn from adults around them. Children should be given constant opportunities to use verbal language. You, the paraeducator, can help children with language development simply by having conversations with them. You may need to name objects for them and help them learn descriptive adjectives. Try to initiate language activities like feel-inside-the-box games and guessing games in which children describe things and use words.

Another important tip for working with communication-impaired children is to allow them to speak, to get the words out. Be patient and wait, rather than jumping in when you think you know what the child wants to say and finishing statements for her (ERIC #E366).

Mentally retarded children may not need any special attention besides having you tune in to activities that may provoke frustration. Your lead teacher may ask you to assist a mentally retarded child during more difficult activities. For example, during a fingerplay song, you may help by holding a child in your lap and by manipulating the child's fingers yourself. The mentally retarded child might also need some extra help with language since slow language development is often a characteristic of mental retardation.

A few other recommendations for working with mentally retarded children are to:

- Give clear and short instructions.
- Help the children to look at the small steps involved in a project rather than overwhelming them with the whole thing at once.
- Stick to a routine.
- Give the children plenty of time to practice new skills and learn new information (ERIC Digest #E366).

If you have a behavior-disordered child in your room, you may be assigned to work with this child closely. If the child exhibits aggressive behavior, this will be a challenge. It is not uncommon for the lead teacher to request that a paraeducator work on a one-to-one basis with an aggressive behavior-disordered child in order to try to control the child's outbursts. It may help to try these tips:

- Hold the child in your lap.
- Allow the child to hit a weighted clown doll or a plastic "bop bag" instead of another child or an adult.
- Use "time out" techniques. Remove the child to the back of the classroom or restrict her to sitting on the bench out on the playground. Tell the child that she must sit in the time out spot until she feels ready to join the group again.
- Let the child throw foam balls.
- Allow the child to squish and punch clay.
- Have the child bite on a leather strap or chew on sugarless bubblegum when he or she feels like biting.
- Let the child run around the playground when he or she feels like exploding.

Remember that behavior modification works well with children who are behavior disordered.

You should be aware that as a withdrawn, depressed child gets better, he or she is likely to become aggressive in what is known as the pendulum effect. Again, it helps to be alert to signs that the child may need to be alone, or be allowed to stomp, yell, or hit without hurting anyone. Time out and the other techniques just listed may be helpful. Whatever you and the teacher decide to do, you may be asked to stay with the child for safety reasons. If this is the case, you can acknowledge the child's anger and other feelings; you may also be able to suggest constructive ways for the child to deal with himself.

One way to work with ADD/ADHD children in your room is to keep them busy. It also may help to let them move from one center to another and not require them to remain in one place all the time. Remember, though, that too many choices may be difficult for ADD children. Often they do better with less stimulation than more. A quiet, somewhat sheltered corner or area of the room may be very beneficial for times when children need peace and decreased stimulation. You may want to limit choices and suggest gently that the child may choose one of two options. You might say, "Look, no one is painting at that easel and your friend Matthew is the only one playing with the blocks. Why don't you paint a picture or go build with Matthew?"

Anna Thompson, an educator and mother of a child with ADHD, has some special insights about what helps. She states:

> From my standpoint as a parent, the most important gift that educators can give my ADHD child is understanding. The most important gift that they can give me is regular, open communication. (Phi Delta Kappan, Feb. 1996)

Since there are several theories about what causes learning disabilities, it is difficult to agree on how to best help the problem. There are, however, several techniques that have been effective with learning disabled children, including:

- Structure. A well-planned classroom. Classroom rules should be posted for older children and repeated often to younger ones so they will be reminded of and understand the limits. You can help with the classroom organization.

- Consistency of discipline. It will be important for you and the teacher to avoid giving mixed signals about what is acceptable and what is not. A united front and consistency is vital.

- Behavior modification. Ask the teacher to always go over any behavior modification plans with you so that you will fully understand how you can help children to succeed and feel good about themselves.

- CARE, that is, being:
  - Congruent
  - Acceptant
  - Reliable
  - Empathetic

  This works with all children, especially ones with learning disabilities.

- Provide a good mix of active and quiet activities. Alternate high energy and participation activities with lower energy activities. Provide opportunities for enough physical exercise to tire active children and allow children freedom to move around at intervals. Don't expect children to sit still for too long or if you are not right there with them.

- Love. Dr. Lendon Smith, a family medicine specialist, made the following statement in 1981 to an audience of early childhood educators: "We have 5,000 children on stimulants to calm them down. All that 4,995 of them need is a little love." Smith was decrying the tendency of parents and teachers to ask medical doctors to place seemingly overactive children on stimulants or drug therapy. Dr. Smith advocates that we use diet, physical exercise, relaxation exercises, and proven educational techniques instead.

If you work with children who have been affected by their mothers' drug use, you may be called upon to give extra TLC. If you work in a day care or preschool center, you may find that little ones from abusing mothers are more difficult to console when they are upset. You may also notice that these children need help adjusting to change. Swaddling infants has been shown to be effective; you should make a special effort to help these babies feel as secure as possible. With older children born to substance abusers, arrange for small groups and also decrease the amount of stimuli in the room.

For more information on how to help children of abusing mothers, contact your local children's hospital or a large city school district. Many cities like Los Angeles, New York, Atlanta, and Chicago have resources with suggestions on how to work more effectively with these children. The Los Angeles Unified School District has a list of classroom strategies that have been successful with substance affected children, including recommendations on adult/child ratios, transition time plans, curricula, and rules (Cole, et al., 1991, ERIC Digest #E 505, 1991). Don't hesitate to contact possible help sources in your area.

Anyone who works with special children needs to be cautioned about tossing labels around. Avoid calling your students your "ADD kids" or your "LD" kids either when talking to them or when talking about them to other people. It is so easy and tempting to do, but please, just stop and think for a second how damaging this can be. Sylvia Rimm says that if you do label ADHD children in your speech you risk altering their feelings or perception about their own responsibility for their behavior (1995). Think about it. If a child constantly hears that she is "off the wall" or "out of control" and that "no one can do a thing with her," then she may feel that she *can't* do anything about her own actions and that she does not even have to try to behave appropriately. After all, she already knows that adults believe she cannot be managed.

Rimm actually cautions against the use of labels in general, saying that if something is said that narrows a child's picture of his or her own prospects, it can be damaging to that child. She goes on to warn that:

> *The resulting peer pressures and lowered parent and teacher ex-*
> *pectations may have permanent debilitating effects on children's*
> *school performance. Although there are some circumstances in*
> *which such designations are absolutely necessary to obtain edu-*
> *cational support, I urge you to consider all the potential nega-*
> *tive consequences before assigning any kind of label to a child.*
> *(Rimm, 1995)*

Instead, Rimm and others recommend using a moderate amount of appropriate and honest praise and speaking positively about children within their hearing. Rimm expresses the view that these patterns of communication are beneficial to children, and are especially encouraging for ADHD children (1995).

The days of paraeducators working with special children will, of course, be as varied and individual as the children with whom they work and the facilities in which they serve. One paraeducator might be assigned to the whole special education department in a school and might be required to run errands and complete task lists during the day. Another paraeducator, such as Linda in Kansas, is assigned to a particular special child. Linda works with a third grade boy with muscular dystrophy. She describes her duties this way:

> *I individualize and adapt third grade curriculum to suit physical and academic needs of a nine-year-old boy with muscular dystrophy. I use a notebook to communicate observations to the parents and other staff members. I provide assistance in toileting and stretching muscles. I move the student daily from the wheelchair to work on conditioning. I also assist other students with skill reinforcement.* (Table 7–7)

Shari, in Georgia, works with children who have learning disabilities. Her day is spent helping children in a self-contained LD class, assisting one child in Adaptive Physical Education and assisting another child during inclusion in a science class. So Shari has dealings with many children during the day.

Schedules and locations vary for special education paraeducators, too. The paraeducator who is assigned to several special education teachers may rove from room to room. Linda, who is assigned to the boy with muscular dystrophy, goes where he goes. A sample schedule for a special education paraeducator is shown in Table 7–8.

As previously stated, many of the guidelines and recommendations from Chapter 4 (about infants and toddlers) may apply to work with special children. If you work with certain categories of special needs children, your day could involve one or more of the following:

- Assistance with feeding
- Assistance with toilet learning
- Diapering
- Less involved educational activities

Refer back to Chapter 4 as needed if you are called on to give extra care and attention to children with special needs.

It is often overwhelming to work with children with special needs and there may be times you will be intimidated by a lack of formal training. Sometimes you may feel that no level of training could completely prepare you for your job as a special education paraeducator. Turn your thinking around at those times. Realize that when you do your best to give compassionate and appropriate assistance, you provide a great service. Shaffer speaks of this training issue, at least in regard to mental disabilities: "The paraprofessional has, in many instances, higher expectations of what the student can do because doubt and theoretical limi-

TABLE 7–7 Paraprofessional Checklist

DEPARTMENT OF ELEMENTARY AND SECONDARY EDUCATION
Section of Special Education School Improvement
Program Review

PARAPROFESSIONAL CHECKLIST

District Name/Code: _____
Teacher(s): _____ Building: _____
Paraprofessional: _____*Linda*_____ (To whom assigned) _____
(Please provide the requested information.) _____

1. What was your date of initial employment as a paraprofessional in this district? ___*9-94*___
2. Indicate minutes per week for which you are assigned to class(es): _____*1950*_____
3. Have you completed a high school program? (Yes) No
4. List areas of teacher certification (if applicable): __*K-8 and Library Science K-8*__
5. How many hours of training will you have received by the end of <u>this</u> school year? _*N/A*_

   Please indicate topics/areas covered by this training:

   N/A   Training in area(s) of disability(ies) served
   N/A   Behavior modification
   N/A   Instruction techniques to be used in the class (i.e., cueing, modeling,
           demonstration, reinforcement, correction, etc.)
   N/A   Other (specify): _____

6. What are the disabling conditions of the students you regularly assist? *(Check those that apply)*

✔ Learning Disabled	___ Behavior Disordered/Emotionally Disturbed
___ Speech Disordered	✔ Physically/Other Health Impaired
___ Visually Impaired	___ Hearing Impaired
___ Multiple Disabilities	___ Early Childhood Special Education
___ Traumatic Brain Injury	___ Mentally Retarded
___ Language Disordered	___ Deaf/Blind
___ Autism	___ Other (specify): _____

7. Describe your duties:

   *I individualize and adapt third grade curriculum to suit physical and academic needs of nine-year-old boy
   with muscular dystrophy. I use a notebook to communicate observations to parents and other staff members.
   I provide assistance in toileting and stretching muscles. I move student daily from wheelchair to work on
   conditioning. I also assist other students with skill reinforcement.*

8. Indicate where you are each period on the school day:

   1. *9-11:50 Third Grade*
   2. *11:50-12:15 Lunch*
   3. *12:15-12:45 Classroom*
   4. *12:45-1:00 — Recess*
   5. *1:00-3:00 Classroom*
   6. *3:00-3:15 Recess*
   7. *3:15-4:00 Classroom*
   8.

9. Comments/Concerns:

Table 7–8 Special Education Paraprofessional Schedule

7:15	Workroom	Run off papers.
7:30	LD Classroom	Take up lunch money, record attendance, etc.
8:00	LD Classroom	Reading—Assist students.
8:45	LD Classroom	English—Assist students.
9:30	Gym	Adaptive P.E. with Amy.
10:00	Workroom or Classroom	Grade papers while the children are in homeroom.
10:30	Science class	Take notes for Drake.
11:15	LD Classroom	Review science with Drake.
11:30	LD Classroom	Spelling—Assist students.
12:00	Lunch	
12:30	LD Classroom	Math—Assist students.
1:15	LD Classroom	Social Studies—Assist students or teacher.
2:00	LD Classroom	Check assignment sheets; homework materials.
2:15	Monitor halls.	

tations have not been learned" (1984). Of course, further training is a wonderful thing, and you'll need to evaluate whether further training would be appropriate for you. However, until additional training is accomplished or if it is not chosen, don't beat up on yourself. Be an advocate for the special children with whom you work. Hope for and work toward the best you can for them.

WORKING WITH PARENTS OF SPECIAL CHILDREN

Research (Chinn, Wynne, & Walters, 1978) has shown that parents of special needs children go through a process similar to the grief reactions described by Kubler-Ross in *On Death and Dying* (1969). Parents have an image of what they expect for their child's life and it's as if they have to let that image go and then grieve for the child-that-cannot-be. It is not uncommon to see denial, blame, and guilt when you interact with parents of special needs children. Parents often experience feelings of disbelief, anger, and helplessness. You may also see parents project feelings of blame onto the preschool, the center, the school, or the school personnel. There is a high rate of divorce among parents of children with special needs; parents seldom go through the steps of the grief process at the same time and in the same way and this often leads to dissension in the home.

When a child has a clear disability that is diagnosed at an early age, parents have to adjust, accept, and cope with associated problems much earlier than parents of a child who has what is called an "invisible handicap"—a learning disability, mild retardation, or a behavior disorder. When you work in a preschool or elementary school you need to be especially sensitive to what stage of the grief through acceptance process that parents may be in.

Much of the initial discussion with the parents will be the responsibility of the teacher. The teacher will need to use all of the communication skills that he or she can muster; he or she still may not be successful in persuading parents that their child needs special attention, evaluation, or help. Some parents are willing to accept that their child has a learning disability or other special education problem; others are not.

In the case of children with behavior problems, you may see a *family* with problems. The term *dysfunctional* is sometimes used to describe families with problems that affect their children. To many parents, even the suggestion of a behavior problem in their child brings out strong defensive reactions, such as, "Are you telling me I'm a bad parent? That I don't know how to raise my own child?"

In talking with parents, teachers and administrators try to avoid terms that are likely to bring on defensive reactions and substitute other less provocative phrases. Look at the following lists to get some ideas.

Better to use:

"acts out"
"does not have friends"
"daydreams"
"tries to hide in the back of the room"
"fights"

Best not to say things like:

"bully"
"temper tantrums"
"anti-social"
"out of it"

Well, you can probably imagine lots of wrong things that people do say. Just remember how some terms would hit you if your child were being discussed and then concentrate on saying things in the kindest, gentlest way you can. You need to understand how difficult it is for parents to accept the possibility that something might be wrong with their children, especially if the parents don't have any idea that their child has a problem with one of the less obvious special education disabilities. It then can be extremely difficult to convince them that there may be a problem.

Think about the work of Kubler-Ross. Facing the possibility that their child may not be perfect, some parents do grieve for the lost image of what their child was to have been. They actually grieve in much the same way they would grieve if the child had died. Parents may become angry and accuse schools and school personnel of prejudice, of gross misjudgment, or of not really knowing their child. Some parents might verbally attack the skills of the ones evaluating their child. Some parents deny that anything is wrong with their child; some continue to deny it. Many parents go through a time of blaming themselves for their child's problems. Support groups, such as Children and Adults with Attention Deficit Disorder (CHADD) may be suggested so that parents can share with other parents; these can be a tremendous help in alleviating tough feelings.

In fact, there may be instances where you and the teacher feel that the parents really are responsible for the child's problems, but you must be very careful not to prejudge or judge. Judgment or a critical attitude will not help the parents cope; judgment and criticism greatly interfere with the kind of cooperative relationship needed between the family and the school in order to best serve the needs of the child.

There may be constant adjustments in the communications between the teacher and you and the parents of a special child. For example, when a formally depressed child gets better, he or she is likely to become aggressive and begin to act out. If this happens the parents may not understand what is going on. They may become angry and fearful and want to stop the educational program because they do not understand that their child needs to release pent-up anger and that it will take time for their child to learn how to deal with anger in socially acceptable ways. The teacher and possibly others will need to reassure these parents that this phase is normal. You both need to let the parents see that you are concerned and that you care about their child.

As the paraeducator, your role will often involve support for the lead teacher; it is draining to have confrontations with parents who are having to face things they may not want to face about their children.

You will also need to support and encourage the child and the parents however you can as well, without undermining the authority of the teacher in any way.

Non-English Proficient Children

Children of immigrant and refugee families are increasingly represented in classrooms and their numbers are expected to continue to grow, and grow dramatically, during the next years. We have children from all parts of the globe in many areas of the United States. As a paraeducator, you may have the important and immediate task of communicating acceptance and respect to children with varying degrees of English proficiency. You and the teacher will most likely do all you can to decrease any feelings of alienation and isolation (Thonis, 1990). Remember that once these children adapt to their new surroundings, many times they can be invaluable as classroom resources. Because of their backgrounds and different cultural understandings, they may broaden the lives and worlds of everybody in the classroom.

Now more and more public school districts are hiring teachers for ESOL, English as a second language. These teachers are often itinerant; they have duties and children they teach at several different schools. ESOL teachers may serve as resource teachers who only see their students for short arranged tutoring sessions. You need to find out from this visiting professional or from your district office some specific ways that you can help any children who have less than standard English proficiency. Some information that might help with planning for these children includes:

- Proficiency of the child in the language of the home.

- The child's understanding of English and ability to speak it.

- Whether the child's language and speech are appropriate for the child's age.

FUTURE TRENDS FOR THE SPECIAL EDUCATION PARAEDUCATOR

Reports to Congress in the last few years indicate that the numbers of paraeducators working with our nation's special children have increased continually. Look at the data in Tables 7–9, 7–10, and 7–11. During the 1989–1990 school year, 154,738 teacher aides worked with special education and the projected need was for almost 6,000 more. During the 1992–1993 school year, the number of aides in special education was up to 178,532, and the states declared that there was a need for 5,000 more. (Information supplied through the National Clearinghouse for Professions in Special Education.)

According to the 17th Annual Report to Congress, paraeducators made up the largest category of personnel employed to serve infants and toddlers with disabilities. The next highest category was filled by special educators, then came "other" personnel, followed by speech/language pathologists. The greatest demand was reported to be for speech/language pathologists. It was stated in the report that the paraeducator category is "defined by individual states."

The numbers for preschoolers with disabilities rose by 8.4 percent between the 1991–92 school year and the 1992–93 school year. The number of three- through five-year-old children with disabilities increased to 493,425 in the 1993–94 school year; that number was up by 8.3 percent over the previous year. The reports from the states indicated that part of these increased numbers may be due to improvements in the individual states' reporting systems (17th Annual Report to Congress). There is no way to predict the future, but it is safe to say that right now the need for paraeducators who are willing to work with special children is strong.

There are also moves toward increased training for paraeducators in special education. Under the Early Education Program for Children with Disabilities, there were eight new projects funded in 1994 for training special education personnel, including paraeducators. There was also an experimental project for evaluation of paraeducator training systems which was supported by federal funds (17th Annual Report to Congress).

In the 17th Annual Report to Congress, there were some interesting observations from the states concerning numbers and the use of paraeducators. Georgia reported that they have an increased number of aides because they are needed to support inclusion. In New Mexico, the need for preschool teachers actually went down because the number of three- through five-year-olds was not as high as anticipated and the personnel shortage they expected did not happen. California said that their higher number of children who received early intervention services was because of increases in available federal funding. Illinois verified that the

TABLE 7–9 School Staff OtherThan Special EducationTeachers Employed and Needed to Serve Children with Disabilities Age 3–21. Source: Division of Innovation and Development "To Assure the Free Appropriate Public Education of all Children With Disabilities," *Sixteenth Annual Report to Congress on the Implementation of the Individuals with Disabilities Education Act,* Washington, DC: U.S. Department of Education, (1994).

| | TEACHER AIDES | | | | | |
| | 1989–1990 | | 1990–1991 | | 1991–1992 | |
State	Employed	Needed	Employed	Needed	Employed	Needed
ALABAMA	1,525	245	1,641	248	1,630	140
ALASKA	527	23	604	36	692	1
ARIZONA	2,182	39	2,321	41	2,368	24
ARKANSAS	748	21	936	12	940	31
CALIFORNIA	21,189	632	22,048	1,047	22,814	702
COLORADO	1,975	58	2,093	43	2,367	40
CONNECTICUT	2,619	17	2,687	32	2,599	21
DELAWARE	377	18	354	32	353	52
DISTRICT OF COLUMBIA	324	43	322	26	327	7
FLORIDA	6,732	724	7,041	812	6,639	516
GEORGIA	3,447	209	3.727	121	3,774	148
HAWAII	489	12	532	21	476	17
IDAHO	813	114	875	60	901	41
ILLINOIS	10,577	11	11,356	0	11,796	5
INDIANA	2,755	620	2,960	229	3,074	255
IOWA	2,139	7	2,312	2	2,340	25
KANSAS	2,594	7	3,236	0	3,310	1
KENTUCKY	1,514	99	1,596	161	1,759	174
LOUISIANA	4,294	123	4.664	56	4,820	72
MAINE	1,313	117	1,434	65	1,715	97
MARYLAND	2,504	78	2,681	25	2,834	35
MASSACHUSETTS	4,819	0	4,974	.	4,970	.
MICHIGAN	1,853	61	1,965	0	2,122	9
MINNESOTA	3,874	15	4,490	63	5,061	479
MISSISSIPPI	681	40	672	27	740	23
MISSOURI	2,859	0	2,848	0	3,478	12
MONTANA	667	246	816	155	893	127
NEBRASKA	1,114	0	1,363	0	1,448	1
NEVADA	361	38	484	30	576	18
NEW HAMPSHIRE	1,346	283	1,530	342	1,687	295
NEW JERSEY	6,196	66	6,030	48	7,017	174
NEW MEXICO	1,527	10	1,640	30	1,594	42
NEW YORK	13,018	.	12,141	0	12,485	0
NORTH CAROLINA	3,531	543	3,521	533	4,004	516
NORTH DAKOTA	495	51	632	13	691	33
OHIO	3,154	97	3,410	258	3,419	80
OKLAHOMA	1,069	61	1,180	23	1,326	34
OREGON	861	80	880	81	1,689	120
PENNSYLVANIA	6,043	239	5,550	358	5,620	115
PUERTO RICO	535	14	535	0	665	0
RHODE ISLAND	635	10	697	9	740	12
SOUTH CAROLINA	1,761	101	1,898	198	2,024	182
SOUTH DAKOTA	329	37	541	102	533	24
TENNESSEE	2,933	62	2,812	91	2,779	68
TEXAS	10,683	.	11,079	250	12,531	120
UTAH	1,711	114	1,580	63	1,300	60
VERMONT	1,146	0	1,295	4	1,328	7
VIRGINIA	3,517	347	3,797	357	4,283	300
WASHINGTON	2,179	36	2,415	35	2,621	51
WEST VIRGINIA	1,062	1	1,135	60	166	104
WISCONSIN	3,010	18	3,358	16	3,696	6
WYOMING	767	113	799	116	805	0
AMERICAN SAMOA	4	0	3	0	3	0
GUAM	.	.	165	40	179	1
NORTHERN MARIANAS	35	3	32	1	37	1
PALAU	.	.	.		.	
VIRGIN ISLANDS	.	.	95	1	92	5
BUR. OF INDIAN AFFAIRS	310	44	261	45	264	29
U.S. & INSULAR AREAS	154,738	5,939	162,043	6,413	170,397	5,448
50 STATES, D.C., & P.R.	154,389	5,893	161,487	6,326	169,822	5,413

TABLE 7–10 Special Education Teachers, Occupational Therapists, Physical Therapists, and Teacher Aides, Employed and Needed to Serve Children with Disabilities, Ages 3–21, 1992–93 School Year. Source: National Clearinghouse for Professions in Special Education, 1920 Association Drive, Reston, VA.

State	Special Education Teachers[a]		Occupational Therapists[b]		Physical Therapists[b]		Teacher Aides[b]	
	Employed	Needed	Employed	Needed	Employed	Needed	Employed	Needed
ALABAMA	5,249	450	40	12	33	13	1,685	68
ALASKA	1,039	14	27	1	25	0	722	0
ARIZONA	3,975	176	49	19	22	6	2,575	68
ARKANSAS	3,009	72	23	13	27	17	974	24
CALIFORNIA	27,620	1,228	45	16	16	9	23,825	541
COLORADO	3,862	17	150	10	41	4	2,402	9
CONNECTICUT	4,544	69	122	3	77	1	2,758	44
DELAWARE	1,020	75	10	3	9	0	346	54
DISTRICT OF COLUMBIA	832	74	28	2	11	1	327	66
FLORIDA	14,845	1,835	184	45	131	35	7,106	279
GEORGIA	8,657	277	85	16	86	13	4,629	200
HAWAII	1,193	82	21	3	30	2	529	22
IDAHO	1,106	326	23	8	15	7	925	40
ILLINOIS	18,319	207	347	35	205	31	12,451	2
INDIANA	6,334	658	96	8	82	4	3,298	37
IOWA	4,519	549	51	1	38	0	2,376	1
KANSAS	3,481	99	72	13	40	15	3,818	8
KENTUCKY	4,846	249	26	28	38	18	1,972	61
LOUISIANA	6,838	2,024	89	41	63	33	4,949	109
MAINE	2,074	210	74	13	44	6	1,677	132
MARYLAND	6,738	112	137	7	96	6	2,999	42
MASSACHUSETTS	8,315	43	173	6	107	4	5,580	*
MICHIGAN	13,470	615	337	2	189	1	2,155	10
MINNESOTA	7,644	962	261	44	110	21	5,638	439
MISSISSIPPI	3,951	344	5	1	14	3	740	17
MISSOURI	7,658	721	94	0	46	0	3,710	6
MONTANA	1,044	185	13	5	11	3	949	161
NEBRASKA	2,316	26	20	1	18	5	1,413	4
NEVADA	1,456	99	10	3	11	1	434	12
NEW HAMPSHIRE	1,760	246	99	6	35	2	1,880	522
NEW JERSEY	15,521	278	160	18	142	17	6,975	69
NEW MEXICO	3,418	437	132	25	69	14	1,654	57
NEW YORK	29,115	8,863	361	*	249	*	12,173	*
NORTH CAROLINA	7,687	1,068	108	91	100	73	4,268	591
NORTH DAKOTA	962	91	15	1	12	2	748	44
OHIO	12,876	481	240	33	215	32	3,090	140
OKLAHOMA	4,070	173	51	13	76	11	1,396	25
OREGON	3,432	241	56	10	16	2	1,689	120
PENNSYLVANIA	13,489	46	162	2	149	5	6,174	17
PUERTO RICO	2,609	272	17	26	11	23	665	0
RHODE ISLAND	1,439	9	28	2	25	1	749	3
SOUTH CAROLINA	4,434	289	40	14	34	14	2,023	87
SOUTH DAKOTA	1,007	10	32	3	24	3	637	1
TENNESSEE	5,071	143	55	7	52	6	2,754	14
TEXAS	16,893	1,189	147	25	83	5	11,312	256
UTAH	2,118	104	22	11	20	8	1,605	65
VERMONT	972	10	11	1	8	1	1,601	6
VIRGINIA	10,356	1,131	178	45	232	31	4,747	462
WASHINGTON	4,848	95	174	29	79	30	2,964	24
WEST VIRGINIA	2,831	78	6	5	23	3	1,224	30
WISCONSIN	7,824	823	224	4	174	18	3,836	6
WYOMING	867	7	36	5	20	2	844	0
AMERICAN SAMOA	64	8	0	0	0	0	3	0
GUAM	139	19	2	5	1	4	188	0
NORTHERN MARIANAS	39	30	3	3	0	3	50	2
PALAU	*	*	*	*	*	*	*	*
VIRGIN ISLANDS	84	11	1	0	2	1	96	5
BUR. OF INDIAN AFFAIRS	229	92	3	12	15	16	226	0
TOTAL	330,198	28,038	4,973	749	3,504	583	178,532	5,000

Note: Data for speech-language pathologists are included in the numbers for special education teachers.
[a] Data for special education teachers were taken from Tables AC1, page A-147, and AC2, page A-148. [b] Data for occupational therapists, physical therapists, and teacher aides were taken from Table AC3, pages A-152 and A-153.
*No data reported.

TABLE 7–11 How much is spent on special education? Source: From *Teaching Exceptional Children by the Council for Exceptional Children,* Vol. 26. Copyright 1994 by The Council for Exceptional Children.

While no data are collected on the total amount of money expended to educate students with disabilities, is it possible to estimate. In 1990–91 the average cost of education in the U.S. was $5,266 per student. On average, the public spends 2.3 times this amount on students with disabilities. For a student with disabilities, it is estimated that an additional $6,845.80 was spent. In 1990–91, 4.8 million students with disabilities received special education for a total additional cost of $32.86 billion.	**Where does the money go?**	

Where does the money go?

	General Education	Special Education
Instruction	54%	62%
Support Services/Administration	35%	11%
Transportation	8%	4%
Related Services	—	10%
Public Services	3%	—
Assessment	—	13%

Source: Moore, 1988

number of children served in that state will continue to rise over the next few years, and that they will also have an increased need for personnel. The state of Indiana reported an increase in numbers of children served from 1992–93 to 1993–94 and indicated that the increase was because of an increase in the at-risk population. In Indiana there are efforts being made to "identify biologically and environmentally at-risk children" (p. 250, 17th Report, made available through the National Clearinghouse for Professions in Special Education.).

No matter what type of educational setting you work in, if you work with children at all, you will need to be familiar with what is going on in special education. You need to be familiar with the protections and privileges the law gives to all children and you need to be in an informed position to help the lead teacher or director spot children who may need some extra care and attention. Staying in tune with the children in your care, seeing special needs and discerning when further evaluation is called for, is really one of the most important parts of your job as a paraeducator.

CHAPTER 8

Ways and Means for Good Behavior

It would be wonderful to work in a classroom where all the children are always upbeat, agreeable, and eager to learn and where everyone gets along all the time and no one ever behaves inappropriately. Well, you already know that will not happen in this lifetime. Discipline is part of life and it is part of days at school, too. Punishment is often what jumps into minds when the word discipline is spoken, but discipline is a whole lot more than negative consequences; it also involves positive consequences and training and learning to behave in acceptable ways. Joanne Oppenheim says in her book, *The Elementary School Handbook,* that "...the real objective of discipline should be to help children discover self-control" (1989).

As you prepare for your job as a paraeducator, and also periodically as you perform the job, you will be wise to discuss and develop ideas, philosophies, and expectations about discipline. You will need to talk about classroom management with the teacher before you jump into your involvement with the children. You will need to align yourself with the methods that the lead teacher uses and then use additional techniques as appropriate. The lead teacher will have procedures she uses to encourage good behavior and consequences for times when the desired behavior does not occur. Your job will involve supporting the teacher's discipline plan so that there is consistency for the children and also to help the teacher decide on behavior plans for individual children.

Developing discipline ideas and deciding on consequences for misbehavior will be done primarily by the teacher, but there will probably be many times when you are alone with a small group and the management will be up to you. In fact, knowing where your boundaries are as a paraeducator is vital to working out a good cooperative relationship with the lead teacher and to doing a good job. You really need to know just what role the school and the lead teacher expect you to take in disciplining the students because there can be tension if you take on too big a role in this or if you hang back and do not act when you are expected to. So, have the philosophy and boundary talk before the action begins with the children and then keep on communicating about your balance with the lead teachers and any other adults in the room. It will be your responsibility to understand what the teacher wants in the way of classroom behavior and then to help maintain that order.

There will also be times when you and the teacher will puzzle together over "What do we do with this one?" What works for one child does not necessarily work for another and some children can be quite challenging. Whenever possible, find the *key* to individual students and make consequences and rewards work for particular students.

The age of the children, their level of development, and the particulars of situations are factors to consider. You certainly should not expect the same standards of behavior from four-year-olds that you expect from eighth graders. Sometimes the same action should not have the same outcome, either. For example, consider Kubi. The other children have swiped his toys all morning. Kubi has whined but otherwise let it happen. Finally, though, Zachary grabs Kubi's toy and Kubi strikes back by hitting him on the arm. Also consider Elida, who hits other children over the head rather often without any apparent provocation. True to form, Elida has to walk around Brittany to go to the bathroom and she bops Brittany on the head as she goes by. Should Elida and Kubi be dealt with in the same way? You and the teacher will treat incidents such as these differently. Over time you will work out a variety of strategies and you will use them. You will need to pay attention to what is going on with children and also to their intentions.

You and the teacher should discuss what is considered major and what is considered minor. You need to think about your own values concerning appropriate behavior. What really is important and what can be overlooked? Brown and Kritsonis tell about a math teacher who made a very big deal about bringing pencils to class. The teacher threatened that anybody who did not bring a pencil to class would be sent straight to the principal's office. The students responded to the challenge and then the teacher was obligated to involve the principal. Pencils became a bigger problem than they needed to be! Brown and Kritsonis say that, "Some teachers find themselves taking an inflexible stand on issues that are of minor importance, and this is most unlikely to promote a good learning environment" (1992). There are things that have a tendency to drive paraeducators and teachers crazy, but you really need to evaluate what the most important goals are and what consequences are fitting and reasonable.

Something you will want to discern quickly is what the teacher expects from the classroom environment. What is an acceptable noise level for group learning activities? How much is too much noise at seatwork time? What about the movement around the room? When is it okay for children to move around freely and when does the teacher expect them to remain in their seats? Observe closely and clarify your perceptions by communicating with the teacher. The two of you will need to have a clear idea of what type of classroom atmosphere you both are comfortable with. Part of your job will be to facilitate the teacher's goals for the learning environment, so obviously you must have a good feel for what those goals and expectations are before you can help accomplish them. You will need to discuss any serious differences in opinions, but again the teacher is the leader in the room and you must yield to the teacher's preferences.

If you ever work with a teacher with whom you have strong disagreements concerning the classroom environment, you need to respectfully try to come to some understanding of each other's positions. Let's say the teacher expects absolute quiet during "morning work" and you are more lenient, and feel comfortable with a low hum and some movement around the class. You might feel tempted to let the children "loosen up" whenever the teacher is out of the room. It will not work, though, for you to go against the teacher's wishes. First of all, it will be confusing and unfair to the students, and secondly, it will not help the relationship between you and the teacher. You must come to some sort of understanding, or you'll either be miserable or drive each other crazy!

KNOW YOUR STUDENTS

Something that will help you in dealing with children as much as anything is really knowing the children. It helps to know normal child development as you decide on techniques to use with children of different ages. If you work with infants and toddlers, you will likely find that it works best to physically remove objects or children from certain situations. Even at these young ages you should explain to children what you are doing and why in a simple way so that eventually they will begin to put actions and responses together. During the preschool years, there is a lot of focus on changing the surroundings, plans, and methods in order to help little ones comply with the rules. As children grow older, though, there is a shift from adult actions to more self-control on the students' part.

It is also vital, and so necessary, to observe individual children so that you can judge whether your methods are effective or not. For example, the worst thing in the world to Katie is to be put in time-out or restricted from her social interactions in any way. Brent, on the other hand, seems to have a pretty good time in time-out; he just sits in his own little world and counts the dots on the ceiling. So, get to know your children. Learn about what you can expect from them based on developmental maturity and assess them individually based on their personalities and temperaments.

You will also quickly become familiar with the kind of behavior strategies your students use to get their own way. Remember that "child strategies to remain in control are natural and normal." From a child's point of view, rules and expectations in a classroom or center can be pretty constraining. Children use some (hopefully not all!) of the following methods when adults try to "cramp their style":

- Crying
- Whining
- Pleading
- Screaming
- Arguing
- Pretending not to hear
- Refusing to meet your (adults') eyes
- Running away
- Putting their hands over their eyes or their ears
- Becoming stiff
- "The silent treatment"
- Tantrums
- "Acting out" anger and aggression
- Changing the subject
- Name-calling
- Threatening to "tell"
- Threatening that they don't or won't like or love you anymore
- "Talking you to death"
- Ignoring the rules

Your students may try many of these strategies at times, but most of the time they will more likely cooperate and care about following the rules, especially later as they get more involved in making classroom rules themselves. It is a pleasure to watch little ones, with their straight-forward relationships and their growing sensitive concern for others, as they learn to interact cooperatively. It continues to be a pleasure seeing children grow in self-control as they learn how to make good decisions and behave appropriately. You just have to give them time and room to grow by holding realistic expectations and standards.

As discussed in the preparation chapter, there will be times you are more or less drawn to some children. You will be able to relate more easily to some children than others. If you maintain a fair and friendly manner with all the children, this should not be a problem. Occasionally, there may be children whom you have a real problem liking. When this happens, you will need to "consciously reach out to them" and try to figure out why you feel the way you do. One educator told of a teacher who had five girls whom she had trouble liking. The girls were clingy and constantly wanted to touch or be near her until it about drove her to distraction and she was afraid she would "lose it" with these girls. After a dream the teacher realized that she herself acted a lot like the girls when she was in the third grade.

You might be able to figure out that Terrence, one of your least favorite students, strongly resembles the neighborhood kid who stuck your head in the sewage creek when you were a kid. Now is that really Terrence's fault? Your job as a paraeducator will be to treat each and every child fairly and compassionately, no matter what they look like, who they remind you of, or how they act.

RULES

Children do need limits, and that's really what rules are. Rules give guidelines for behavior and children need those guidelines. They feel more secure when they know what the rules are and when they know what is expected of them. Children generally want to please, but how can they if they don't know what it takes to do that? Elizabeth Ellis, a clinical psychologist and author of *Raising A Responsible Child: How Parents Can Avoid Overindulgent Behavior and Nurture Healthy Children*, says this about rules:

> *All the child development research shows that young kids need security, predictability, and regularity of schedules. Rules make young kids feel secure and able to view the world as a predictable place, where they understand what's going to happen, who's going to do it, and what they're supposed to do.*

Your job will also involve helping the teacher enforce important rules of good behavior and teaching the children how to get along well in your room, in the school, and ultimately in the world. Rules, either spoken or unspoken, will be present throughout life. Children find out early that there will always be expectations concerning their behavior. Sometimes they get confused and mess up when they do not know exactly what those expectations are. That is why it is so important that rules be made clear to children. It also helps them when rules are made for good reasons and the children understand the reasons.

Some school rules are unique. The rules might be unique because of the particular physical environment or staff schedules. The social climate, the weather climate, and even the financial climate can have a bearing on rules.

There are some general consistencies about rules, though, no matter how different the facilities in which they are found. From the early childhood center on through elementary school, all rules are related to four basic categories:

1. Safety
2. Consideration for others
3. Respect and care for the surroundings
4. Cooperation for cleaning up

In other words, children should not do anything to hurt themselves, they are not allowed to hurt others, they must not destroy the environment, and they have to pitch in and help after they contribute to messes. As children get older and group instruction begins, then another category emerges: respect for other children's right to learn.

Rules in this category boil down to the idea that children should not be allowed to interfere with other children's learning. Some examples of some unacceptable behaviors in this category are interrupting and talking to others while they are trying to do their work. A common practice in preschool, prekindergarten, and lower elementary school grades is to open up a discussion about classroom rules. Children are allowed some input in deciding behavior expectations for the room. Students brainstorm for rule ideas. Sometimes teachers even allow the students to seriously consider a list of rules and vote on which ones they think are most important. The class members have then contributed their own ideas about appropriate behavior and what it takes to have a classroom where everyone can learn and get along together. When this kind of discussion takes place, children can gain a greater understanding for the reasons behind rules and may be able to help "trouble shoot" with their peers. The adults in the room are still the ultimate authority but children feel better about the whole process and grow to understand that rules protect everybody. The classroom rules become "our rules" instead of the "teacher's rules."

You and the teacher should evaluate the rules in your classroom. Are there too many or are the rules too picky? When you see that you have gone overboard on rules, it may mean that you are overusing or pushing the limits of "teacher power." Guard against this. Some student teachers shared some of their observations of rules. One told of a child who got in trouble for eating his "pusher" first at lunch. The child did not understand what a "pusher" was or why it mattered what she ate first. She found out that a "pusher" was her teacher's word for a piece of bread. Another student teacher shared another strange mealtime rule; children were not allowed to eat "just the frosting off their cupcakes." Every now and then you and the teacher should check your rules for the children and make sure you are focusing on the most important things and that you are not being unreasonable with or overloading on rules. When there are too many rules, children may get overwhelmed and frustrated and *ignore* the rules. You and the teacher would do better to establish only a few understandable rules with clear consequences for not following them (ERIC #E408).

As a paraeducator, you are an authority who must help assure that rules are followed, especially when they concern the safety and well-being of children. That is one of your responsibilities. Sometimes the children will not appreciate you exercising your responsibility. There will probably be many times when a child will be angry with you because you block him from his desire or goal. Just endure the momentary anger; hopefully it won't last long. It is not realistic for you to think that the students will always be happy with you. They really do want and need guidelines; they just don't always know that.

You can be a big help when you reiterate rules or give instructions if you are very clear and definite, rather than vague. Picture this idea in family life. Think of a mom saying, "Kids, I need you to help some this afternoon." Compare this to another mom saying, "Here's a list for you, Carlos, and here's one for you, Christina. There are three tasks on each list; I want you to have them finished by 5:30." Which mother do you think will come closest to being satisfied around 5:45? The first mother will probably look around and think, "Where are they? I told them I needed some help this afternoon?" (Well, the children left the vicinity so they wouldn't have to do any work!) The other mother might not be totally pleased with how tasks were done, but at least she will have a specific base from which to address the issue. Brown and Kritsonis discuss the need to be definite in *School Discipline: The Art of Survival,* saying that students need clear directions so that they will know what they are really supposed to do, and if they are given vague instructions they may be more likely to behave inappropriately. Brown and Kritsonis give three assignment instructions, ranging from "real loose" to very precise; they suggest that the vague direction is "an open invitation to 'goof off'," and that the clear definite instructions are more likely to bring good results (1992). Think of these classroom scenarios:

- One teacher tells her class that she would like them to "review for a while." Then she goes to her desk, sits down, and begins to grade the spelling tests.

- Another teacher says, "This Friday there will be a test on fractions. You may use this time to study and turn in late work." Then he goes to his desk, sits down, and begins to grade spelling tests.

- A third teacher says, "This Friday there will be a test on fractions. Open your math books to page 57. Get out a pencil and a piece of paper. I'm going to set the timer for eight minutes. See how many of the review problems you can do in that time. If you have any questions or just don't understand something, come see me." The teacher sets the timer. Then she goes to her desk, sits down, and begins to grade spelling tests.

Obviously, the student responses will be different. You can see that the things you say and the things you do can greatly affect how the children follow directions and keep the rules.

COMMUNICATIONS AND ACTIONS THAT FACILITATE COMPLIANCE

One of your goals in your job as a paraeducator should be to interact with students in such a way that maximum learning potentials are achieved. There are ways to speak to children that enhance their sense of self-esteem and make them open to doing their best. Expect good behavior rather than predicting trouble from children. It should be your practice to respect the children and avoid humiliating them, even when they really blow it. Then when they do really blow it, expect better behavior next time. Let your attitude be one of confidence that children can and will improve their conduct.

"I" Messages

A frequently heard missive is to *label the behavior, not the child.* One way to do this is to use what Gordon (1974) calls *"I" messages* in contrast to *you* messages. In an "I" message you shift the focus from "you are so........." and "I don't like you" to "I don't like what we have to do as a result of your action" and "I don't like what you are doing." Sometimes an "I" message indicates that you recognize your part in the problem. For example, if one of your three-year-olds accidentally spills paint, you really may not be angry because the child spilled the paint, but because you have to clean up the mess. Your first impulse may be to lash out at the child and say something like, "Good grief, don't you ever look what you're doing?" or "Why are you so clumsy?" Make sure you refrain yourself, though. The child probably feels bad already and your accusing statements will only make her feel worse, and the accident might not have even been the child's fault. The paint may have been placed too close to the child or to the edge of the table. In that case the spilled paint may have been more your problem than the child's. It would be much better to say something like "I really hate to clean up paint!" This is the truth about what is annoying you. Even little children can understand a dislike for cleaning up messes.

Of course there will be times when you honestly feel that a child is responsible for a mess or misbehavior, especially if the child is one you have trouble liking. You need to let the child know it is the wrong or careless behavior you don't like, rather than the child. It is more effective, fair, kind, and professional to say "I don't like it when you hit" than to say "I don't like you." The latter statement puts a blanket of disapproval over all of a child's behavior and his whole self; the former relates only to unacceptable behavior. When you need to discipline a child, be so careful to convey to him or her that you do not approve of the behavior, but that does not mean that you disapprove of him or her. Be sure to separate the person from the person's actions.

You can help teach even young children to send "I" messages; even little ones can learn this technique. As the paraeducator, you can direct children to say "I don't like it when you do that!" to other children instead of shouting "I don't like you!" or "You're mean!" When you label behavior that you dislike, the child who needs correction learns what is acceptable behavior without being made to feel unacceptable himself. When children learn to use the "I" message technique themselves, they also learn more about what kind of behavior is acceptable. Eventually, the children will learn to differentiate between who a child is and how that child behaves. We all need to learn and practice this.

Be Positive

Another way to encourage good behavior and help children remain open to doing their best is to state rules and instructions in a *positive* way. The *don't* words trigger a different response in all of us than more positive ways of saying the same things. Look at the difference in the following statements:

- "DON'T RUN!" versus "Walk inside; run outside."
- "Do not open your mouths during the spelling test." versus "Keep your mouths quiet during the spelling test."
- "Don't leave a mess after snack." versus "After you finish your snack, pick up your garbage and put it in the trash can."
- "If you don't study this material, you are going to do poorly." versus "If you study this material, you will do well."

Stating rules and instructions in a positive way can serve as a helpful reminder of what is expected and considered appropriate.

Be An Example, Use Examples

You probably will use *modeling* to encourage appropriate actions. This technique involves pointing out a child or teacher example, such as:

- "The paint stays on the paper. That's the way, Kerry."
- "See how slowly I am pouring the milk so it doesn't spill."
- "Laney is ready. Her eyes are on me and she is listening."

Be careful when you use modeling statements, though, that you do not use the same child all the time as your example. Using the same student as a model all the time will bring on claims that you have a "teacher's pet." Most teachers try to use every child as a model, and you should, too. When children hear a modeling statement, they frequently chime in "me, too." While you may not be able to take the opportunity to recognize and reinforce all of the positive models, you may want to reply in this vein, "Yes, and I'm so glad many of you are using the glue carefully" in order to acknowledge that there are others doing a good job besides just the one you singled out.

Redirection

Redirection is another verbal behavior strategy that works by redirecting a child's focus to something else—another activity, toy, area, or playmate. Here are some examples of redirection:

- "Here are some green stompers for you to use, Keiko."
- "You can stretch this muscle guy, Danielle."
- "While you're waiting for your turn at the computer, you may choose the puzzle with the hot air balloons or the weather puzzle."
- "I know you wanted to read a dinosaur book, Raoul, but they are all taken right now. Since you like spaceships, would you like to pick one of these?"
- "Karen, while you are waiting for Vida and Brenna to finish their game of Boggle, why don't you find a partner and choose another game from the middle shelf?"

Little ones under three can be awfully intent on holding on to toys and other objects, but they usually do accept substitutions. If you work with young age groups you probably will find that the rooms are already equipped with many duplicate toys. Younger preschoolers have some strong "I want what he has" tendencies. In these young ages you will probably use redirection a good bit.

In kindergarten and early grades, however, the use of redirection can send a message to the children that they have opportunities for multiple choices after they are disappointed over not getting their first choices. You and the teacher may not always want on-and-on multiple choice options to be available.

A possible pitfall in using the redirection strategy too frequently is that it may give the children the idea that something better will be offered every time they don't get to have or do what they want. Offering an enjoyable alternative every time there's a balk may inadvertently teach a lesson you don't wish to teach. A child may become difficult and uncooperative because he learns that being so gets lots of attention and brings a desired change in circumstances. So be discerning about how and how often you use the redirection technique.

There are other kinds of redirection statements that may work well with groups as well as individuals. Try saying things like "Let's take giant steps to the corner. Can you stretch to make giant steps like this?" and "We're going to tiptoe back into the room. Let's be so quiet that we sneak up on Mrs. Rizzel without her even hearing us until we get to our seats." These kinds of directions may capture the children's imaginations and make them eager to join in. The key to redirection is to make the alternative idea or method desirable.

Be cautioned against using the same ideas too often, even if they are fun and the children respond well. Any specific spark can lose its glow after a while. If you use the "let's tiptoe as quietly as mice" statement every day for a week, it certainly will not bring the same eager response on Friday as it did on Monday. Rather than becoming stale, it is best to use a variety of redirection statements and to bounce them around sporadically.

Teach Cause and Effect

Cause and effect statements are simple ways to encourage good action choices. If you simply state the facts about a situation, you may provide the information children need in order to make a positive choice. Some examples of cause and effect statements are:

- "If you pick off all the leaves, the plant will die."
- "It hurts to have sand thrown in your eyes."
- "If you eat your lunch now at snacktime, you may be hungry and bored at lunch time."

Each of these statements gives information that helps children decide the appropriateness of their actions or realize the consequences of what they are about to do.

Give Choices

Another way to encourage good behavior with your communication is to *give a choice.* You will, of course, want to refrain from leaving choices open-ended; you should limit any choices to things you would actually like the child to do. As warned about, you don't want children to get the idea that the choices are endless, or you'll have to deal with a lot of manipulation. However, giving children choices appeals to their sense of independence and helps them learn about making decisions. Here are some examples:

- "Are you going to put your used napkin in the trash or on the tray?"
- "Can you walk to the gate yourself or are we going to hold hands and walk together?"
- "You may work on math homework alone or play the computer review game with a partner."
- "You may choose to rest quietly next to your friend or on a cot somewhere else in the room."

Expect Respect and Give Respect

If you want the respect of your students, you need to set the right tone with them right from the start. It generally does not work to try to be a buddy to your students. Don't invite too much familiarity. For example, consider that how you have students address you will affect the way you are perceived. Think about it. When children address an adult by a first name, they feel permitted to relax their behavior more than if they address an adult by *Ms.* or *Mr.* You need to maintain a certain amount of reserve and remember that, yes, though you love them, you are not on the peer level with your students, but in a position of authority over them. Brown and Kritsonis also suggest that you act your age even if you are not much older than your students, because they really do "expect you to be a mature adult" (1992).

Be as consistent and fair as you possibly can in your speech and interactions with the children and your manner will be more conducive to good behavior on their parts. Anybody can have a bad day and children can certainly understand that, but they do need consistency from you and the teacher in order to understand what is expected from them. If you let "Action Z" go on Thursday, and you fly off into orbit when they do the same "Action Z" on Friday, then you will confuse your children. Children need to see consistency in your responses to them and their actions. They need to know and trust that you will treat them fairly and with respect and that you care about their feelings. Even if you feel a greater affinity for some children, you need to be even in how you deal with all of them. If you do not do your part in setting up a consistent, fair, and respectful atmosphere in your room, then you may send a message to some children that their inappropriate behavior does not really matter. Children can come to feel that no matter what they do, you and the teacher will not treat them fairly or be pleased with them. The way you treat children will have tremendous bearing on how they act in your room. You need to consistently reinforce the kinds of behavior you and the teacher feel are appropriate and also consistently deal with behaviors you find to be inappropriate. If you are as consistent and fair as possible, and treat the children with respect, they are more likely to be consistent in their behavior, and to treat you and others fairly and with respect. Remember that as their paraeducator, you are one of their examples.

ANTICIPATING AND PREVENTING INAPPROPRIATE BEHAVIOR

The atmosphere of your room may really have an impact on how the children act. The quality of the classroom atmosphere includes intangible and tangible factors such as:

- Consistency
- Fairness
- Respect
- Physical layout of desks and tables
- Room decor
- Noise level
- Routines and schedule

The consistency, fairness, and respect aspects of the classroom atmosphere should be permanent fixtures. The other aspects will vary. Hopefully your classroom setting will be pleasant, with physical features that appeal to the children. The classroom setting and activities should be changed frequently enough to prevent boredom. If children become bored with what they see and bored with what they are supposed to be doing in the classroom, they sometimes will be inspired to become more innovative in their behavior in attempt to liven things up.

If you and the teacher are not well-organized, you may invite inappropriate behavior, too. Just picture this scene. The children have just returned from a school assembly and are settling back at their desks. Mrs. Peacock had planned to immediately begin the unit on the skeletal system, but the overhead projector she needs is in the room next door. Mrs. Peacock asks you to go get it. Uh-oh. You take the time to retrieve the overhead projector. Now she can't seem to put her hands on the transparencies she asked you to prepare. What's more, you can't find them either even though you know you did them and then you put them on the......Well, where did you put them? As the two of you scramble and consult, the settling at the desks gives way to shuffling and then some out and out rambunctiousness as Serena starts throwing used, crumpled tissues at Peter's head. There will always be the potential for unexpected glitches in the schoolday, but you can really cut down the amount of time that it takes to move to the next lesson or activity if you have good organization in your room, thereby lessening opportunity for the students to act up.

Snatches of unplanned time can provide open invitations for children to look for ways to fill that time. Sometimes lessons are shorter than predicted, the class has to wait for the office to call them to an assembly, or one group finishes an activity before another group. When the lesson is finished and there are still five minutes to go before lunch, you may be called upon to keep the students engaged in something worthwhile. You need some ideas on how to constructively use such waiting times. Some ideas for effective time fillers are listed below:

- Open-ended phrases—One student may be given an open-ended phrase such as "Something that makes me feel good is..." or "If I could give everyone in the world something, it would be..." and so on. After the first student completes the phrase, he chooses another student to share her ideas with the class.

- Riddles—Keep a good supply of riddles readily available. You might even want to keep riddles in an index card file so that you can keep track of which ones you have used already. Some children's and teachers' publications are good sources for riddles. (*Highlights* and *The Teacher's Almanack,* for example)

- Academic trivia questions—Keep the Brainquest set for your students' level on hand all the time. Depending on the amount of spare time, you can ask the questions to the entire group or quickly divide the group into teams. Correct answerers could be awarded something simple like front place in line for lunch.

- Reading out loud—Have a book with short chapters or poems to read to the students at odd moments. You might also teach the students a poem line by line, with them repeating the lines after you, until they memorize it. You could also ask volunteers to act out a poem as you read it.

- Silent reading—Students should keep a pleasure book at their desks for those little snatches of time between activities.

- Visual brain-teasers—Draw a quick puzzler on the board (such as a large numeral *1* with a shaded circle in the middle of it, for *hole in one*). One second grade teacher puts a new puzzler on the board every morning. No one is allowed to tell the solution until the end of the day so that they will not ruin the fun for everyone else. Those who do guess early are encouraged to think of their own puzzlers. At odd times during the day, Mrs. Ball points the teaser out again. Find a book of these at an educational supply store and use them as "get those wheels turning" time-fillers.

Just be sure that you and your teacher are always prepared for vacant time. Use spare time, even little bits, for something worthwhile rather than tempting creative young minds to invent inappropriate time wasters.

Develop some strategies for routine happenings that provide opportunities for things to get too crazy. When the children break into groups for learning projects, you may put a classical music tape on and tell them that they may confer together as long as it doesn't get too loud for you to hear the music. When you are asking a small group review questions while the teacher is conducting experiments with the other groups, use the "beep system" to control the responses. Ask a question, have students raise their hands when they know the answer, but keep their mouths closed tightly until you say, "beep." You can "beep" individuals or the group as a whole (DiPaolo, GA Preschool Association 1990 Conference).

Anticipating inappropriate behavior and intervening before it breaks out is a technique that takes time and experience to learn. If you watch your students and study their behavior patterns, you can learn to anticipate some situations. Many children are fairly predictable. You might observe, for example, that a child becomes aggressive whenever he plays with more than one child, so you and the teacher simply take precautions for allowing the child to play with only one other child at a time. If you know that another child really does better with time by herself before lunch and seems to fall apart without it, you can see what you can do to arrange for that "alone space" time. Likewise, if you've noticed that time and time again a little one gets tired and irritable just before it is time to go home, you might see about some extra rest time for that child. Some children are easily overwhelmed by stimuli (sights, sounds, and actions) and can only deal with them a little while before they react negatively. Be a careful observer of the children in your room and you may be able to figure out what causes them to "blow it" and help them avoid the situation next time.

When you see a student teetering between doing what she's supposed to be doing and adding some extraneous activity, you may not have to say a word to her to bring her back in line. Eye contact alone can be very effective. Eye contact has a great deal to do with discipline; be sure to really look at the children. Or as you walk around the room, simply put your hand on the child's shoulder for a few seconds and then move on. The touch itself gives the message: "I see you. Stay on task."

When your class becomes too noisy or you sense a situation is getting out of control, speak in a lower volume, with firmness and calmness, rather than raising your voice. Whenever possible, have the children conform to your reasonable voice level, rather than you compensating for their unreasonable noise levels. Often if you speak more softly, it will have a soothing effect and children will quieten so that they don't miss anything.

No matter what you do, though, you will encounter some resistance. Resistance to rules and not conforming to what is expected can be seen in both children and adults. While we usually view this resistance as negative behavior, resistance may be regarded in a more positive light. Moustakas believes resistance is healthy. So...when you are dealing with a little precious who seems intent on breaking the rules, it may help you to remember what Moustakas said:

> *Resistance is a way for the child to maintain his own sense of self in the light of external pressures to manipulate and change him. It is a healthy response, an effort of the individual to sustain the integrity of the self. (1966)*

CONSEQUENCES FOR UNACCEPTABLE BEHAVIOR

Even if you do all you can do to promote the kind of atmosphere conducive to good behavior and you try to anticipate and prevent inappropriate behavior, there will still be times when your students resist rules and make wrong choices concerning their actions. Talking out, interrupting, not following directions, making fun of other children, bullying, and fighting are common problems that cause disruptions in the classroom. There will be times when you and the teacher will have to follow through with the consequences for disobedience. Consequences for inappropriate behavior include:

- Time out
- Loss of free time
- Loss of a privilege
- Reprimand
- Communication with parents

As stated, the teacher will be the one who is primarily responsible for the discipline philosophy in the room and for decisions about consequences, but as you work together, you will work more interdependently and make more decisions together. Even if you do not have much or any input at first, you will probably have plenty of input eventually! Store away this information for that time. Whenever possible, the consequence for any inappropriate action should be one that:

- works for that particular student. (Remember that some children actually enjoy time out, for example.)
- is administered as soon as possible after the event (or it will lose its effectiveness).
- does not single the student out. (You sure don't like to be singled out, do you?)
- does not include ridicule or humiliation (same thing—back to the respect issue).
- you and the teacher are comfortable with. (You have to feel right about administering the consequence.)
- fits the crime. (You do not want to give a consequence that is way out of proportion to the action—too severe or too lenient.)

Time Out

Let's look at those consequences again a little more closely. The first one mentioned was *time out*. This can be done in your own classroom, in another classroom, or in the office. You should avoid using the hall for time out unless someone is able to monitor the child at all times. A child who is already in trouble may be tempted to vacate the premises. There is also the possibility of someone coming in from the outside. It is vital that safety issues be considered when you are deciding on a place for time out. Preschoolers, especially, need to be closely watched during their short times of chair-sitting. Wherever you choose, the isolation area needs to be supervised, safe, and unrewarding.

If a student is being inattentive or disturbing others, using a time-out place within the room can be effective because it may help the student to focus less on nearby attractions and more on school work and staying on task. Some classrooms have carrels for this purpose. Some classes paint and decorate refrigerator boxes to make "offices;" these portable, makeshift partitions provide quiet areas where students may work with fewer distractions.

Another possibility is to have an agreement with another teacher to use each other's rooms occasionally for time out. It may be helpful to remove a child from your classroom for a short time and take him to another room to do his work and consider his actions. You must be careful, though, not to humiliate any child. Be sensitive about the different classroom's grade level and student composition. Shaming, humiliating, or ridiculing a student is destructive. Remember that the children who cause you the most trouble have probably already been hurt in many ways, and are needy for attention and peer acceptance.

In some places a child may be taken to the office for time out. The office may be a place for disruptive children to reflect and do work separately from their cronies, but still be under adult supervision. You will need to find out how the administration feels about this possibility.

As already stated, even or especially when a child is "in trouble," you need to avoid ridiculing or disgracing and seek to have positive communications with your students. Consider the difference between "GO to Time Out!" spoken in harsh anger and "You need to sit for a few minutes until you are ready to...." spoken with calm matter-of-factness. The second statement gives a child an open invitation to rejoin the group and to live up to rules and expectations.

Loss of Free Time

Another effective consequence is *loss of free time*. Loss of free time may mean that a child does not get to participate in free play time within the classroom or outside, the child may miss being able to socialize with friends during snack breaks, or the child may have to stay after school.

If you use the loss of free time technique, always remember that children may not be left unattended. You cannot leave a child or two in the room without supervision while everyone else goes out for recess. You and the teacher should not leave a child who has been kept after school in the room alone while you spend the time in a meeting or making copies.

Again, it is so important to know your students. You may have children who really do not like to go out on the playground because of the weather or because they are having trouble "fitting in" with the other children. You need to key in to this, because such children may even go out of their way to make sure that they will *not* be allowed to go outside, because that is exactly what they want. They may neglect getting their work done or act out just so they will hear the longed-for words, "You may not go out to the playground. You must stay inside." If you are sensitive to your students, you'll be able to discern whether this consequence is a deterrent or a cause for private celebration for individual students. Sometimes it takes time to find the best consequence for a particular child. Watch closely. You and the teacher will know that you have not found the right consequence and that you need to try another approach if the nondesired behavior continues.

Of course, you must make arrangements with parents before keeping children after school for any reason. This will likely cause the consequence to be postponed because you must have time to notify the parents and give them time to make transportation arrrangements. The necessary delay may cause this consequence to lose some of its effectiveness, in that the tie between the action and the consequence is stretched and a child's memory of exactly why he is being disciplined may fade somewhat. On the other hand, in cases where children ride buses to school and parents have to get off work to pick them up, this consequence can be very effective. When the parents are inconvenienced it is likely that they will let their children hear about it, thereby reinforcing the discipline.

Loss of Privilege

The *loss of a privilege* can be an effective consequence as long as the privilege is sufficiently and significantly important to that child. In a Georgia elementary school, the sixth graders take an overnight trip to Huntsville, Alabama, to Space Camp. From the beginning of the school year until the spring trip actually arrives, the sixth graders are reminded that they must maintain a certain level of behavior in order to go on the

---

Rules from a Sixth Grade Class from a Student's Perspective

1. No fighting (or you get a yellow break miss).
2. No talking while a teacher is talking (yellow break miss).
3. No running (yellow break miss).
4. No gum (yellow break miss).
5. No cheating or you get a yellow break miss.
6. Do not tear up the break misses you get or you get two more.
7. Turn your work in on time (white break miss).
8. Bring all the stuff you need for class to class or you get a white break miss.

Note: Eight white break misses (for work-related transgressions) means after school detention. Three yellow break misses (for behavior-related transgressions) means after school detention. If you get three after-school detentions, you have to spend one day in in-school suspension.

---

trip. If they step out of bounds too far or too often (have a specified number of "break misses" or "in-school suspensions"), they will not be allowed to go on the trip, and the trip is a Big Deal. In this case the loss of a much-anticipated privilege is compounded by the community awareness of the trip. It's bad enough to miss out on the trip, but then to have everybody else's parents know that you are not allowed to go on the trip is really awful! (See the chart of a sixth grade break miss system.)

Removal of a privilege can involve restricting use of a particular toy or piece of equipment or the use of a play area for a short time period. After the "off-limits" time, the child should be encouraged to try again, with a quick positive reminder of rules and consequences.

Reprimands

Reprimands are another consequence of inappropriate behavior. When children break one of the rules that have been discussed previously, you need to point it out to them. You can do this literally if there is a chart of classroom rules posted on the wall. Simply getting their attention and walking over and quietly pointing to a specific rule may be all you need to do.

A reprimand does not have to include a loud and long tirade. One basketball coach told his preteen players not to shoot the basketball until it had been passed three times to try to curb their "run and gun and shoot bricks" style. One player continually ignored the coach's edict, so the coach finally pulled the boy from the game. As the boy approached the bench, with a "what did I do?" look written all over his face, the coach did not verbally fuss at him at all. The coach just held up three fingers, the boy immediately understood, and changed his basketball behavior when he was put back in the game. Very effective, but also very respectful of the child.

When you need to reprimand an individual child, it is best to speak to that child privately. It also helps to listen to what the child has to say. There may be factors that you and the teacher really don't know about. If you listen you may be able to pick up that a child is frustrated with the work, bored by the work, or having a problem with another student. Sometimes a child may feel she is being treated unjustly and may need to talk it out. You do not want to give in to manipulation, but sometimes it is very important for a child to know that you value her enough to listen. You can then point out how the child behaved inappropriately, and hopefully this will help the child learn from the experience.

Communication with the Parents

Communication with the parents can be used as a consequence of unacceptable behavior. There may be occasions when a *call* or *a note to parents* will be appropriate. Sometimes just the threat that you or the teacher will get in contact with parents is enough to deter many misbehaviors. When a child knows that the teacher is perfectly willing to call his parents, he may try harder to keep himself in line. One teacher was challenged by one boy's highly disruptive and destructive behavior. She knew that the boy's father worked nights and she made the deliberate decision to disturb the father by calling him during the day. Naturally the dad was not pleased, so it did have a real impact on the little guy's subsequent behavior.

As a paraeducator, you should not make initial calls to the family concerning unacceptable behavior. That really is the teacher's responsibility. After the initial communication about the problem behavior has been established, then you and the teacher may possibly share follow-up phone calls. Communication with the family is important and should not be used solely as a result of misbehavior. It is encouraging to call the parents when their child has had some better days following some problematic ones. You should become knowledgeable of the family situation before making calls to the home. If both parents work, call the home in the evening. Call a parent at work only if you have specific permission to call in nonemergency situations.

The consequences we've discussed are the most frequently used. Your job will be to follow through with the teacher's suggestions and to offer suggestions when appropriate. Remember that no one consequence is right for every child and no consequence should be used for every child even in similar situations. Children and the homes from which they come are so different; their responses to behavior consequences will be different. For example, Morgan may have been yelled at so much at home that she seems immune to loud or raised voices; yelling does not even faze her. Then there's Sam who is so sensitive that just a severe look withers him and if you actually have to reprimand him, you may see a glint of tears in his eyes. Again, know your children and be discerning.

Lovitt, in *Managing Inappropriate Behaviors in the Classroom,* says that "punishment can be defined as a technique that decelerates the frequency of a behavior when it is given contingent on that behavior"

Teacher/paraprofessional responses to students' conduct, recalled by a group of children of various ages:

- Book thrown
- Demerits
- In-school suspension
- Put in a corner
- Ruler hit across hand (Yes, in the 90s)
- Candy given
- Tokens earned
- Coupons earned, visit to classroom "store"
- Cussing in Spanish

Worst punishments recalled by the same group:
- Being expelled
- Alternative school
- Isolation (doing work in a room all by yourself)
- Points taken off grade for talking too much
- Assigned seats
- Having to eat the combination of food they had made while playing with food in the cafeteria

Best rewards, recalled by the same group:
- Getting to talk
- Getting to work in groups
- Extra time on the playground
- Potato chips or popcorn and soft drink
- Candy
- Pizza party

(1978, and ERIC Digest #E408). Lovitt reminds us that "reprimands, frowns, reminders, and other subtle expressions can serve as punishment," and that these "can be very effective when used appropriately." He does caution, though, that sometimes the effects of punishment splatter too far and the punishment snuffs out more behaviors than originally intended (ERIC #E408). The point is that whenever you do send out punishment messages, you need to make sure that the children understand clearly what the message is, what specific behavior is unacceptable, why you are frowning, and what they need to do to correct the behavior. If children know they are the recipients of frowns and reprimands, but are not really sure why, then they will be confused and may begin to associate those frowns and reprimands with the way they feel about you (Lovitt, ERIC #E408).

TECHNIQUES TO USE WITH INAPPROPRIATE BEHAVIOR

The whole goal of classroom discipline is to teach children how to act in a responsible, acceptable way. Sometimes techniques are needed to decrease unwanted behaviors. There are arguments among the experts over what works and what does not, and what is too harsh or too lenient. Positions range from Dr. Dobson's *dare to discipline* stand to Gordon's *participative management* approach. You will again need to make sure that you have a good understanding of your school's procedures and policies and those of the teacher with whom you work. This is an important area that demands at least some sort of agreement. If you personally tend to be very strict, with firm ideas of how children should and should not behave, you could go crazy working in an ultra-permissive environment. The opposite is also true. If you tend toward the lenient end of the scale, you will not be very happy in a more regimented school. You really need to get a feel for the school's ways before you ever accept a position and then further clarify your role in discipline matters on an ongoing basis. For our purposes here, we certainly will not touch on the controversies surrounding school discipline except to say that debates definitely continue. It will be up to you and your teacher to consider your students and decide which techniques seem best and agreeable to you. Thomas Gordon suggests that in actuality most parents and teachers are more comfortable with a style that does not fit on the authoritarian versus permissive scale, but has characteristics not especially related to power or control and contains an emphasis on internal controls ("Teaching Children Self-Discipline," 1989). Once you have accepted employment, don't be caught up in either-or semantics; you and the teacher may incorporate aspects from several major approaches to discipline to form your own particular style. The important thing is for you and the school and you and the teacher to be able to work out a style that suits all of you.

One technique for decreasing unwanted behavior is to use DRO, *differential reinforcement of other behaviors.* You and the teacher can reward a student when he refrains from specified undesirable behavior or when he controls himself better by performing that same specified behavior less often or for less time. Let's say Charlie has a bad habit of interrupting during class discussions but he is really trying to do better. You notice that Charlie starts to blurt out something while a classmate is asking a question but catches himself and closes his mouth tightly and raises his hand. After the discussion, you could go by Charlie's desk and quietly commend him for his effort (ERIC #E408).

Overcorrection is another technique used for decreasing undesirable behavior. In overcorrection you or the teacher would have a child "fix" what she had done wrong. A child who wrote on the wall in the bathroom might be required to scrub and repaint the wall. A child who spits could be required to vigorously clean up where he spits every time he does it. A child who does not proof her work could be asked to overcheck by reading directions and work before turning new work in.

The *satiation* technique is when you give students more opportunities to do or have whatever it is you are trying to eliminate. If Greg steals Anna's pencils, you could supply Anna, Patrick, and Pedro (the children who sit around Greg) with pencils and have them each give Greg a pencil every day until he decides he does not need to steal anyone's pencils anymore. Another commonplace example is inviting a clowning child up to the front of the room to share jokes with everyone.

A unique variation of the satiation technique was used by a first grade teacher who had a problem with widespread tattletaling in her classroom. No matter what she said in attempts to curb this behavior, the numbers of tattletale practitioners and tattletale practices continued to escalate. Her students were making her crazy with their constant whining about inconsequential matters. She changed tactics. She installed a "whisper box" in a secluded corner of the room, and informed the class that if they just had to tell on somebody they were welcome to go tell their woes to the box. Of course, she helped them understand that important matters, especially those concerning safety, needed to be brought to her attention. It took a while, but eventually the tattletaling in the classroom decreased. At first, the teacher would look up from reading groups to see a line waiting for the box, and frequently she had to remind children that "that sounds like something you should tell the box." Later, the children seemed to decide on their own that the supposed wrongs imposed on them were not so significant that they were worth losing time doing seatwork in order to whisper into the box. On the other hand, when the teacher noticed that a particular child seemed persistently upset and was seen often with her head leaning over the box, she was able to pull that child aside and find out what was bothering her so much.

Sometimes the best thing you can do with undesirable behavior is to ignore it. If you ignore demands or whining or tantrums, children may realize that extra attention is not forthcoming and may decide that the behavior just doesn't bring desired results, so it's not worth it. *Ignoring* is a usable technique with new actions that are annoying or irritating but of minor consequence. You will be wise at times to decide to deliberately *not* hear or see some things, and with experience you will learn when to employ suppressed vision or hearing capabilities. Children do many things just to test an adult's reaction or to get attention. Sometimes there may be comments directed toward you that are offensive and are intended to "get a rise out of you." For example, a child may say something like "you're ugly" or "you're fat." You may decide to ignore such comments completely, without responding in any way, or you may want to respond very matter-of-factly, with a comment like, "That's right, I don't look so good this early in the morning." Withholding any reactions that might reinforce the behavior and minimizing responses is a form of ignoring and usually ends the undesirable interaction. Margaret Maggs says in her book, *The Classroom Survival Book,* that a good guideline to follow is: "Notice what's happening when it begins to detract from the learning of other students" (1980).

Another procedure for decreasing unwanted behavior is to assign a token or point value to inappropriate actions. This is called response cost. Whenever a child does something that goes against the clearly understood class rules, then the child is fined by having to give up something. In one second grade classroom the children have cloth drawstring bags hooked on their desks in which they accumulate "tickets." Tickets are given out for all sorts of good behavior, for staying on task, for listening well, for acts of kindness. Tickets are taken up after inappropriate actions. At regularly scheduled times during the school year, the children are given the opportunity to "shop" at the teacher's store and to "buy" items with their tickets. The teacher sells things like fast food "kid meal" toys, items that her own children have outgrown, donated items, and garage sale stuff. She does not spend much, if any, money on the "store" items, but the children really love to shop and seem to appreciate their "treasures." This teacher's students make an effort to hold on to their ticket supplies until shopping day, so the system does seem to make a difference in the behavior of these second graders.

You will probably need to use *calming down periods* for out-of-bounds children at times. Sometimes this technique is helpful in giving you and the child a chance to gather your wits before you try to talk about the inappropriate behavior. You may need to rock or hold a little one after a tantrum or outburst, or you may need to allow a child to sit calmly by himself for a short while. When the child is calm and not angry anymore, then you need to clear things up.

The techniques mentioned so far are generally used on an individual basis. There are times when the teacher will use group methods to manage classroom behavior. For example, time out on the playground may be dependent on the whole group's behavior, and one child's inappropriate actions may impinge on the reward for the rest of the class. Another example is when a child has trouble staying on task, and the teacher calls on the whole class to help her do better. A class reward could be contingent on that child getting her work done, so the rest of the class might be inspired to be supportive of that student's efforts to do her work and not encourage her in off-task diversions. Group methods with whole class contingencies and consequences will likely be up to the teacher, but you need to be aware of the difference between individual and group methods (ERIC #E408).

C O N F R O N T A T I O N S

Conflicts are inevitable in any classroom. Hopefully, the ones in your room will be minor. You will likely witness or participate in times of confrontation between students, between students and you or the teacher, between you and the teacher, and with your own self.

There will probably be many times when children do not get along. There may be occasions when you will need to set up direct communication between two arguing children. You may say something like, "Look at his face; he's not happy. It hurts to be hit with a flying Frisbee.

Listen, he wants to tell you how he feels." This is where those "I messages" are especially helpful. If you can teach children to express how they feel rather than being accusatory or abusive, you will hopefully help them learn to respect one another. Taking a child by the hand and helping her confront another helps provide a safe forum for the expression of wishes and feelings and lets both children know that you will defend their rights. It also lets the children know that you care that rules are observed by all.

Children can learn the ignoring technique just as adults can. You may be able to teach children that the best thing to do in some circumstances is to ignore whoever is annoying them. For example, if someone says, "You're so stupid you could get locked in a grocery store and still starve to death" and really upsets some little tender-hearted soul, you could say, "If I were you, I'd ignore _____. I wouldn't pay attention to such a ridiculous comment." Help the injured party learn to take the focus off the antagonizer, and the antagonizer will hopefully lose his momentum.

Brown and Kritsonis (1992) suggest that you "develop a thick skin" when it comes to your interactions with students. The language and ways of verbal expression in your students' homes may be very different from what you would hope. There may be times when students will speak to you in ways you find offensive, but seem perfectly normal and acceptable to them. Try to avoid getting angry, feeling sorry for yourself, and taking things personally. Do try to teach them better ways to say things but be careful not to expect too much too fast. You and the teacher will have many times when you will have to discern whether a student's words are a cause for training or for negative consequences.

Tony DiPaolo said, "Anger is the outergarment of fear" (Georgia Preschool Association 1990 Conference). Remember his words when you face an angry child. Some of the most hostile children are the ones who live the most insecure, least loved lives. If you can find some compassion even when a child is blazing mad at you or at a situation, you will make an impact on that child. If you react with the same anger that "everyone" else in his life demonstrates, you will send a message that anger is the normal way to respond to life.

Guard your own reactions whenever you confront individuals or groups of children. Be careful about demonstrating anger or other emotional responses. If you do succumb to flaring up or, worse, crying, then the students will win that particular battle in a big way. You will have to find your own way to deal with those moments when the children really get to you, but the worse thing you can do is let them know that they did really get to you. James Dobson says, "A teacher, scoutmaster, or recreation leader who tries to control a group of children with anger is due for incredible frustration. The children will discover how far the adult will go before taking any action, and they invariably push him or her right to that line," and "Your anger is the least effective motivation I can imagine." ("The New Dare to Discipline," 1992) Brown and Kritsonis say that, "The system that will work best has to evolve, but the system that is least effective is undoubtedly to pitch a temper tantrum or burst into tears" (The Education Digest, Dec. 1992, excerpt from *School Discipline: The Art of Survival*).

One approach that will help you avoid "losing it" is to promptly deal with situations so that they do not have a chance to build to explosive proportions. When a student does something inappropriate that cannot be ignored, but must be confronted, do not avoid the confrontation, even when the teacher does not want to hear about it or the child is hostile or vengeful. Likewise, if there is a significant problem between you and the teacher, it will be best to go ahead and address it. You will not accomplish anything by putting problems off, except for opening possibilities for them to escalate.

However, this does not mean that you should just jump right in there. You should take enough time to consider the right place and time and approach for confronting problems. Of course, whenever possible, you should discuss problems with others privately, and when both parties are free to focus on a resolution. The best approaches are always ones that you would want to be used with you. Some good questions and statements for opening discussions about conflicts are:

- "This (explain what 'this' is) seems to be a problem. What do you think?"
- "Let's figure out a way to solve this problem together."
- "That's one way to handle this; here's another idea."

Of course, many confrontations with students have non-negotiable consequences and solutions. When clearly established rules have been violated, there is no choice but to follow through with the stated consequences. That's why it is important for you and the teacher to decide on consequences you will feel comfortable administering. If you balk at or do not intend to follow through with what has been established, the students will pick up on your reluctance.

Open communication encourages both parties to cooperate. A willingness to look at other possibilities promotes joint agreement. When you or the teacher has a do-it-my-way attitude, mutual support and cooperation are thwarted. Consideration of alternate solutions brings an admission that there are probably a number of viable possibilities, and is a more realistic approach. Sometimes it will be helpful for you and the teacher to agree to think over alternatives and discuss them together later. When you do tentatively decide on a solution, you may agree to try it for a week or so and then evaluate the effectiveness.

Let's say you and the lead teacher agree that there is a problem with noise and confusion right before lunch when the children go to the bathroom and wash their hands. You have been trying to send one table to the bathroom at a time, while the children at the other tables continue with their seatwork. The children are allowed to go to centers when they finish their morning work, so some children are not even at their tables, but are scattered around the room's periphery. The teacher is usually finishing the last reading group at a table in the back. You, meanwhile, are trying to stand in the doorway so that you can monitor the students across the hall in the bathroom *and* keep an eye on the room activity, as well as remember who has been to the bathroom and who has not. Your goals are to make sure people stay on task, make sure that no one experiments with water, toilet paper, or routes, and see that twenty-seven pairs of hands are clean and ready for lunch. Help! You and the teacher will need to brainstorm for different solutions, and decide which alternative to try. This will take a little bit of time and clear heads. The conversation might end with, "We'll try it this week and discuss whether it works next Monday."

There is so much going on in a classroom that sometimes there is little time for the adults to speak together while the students are there. There may be many opportunities for misunderstandings between you and the teacher. Be sure to clarify matters as soon as possible and as often as needed. Hopefully, your personalities will mesh well as you work together, but this is not always the case. Whether you get along well from the start or you are a little leery of each other, there may be times when you will have to work at the relationship. The relationship between a lead teacher and a paraeducator is different from the relationships in many other work environments, in that one of you has more responsibility than the other and you work in close proximity to each other for a long period of time. There probably will be a few days when you feel tension mounting between you. It will take getting to know each other to decide when to initiate a discussion. Sometimes if you leave it alone, the next day will be better. Other times you may need to say something like:

- "Is there anything we need to talk about?"
- "I'm really feeling uncomfortable because I sense there is something wrong."
- "I have this concern. What do you think?"

Jean Jackson, who trains paraeducators for a Georgia county school system, says that communication is the biggest problem between teachers and paraeducators. She recommends that last question to start communication flowing. Be aware of the possibility of communication problems between you and the teacher and make an effort from the start to prevent as many as you can, but when problems do occur, have the courage to confront them.

There is another person besides students or the teacher that you may have to confront while you work as a paraeducator. That person is you. If there are problems with relationships or with behavior in the classroom, check to see if any of your own actions have contributed to the problems. Brown and Kritsonis use the titles, *13 Ways Not to be Part of the Discipline Problem* and *How Teachers Can Avoid Contributing to Discipline Problems in Schools: Could I Be Part of the Problem?* (The Education Digest, Dec. 1992). They suggest that instead of placing total blame on the student, teachers should do some self-evaluation to determine if they themselves should share the blame. Including some of their suggestions already mentioned, Brown and Kritsonis recommend the following for preventing discipline problems:

- Be organized.
- Be definite.
- Be natural.
- Act your age.
- Be consistent and fair.
- Develop a thick skin.
- Avoid arguments.
- Avoid temper fits.
- Develop a set of values.
- Do not threaten.

Classroom Management Self-Evaluation

Discipline problems inevitably occur in any classroom. If there is a persistent pattern to problems, it is definitely time to try to locate the root cause. A discipline pattern may be due to actions or inactions by the students, by the lead teacher, by paraprofessionals, or, more likely due to some combination of these. You cannot control anybody but yourself, so when problems occur, perform a little bit of introspection to make sure you are not doing anything to contribute to or cause behavior or relationship problems in your classroom. Ask yourself the following questions:

1. Am I trying to be a buddy to the children?
2. Do I give clear instructions about what I expect the students to do?
3. Do I show favoritism?
4. Do I provoke the children?
5. Am I too lenient? And then get angry because the children are not acting according to my expectations?
6. Are my expectations too low? too high?
7. Am I so harsh that students could feel that there is no way to please me, so why bother?
8. Am I consistent?
9. Do I treat the students like "babies"? Do I do things for them that they should be doing themselves and then become frustrated because they aren't more mature and responsible?
10. Do I have my tasks organized well enough that I prevent unnecessary distractions or delays?
11. Do I show kindness and respect to *everyone* in the classroom through my words, my actions, and my attitudes?
12. Do I support the teacher? Is it possible that my actions unwittingly undermine the teacher?
13. Are there any actions I can take to be a solution to the problem?
14. If I really do not think there is anything I can do to help this problem within the classroom, is this problem significant enough that I should discuss it with an administrator?

These are tough questions, but if you are honest, they may reveal ways you contribute to classroom problems without even being aware that you are doing so. If you find out that you yourself may be helping a problem along, do what you can to correct your own actions or attitudes. You may want to talk to another paraprofessional or the teacher for some suggestions about what you can do to be a part of the solution. You never know, but if you are willing to acknowledge your part in a problem, the teacher may also be willing to do a self-evaluation. If you can get through these questions and feel that you are not a contributor, that is great. You may then be more able to accept that some things are out of your control.

- Avoid humiliating the pupil if possible.
- Give the students responsibility if they can handle it.
- Do not rush to give absolution.

Brown and Kritsonis stress that an important guideline to remember is to "make every effort to avoid a teacher versus class atmosphere" (1992).

You need to remember that you never win when you are in a power struggle. You won't accomplish anything by entering power struggles with the students or with the teacher.

The recommendation for self-evaluation holds true for paraeducators as well. Self-evaluation does not always show a pretty sight, but can be beneficial for helping you to give your honest best effort, both in school relationships and in classroom management.

There is one other area related to classroom discipline that will require great care. Remember that discipline matters and work relationship problems should be confidential. Do not broadcast offenses. Also, once a matter has been dealt with, move on. Don't hold grudges with the children in your room or with your coworkers.

STRATEGIES FOR MAINTAINING ORDER

Some effective teachers use variety in their methods so that their children are not bored and will stay alert to instructions. If you want to really keep your students on their toes, try singing or rapping directions occasionally. For example, sing the following to the tune of "The William Tell Overture:"

> *Clean up, clean up, clean up the toys*
> *Clean up, clean up, clean up the books*
> *Clean up, clean up, clean up the games*
> *Clean up the room right now!*

Or, sing:

> *If you want to hear a story, a story, a story*
>   *If you want to hear a story,*
>   *Come sit on the rug. (to the tune of "Did You Ever See a*
>   *Lassie?")*

Make up your own raps to suit whatever the situation. The students may think you've lost your mind, but they will not ignore you.

When you do need to get the students' attention, and you would rather not sing or rap, think of things to say other than just "Shhh!" and "Attention" all the time. Some other ways to get children quiet and get their attention include:

- Ringing a bell
- Playing "freeze" when the lights are turned off
- Counting backwards and letting the children know they are to be quiet and still by the time you reach zero, using different beginning numbers sometimes
- Saying a previously discussed secret code word, such as "serendipity"
- Playing a music box
- Writing the names of students on the board as they catch on and become quiet

Children like to use hand or body signals. Plan some signals for frequently used instructions, such as instructions to listen, pass papers, or sit down. Quiet signals may be used for the class as a whole or may be specially arranged with individuals who need reminders about their behavior. A private signal may be a way to help a child learn to control inappropriate behavior without embarrassing the child in any way. Be creative and let the children supply ideas for signals, too. (See Figure 8–1.)

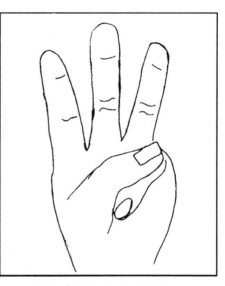

FIGURE 8–1 Quiet Signal.

Many classrooms for younger children have visual warning systems concerning behavior. Just having something that children can see as a reminder may be helpful. The most simple example is writing a child's name on the board after the first offense and putting a check mark by the name after the second. Sometimes a note is sent home after a third goof-up. This idea can be elaborated on and varied to great extents. Your teacher may want to use a system using clothespins or magnets with all the class names. The child's name may be moved from one area to another depending on behavior. For example, you could have the job of cutting out enough laminated construction paper cars for everyone in the class. Then you could attach an adhesive magnet strip to the back of each car and write each child's name on the front. Then you could make a giant construction paper traffic light and laminate that. The children's name cars would be placed around the green section of the light. If a child has to be warned about inappropriate actions, then that child's car would be moved to the yellow light. If a child continued with inappropriate behavior, then the car would be moved to red as an indication to that child to "stop" the undesired activity. If the child persisted at that point, then a previously determined negative consequence, such as time out, should be administered, and the car removed from the traffic light for a time, to indicate that the child needed to switch gears or change directions. Look at Figures 8–2, 8–3, and 8–4 for some other

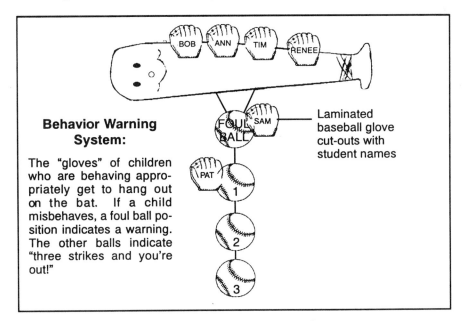

Behavior Warning System:

The "gloves" of children who are behaving appropriately get to hang out on the bat. If a child misbehaves, a foul ball position indicates a warning. The other balls indicate "three strikes and you're out!"

Laminated baseball glove cut-outs with student names

FIGURE 8–2 Behavior Warning System.

Children may color and write their own names on hot air balloons. The balloons may then be laminated and "magnetized."

When children behave appropriately, their balloons float up in the sky. When a child is warned about his behavior, his balloon lands in the trees. When a child is reprimanded, her balloon is "grounded."

FIGURE 8–3 Behavior Warning System.

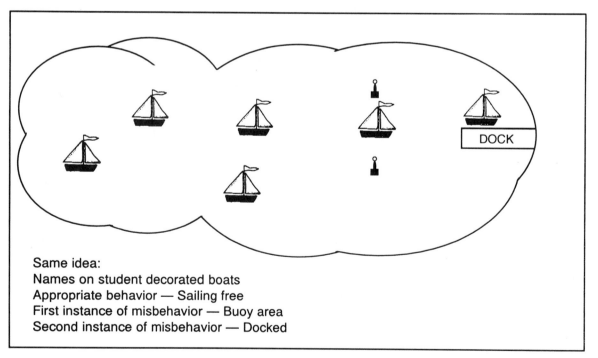

Same idea:
Names on student decorated boats
Appropriate behavior — Sailing free
First instance of misbehavior — Buoy area
Second instance of misbehavior — Docked

FIGURE 8–4 Behavior Warning System.

ideas. Use your imagination; there are lots of possibilities. If you and your teacher want to use this kind of system, you may even want to use a theme that goes along with one of your learning units, such as space ships or pioneer life.

Many schools use a form of behavior management called *assertive discipline* (L. Canter, 1970,1974; L. Davidman and P. Davidman, 1984). While an inappropriate technique for preschools, assertive discipline has been widely used in elementary school settings. Assertive discipline has been shown to work best when an entire school staff is committed to using the technique. It can also be effective with an entire grade level. In assertive discipline teachers and paraeducators must initially establish their classroom rules. This works best when the rules are elicited from the children themselves, set up at the beginning of the school year, and posted prominently in the classroom. Teachers and paraeducators must be consistent in applying the rules; they also need to learn to use "I" messages to indicate their displeasure or pleasure. Statement forms such as "I don't like it when someone interrupts another student, Aisha" and "I like the way you are listening politely to Martin" should be common. With the assertive discipline technique, consequences for misbehavior must be clearly understood and consistently applied. At the first incidence, the teacher (or you) writes the child's initials on the board in a place reserved for assertive discipline markings. At the second misbehavior occurrence, a check mark goes by the child's name, and a specific and reasonable consequence is related to it. This may be having to remain in the room during recess or having to move to an isolated area of the room. After a second check, the consequence may be a phone call to the family or a request for a conference. In the event of a third check, the child may be sent to the office, and the parents may be notified that their child must serve detention the next day or that their child will be kept in in-school suspension.

Some schools have specified places and adult monitors (special teachers or paraeducators, sometimes) for in-school suspension, ISS. Students in ISS are expected to complete the assignments their teachers send with them. Sometimes the ISS is for a designated amount of time, such as half day, one whole day, or two days. In some schools, children may be assigned to ISS until the parent(s) make an appointment for a conference with the teacher and the principal.

The element that is crucial to the success of assertive discipline is following through with predetermined consequences. The students

---

Middle School Merit/Demerit System

Students earn a "gold card" if they go four weeks without getting any demerits. A gold card entitles them to:

    2 locker passes
    2 free CD passes
    2 homework passes

Students may also earn more of these privilege passes with merits.

     7 demerits = loss of activity
     9 demerits = detention
   11 demerits = second detention
   13 demerits = third detention
   15 demerits = in-school suspension

---

have to know that the teachers and other staff members mean what they say; empty threats do not work.

While assertive discipline has been highly successful, it has also been criticized. Canter insists that the "assertive teacher is one who *clearly and firmly communicates needs and requirements to students, follows those words with appropriate actions, responds to students in ways that maximize compliance, but in no way violates the best interests of the students*" (Charles, 1989, p. 106, emphasis in the original).

In one large school a "break miss" system is used across the entire sixth grade. (Look back at Sidebar A on page 255). Students are told clearly what is expected from them, and what is not considered acceptable. All of the teachers give break misses for the same infractions and the system is used from the very beginning of the year through the end.

Peer mediation is a strategy now being used in some schools to involve students in decisions and to encourage problem solving and good communication skills. Volunteer students who have been specially trained in listening and conflict resolution meet with students who are involved in disagreements. Following predetermined guidelines, together they discuss both sides of the controversy and attempt to reach an agreeable conclusion. The hope is that the students themselves will learn to work out relatively minor problems before they grow to larger proportions.

Children can be very cruel, but they can also be very supportive. Be sensitive to the children. By fostering a supportive classroom climate, you will simultaneously encourage children to include insecure, less accepted children. These less confident, less accepted children often tend to be discipline problems as they seek attention. Watch for occasions to encourage interactions with a usually rejected child. If you see some of the more popular children playing with a lonelier child, be sure to carefully and privately commend them by saying something like, "I enjoyed watching you play with Deneisha today. You were very considerate and I am really proud of you." These types of observations help to create a good interactive group and good class support. Your encouragement of good communication and problem-solving skills among the children will go a long way toward encouraging appropriate behavior as well.

Keep notes about what strategies seem to work well with your students. Collect ideas from other paraeducators and teachers. When you observe others effectively managing a group of students, learn from them. Actually write down what you observe so you won't forget it. Use a variety of techniques with your children and don't be afraid to combine approaches. For example, you might want to positively reinforce appropriate behavior with praise or rewards and be selectively inattentive to some inappropriate behavior at the same time (ERIC #E408).

POSITIVE REINFORCEMENT FOR APPROPRIATE BEHAVIOR

Take a genuine interest in working with the children, exhibiting pleasure and enthusiasm as you assist them. This will help stimulate the children's attention and responses. They are quick to pick up on your feelings and attitudes. It is not realistic to expect that you can always be cheerful and brimming with energy; but if you usually are, the children will understand when you have an occasional bad day.

Helping to create a positive environment may take some additional time each day to create a sense of family and community within the group. Children come from different families with great diversity in their abilities to interact and get along with others. They can be guided to see their class as a "family away from home." They work together, play together, eat together, and can benefit from one another through the teacher's leadership, and yours as well. Start early to help them assume responsibility for their actions and to keep their classroom and belongings in order. Give positive responses to cooperation, and acknowledge and encourage considerate behavior while helping them be aware that each is a separate, unique individual. They will not always get along with their siblings and they will not always get along with each other, but you can help guide them to find solutions to their differences.

Unfortunately, too many times teachers and paraeducators accept proper behavior as the norm and fail to acknowledge and reinforce it by making a comment. Take the time to notice and appreciate your students' good actions and attitudes. Do not fall into a pattern of focusing only on negative behaviors. Encourage your students with comments like, "It makes me feel so good to see all of you working so well" and "Isaac, I like the way you waited patiently for your turn at the water fountain." Reinforcement may often keep disruptive behavior from occurring.

When you give positive reinforcing responses and accentuate the positive learning in situations, good feelings are emitted in both you and the children, and the children are encouraged to try again. Remember what we said about positive communications from the adults being more conducive to good behavior. Use positive statements to give instructions in the "do" mode as opposed to the "don't" mode. Instead of saying, "Don't take too long in the bathroom," try, "You have ten minutes for a bathroom break before we board the bus." The first comment suggests you believe they will waste time, while the second comment clearly tells the students that you trust them to do right. Try hard to remember that how you say things is so important, even in the heat of the moment. Asking a child who is using a crayon to write on the wall, "What is wrong with you?" is less effective than, "Stop writing on the wall!"

How you respond to the children's behavior is crucial. Positive reinforcement of behavior is preferable to negative consequences for misbehaviors. Here are a list of some positive reinforcers you may want to use:

- Praise—Use a variety of response statements; these need to be personal and specific.
- Nonverbal approval such as a smile, a pat on the back, or a hug.
- Recognition—"Sarah is sitting quietly."
- Privilege—being a line leader, a messenger, or project captain.
- Earn time to work on a special project or go to a learning center.
- Class party for something done especially well by the class.
- Special movie.
- Free time for game activities.
- Time alone with you or the teacher.
- Lunch with you or the teacher.
- Taking a special item or a classroom pet home overnight or for the weekend.

Dear _____,

We are happy to report that today _____:

____ a good job _____

____ really tried to do better with _____

We are proud and know you will be, too!

_____
Teacher's name/Paraprofessional's name

_____
Date

FIGURE 8–5 Happy-Gram.

- A happy-gram to the parents. (See Figure 8–5)
- A call to the parents by the child, you, or the teacher to relate good news.

Reinforcement must be sincere, not overdone, and given as appropriate. In a workshop at the Georgia Preschool Association's 1990 Conference, educator Tony DiPaolo reminded listeners that you can never encourage enough but you *can* praise too much. Children are pretty savvy; they know when they are being bamboozled. Look for opportunities to compliment children honestly. Do not try to use positive reinforcement unless the behavior warrants it. All children know whether they really deserve a compliment; do not try to fool them.

On the other hand, children respond to sincere praise and encouragement. (Don't we all?) Dobson says that, "Most children and adults are keenly interested in what their associates think and say. As a result, verbal reinforcement can be the strongest motivator of human behavior." He goes on to give examples of the force that negative comments can carry. In your job as a paraeducator, you should never even unconsciously tear down children with your words but should always encourage them to be the best that they can be. You might even want to collect

To survive as an adult in this society, one needs to know how to work, how to get there on time, how to get along with others, how to stay with a task until completed, and yes, how to submit to authority. In short, it takes a good measure of self-discipline and control to cope with the demands of modern living. Maybe one of the greatest gifts a loving teacher [or paraprofessional] can contribute to an immature child, therefore, is to help him learn to sit when he feels like running, to raise his hand when he feels like talking, to be polite to his neighbor, to stand in line without smacking the kid in front, and to do language arts when he feels like doing football.

James Dobson, *The New Dare to Discipline*, 1992

new and different ways to send the message, "I'm proud of you; you did a good job."

You, as a paraeducator, will have a lot of influence on the behavior in your classroom. Remember to communicate well and as often as necessary with the teacher about your role in classroom discipline. Be supportive of the teacher's efforts to promote responsibility and appropriate behavior choices in the children. Remember to keep your sense of humor and treat even and especially unruly children like you would want to be treated yourself.

CHAPTER 9 Classroom Organization

The best classrooms are well organized. While you may know a creative teacher who has not seen the top of her desk since the beginning of the school year, and who does not pay much attention to classroom organization, for most, getting organized is a huge component of successful teaching and will pay big dividends. You, as a paraeducator, can be a key to effective organization.

THE PHYSICAL ROOM ORGANIZATION

Back in Chapter 3, there was a discussion of a few classroom organization ideas for you to consider in your first days as a paraeducator. Refer back to those and consider these new ideas, too.

Room arrangement is an important factor in determining the organizational flow of the days of school. However, you may not have much input on how the room is arranged at first. If this is the case, don't despair. As with so many aspects of your job as a paraeducator, your input into room arrangement will most likely increase as rapport is built between you and the lead teacher. Just work on the factors you are given freedom to work on. Then when you do a good job, you will probably be given more and more freedom. Continue to ask questions and go visit other classrooms to learn firsthand how others organize their rooms and materials.

A good beginning point in periodic evaluations is to look around for anything that seems to detract from the room's appearance. Generally, if there is an overflow of "stuff" in the room, much of it will be fairly inaccessible. Classrooms of bonafide packrats who keep everything stored on sagging shelves, in bulging cupboards, and in brimming boxes all over the room, will be less attractive to the children and others, will have less space for the "important stuff, " and will have many unnecessary and unwanted materials. Too much time will be wasted in finding what you need. Work toward an uncluttered environment. It will be easier for you to efficiently make use of the right materials and create a more pleasant classroom environment for the children. If you and the teacher want your students to develop strong work study skills and good school housekeeping habits, then it begins with you.

Storage

If you do indeed need to store less frequently used materials in boxes, try to find boxes of fairly uniform size and shape. You might even want to cover the visible ends with colored adhesive paper. You and the teacher might want to try this idea: label each box carefully, with a brief description and large letter or number. Inside the top of the box tape a list of everything in that box. Make a duplicate of this list to store in a file box at your desk; each list must include the box identification letter or number. Then when you need something from one of the boxes, you can look at the lists from your file box to determine which box to go to instead of following the "I know it's here somewhere" routine.

Some classrooms exhibit quite a bit of creativity. One teacher put up colorful curtains to hide stacks of "stuff" above the cabinets. In another room there is a lot of varied paraphernalia underneath the open sink counter. It would look really sloppy if you could see it, but you can't, because it is hidden by a different kind of curtain. You may be able to help the teacher come up with all kinds of ideas for your classroom.

Classroom Filing Systems

As mentioned in other chapters, begin your own file. You will have to make a decision about whether to keep your own file separate from the one in the classroom. Accumulate ideas as well as materials. Take pictures of great bulletin boards, jot down sketches of good art projects, collect patterns, poems, and anything else that warrants saving.

If you and the teacher subscribe to any teacher or educational resource publications, you need to figure out what to do with them after you read through them once. You will probably want to read or glance through them while they are current or at least as soon as possible. You may see lots of ideas that you want to go ahead and use and some that you know you'll want to use in years to come. So do you save the whole thing? You might find it helpful in the long run to cut out only what you want to save and file these items immediately. Right now you think you will definitely remember THIS idea next year, but that charming poem on Thanksgiving pilgrims will elude you next year unless it is already in your November file. You will not use all you save, but you can add or discard. Be selective. The benefits from this kind of system are that you eliminate a messy stack of saved magazines from cluttering up your room and you save some valuable time later down the road.

Materials: On Hand and At Hand

Take an occasional inventory of your materials supply. Review the list of materials in Chapter 3, and refurbish important items such as pencils, highlighters, "sticky" notes, and folders as needed. Don't sacrifice maximum efficiency by not being organized enough to obtain or request the items that will most help you. Keep a running list of anything you need so that you will be ready to requisition appropriate supplies when you have the opportunity.

As mentioned in Chapter 3, whenever possible, make sure that things you use frequently are accessible for quick use. When you consider your everyday actions, think about logical placements for things such as staplers and teacher desks. Do you and the teacher really need to have your desks on the same side of the room? Do the two of you share ideas and duties constantly so you need to have your work bases pretty close together? Or do you have fairly set independent tasks? Would it make more sense now that you have learned more of the routine for your desk to be closest to the door and the teacher's desk to be placed toward the back? What do the children do and where do they go when they first come in to the room? Do they check in with you or do they go straight to their desks or to a rug area? The answers to these questions will influence something so basic as desk placement. Instead of keeping two staplers on two desks, you and the teacher may realize it makes more sense to put one on your desk because you deal with more of the clerical duties and another at the table where the teacher conducts reading groups because she likes to staple each student's worksheets together after she goes over them with the students.

Keep materials where they are to be used. A rolling cart or a large dish pan may be used to keep reading workbooks near the reading circle where they will be used, and will keep them from cluttering up the reading table or your desk. Think through your day, think of the materials you use, and place those materials where they will be as accessible as possible to you at the very time you'll use them.

In summary, as you continue to help with classroom organization:

1. You will again need to evaluate and gather tools to help you to do your job in the most efficient manner possible.

2. You should also reevaluate the existing filing system and possibly set up a new one for the classroom.

3. You should also continually evaluate placement of materials and structures used in the classroom to make sure that things are arranged in such a way that they maximize time and minimize effort.

PAPERWORK

The paperwork in a classroom is never ending. There are daily and other forms to fill out, evaluations to write, and papers to correct. Report cards, progress reports, cumulative files, and the students' permanent records must be completed. If you work with infants and toddlers, you will keep track of schedules, feeding, and toileting reports. In special education, there are IEPs to keep current.

The mountain of paperwork can be overwhelming! In fact, recently a Chicago principal said that the teachers in his school indicated their second biggest problem behind discipline was coping with all the paperwork. This remark was given support by a National Education Association (NEA) survey in 1985, in which 92 percent of the teachers reported they loved to teach, but spent too much time on paperwork and administrative tasks. One of the most important jobs you will be called on to do is assume some of this clerical responsibility from the teacher, subsequently freeing the teacher to instruct more effectively. The paperwork burden is significant, and you both need to find ways to lighten the load as much as possible.

The best motto in dealing with paperwork is to try your best to deal with a paper only once. The *fastest* way to get paperwork done is to complete it immediately when you first get it or learn about it. Do not bury the paper and think you will get to it later.

Do your paperwork correctly the *first* time. Follow all the directions to ensure that you do not have to do it all over again. If you do not understand exactly what to do, go ahead and ask for explanations so that you can record the information correctly. When you make it a practice to complete paperwork promptly, you free yourself and the teacher from having to think about it any more. Turn in your completed forms to the right person and then they won't get lost in anybody's shuffle. Then your paperwork task is done and you won't end up misplacing papers and wasting time finding new ones.

Do not let paperwork build up and become overwhelming, because it certainly will if you allow it to. Paperwork is kind of like laundry and kudzu. It grows and grows. Kudzu is a nuisance plant that grows in Georgia, and seems to overtake whole forests in the space of one summer night. There are lots of tales about the resiliency and persistence of kudzu. You can't kill the stuff. That's what paperwork is like. You can't get rid of it, so you might as well learn to deal with it quickly rather than thinking you can ignore it and it will go away, only to find that it has overrun its bounds and smothered everything else.

Forms not turned into the office can generate even more paperwork, such as notices and nasty-grams that state: "Your student of the month form was due last Thursday. Please get it in ASAP;" "Physical fitness reports were due last Friday. Turn yours in today!" You don't want to look at this kind of communication, and the office staff or principal does not especially like to send this kind of message. However, neither does the office staff nor principal appreciate it when you do not get items in on time. Remember that a large part of your job may be to free the teacher from clerical duties so that more time can be spent on actual teaching. You need to strive for efficiency in this component of your job, even if it is your least favorite part of your job. Try to take time, to complete forms on the very day you receive them. Maybe Thomas Henry Huxley had a vision of twentieth century paperwork when he wrote the following words:

> *Perhaps the most valuable result of all education is the ability to make yourself do the thing you have to do, when it ought to be done, whether you like it or not; it is the first lesson that ought to be learned; and however early a man's training begins, it is probably the last lesson that he learns thoroughly."*
>
> Thomas Henry Huxley, 1825–1895
> *Technical Education* (1877)

Occasionally, it is truly not possible to do the paperwork immediately. There also is paperwork that presents itself and must be dealt with on a periodic basis. In these cases, you need to move from the fastest way to the *surest* way to get paperwork done. Schedule it on your calendar or directly into your lesson book, whichever you are sure to use. Use bright colors of ink to write or flag reminders to yourself. You will be looking at your calendar or plan book every day anyway; now, you will see reminders for anything you need to do. Put a check after your reminder once you do the task. Then it is finished and off your mind.

If you or anyone else needs to verify later that it was done, you can go back to your mark to reassure yourself that, yes, you did do that. Your days will be busy and filled with all sorts of details; it will really help you to develop and use a system that reminds you of easily forgotten tasks and keeps you organized. Scheduling paperwork tasks on your calendar or in your plan book will help prevent you from feeling overburdened, will allow you to get everything done, not forget anything, and have your paperwork done on time, too.

Another method for dealing with paperwork is to use the method mentioned in Chapter 3. Sort everything that comes across your desk into three stacks as follows:

1. Stat!!! (Check this stack over several times during the day to make sure you keep current.)

2. Hanging over your head—stuff you have to tend to but not necessarily this minute. Check this stack at least once every day.

3. Lower priority—probably the biggest stack. Check this stack once per week.

Student papers that need to be graded, recorded, and returned are a big part of the paperwork load in a classroom. You and the teacher will have to work out a system for checking the children's papers. The teacher may want and need your constant help in this area. You will have to know how much responsibility the teacher wants you to take for student papers. It will be important for papers to be checked as quickly as possible, especially for the very youngest students, because the feedback has to be immediate for early ages or they won't remember what they did originally and associate corrections properly. All students need prompt feedback so that they can see how they are doing. It is also important for the teacher to see what, if any, reteaching needs to be done. It is important for you, too, to see how you can best help with reviews and reinforcement.

The teacher may want you to grade papers, then leave them for her to glance over and record in the gradebook. You may also develop a classroom system where the students put their papers in colored folders in a basket. The folders could be different colors for different subjects. Maybe you would be responsible for grading certain subject papers and the teacher would be responsible for grading the rest, or you both could share the responsibility and whoever gets to them first, grades however many as possible. If you work in kindergarten, the teacher may have you check over all the morning work while she is involved with reading groups. In some kindergarten classrooms, the children take their completed papers to the paraeducator, who goes over the work with them before they are allowed to move on to "centers." If there is any cause for concern over a child's work, then the paraeducator saves the papers for the teacher to examine. With this method, the children are given immediate feedback and papers are not allowed to stack up.

A huge stack of uncorrected papers can be overwhelming. Depending on the grade level and competency of the students, the teacher may have them self-correct a good bit of the work. In such a case, you may be asked to monitor the children as they correct their own papers, so that you can encourage honesty and also help pick up on comprehension problems. Sometimes a teacher will have older students help correct papers, or at least separate, stack, and staple sets of papers to be returned. If a lot of the paper-grading responsibilities fall on you, utilize the help of older students if it is alright with the teacher. Even if your students are too young to help, often older students are delighted to offer their services during off times such as bus duty or in the afterschool program. If student helpers are an option for you and your teacher, then you may be the one to coordinate the efforts.

There may be time slots during the day when you can help grade papers without taking any time away from the children. Think ahead for times when you may be sitting either with your class or waiting for the class. For example, if your class is settled in front of the stage and you are waiting for other classes to file in before an assembly begins, you may be able to get through quite a few papers and still keep an eye on your little preciouses; or when your class is in the media center and you are required to stay with them but you are just sitting because the media center paraeducator has all of your students enthralled with storytime. Times such as these may be good opportunities for you to help with the paper press. Instead of being frustrated over waiting, you can think of all the paperwork you accomplished and feel satisfied that you did something productive.

Follow this system and you will be more likely to keep a handle on paperwork:

1. Complete paperwork correctly and thoroughly, and return it to the right person immediately.

2. Use "waiting time" to correct papers and complete forms.

3. Enlist student help.

4. Use bright-colored pens to write reminders of what is due and when it is due directly in plan book. Check off the item when it is completed.

You may be tempted to take paperwork home with you, but think twice before you do that. First of all, paraeducators (and teachers) may not be allowed to take the most important papers home with them. Some records, for example, are not permitted to leave the school building. Also, you might consider whether your salary as a paraeducator warrants you getting into a pattern of taking work home with you. Of course, that decision is very personal. You need to remember, though, that if you ever do donate your time away from school, then it will be easier for others to expect you to continue to do so.

Color-coding may be used in several ways to simplify your life. Different color folders, files, markers, and highlighters may be used to give you information at a glance. For example, you may house emergency information in a red folder in a stand-up file on your desk. If you need a parent number in a hurry, you will know to just grab that red folder. Not having to look through stacks, or even go through files in the file cabinet, may save you some valuable time. Another idea is to use different colored highlighters in your attendance record book. For example, you could mark the record slot of all the children who will be staying in the after-school program (ASP) that day with a specified color. That way at the end of the day when you are tired and the children are confused you can check quickly how many children from your classroom are supposed to go to ASP. You may also want to color-code student files by placing a red circle or sticker on files of students with medical problems or special instructions from the parents. You can be reminded at a glance that Rebecca needs to wear her glasses every day or that Osama's file includes a letter requesting no corporal punishment. After you make copies of morning work activity sheets, you and the teacher might want to go ahead and arrange the work for the days of the week. You could have a different colored file for each day of the week. The uses of color-coding are limited only by your imagination. If you adapt color coding ideas to your particular classroom organizational needs, you will find that color-coding can help considerably in bringing order to busy days.

RECORDS

Daily Counts and Records

You might be required to keep both a roll book and attendance records every day. Your roll book is probably more for you, supplying you with a record of all sorts of information that may need to be checked later in the day or even three weeks or months from now. The attendance record is generally a sheet with absences and tardiness noted on a chart of student names. The attendance record will most likely have to be turned in to the office each morning by a certain time. A secretary may then compile all the attendance record information into a school record of total number present and the total number of students who are absent.

Sometimes you might wonder why these records are so necessary, and why getting that piece of paper turned into the office has to be a priority in your day. Well, you need to remember that state and federal monies are tied to numbers. The numbers on those attendance records ultimately have a bearing on funds for supplies and for salaries, yours included. Also, there are times when attendance information is used in making important decisions, including legal ones, for students (Maggs, 1980).

Whether you are required to keep a roll book or not, it is a good idea to keep your own records in the classroom, rather than only turning in what is required by the administration. If there is ever a question about what you have turned in, you need to be able to show something that will back you up. So keep a roll book; you can use it to record lots of information besides just attendance.

Even though you may never have to turn in your roll book, be accurate and neat! You may never have to show your roll book to any one other than the teacher and ones who substitute for you, but you need to be prepared for the possibility that you do. Your roll book could even be subpoenaed by a court in the case of a student getting into trouble or being the subject of a custody battle. You never know when you might be called upon to provide information about one of your students and will have to lay your whole record-keeping system out for other eyes.

Look at Tables 9–1A and B for an idea of how two kindergarten paraeducators record information in their roll books. They have each developed systems that work for them. Your needs may be different, you will need to record other types of information, so you will work out your own system. Have fun! Make your records work for you instead of you having to work endlessly on your records.

Lunch Count. Besides attendance, another count you may have to do every day is the lunch count. If your school has a cafeteria or food brought in, then you must count the students who brought their lunches from home and the ones who are buying lunch through the school. Of course, the lunchroom workers appreciate this information as fast as you can possibly get it to them! They have to know how many

TABLE 9–1A Lunch Lists.

Teacher's Name _____ Date: _____

Child's Name	M	T	W	T	F
Amaker, Ahmad	Pd $5 J	Pd	Pd J	Pd	Pd
Benater, Antonio	Pd $1	B	B	A	Pd $1 IC
Cooper, Ted	c/o Pd $4	Pd	Pd	Pd J	Pd
Dhahis, El	B J	B J	B J	B J	B J IC
Eidson, Kym	B	B	B	B	B

Key:
Pd $5	— paid for week	ink color 1
Pd $1	— paid daily	ink color 1
B — brought lunch		ink color 1
F — free lunch		ink color 1
J — juice		ink color 2
IC — ice cream		ink color 3
A — absent		ink color 4
c/o —	carry over from	
	previous week	ink color 1

Outline box with a specified highlighter to indicate ASP attendance

TABLE 9–1B Lunch Lists. Courtesy of Bobbie McCord.

Mr. Passanante's Lunch List

Name	Monday				Tuesday				Wednesday				Thursday				Friday			
	L	M	S	I	L	M	S	I	L	M	S	I	L	M	S	I	L	M	S	I
Aja	T	✓	✓	✓																
Annay																				
Blake																				
Bonnie																				
Christine																				

Key: L — Lunch
        M — Milk
        S — Slushie
        I — Ice Cream
T for Ticket or D for Daily
   under L for Lunch

children to prepare for. Years ago, the lunch count was not so complicated as it is now. You simply distinguished between those who brought
from home and those who bought from the cafeteria. Now, you may
need to give other information as well. Many schools provide menu
choices. For example, students may be allowed to select a salad lunch
or a hot lunch. Sometimes there are even multiple hot lunch options.
The students, then, have to be informed of their choices for the day,
must make a decision, and then tell or record their decision. You, the
paraeducator, will probably have the job of making sure this information makes it to the lunchroom ladies. You might have to send a count
such as the one in Figure 9–1.

In early grades, this may take a while. One kindergarten
paraeducator, Holly, has the children line up at her desk immediately
as they come into the classroom from bus duty. She states the choices
for the day repeatedly because the kindergarteners tend to forget. Holly
greets the students one by one as they reach the front of the line, and
she elicits whatever information she needs from them for the day. If
there are any notes or any money envelopes from home, they dig them
out of backpacks at this time. This paraeducator then finds out the following information from each child:

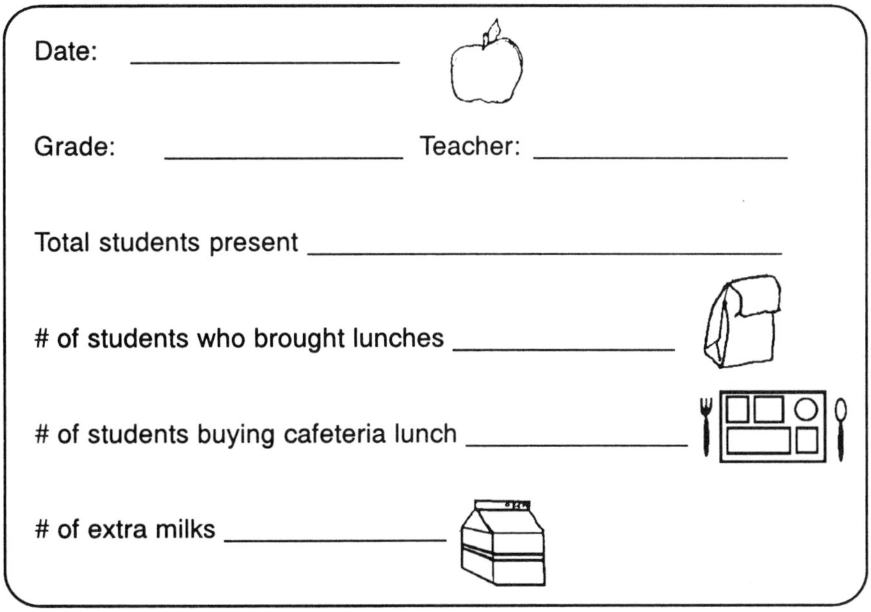

Date: _____   🍎
Grade: _____   Teacher: _____
Total students present _____
# of students who brought lunches _____
# of students buying cafeteria lunch _____
# of extra milks _____

FIGURE 9–1 Lunch Count.

- whether the child is buying a school lunch or not
- the child's choice of the school lunch options
- whether the child is going home or staying in ASP
- whether the child is deviating from his usual transportation routine to ride the bus or go in car pool
- whether the child is buying juice or ice cream

The children (and parents) know that Holly expects them to make up their minds during this time, and they have to stick with their choices. They also know that money from home must be in a labelled envelope. Having learned from experience, Holly wants to avoid the confusion of issues such as whether the money in the bottom of the backpack is for lunches for the whole week or for a book from the bookfair. Holly's method works for her and the teacher with whom she works. Holly finds out whatever she needs to know from the children at one shot and then the teacher knows all the morning business is being taken care of and the children are free to move on to group learning activities with her. Once she has spoken to all the children, Holly finishes the attendance report, completes the lunch count, makes notes to herself about changes from routine occurrences, and leaves the classroom to turn in various forms and do necessary errands, such as make a few copies, sign up for the VCR or computer lab, and check on requisitioned supplies. Later, before lunch, Holly reads down the list, and the children line up in groups according to which lunch option they chose. She also takes her list with her when she takes the class to the cafeteria because her students are prone to forget what they said they wanted and argue about it in the line. Since rapid movement through the lunch lines is a priority in this large school, having the list with her is beneficial because referring to it stops line-bogging discussions quickly.

At the other end of the grade range in this elementary school, a sixth grade teacher does not directly ask the students about lunch choices. Each student is expected to sign in on a chart placed on a table by the teacher's desk. Just by signing in they signify their presence, and they mark a "B," an "S," or a "1" or a "2" by their names, to indicate whether they brought their lunches, want the salad lunch, or want the first or second hot lunch option (Table 9–2). Students are expected to remember and stick with their choices.

As the paraeducator, you may develop your own system that works for you and the teacher. Whether the bulk of the responsibility is on you

TABLE 9–2 Lunch Sign-in Chart.

Name	3/20	3/21	3/22	3/23	3/24	3/27	3/28	3/29	3/30	4/1	4/2
Braves, A.	1	B	2	B	B	1	A				
Carry, B.	2	1	1	1	B	2	1				
Carr, J.	A	A	1	1	1	1	1				
Lake, O.	B	2	2	B	B	B	B				
KEY											
1 = The first Choice on menu B = Brought Lunch											
2 = Second choice on menu A = Absent											

or the students, though, you need a system that makes sense and takes up as little teaching time as possible.

Records Not Done on a Daily Basis

Progress reports, report cards, and permanent records are ones that you will complete periodically, but you will not deal with these on a daily basis. Primarily your work on progress reports and report cards will be to fill them out, but not to make decisions about the grades that go on them (Figure 9–2). You may be asked to write out the basic information such as name, grade, subjects, and days absent. The area for which you are most likely to be asked for input is conduct. You will be as much an authority on the conduct of your students as the teacher.

Many schools do a monthly computerized attendance report. The secretary may send you the information pertaining to your class and ask you to verify it before it is counted as official. This is where you will need to look back at your daily records to check for any discrepancies.

Your students' permanent records are the ones that will go with their cumulative files. Oftentimes these are not even thought about until the very end of the school year and then there's scurrying to complete them for the office. You could be a big help to the teacher if you think about the permanent records earlier in the year. If your students have hearing and vision screening tests, these results may be entered on the permanent records as soon as you get them. Other test results may be

3/07/96

GRADE REPORT

Student Number:

Name:

COUNTY SCHOOLS

School:
Year: **95–96**   Grade **08**
Homeroom:
Page: **1**

Course Number	Description	Teacher	Per.	First 8 Weeks Grade	Con	Second 8 Weeks Grade	Con	Third 8 Weeks Grade	Con	Semester 1 Average	Fourth 8 Weeks Grade	Con.	Fifth 8 Weeks Grade	Con.	Sixth 8 Weeks Grade	Con.	Semester 2 Average	Final Average
8502 01	Science 8C		1	99	S	93	S	90	S	94	90	S						
6104 02	AIM Lit.		2	70	S	83	S	92	S	82	88	S						
0820 03	Gen. Music I		3	94	S													
0900 03	Home Econo I		3			98	S											
0980 03	Careers I		3					96	S									
0960 30	Computer Tech I A Joy to Have in Class		3								97	S						
0700 22	P.E./Health A Joy to Have in Class		4	86	S	93	S	92	S	90	95	S						
8602 05	Soc. Studies 8C		5	97	S	94	S	92	S	94	100	S						
8302 20	Language Arts 8C		6	92	S	96	S	89	S	92	91	S						
7433 07	Pre-Algebra 8B		7	94	S	86	S	85	S	88	97	S						

HOMEROOM ATTENDANCE: PRESENT/ABSENT 116/1

Comments:

Exploratory Average: 96
NEXT TO COURSE INDICATES PARENT CONFERENCE REQUESTED

Explanation of Grades
A+ = 98–100 A = 93–97 A– = 90–92 B+ = 87–89 B = 83–86 B– = 80–82 C+ = 77–79 C = 73–76 C– = 70–72 F = Below 70 (Not passing)
CONDUCT: S = SATISFACTORY U = UNSATISFACTORY N = NEEDS IMPROVEMENT

FIGURE 9–2 You may have the honor of filling out report cards.

recorded, too. Margaret Maggs, in her book, *The Classroom Survival Book,* suggests that you update permanent records around February, by verifying addresses and telephone numbers and entering any test results to that point (1980).

Remember to use the specified color of ink if your school system or principal has a preference, especially on the permanent records. Remember, also, that there may be strict rules about where report cards and permanent records may be taken in the school building. You may not be allowed to take permanent records out on the playground with you, even to fill out the basic information such as names and addresses while you are watching the children play kickball. The information on report cards and permanent records is confidential, and many schools have guidelines about where they may be taken so as to prevent even accidental breaches of confidentiality, damage to, or destruction of these records.

You may want to keep a special kind of record for your students to take home at the end of the year. Keep samples of their work throughout the year and assemble booklets. A kindergarten teacher and her paraeducator do this for their students every year. They call these collections *Me Booklets* and include such entries as:

- Photograph of the child taken at the beginning of the year
- Height and weight measurements from the beginning and the end of the year
- Work samples
- Checklists such as the one in Table 9–3
- Copies of report cards
- Pictures and narratives related by the child after field trips
- Lists of words the child is able to read at different points during the year
- End of the year assessment of the child's strengths and weaknesses

This teaching team uses colored folders with brads for the *Me Booklets*. The front is decorated with white-painted handprints and a cute (and sentimental) poem (Figure 9–3). The entries are ordered chronologically. It takes ongoing but occasional effort and attention to put these together. Believe me, parents find them to be a treasure and are most appreciative (Wofford and Hogan, Johnston Elementary School, Woodstock, GA).

Another type of record you need to keep is a log of any problems or incidents with students. An index card file box has already been suggested for this. Maggs recommends using a loose leaf notebook with a

Table 9–3 Progress Check Sheet

CHECK-UP

Identifies shapes

_____ ◯   _____ ▭   _____ ▢
_____ △   _____ ⬭   _____ ◇

Identifies colors

_____ pink   _____ white   _____ purple

_____ yellow   _____ orange   _____ red

_____ blue   _____ green

_____ brown   _____ black

_____ knows phone number

_____ knows birthdate

_____ knows address

page for each student. ("The Classroom Survival Book," 1980) Whenever you are most directly involved with an unusual or controversial occurrence, you need to document what happened from your perspective. Just a simple jotting of facts, such as date, place, people involved, will do. Also, if there is a persistent behavior pattern with a student, you should record occurrences. Be sure to give specifics when you write incident entries. Write: Marshall said loudly, "I don't have to do anything you say. You're a jerk." This tells a lot more than if you were to write: Marshall was disrespectful.

Probably the most awful but necessary reason for documenting information is if child abuse is suspected. If you have any reason for thinking that one of your students might be abused, then you must notify the proper authority, and you should begin to record your observations about that child. It is very important that you keep an account

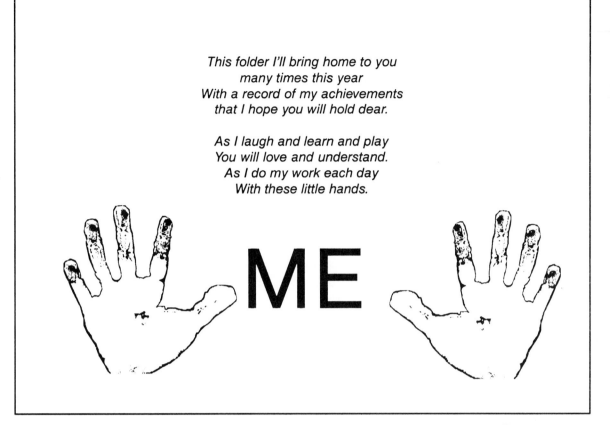

This folder I'll bring home to you
many times this year
With a record of my achievements
that I hope you will hold dear.

As I laugh and learn and play
You will love and understand.
As I do my work each day
With these little hands.

FIGURE 9–3 Cover of "Me Book"   Courtesy of Jo Hogan and Mary Wofford

of what you see in case your testimony is required in court or by the Department of Family and Children Services (DEFACS). Your number one concern should be the welfare of all the children in your class, and if you can promote any child's safety by relating what you see and hear, then you are obligated to be diligent in accurately recording your observations. This information should be kept confidential, of course.

If your facility has regular staff meetings, either take notes and save them or hold on to notes that are distributed after the meeting. It's a good idea to keep old staff meeting notes on file for a while, because nobody can remember all the details a few months later. You might be able to remember only part of the information: "Oh, yes, the principal did say something about afternoon car pool duty while the road is being widened but I don't remember what she wanted us to do." In such a case, you can easily check your file and know for sure what the principal said.

As has been mentioned already, some paraeducators may be very involved in making lesson plans, and others may not have much responsibility in this area. No matter what your extent of "free reign," there will be activities or art projects over which you have some input. Keep plans for these on file, along with a quick evaluation of the activity or project, and recommendations for changes or adaptations in the future.

TIME MANAGEMENT

Time management is more difficult and broader than organizing the classroom and materials, although if you do preliminary organization work, it will certainly help you manage time better. A classroom teacher must be fully prepared before the students' day begins to utilize time to the fullest extent. So much of a paraeducator's job involves helping the teacher with preparation. Therefore, a paraeducator becomes essential to effective time management.

It is easy to become overwhelmed with too little time to do too many tasks. One contributing factor to feeling powerless over time is having no definite goals. Without definite plans, it is hard to stay on the right road. The key to best helping the teacher with time management is understanding and effectively working toward goals. So, one of the first steps in managing your time is to identify your classroom goals. Write them down and put them somewhere where you will see them often.

Second, make appropriate decisions with classroom goals in mind. An educator tells about one of her major goals. The goal was to improve the lives of the seriously mentally ill. When asked to serve on the state Board of the Alliance for the Mentally Ill, the response was a quick *yes* because it had direct bearing on her goal. It was a time-consuming commitment, but because she set priorities, the time was available. If you know what the goals are, then you are more likely to make time for high priority tasks. There are lots of good possibilities that may come up, but if they do not concur with the identified goals, then maybe they are not the best possibilities.

Third, take a step in the direction of your goal, no matter how small. Divide a big goal into smaller objectives; begin with small steps. Take for example, learning to fly. Some preliminary steps would be to visit a pilot's lounge and talk with other pilots, check out books and videos on learning to fly, join the Civil Air Patrol, and fly as an observer with a pilot. Fill out a questionnaire or make a call. Take a first step, even if it's a small one, toward meeting your goal today. Especially if your goal seems formidable, it is easier to set out on the journey lap by lap rather than looking ahead at all the miles you have to go.

Once you understand the teacher's and classroom goals and priorities, you can plan your calendar. Take a few minutes to evaluate how what you do goes along with these goals and priorities. Start by planning next week's calendar. Allow a column for each day of the week. Schedule all of your responsibilities and activities. Add other things from the teacher's "to do" list when you find an open block of time. Then take a red pencil and star every activity that is goal related. You might be surprised at what you find out from this activity. Many times we find out that most of our days are not spent on goal-related or high priority activities. Also, you may find that your schedule is so full that there's no room for anything else! Now is the time to fix this. Look at your activities and decide which ones are least important and relevant to the classroom goals. Try to limit your involvement in these. You cannot protect your priorities unless you learn to decline requests that do not help you achieve your goals. Other people and circumstances will determine your priorities if you do not protect your own.

All of this discussion about time management and priorities may seem reasonable, but on a day-to-day basis, it may be difficult to put into practice. For example, one goal that you and the teacher share is to provide a stimulating learning environment for the children. As one of your steps toward meeting this goal, you change the back bulletin board every month to go along with the social studies unit. Your bulletin board on community helpers is scheduled to go up tomorrow, which is a good thing because the PTA open house is tomorrow night. The teacher wanted you to purposely delay putting up the new one until now because she wants it to be a surprise for the parent volunteers since they are going to be shown on the new bulletin board. You've already taken the old bulletin board down. Everything is traced out—letters and objects and crazy characters—but there is still some cutting to do. You figure you can do the rest of the cutting out while the students do their morning work, after you do all your paperwork and get all the reports and counts in. But the next morning one of your little ones blubbers over her seatwork. It seems she just can't get the concept that pennies and nickels have less value than dimes. Another classroom goal is to place high value on each child's self esteem. The teacher is trying to conduct reading groups. Your first thought is, oh well, you'll just have to stay for a while after school if you have to in order to get that bulletin board up, but then you remember that you have a long-standing dentist appointment this afternoon. Maybe you can see that it's not always easy to decide priorities or to act on them even when you know what the right choice is.

A factor to consider regarding time management is whether you have a tendency to be a perfectionist. Do you put too much pressure on yourself, operating by the admonition, "Do it right or don't do it at all?" There are areas where you may need to let go a little bit. Do not compromise your standards but look at some alternatives. Two examples are the marks you put at the top of student's papers and responses to the homes. It may be the desire of your heart to draw a cute smiley face and write a personal message on each paper. You may think that for your notes home to look professional that you need to type them. In actuality you will find that you need to use a stamp, a sticker, or develop a fast grading mark and save the personal written messages like "This is so much better, Tommy; I am proud of you" for occasional use. The classic check mark indicates that you've checked work and found it acceptable. You may also find that it is fine to write a quick response on the bottom of the note sent to you from home rather than starting a completely new note. You may find that handwritten newsletters are okay, too. As with everything else about your job, you will have to find your own system. Just be sure that you don't waste time on things that may not make a difference until the times when they will definitely make a difference or you have the time to waste.

Time management skills are not established overnight. They need to be considered on a continuing basis. There may be times in your day when things seem to get out of control timewise. Take a hard look at those moments during the schoolday when the action seems to get bogged down, and ask questions like:

- "Why does everything slow down during this time?"

- "What is the priority here and how can I get this done faster?"

- "Is something that I am doing causing unnecessary delays?"

- "Are we trying to squeeze too much into this time? What is most important and what can we eliminate or postpone?"

Sometimes good time management is simply a matter of taking the time to stop, step back, and evaluate the efficiency of your actions and procedures. Don't get so caught up in your hustle and bustle that you keep on doing ineffective actions just because you're too busy to slow down and think. That's probably exactly when you need to slow down and think things through the most.

Hopefully these ideas should give you a foundation upon which you can continue to develop or improve your own time management skills. There are many books on time management in most libraries. While many are written for corporations they may include some ideas you may adapt for your work.

Schedules for your students may give some special challenges. If you work in a regular education classroom it is likely that you will have some children who leave the room for special services. You and the teacher will need to help the children remember when it is time to go to speech, to English as a Second Language (ESOL), to physical therapy, or another session. If the child does not leave for a special service at the same time every day, or even if he does, it may be easy for you to forget to send him or take him. Write out the schedule and highlight information pertaining to special schedules. It may be helpful to set a timer. For example, every Wednesday right after lunch you may remember that Stephanie is supposed to go meet with the guidance counselor at 12:30, but it escapes your mind forty-five minutes later when that time actually comes. The teacher does not remember either because that is right in the middle of a health lesson. Next time when you come back from lunch, set a timer to go off at Stephanie's appointed time so you'll be sure to send her off promptly.

If you work in special education, you will understand varied schedules already. The practice of inclusion means that many children who spend the majority of the schoolday in special education classes are likely to spend at least part of the day being mainstreamed. If you work in a special education classroom, you probably see kids going and coming all day long. It may get pretty crazy trying to figure out who is supposed to be where when. Use whatever tools you need. One special education teacher keeps huge posters of her students' schedules with times and places color-coded for different children so that she and her paraeducators can quickly look up to see what they are supposed to be doing (See Figure 9-4).

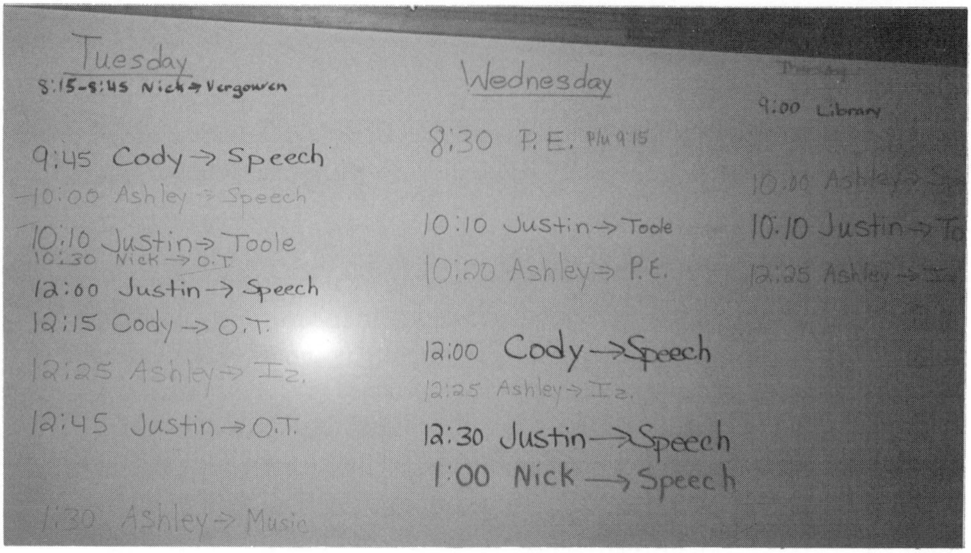

FIGURE 9–4 Color-coded schedule in special education classroom.

CLASSROOM PROCEDURES

Daily Procedures

By now you have probably heard the terms *make effective use of your time, get organized,* and *develop a plan* often enough to understand that the people saying these things feel that the sooner you follow these admonitions, the better off you will be. Think about a typical beginning to a Monday in a classroom. The bell rings and the day is about to begin. You have three administrative tasks that must be handled immediately: take attendance, take the lunch count information and collect lunch money, and find out who will be staying in ASP this week. Meanwhile, the teacher oversees the Pledge of Allegiance and encourages the children to listen to the fuzzy announcements coming through the public address system. On this particular day Mary has brought twenty-five cupcakes for a birthday treat later in the day; Joey and Cham have been fighting since they met up in bus duty and the bus duty monitor wants a word with either you or the teacher before she hurries to her own class; and you notice that Stevie, who has a rough home life and very low self-esteem, looks even more unhappy than usual.

Even with two of you, you and the teacher keenly feel the conflict between nurturing and administrative demands. One of you needs to speak with the bus duty monitor so that she can be on her way. You both feel a pull to set an upbeat tone for the day by wishing Mary "happy birthday" and getting out the birthday hat and a birthday ribbon. Someone needs to get to the bottom of the fight between Joey and Cham, and find time to give Stevie a special smile, hug, or friendly listening ear. On the other hand, you dare not risk the displeasure of the secretary and the cafeteria manager by being late with the attendance report or the lunch count.

What are some ways you might resolve all this? How can you be most helpful to the teacher? to the students? One solution might be to share some of the responsibility with the students. Taking attendance and lunch count information is much easier when the children play a part. Of course, if you work in kindergarten, one of the reasons you are there is that the little ones really do need extra time and help with the business of school. But even though you are there partly to take the load of clerical duties off the teacher, don't take every bit of the load on yourself. You will help the children, and yourself, if you gradually teach them to be more and more independent and responsible. Of course, in the early years it takes someone to oversee their first moves toward independence and responsibility, so your presence is very important. Sometimes it seems easier and faster to just do everything yourself, but in the long run you won't help the students as much if you do for them things they can and should learn to do for themselves.

In one successful system, students take colored tags from a box and hang them on pegs. The pegs may be labelled with the names, initials, or number of the students. The tags may be colored so that red indicates hot lunch, green indicates the salad lunch, brown indicates lunch brought from home, and so on. At the end of the day one of the students is assigned to remove the tags from the pegs and place them back in the box.

You and the teacher can appoint students to do all kinds of classroom housekeeping tasks. You may have the responsibility of supervising and prodding the helpers, but they can be a big help with many chores around the classroom, and children are generally proud to be given responsibility. Rotate the tasks among the students. You might want to change once a week. Some jobs you may assign to student helpers are:

- Cleaning the board
- Passing out papers
- Running errands, being the office messenger

- Feeding the classroom pet
- Emptying the garbage can
- Taking scrap paper to the school recycling bin
- Leading the class in the pledge

One way to aid in a good start to the day is to make sure the students have something to do when they walk in the door. The teacher will probably be the one who determines what this is. Some teachers set the timer and give an allotted time for students to sharpen pencils, go to the library, finish writing in their journals, or whatever task is appropriate. You will need a good balance in your room. Be aware that students need a balance between the structure involved in getting the group started in an organized way and allowing for social interaction among the students and between the students and you and the teacher. Children often have a lot of news to tell, tidbits that seem very important to them, and they need to have a chance to relate them. You may think this is unnecessary but you should consider that your students may settle in better once they have had adequate opportunity to share with you or the teacher.

By now you know that you've got to figure out the best way to collect lunch money, send children to wash their hands, allow students to sharpen pencils, and conduct other daily routines. The best way for your classroom may be different from the best way in the classroom next door. The point is, though, that you and the teacher will need to agree on a plan for daily procedures, and your procedure plans will need to fit your specific classroom needs.

Some recommendations for handling bathroom breaks include:

- Allow limited pass use
  (example: six people allowed to leave the room in one period.)
- Unless mandated by school rules, try to develop a policy that avoids lining up the whole class and having to keep children quiet in the halls.
- Develop a process that does not interrupt teaching—perhaps a red/green signal by the door. When it is red, students know someone else is out and they must wait their turn. A green signal means students may go to the bathroom one at a time.
- Watch for students who seem to make several trips to the bathroom every couple of hours. You need to follow up on this. If the child is just goofing off, then by your checking to see if she has a

problem, you make her aware that you know what is going on. This usually works very well to end unnecessary trips to the bathroom. On the other hand, the child may really have a problem, and in that case you and the parents need to know it. Remember that frequent trips to the bathroom can be signs of urinary tract problems or diabetes.

- In some classrooms, as long as the teacher is not talking, students are allowed to use a pass to go to the bathroom without asking anybody.

- In some classrooms, students have to record the time out to and the time in from the bathroom.

- In lower elementary grades, most teachers make the time for their students to go to the bathroom at least twice during the schoolday.

If you are a beginning paraeducator, you may wonder what the big deal is about sharpening pencils. Why do you need a *policy* on sharpening pencils? Doesn't it make sense to let students go to the pencil sharpener whenever they have a broken pencil? After you observe an epidemic of broken pencils, see the tendency to poke each other with sharp tips, and watch the constant social grouping around the pencil sharpener, you may understand why teachers and paraeducators find it necessary to have a *pencil sharpening policy.* Some possible guidelines are:

- Pencils may be sharpened at any time as long as an adult is not addressing the class.

- Pencils are sharpened only during a designated time during class. The time may be controlled by a timer bell or by watching the clock.

- Sharpened pencils that students may use may be kept on the teacher's or paraeducator's desk, or on a special pencil bulletin board.

- Students may be requested to sharpen several pencils at one time.

- In upper grades where students change classes, students may be required to have their pencils sharpened and be in their seats by the third bell. In some schools and in some classes, students without pencils are given one demerit for being unprepared for class.

You and the teacher will also have to work out how you want students to put away materials, share computers, and make individual visits

A simple idea for managing line behavior with little ones is to rotate positions and to have students pretend the line is a train. The "caboose" is the monitor. If the caboose does a good job (makes sure the other "cars" stay "on track"), then that student gets to be the "engineer" next time. A system such as this can teach responsibility and cut down on constant demands to be "line leader."

to the library. As with all the other procedures, you will want what you do to be efficient, constructive for the students, and fair for all the students.

Good organization also involves anticipating problems that may arise in the daily routine. You may want to wait on the teacher's solutions to these problems, but you probably would do better to think through your own. You are there to provide support for the teacher, and chances are if you both work out the logistics to daily routine problems together, your solutions will be stronger and more effective. A well-organized classroom teacher anticipates situations and prevents them from becoming problems. So does a well-organized paraeducator. If the teacher has already worked out solutions before you come into the classroom, follow the teacher's lead and then adapt your own productive personal touch. A well-planned classroom will eliminate many discipline and time problems.

Less Frequent Than Daily Procedures

Tests are not likely to happen every day. You won't be making up the tests, but you may be grading many. As mentioned earlier, it is best to grade papers promptly so the children get quick feedback. This is especially true for tests; kids are eager to find out "how they did." You may be asked to help arrange the students for taking a test. You may also be asked to monitor during tests. It is helpful to really know your students at these times. When she feels it is crucial to know what each individual child knows and not have any confusion over straying eyes, one kindergarten teacher has her students sit in "offices." She and the paraeducator set up large manila folders on their ends to make a crazy divider system. The children think it is fun to stay behind their own "office" walls and the teacher feels more confident about the validity of the testing.

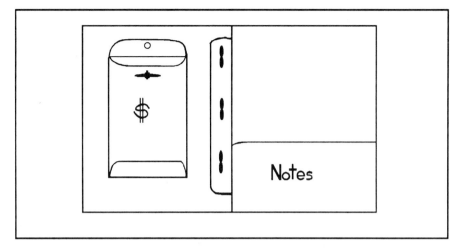

FIGURE 9–5 Field trip organizer. Courtesy of Bobbie McCord.

Field trips can be a special challenge for a paraeducator. In addition to collecting permission forms and collecting money, you may also make some of the arrangements over the phone, and you may have to help the teacher solicit volunteers to chaperone and assign groups of students to each chaperone. Paperwork for field trips can get confusing. Schools generally have a standard field trip information/permission form to send home. Most likely you will just fill in this standard form with the place, description, and date of your field trip and then make enough copies for your class. It helps to have a master list for every field trip, where you can mark off each child's name, whether a permission slip has been returned, whether the fee has been collected, any special considerations, and whether a parent (or grandparent!) is willing to go along as a chaperone. (Get some ideas from Figure 9–5 and Tables 9–4 and 9–5.)

If you help the teacher divide the students into groups and assign them to chaperones, be sure not to give the sweet volunteer parent who is dedicated enough to go on every single field trip the worst behaved child in the class for three trips in a row. Actually it's a good idea for you or the teacher to take charge of your most challenging children. Make out little lists for chaperones with the names of their charges.

Students and chaperones need nametags, especially if they don't know each other yet. Later in the year, depending on where you go, this might not be necessary. It is a good idea to have students wear school t-shirts or the same color shirts if you are going to a busy place with lots of other school groups. Another idea is to have everyone wear identical

TABLE 9–4 Field trip organizer. Courtesy of Bobbie McCord.

	Name	Permission Slip	Money	Bring Lunch	Buy Lunch Money	Wants to Chaperone

*(Table title spanning all columns: **FIELD TRIP**)*

nametags showing the school name and mascot or symbol. Especially if you are going somewhere where groups will be separated and there is a lot of ground to cover, it is helpful to have a way to easily identify people in your class or school group. Nametags don't have to be elaborate; you may even want the students to make them. When the group is assembled, and ready to move to a different area, or on the bus back to the school, you and the teacher both need to check your lists and numbers. You can't have too many people making sure that the exact same number of people who left the school are returning to the school!

There are a few items that may not actually be used but are handy to have "just in case" when you go on a field trip. Gather these and add your own:

- few band-aids;
- tissues;
- bags for garbage and other gross things;
- a little extra money;
- wipes;

TABLE 9–5 Field trip organizer.

FIELD TRIP ORGANIZER					
Field Trip to _____					
Date _____					
# of chaperones recommended _____					
Names	Permission	Paid	Will Bring Lunch	Will Buy Lunch	Chaperone
1.					
2.					
3.					
4.					
5. ↓ 23.					
24.					
25.					

Chaperones   Phone #   # of Students in Group

  1.

  2.

  3.

  4.

  5.

  6.

  7.

Need to remember:

- safety pins;
- pain reliever for your headache!

Field trips are a lot of fun; it's great to have a change of pace from the classroom. However, field trips will not always be very relaxing for you and the teacher. You will both be very conscious of the children's safety and well-being. You will also need and want to interact with the volunteer chaperones in your group. If anybody needs anything, they will come to you or the teacher for help and information. If a child gets sick on the bus, guess who will get to sit with that child? There is a lot of responsibility associated with taking a school group on a field trip. There can be a lot of enjoyment and benefit, too. Don't be surprised, though, if you feel "wiped out" after field trips. Treat yourself to some "down time" when the schoolday's over.

Like field trips, *parties* in the classroom can be a delight and a headache for the paraeducator and the teacher. Your school may have rules about the number of parties allowed per year. Some public schools allow for four parties during the school year: Christmas/Hannukah, Valentine's Day, Easter/Spring, and End-of-Year/Last Day. Many classrooms corral a mom or a committee of parents to be *room parents*. If your class has a room parent, then that's great, because the room parent will probably have the job of planning and arranging for refreshments for parties. If not, then you and the teacher can divide up jobs and ask for donations at party time.

The best rule of thumb for school parties is to *keep it simple*. After a while you'll find that children don't like simple, more plain refreshments any less than they do more elaborate ones. In fact, sometimes they seem to prefer them. That's hard to take if you are the baker of beautifully decorated petit fours watching children overlook your offerings in favor of snarfing down Rice Krispie treats and M & Ms. Cupcakes, popcorn, and cut-up fruit usually go over pretty consistently. Simple works well for games and activities, too. Children just want to have fun at parties; they may not respond well to learning new complicated games.

Sometimes it is fun to have a class party along a theme of study, as in a Western party or a luau. Children can wear and eat and do something that goes along with the theme. For example, they can make and wear grass skirts and leis, and eat pineapple. Some other school party ideas follow:

- Space theme—moon pies, rocket cupcakes, dehydrated fruit
- Harvest fall party—make applesauce and share it with parents or another class
- Explorers and pirates—tuna fish sandwiches, Peppridge Farm "Goldfish", and root beer floats

  Factors to consider when planning a class party are:

- Location.
- Refreshments—who will bring, the cost, and who will pay.
- Storage at school of any perishable items—sometimes you will not be allowed to use cafeteria refrigerator or freezer space, or there is no more space available. Then you'll need coolers and ice.
- Who will serve the food—children get their own or adults take the food to the children
- Party activities—what to do; who's in charge; materials needed.
- All school guidelines followed.
- Cleanup!

ROOM ARRANGEMENT

Every now and then during the year you and the teacher may want to shift the desk arrangement around. No matter how perfect the desk arrangement seems at the beginning of the year, the children will probably grow sick of it. You and the teacher might be tired of it yourselves. If you are ready to make a change, consider the following. By the time you're ready to shift desks, you'll know more about the children and how they interact. There will always be some distractions no matter how you seat children, but you know that some arrangements will work better than others. You and the teacher can glance at some combinations for two seconds and immediately know that they will not work. It is a common practice to put the more disruptive individuals toward the back of the room where they will not bother others so much. Remember, though, that so often when children misbehave they are really crying out for attention. When they are placed farther away, rejection is stacked on top of their need for attention. Children need our acceptance and approval on a daily basis.

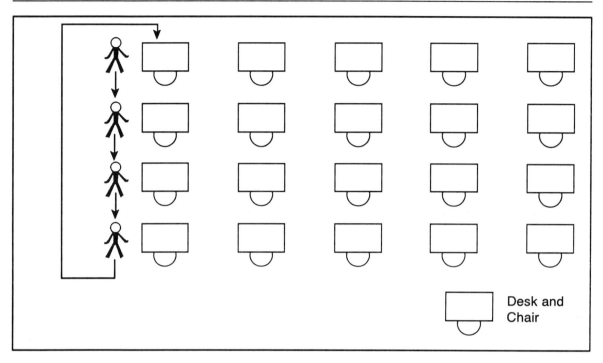

FIGURE 9–6 Rotated Seating Arrangement

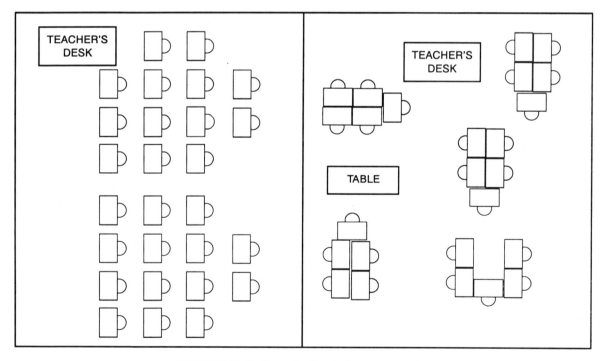

FIGURE 9–7 Sample Desk Arrangements

If your classroom has rows, watch out that your rows do not indicate any pecking order. You may feel that rows are good, but if you encounter behavior problems, give at least some consideration to this possibility. Some teachers still use rows, but do so with an important modification. Children move one seat back on a regular schedule so the child who sits at the back of the row will rotate next to the very first seat. This may be something you can suggest for your classroom (Figure 9–6).

As implied already, there will probably be at least one glitch in any desk arrangement you try. However, you do need to consider that children do have needs for social interactions. You and the teacher may find that the children do better when you acknowledge and allow for their needs for social groupings if you give them rules to make the groupings work, rather than when you arbitrarily arrange them and they end up fulfilling their social needs in mischievous or devious ways (Figure 9–7).

Even the most wonderful bulletin boards and the best displays become stale after a while. You may have the job of changing these on a regular basis. If you don't make changes, the kids just won't see the displays and bulletin boards anymore. They will just become part of the wall. Maggs warns that the same old thing can get boring, and "...eventually the students simply stop seeing what is around them" (1980). She gives a "room calendar" with ideas for bulletin boards and displays for every month of the school year. The calendar ideas are great and include memorable dates such as the start of the Great Depression, the Wright Brothers' first successful flight, and when W. F. Semple patented chewing gum (sure to interest kids!).

As a paraeducator, you may have a good part of the responsibility for how the room is decorated and arranged. Maggs says that room decor is important. There are some things about your classroom that you will not be able to change, but there are many other things you *will* be able to change, depending on your ingenuity.

Did you catch that? The room decor is dependent on the ingenuity of the teacher. Most likely your presence in a classroom will mean that the appeal of the surroundings will at least partly be dependent on you. Many teachers may really like to design bulletin boards and all that kind of stuff, but often if teachers have paraeducators, the area of room decor is one where they choose to have their paraeducators support them. So get creative and have fun.

When you start looking, you'll find ideas everywhere: from teacher magazines, from other teachers and paraeducators, from things the children say, from the news, and on and on.

Maggs goes on to suggest inexpensive ways to decorate classrooms, including using plants, posters, the students' work and art projects, and teacher- (paraeducator-) made displays. She has some excellent, economical ideas for displays and decorating themes, including using collections of various items and adopting a country and its culture as your classroom decorating theme (1980).

COMMUNICATIONS AND CHAINS OF COMMANDS

It won't take you long to find out who is really in charge at your school and to find out who you need to go to for what. If you pay attention, you will find out exactly who is the best person to ask in particular situations. You need to go through proper channels when you order supplies, ask for a personal day off, make a complaint, or schedule *anything*. Learn the hierarchy in your school or center (Figure 9–8). Knowing who is in authority over whom can help you understand situations, keep out of trouble, and communicate effectively and appropriately.

Clear, effective communications will aid your classroom organization. In all your communications, whether with administrator, teacher, parent, or student, be clear in your speech and maintain good eye contact. Hold your head up and look people directly in the eye. This is really important especially in situations where there could be tension or misunderstanding. When taking instructions, make sure you understand correctly. Take notes and parrot back information to verify it if you need to.

When you give instructions to children, be careful not to give so many directions at once that the children forget them all. Following instructions is hard, especially it there is a whole string of them. Listening is a skill that takes some effort to acquire. When a person listens to a cluster of directions, the person has to go through several processes at once: (1) listen and hear what is being said, (2) hone in on what is being asked, and (3) decide how to do what is being asked. This can be difficult for children, so you need to do what you

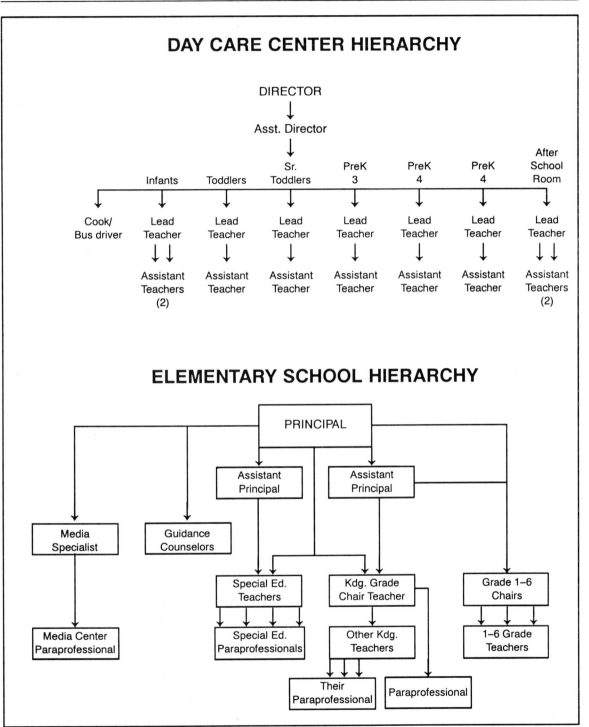

FIGURE 9–8 Day Care Center/Elementary School Hierarchy.

can to help children become good listeners. First of all, when you give children instructions, make sure they are in a position to actually hear you, that they are where they can concentrate. Have instructees look at you; teach children to look at people when they speak. Make sure they understand what you have told them to do. Ask them to explain back to you what it is that you are telling them to do.

A good bit of correspondence is sent home from some classrooms. This may include a weekly or monthly newsletter, behavior notes, forms for parents to complete, as well as many other informative types of communication. What you do and what the teacher does will be up to the two of you. You may be in charge of most of the communications with the home. As discussed in the last chapter, though, be sure that you do not make initial contacts about misbehavior, because that really should be the teacher's responsibility. But once the teacher and the parents have discussed a problem, you may be the one who informs the parents about subsequent behavior. If there is some kind of communication that is repetitive, then you may want to make it easier on yourself by making up a pertinent form such as the one in Figure 8–5 in Chapter 8. (See Table 9–6a and b here.) Sometimes kindergarten teachers and paraeducators even send home baby teeth taped onto duplicated notes for the tooth fairy. In their book, *Good Behavior Made Easy,* Garber, Garber, & Spizman have several great forms that may be sent from school to home, including one on which timid children tally the number of times they participate in class discussions (1992).

Just as in the case of your records of incidences, information sent home should be specific, rather than general. Rather than reporting that Jacques misbehaved, go ahead and report that Jacques threw squash in William's hair. Rather than saying that Wanda had a little accident on the playground, say that Wanda deliberately jumped into the mud puddle.

Make sure that *anything* you send home has correct grammar and spelling. Take special care with this. What do you think it does to parents when they pick up on misspellings or grammatical mistakes made by one of the ones who teaches their child? It does not look good! As stated before, it is not necessary to type or use calligraphy on embossed paper, but you should make sure that even your responses written on the bottom of original notes are neat and legible.

TABLE 9–6a Parent Communication (Courtesy of Jan Holbrook).

DATE: _____

☺ : GREAT	X: OOPS! NEEDS IMPROVEMENT		
Subject	**Began Work Promptly**	**Remained on Task**	**Completed Assigned Tasks**
Morning Management			
Seatwork			
Calendar			
Work Job Tasks			
Computer Activities			
Lunch			
Grooming			
Reading			
Storytime			
Art			
Leisure Skills			
Domestic Skills: (Laundry DW)			
Specials (Music PT, PE)			
Specials (Speech, etc.)			
C.B.I. (Community Based Instruction)			
Other (Assembly Delivering Lunch Tickets)			

Interventions: V–Verbal prompt   P–Physical prompt   T–Time out

Comments:

TABLE 9–6b Parent Communication (Courtesy of Jan Holbrook).

Sai Zaslow   DATE: ___2-12-96___

☺ : GREAT	X: OOPS! NEEDS IMPROVEMENT		
Subject	**Began Work Promptly**	**Remained on Task**	**Completed Assigned Tasks**
Morning Management	X	X	X
Seatwork	☺	☺	☺
Calendar	X	☺	☺
Work Job Tasks			
Computer Activities	☺	☺	☺
Lunch	☺	X	X
Grooming	☺	☺	☺
Reading	☺	☺	☺
Storytime			
Art	☺	☺	☺
Leisure Skills	☺	☺	☺
Domestic Skills: DW	☺	☺	☺
Specials Music	☺	☺	☺
Specials P.T.	☺	X	☺
C.B.I.			
Other Lunch ticket Deliveries	☺	☺	☺

Interventions: V–Verbal prompt   P–Physical prompt   T–Time out

Comments:

USING EQUIPMENT, DEALING WITH MACHINES

A variety of machines are available to make your job easier. First on the list is the copier. If you are very blessed, you may have access to one that staples and collates. Use your copier wisely. It will not take you very long to realize that you do NOT want to be the one who is using the copier when it has an attack. Make sure that you are trained properly on using the copier. If there is something you do not feel confident doing, then don't do it. Ask for help. It's better to wait for assistance than to fiddle with and "kill" the copier.

It is a big help if you copy sets of test forms, book report evaluation forms, class behavior notes, reading incentive forms, progress reports, clinic passes, and so on, for the entire school year. Store them in a cabinet.

Another machine you may use is the Ellison die machine. It cuts out different types of letters and designs, such as bunnies, snowmen, and school buses. Look at the samples and some of the possibilities from the Teacher Center in Canton, GA. (Table 9–7 and Figure 9–9). You will find innumerable uses for die cuts if you have access to a die cut machine. In kindergarten, a little boy had trouble controlling himself during naptime every day. Although he did not initiate the bad behavior, he consistently laughed at the boy who did, and things got out of hand with a whole batch of small boys. Of course, the little boy blamed his own behavior on the instigator. His wise teacher and paraeducator told him that they knew he wasn't starting the problem but he sure was adding to it. His teacher told him he had to learn that he himself was responsible for his own behavior no matter what someone else was doing. She told him she knew he could learn to control himself, and every day that he controlled himself during naptime he could have a little red heart (from the die cutter) to take home to his mother to put on the refrig-

TABLE 9–7 Die Cuts at Teacher Center

Airplane	Brontosaurus	Christmas Tree	Meat Group	Star
Bicycle	Butterfly	Clock Face	Oak Leaf	Stegosaurus
Bird #3	Button Maker	Frog	Owl	Strawberry
Birthday Cake	Caboose	Jack O' Lantern	Panda	Sun/ Happy
Boxcar	Camel	Lamb	Peach	Face
Boy	Candle	Lincoln	Snowman	Tank Car

FIGURE 9–9 Sample of die cut objects.

erator. She asked him if he didn't think it would be wonderful to have a whole refrigerator full of little red hearts. It worked! By the time the little boy took a row's worth of hearts home, he had learned to control his response to the other child's behavior, and the teacher and the paraeducator and the mother all agreed that they didn't even need the red hearts any longer. Just tiny paper hearts, but they helped set the foundation for a child to learn how to behave in school. That boy is in the sixth grade now, is an excellent student, and truly enjoys school. Who knows what *you* can do with paper and a die cut machine?

The video camera can be used to tape class speeches, puppet shows, dances, and so on. The students love watching themselves on screen later. A VCR is great to have in the classroom.

The overhead projector can be used in many classes. An overhead transparency may be placed on the overhead projector to teach a lesson in writing, math, or many other subjects. Varied colored overhead pens may be used to write on overhead transparencies. The different colors will show on the screen. Temporary transparencies can be wiped clean with water and a paper towel. Already prepared transparencies may also be used to project material on the screen to assist with lessons. Professionally prepared transparencies come with some reading and math series. Transparencies may be purchased at educational supply stores. Some transparencies are pretty fancy and come with overlays. You can make transparencies for your classroom by sending a copy of the desired material attached to a blank overhead transparency through a thermofax machine.

The overhead projector can also be used to enlarge outlines. To do this, tape a large piece of construction paper or butcher paper to the board. Place the figure (a small boat, for example) on the overhead. Move the overhead projector the necessary distance from the paper to produce the size you want. Then trace the outline on the paper. You can do a similar process with an opaque projector. Both the overhead and opaque projector processes can be used to make patterns for art projects or for large figures for bulletin boards. For example, an enlarged teddy bear can be traced on to pieces of tagboard. Lines can be penciled on the tagboard bear to split it into eight or ten sections of various shapes. Different selections of wallpaper can then be outlined with Xs in black marker to look like quilt stitching. Then the bear may be given eyes, nose, and a mouth.

Some of you may also use several other machines on occasion: the thermofax, the ditto machine, the film projector, slide projector, and CD player. If you are like many others, you may feel intimidated by machines that you do not feel confident running. Be sure to get inserviced on these machines so that you can use them rather than avoid them. Set up a time to meet with your school media specialist if this is an option.

Don't forget a simple machine like your camera. Students love to have their pictures taken and then they love to see the pictures displayed. It's fun to take pictures of the children at the beginning of the year (and record their height and weight) and then again at the end of the year to see how much they change while they are with you.

Many schools have their own laminating machines. These are wonderful. When you laminate materials, the plasticlike coating protects them from wear and tear and also from fading. There will probably be a multitude of materials that you and the teacher will want to preserve by running them through the laminator.

Another machine you may be asked to operate is a videodisc player. Each side of a videodisc holds regular video material, like news reports and presidents making speeches today and in the past. The discs also have thousands of numbered still frames on each side. To access the discs, you can use a remote control, a bar code reader, or computer software. When you access the disc, bingo! What you want appears immediately. The disc can be listened to in stereo in one language, or it can be listened to in two languages, English and Spanish, at the same time when students have on headphones.

Yet another interesting, ongoing activity involving a machine is the Electronic Bulletin Board, a development in telecommunications. To use this, your school needs a modem and a cable hookup. You may be able to help your students send ads or write letters to students at other schools. You might also suggest to the teacher that the class send messages to people in retirement homes or long-term health care facilities.

More and more classrooms and schools have computers and computer labs. When your students are on computers, you may be called upon to problem-solve, to answer questions like, "How do I get out of this?" and "How do I get back to the main menu?" or "What's wrong with the printer?" Students can learn all sorts of things through computers, including keyboarding skills, word processing, and how to make graphics, fonts, and borders. (In fact, *you* will probably use software packages like Printshop, Deluxe to make cards and parent notes and banners.) The Minnesota Educational Consortium (MECC), as well as many other software developers, produces a good amount of software with math drills, reading skills, and so on. As mentioned in Chapter 6, there are many educational games for the computer. A continual favorite is *Where in the World is Carmen Sandiego?*, in which students learn about other countries' flags, money systems, monuments, cities, and so on, all while trying to catch a thief who has stolen some national treasure. You'll have fun watching the students have fun on today's computer resources.

Many schools are now connected to the InterNet. The InterNet is a fast-evolving resource for worldwide research and communications. Through this students can *surf the net* to find most any topic of interest.

The idea of being called upon to operate some of the aforementioned pieces of equipment might give you nervous shakes. Stop that right now. Don't let any inanimate machine intimidate you, a human being with a good mind and the capacity to learn new and exciting things. Over time, try to master them all. Go through this checklist periodically and see how many you learn to use and use well:

- Copier
- Thermofax
- Opaque projector
- Overhead projector
- Cassette recorder/player
- Videocamera
- VCR
- Laminator
- Videodisc player
- CD-ROM
- Printer
- Computer
- Camera

Whew! That's a lot, but once you gain knowledge of the equipment available at your facility, you will also gain confidence. Remember that everybody has to learn sometime. If you are unsure how to use something, ask, but do so before you're in the middle of something with your students if at all possible. A large part of being organized is being prepared. So a big factor in your classroom organization may be your preparedness in using the equipment available to your classroom.

ORGANIZATION CAN HELP STRESS LEVEL

If you are disorganized, you will most likely be more frazzled in your job as a paraeducator. Stress is a part of life in an educational facility. There will probably be times when you will want to run screaming from the place. But there won't be as many if you are prepared, manage your time wisely, and keep as organized as possible.

If Margaret Maggs is right, you may even be able to plan your lowest point of the school year. She says:

> *In terms of your day-to-day planning, you will find that by March the drear-and-drudge syndrome will have caught up with you. Although calendars do not indicate it, March contains the largest number of long school days in psychological terms.*

and then:

> *When you are overcome with that pre-spring hopelessness, don't give up. Try to learn from it.   (1980)*

She offers some suggestions for this predictable "blues" time. She suggests doing something different, really evaluating your methods, and looking back to see what you and the students enjoyed back at the beginning of the year. Maggs has a helpful "Blue Monday Checklist" in her *Classroom Survival Book* and gives the advice that when stress or blues grow, it's a good idea to remember why you're in the classroom.

She believes that some people continue teaching just because they enjoy the act of teaching. Although they know that feelings of satisfaction may not come every day, they place great value on contributing to a child's education. They acknowledge and accept the down sides to days in the classroom because they anticipate the days when that "one golden gleam of interest in a child's eye" make it worth it. (Maggs, 1980)

The reasons that paraeducators continue to do what they do may be very much the same. Sometimes it will help you to get back to those original reasons.

CHAPTER 10

Resources for the Productive Paraeducator

Resources have been mentioned over and over again in this book. There are a vast number of resources available for teachers and paraeducators. Resources can be found in the most unlikely places, so make it your practice to keep your eyes open for materials and ideas for your classroom. Resources include: journals, educational supply stores, books, area attractions, newspapers, hotlines, offerings through the mail, community resources, and people. Good resources are so valuable, and among the most valuable are the people around you. As mentioned continuously, the other paraeducators around you can be immeasurable help in practical, hands-on training. Learn from what a more experienced paraeducator does and rev up your own enthusiasm by watching the fresh ideas of a new paraeducator. Some of your best mentors will be people already at your workplace. Learn from each other and be supportive of each other. Don't overlook your retired neighbor who taught school for twenty-seven years. That neighbor might be able to share insights that could really help you do your job. People can be wonderful resources not only for you, but also for your students. Check out these possibilities and think of others:

- Classroom volunteers
- Parents demonstrating crafts or skills
- People from the community telling about their jobs
- Neighbors, friends from other countries sharing about their homeland and life experiences
- Storytelling
- Grandparents telling about changes they have seen in their lifetimes

COMMUNITY RESOURCES

Get into the practice of scouting for opportunities for your students while you read through the local newspaper and listen to the radio. Keep your eyes and ears open for offerings from local businesses, large corporations, and public organizations. Some possibilities along this line include:

- Free storytelling at libraries, bookstores, and museums.
- Free concerts at churches and community areas.
- "Baby Think it Over" dolls were presented to a local school board by the March of Dimes.
- A large regional supermarket chain has contributed "grocery stores" to schools to use for hands-on learning of consumer math, nutrition, and other subjects.
- A nationwide HMO has put together a community service program called *Professor Bodywise's Traveling Menagerie.* This 45-minute performance teaches children about health and safety.
- Free programs and information from local hospitals.
- Free handouts and visits through the fire department.
- Tourism packages available in most states.

Area Attractions

Oftentimes the tourists are the major enjoyers of local attractions, and the "natives" are heard to say, "I've been meaning to go there..." Take a look at what your area has to offer and take advantage of the proximity. There may be some great attractions that you tend to take for granted. Check to see if you are within bus distance of a:

- Cavern
- Waterfall
- Hiking trail
- Historical monument
- Sea aquarium such as the one in Chattanooga, TN
- Manufacturing plant that gives tours
- Museum
- Planetarium
- Botanical garden
- Wildlife preserve
- Hands-on learning facility (such as the Boston Children's Museum, Philadelphia's Franklin Institute, San Francisco's Exploratorium, or Atlanta's SciTrek)

- National or state park
- Overnight educational facility such as Space Camp in Huntsville, AL
- Periodic exhibit or festival

Encourage the teacher to authorize field trips to places of importance right in your area. If field trips are not an option, then learn from individuals who have been able to go to area attractions. Give them an opportunity to share about the experience and to show something they brought back (pictures, brochures, or video).

FREEBIES THROUGH THE MAIL

Some companies and associations will provide individuals and classrooms with free materials. Some of these are heavily promotional but often there is a lot of valuable basic information as well. *The Educator's Guide to Free Teaching Aids* is a guide that briefly describes free educational materials and tells how to receive them. The guide is published annually by Educators Progress Service. Your media specialist should be able to obtain one for your school. Also, many colleges and universities keep the current guide. Obviously a listing here would be impractical because of the temporary nature of such offerings. An example of a free classroom resource mentioned in February 1996 in the *Atlanta Parent* newspaper is *The Real Deal,* a 12-page activity booklet published by the Federal Trade Commission (FTC) and the National Association of Attorneys General. Using cartoons, puzzles, and other activities, this booklet teaches students to be smart when they shop. For free copies, call the FTC at (800) 769–7960. If the FTC does not distribute this particular booklet anymore, they may offer some other classroom aid.

Another great source of information about free things for your classroom is *100s of Free Things for Teachers* (1995) by Dawn Hardy and the editors of Consumer Guide. This includes resources pertaining to nutrition, economics, environment, and many other subjects. For more information, write to:

Publications International, Ltd.
7373 North Cicero Avenue
Lincolnwood, IL 60646

Be on the lookout for blurbs about free material in magazines, news shows, and newspapers.

TELEPHONE SOURCES

Some great information may be as close as your telephone. In Georgia, the public has access to the Cooperative Extension Service of the University of Georgia. People are welcome to call their local county extension to find out data about agriculture, horticulture, environmental concerns, nutrition, and many other subjects. (The Extension Service also coordinates the 4-H youth program.) Check out your county and colleges and universities in your state to see what kind of resources they offer the public. Probably a lot more than you think.

Free brochures are offered to parents as an outreach of the U.S. Department of Education, through ACCESS ERIC. These brochures offer recent research information and give possible resources for educational concerns of today's parents. Brochure titles include *What Should Parents Know About Performance Assessment?* and *How Parents Can Identify a High-Quality Preschool Program?* To find out more, call 1–800–538–3742 or write to:

> ACCESS ERIC
> 1600 Research Boulevard
> Rockville, MD 20850-3172

There is also a federally funded national information network that provides research services for educational personnel. This is ERIC, the Educational Resources Information Center. There are 16 separate subject-oriented clearinghouses under the ERIC umbrella, including:

> ERIC Clearinghouse on Disabilities and Gifted Education
> (ERIC EC)
> The Council for Exceptional Children
> 1920 Association Drive
> Reston, VA 22091-1589
> 1-800-328-0272 (toll-free)
> ericec@inet.ed.gov (Internet)

> ERIC Clearinghouse on Elementary and Early Childhood Education
> (ERIC PS)
> University of Illinois, College of Education
> 805 W. Pennsylvania Avenue
> Urbana, IL 61801-4897
> 1-800-583-4135
> ericece@ux1.cso.uiuc.edu

Many large public libraries and university libraries keep RIE, *Resources in Education* and CIJE, *Current Index to Journals in Education* on the reference shelf. These indexes provide abstracts of ERIC documents and articles.

The Department of Education funds other information clearing-houses as well, including:

NICHCY, National Information Center for Children and Youth
with Disabilities
P.O. Box 1492
Washington, DC 20013
1-800-695-0285
nichcy@capcon.net

DB-LINK, The National Clearinghouse On Children Who
are Deaf-Blind
345 N. Monmouth Avenue
Monmouth, OR 97361
1-800-438-9376
leslieg@fsa.wosc.osshe.edu

FREE NEWSPAPERS

The Wal-Mart Corporation has underwritten a news magazine called *Kids F.A.C.E.,* which stands for Kids For A Clean Environment. The theme of this newspaper is environmental concerns and it has ideas for projects, informative articles, activities, and write-ups about what kids all over the United States are doing to help the earth. This newspaper can be picked up just inside the door at your area Wal-Mart store. For more information, contact:

"KIDS F.A.C.E."
Kids For A Clean Environment
P.O. Box 158254
Nashville, TN 37215

Atlanta Parent is an excellent newspaper published monthly and distributed at no charge all over the metropolitan Atlanta area at stores and public libraries. The contents run the gamut from party theme and craft ideas, to suggestions on behavior, to toy evaluations, to health in-formation, and so on. The newspaper is written specifically for parents, but anyone who works with children could glean from the ideas and information. Subscriptions are available also.

> Atlanta Parent, Inc.
> 4330 Georgetown Square
> Suite 506
> Atlanta, GA 30338

Don't overlook the freebies at restaurants, libraries, hospitals, and other public places. You might find some treasures.

MAGAZINES AND JOURNALS

An exciting array of magazines with ideas for bulletin boards, art projects, individual and unit lesson plans, and tips on discipline, curriculum, ways to deal with parents, and so on, are available along with the usual subject matter journals. For the beginning paraeducator, the problem is not availability, but making a choice of which publication suits your needs best. This list of magazines is designed to help you make that decision. Should you decide to order one of these publications, it would be advisable to check to see if the address is still current.

> *Instructor, Incorporating Teacher*
> The Instructor
> P.O. Box 53896
> Boulder, Colorado 80322

This magazine should be in university libraries. Many schools also keep a subscription for their media centers. It is a good source for current issues in education and recent ideas to use in the classroom. In addition to a monthly planner, bulletin board, art ideas, poetry and science projects, the magazine also includes articles on curriculum and other informative subjects.

> *Schooldays* (Primary: 800-333-3580)
> *Classmates* (Secondary: 800-421-5565)
> P.O. Box 2853
> Torrance, California 90509

These magazines are published four times a year and are filled with practical ideas for those who work in elementary schools. Both issues include reproducible units, science lessons, art ideas, bulletin boards, and successful teaching techniques.

> *Teaching K–8*
> P.O. Box 512
> Farmingdale, New York 11737
> 800-678-8793

Along with monthly articles on curriculum issues, regular features include education newswatch, teaching math, teaching science, professional growth, the *Teaching K–8* shopper, what is new in teaching aids, and recommended books for the month.

> *Lollipops, Magazine for Preschool and Early Childhood Education*
> Good Apple Publishers
> P.O. Box 299
> Carthage, Illinois 62321
> 217-357-3981

This is an excellent magazine for those who work in early childhood, kindergarten, and first grade. The publication includes timely teaching tips, bulletin boards, cut-and-paste activities, craft projects, songs, fingerplays, game boards, and a monthly calendar.

> *Oasis* (5-9)
> Good Apple Publication
> P.O. Box 299
> Carthage, Illinois 62321
> 217-357-3981

This is a resource for those who work with middle schoolers, but is also useful with upper elementary grades. Five issues per school year include reproducible pages, biographies, calendars, book reviews, composition boards, environmental units, and tips to teachers from teachers.

> *Copycat*
> P.O. Box 081546
> Racine, Wisconsin 53408
> 414-634-0146

Copycat has a newspaper format and contains creative, easy-to-use ideas for every area of the curriculum. There are many seasonal activities, arts and crafts, bulletin boards, and unique units of study.

The Reading Teacher
Journal of the International Reading Association
800 Barksdale Road
P.O. Box 8139
Newark, Delaware 19714

This publication includes sections on evaluation and recommended use of children's books, links literary research with instructional practice, includes practical ideas for classroom use, and recommends books. Included in the fall issues is a complete list of favorite books chosen by students and teachers.

The Arithmetic Teacher
NCTM Dept. M
1906 Association Drive
Reston, Virginia 22091

This journal includes materials to use with K-8. A section on Calendar Mathematics gives weekly activities, further divided into grade-level projects. Also included are articles on putting research into practice, math and technology, reviews of computer materials, and new books on mathematics for children and teachers.

Science and Children, A Journal Devoted to Pre-school Through Middle School Science Teaching
National Science Teachers Association
1742 Connecticut Avenue N.W.
Washington, D.C. 20009

The journal includes recommended books and resources for teachers, ideas for complete science units, early childhood science activities, and important research in science education.

New Directions
NRC for Paraeducators CASE/CUNY
Room 620N
25 West 43rd Street
New York, NY 10036

This newsletter is published four times a year and discusses pertinent issues for paraeducators, such as training, employment opportunities, and personnel practices.

Day Care U.S.A. Newsletter
Day Care Information Service
United Communications Group
8701 Georgia Avenue, Suite 800
Silver Springs, MD 20910

Young Children
Journal of the National Association for the Education of
    Young Children
1834 Connecticut Ave., NW
Washington, DC 20009

BOOKS

Many books have been mentioned in the previous chapters as being good resources. The list below includes them and others that have information or recommendations that can benefit paraeducators. Your school media center, public library, and college library probably have some wonderful book resources, too.

Activities For Enhancing Literature, Creative Teaching Press, 1989. Activities to go along with eight favorite children's books including *The Indian in the Cupboard* and *The Lion, the Witch, and the Wardrobe.*

Art For All Seasons, Evan-Moor Corp., 1993. Great ideas. Permission granted for reproducing for individual classroom use but not for schoolwide use.

Basic Classroom Skills Through Games by Irene Wood Bell and Jeanne E. Wieckert, 1980 (Libraries Unlimited, Inc.). Give permission for individual media specialists and teachers to copy their games to use in classroom or media center teaching.

Chemistry for Every Kid,
Earth Science for Every Kid,
Math for Every Kid by Janice Van Cleave, 1991 (John Wiley and Sons, Inc.). Easy experiments and projects.

The Classroom Survival Book by Margaret Martin Maggs, 1980 (New Viewpoints, division of Franklin Watts). Very practical book about classroom organization and management.

The Cooperative Sports and Games Book by Terry Orlick, 1978 (Pantheon Books, New York). "Challenge without competition."

Driven to Distraction: Recognizing and Coping with Attention Deficit Disorder from Childhood to Adulthood by Edward M. Hallowell and John J. Ratey, 1995 (Simon & Schuster). Includes a list of 50 tips on how to manage ADHD children in the classroom.

Educational Games for Fun by Margaret E. Mulac, 1971 (Harper & Row, Publishers, Inc.). Some wonderful classic style educational games for every subject.

The Educator's Desk Reference: A sourcebook of educational information and research by Melvin N. Freed, 1989 (American Council on Education and Macmillan Publishing Company, New York). Lots of helpful reference information for anyone involved in or interested in education.

Everybody Wins by Jeffrey Sobol, 1983 (Walker and Company, New York). "393 non-competitive games for young children." Recreational games.

Exceptional Children and Youth: An Introduction by Edward L. Meyen. Informative about PL 94–142.

Feed Me, I'm Yours by Vicki Lansky. Helpful hints on nutrition for children and ideas for cooking with children.

Games for Learning: Ten Minutes a Day to Help Your Child Do Well In School—from Kindergarten to Third Grade, written by Peggy Kaye, 1991 (Harper Collins Canada Ltd.). Excellent ideas for parents but could be done very effectively by paraeducators in small groups or with individual students for extra help and fun reinforcement.

Getting Things Done, the ABC's of Time Management by E.D. Bliss, 1976 (Scribner's).

Good Behavior Made Easy by Garber, Garber, and Spizman, 1992 (Family Life Productions). Great ideas for parents and educators to use in dealing with many types of behavior, lots of good insights, practical helps.

Holiday Games and Activities by Barbara Wnek, 1992 (Human Kinetics Books). Physical education and recreational games.

Indoor Action Games for Elementary Children by David Foster and James Overholt, 1989 (Parker Publishing Co.). A variety of indoor recess and physical education activities; mostly just for fun and release of energy, but a few great academic activities as well.

Let Me Do It! by Anne Rogovin, 1980 (Thomas Y. Crowell). Insightful guide to children's learning activities, especially for children with special needs; wonderful ideas for pantomimes, fingerplays, puppet materials, plant projects, and on and on.

Ray Gibson's *You and Your Child...Games* series on different subjects, 1993 by Usborne Publishing Ltd. Ideas for parents to use at home with their children; may be used in the classroom as good small group or one-on-one reinforcement.

School Discipline: The Art of Survival by Jim Brown and William Allan Kritsonis (Book Masters, Inc.). Valuable guidelines for classroom management, tips on how not to be part of behavior problems.

The Seven Habits of Highly Effective People by S. Covey, 1989 (Simon and Schuster).

Story Stretchers,
More Story Stretchers,
450 More Story Stretchers by Shirley C. Raines and Robert J. Canady, 1992 (Gryphon House, Mt. Rainier, MD). Activities to expand children's favorite books; activities for many subject areas including art, science, math, and writing; activities to go along side of such books as *Flossie and the Fox, Two Bad Ants, Amelia Bedelia,* and *Alexander and the Terrible, Horrible, No Good, Very Bad Day.*

Ten Minute Field Trips—a Teacher's Guide to Using the Schoolgrounds for Environmental Studies, by Helen Ross Russell, 1990 (National Science Teachers Association.)

Time Management for Teachers by K. Collins, 1988 (Parker Publishing Company, Inc.). Ideas that may be adapted by paraeducators, too.

Vito Perrone's *101 Educational Conversations with Your...Grader* series for children of different grade levels, 1993 by Chelsea House Publishers. Geared toward parents, but would be a terrific aid to paraeducators beginning to work with a new age group; recommendations for conversation starters and effective ways to communicate with children of different age levels.

Wacky Cakes and Water Snakes by Stacie Hill Barta.

Why Bright Kids Get Poor Grades: and What You Can Do About It by Dr. Sylvia Rimm, 1995 (Crown Publishers, Inc.). Great suggestions and helpful information for anyone who wants to help underachievers do better; has "teacher tips" throughout the book, would benefit paraeducators, too.

SUPPLY STORES

Zany Brainy is a cool store with locations across the United States. Zany Brainy has 36 stores, mostly on the East Coast, but with one in the Chicago area. These stores are fascinating for anyone who works with children and enjoys seeing the "learning light bulbs" turn on.

The School Box is a great resource for those living in or traveling through Atlanta. There are eight locations in the metro area. Search your area for a supply store near you.

HOTLINES

Hotlines and helplines can give you quick, specialized, valuable information. The following are national hotline numbers:

AIDS Hotline 1-800-342-AIDS

Boys Town 1-800-448-3000

Child Abuse 1-800-4ACHILD

Cocaine Baby Help Line 1-800-638-2229

Cocaine Hotline 1-800-Cocaine

Partners for the Planet Hotline 1-800-473-0263

There will also be important hotline numbers for your area. Many of these can be found in the community service portion of your phone book:

Child Abuse Hotline

Poison Control Center

Substance Abuse Hotline

Violence Prevention Hotline

ORGANIZATIONS

Many councils, foundations, and organizations are ready and willing to provide information and help whenever possible. You may be surprised what a phone call or letter may do.

American Academy of Pediatrics
141 N.W. Points Blvd.
P.O. Box 927
Elk Grove Village, IL 60009-0927

American Dental Association
Council on Community Health, Hospital,
    Institutional and Medical Affairs
211 East Chicago Ave.
Chicago, IL 60611-2678

American Printing House for the Blind
1839 Frankfort Avenue
P.O. Box 6085
Louisville, KY 40206
(592) 895-2405

Big Brothers/Big Sisters of America
117 South 17th Street, Suite 1200
Philadelphia, PA 19103

Blind Children's Center
4120 Marathon Street
Los Angeles, CA 90029
(213) 664-2153

They provide informational booklets covering several topics, including play activities and early motor development.

CH.A.D.D.
Children and Adults with Attention Deficit Disorder
        Nationwide Support Group
499 Northwest 70th Avenue
Suite 308
Plantation, Florida 33317

The Council for Exceptional Children
1920 Association Drive
Reston, VA 22091-1589

Earth Force
1501 Wilson Blvd.
12th Floor, Dept. AM
Arlington, VA 22209

FERPA Office (Family Educational Rights and Privacy Act)
U.S. Dept. of Education
HEW Building (North)
330 Independence Avenue, S.W.
Washington, D.C. 20201

Head Start Bureau
Department of Health and Human Services
P.O. Box 1182
Washington, DC 20013

The International Society of Arboriculture
P.O. Box GG
Savory, IL 61874-9902

Learning Disabilities Association of America (LDAA)
4156 Library Road
Pittsburgh, PA 15234

March of Dimes Birth Defects Foundation
1275 Mamaroneck Avenue
New York, NY 10605
(914) 428-7100

NAEYC
National Association for the Education of Young Children
1509 16th Street N.W.
Washington, D.C. 20036

National Association for Perinatal Addiction
        Research and Education
11 E. Hubbard Street, Suite 200
Chicago, IL 60611

National Association for the Preservation and
        Perpetuation of Storytelling
P.O. Box 112
Jonesborough, TN 37659

National Education Association (NEA)
Office of Education Support Personnel
1201 16th Street, N.W.
Washington, D.C. 20036

National Resource Center for Paraeducators
Center for Advanced Study in Education
25 West 43 Street, Room 620N
New York, NY 10036

The Orton Dyslexia Society
724 York Road
Baltimore, MD 21204

CHAPTER 11 — Onward and Upward: Upgrading Paraeducator Status

After a while you will settle into your niche as a paraeducator. You will know what you're supposed to do and you will feel pretty comfortable doing it. You will become used to the students and the teacher and they will become used to you. Is that it? Are there ways to upgrade your position? It may be that you will be perfectly happy with your job just the way it is, or it may be that you'll look for ways to continue to grow and improve as a paraeducator. This chapter is for those of you who have that urge for progress because you will be interested in future possibilities. It is also for those of you who need your jobs badly because you are the workers who are least likely to know or care about how laws protect you or to complain about unfair employer practices.

Informed workers who know their rights can protect other future child care workers by alerting employers to the fact that this career group is becoming savvy, and will use the law in a never-ending struggle to give the child care profession the recognition and compensation it deserves. If you work in a day care center, you know that you are the one who helps the working parents of your little charges keep their employment and their peace of mind.

Part of this chapter has been written in an attempt to connect existing law to our career field's continual effort to upgrade professional status and consequently upgrade wages and working conditions.

KNOW YOUR RIGHTS

Workers entering the caring and giving profession of child care expect employers to be ethical and honest. Sadly, though, as with many other professions, there will always be some who will bend the law, overlook the law, or break the law through greed, confusion, ignorance, or other reasons. Knowing your rights will help protect you from being exploited.

You've chosen paraeducator work for many reasons, including a sincere desire to add to the quality of education and care of children, and because you need the financial support. You may feel that defending your rights is not a part of your employment. Certainly it is true that defending your rights can be uncomfortable, unfortunate, and even detrimental in some rare circumstances. Remember, though, that others will follow after you in this career. Your knowledge can protect their lawful rights as well as your own.

The first step in asserting your legal rights is to know what those rights are. It is important to know which practices are prohibited by law, and to distinguish these from actions that may seem unjust, but which are not unlawful (U.S. Department of Labor, 1992). Appendix G reviews pertinent laws for the paraeducator. Try to keep current on new legal developments that pertain to your job.

In regard to the Equal Pay Act of 1963, consider whether you do maintenance or cooking tasks as part of your job. Since the hourly wages of maintenance workers and cooks may be well above the hourly wages for early childhood workers, it is a wonder that many early childhood workers perform maintenance and cooking duties without equal pay. Something to think about, isn't it?

THE LAW CAN BE USED TO UPGRADE STATUS

How can you personally use the law to upgrade the early childhood profession? What can you do that will help to increase either the public view or compensation for paraeducators? Here are some suggestions concerning the interview stage:

- Report illegal statements in employer advertising for early childhood positions (EEOC).

- Report illegal and objectionable interview questions that have nothing to do with your ability to perform job duties.

- Report it if a prospective employer does not notify you after submitting your name to a credit reporting agency or if the interviewing employer refuses to state the agency's address or the nature and scope of the agency's investigation.

- Report it if a past employer gives untrue information and/or information that is not related to the job when your references are checked. This also includes confidential material in personnel or medical files.

- Report training wages that are not at least 85 percent of minimum wage (U.S. Department of Labor).
- Report Civil Rights Law violation(s).
- Report it if an employer requests/requires you to undergo a medical exam before a job is offered. Report interview questions about your medical history.
- Ask an employer whether required maintenance, cooking, and cleaning job duties will be paid at a rate equal to other such workers in the community.

Note: You have an important obligation in the interview process, too, that is, to be honest. Courts have ruled overwhelmingly that applicant misstatements during interviews or on applications are excellent reasons for not hiring or immediately firing.

Note #2: The reason that many early childhood workers receive minimum wage is that so many workers accept jobs at that pay level. If you are really bold, you can always suggest to a prospective employer that minimum wage is not a fair wage for the required duties and services expected and for your training and experience. This is not done very often, but some things might change if all the applicants pleasantly refused to work for unfairly low wages. What would become of all of the low paying centers and schools needing staff if this happened?

HOW TO HELP YOURSELF AND OTHERS IF YOU ARE OFFERED AN EMPLOYMENT CONTRACT

How can you as a paraeducator act to protect worker interest if you are offered an employment contract? Some possibilities include:

- Get negotiating help from a professional bargaining agent or work group representative.
- Get legal help if you do not understand all the parts of an offered contract.
- Remember that all contract specifics are negotiable.
- Analyze your job using the Internal Revenue Guidelines to determine whether you should be designated as an independent contractor or hourly worker status best describes your job.

MAKE SURE LAWS ARE ENFORCED WHERE YOU WORK

Once you take a job as a paraeducator, you can make sure labor laws are enforced by:

- Awareness of labor laws, first of all.
- Knowing when you are working overtime.
- Knowing about compensatory hours and rate of pay.
- Checking to see if your paycheck is correct, especially if you do split shift work.
- Requesting labor law posters at your place of work if they are not there already.
- Reading your state's lunch and break time policy.
- Letting your employer know that duty-free lunch periods can only be changed by employee-employer agreement.
- Knowing your state requirements concerning employee break and bathroom facilities.
- Knowing that if your employer requires you to work after hours doing such things as preparing written lesson plans, attending night meetings, or making home visits, this should be paid work time.
- Making sure your payroll deductions are correct and appropriate.
- Keeping complete records of all job-related expenses.
- Keeping accurate, timely personal records of job-related facts, dates, times, meetings, etc.

BE CAREFUL WHAT PRECEDENTS YOU SET

It is important to know your rights and consider others when you decide to be accommodating. Each time a worker agrees to work during lunch time or waives legal break times, it affects all workers. Workers in caring professions such as child care and education can be unwise and unaware that "giving" actions may have unanticipated results. When you do things such as work unpaid hours, even though you do them for the children's benefit, you may unwittingly lead your employer to expect every employee to act in this sacrificing way. It is wonderful to be a "giver." So many people who work with children have just the sort of kind, generous natures that make them apt to give of themselves. Changes in worker rights have been hard won, though, and in many cases worker rights protect the health, job satisfaction, and interests of workers. With the long upward struggle toward "comparable worth" salaries and benefits, early childhood workers should guard their rights and recognize exploitation when it occurs. As stated before, there are widespread low pay rates for paraeducators. Though you have such good motives and mean it only for the best, when you give away your time and pay rights to your job, you do not help the cause for better pay for paraeducators. The whole profession gains when workers are knowledgeable, and expect labor laws to be followed. Individual workers gain from decreased burn-out rates and increased job satisfaction. So consider all this when you make your own job decisions.

POSSIBLE CHANGES IN THE FUTURE

There are advocates out there who strongly believe that day care providers should be better trained and better paid. Finkelfor (1988) says this:

> Advocates have latched on to sexual abuse in day care as evidence that providers should be better trained, screened, and paid, that licensing should be more stringent, and that publicly funded facilities should be more numerous. Others see these events as evidence that children have no business in day care at all.

The question is raised about how the image of child care workers could be enhanced and young children could be better protected through child abuse law or licensing law. Some changes that might help would be:

- Criminal background checks and fingerprinting across the board for all center staff and support service contractors.
- Strict rules and procedures concerning all adults, parents, and staff family members entering day care center child use areas.
- Mandatory screening of student early childhood majors in student teaching classes.
- Child care law and abuse detection training curriculum made mandatory for all staff members.
- Unannounced site inspection by licensing agencies.
- Mandatory distribution of information and/or parent sessions concerning child abuse in all licensed centers.

When you see these kinds of changes, do not balk at them. You might not like submitting to fingerprinting or having surprise observation visits to your room, but you need to recognize that these are ways to pull up standards. If standards are raised and you are a part of the higher ones, it can only benefit you. Recognize that strict policies for entering rooms in day care centers really protect everybody. You might not like it when your sister comes to bring something by for you and she is given the tenth degree in order to get past the front desk, but you sure would be glad if a hostile estranged divorced parent was stopped from coming in and kidnapping a child in your care.

In fact, you can do more than simply refrain from resisting such changes; you can work toward them. Career workers in any given state can unite to make sure their state's licensing law does require fingerprinting and criminal background checks on newly hired workers in licensed centers. See about your state. Encourage student teaching training with classes that monitor and observe candidates before graduation or licensing so that unsuitable candidates could either receive further training before working with children or could be steered in other career directions. Support or initiate recommendations for continued training and higher standards for paraeducators.

U N I O N S

Workers may also band together in unions. This is an option that may be available for you to consider. According to a profile that Morin (1991) calls "the foremost unions representing the child care teacher," the following estimates of union workers were cited:

- American Federation of State, County and Municipal Employees (AFSCME), 10,000 child care workers
- United Auto Workers/ District 65, 1,500 child care employees
- American Federation of Teachers (AFT), 6,000 child care workers
- National Education Association (NEA), 8,000 preschool workers
- Service Employees International Union (SEIU), 1,000 to 1,500 child care workers

To be covered under the National Labor Relations Act, a company, individual owner, or school must either (1) be engaged in interstate commerce, or (2) the volume of business must exceed $250,000 per year. NCECW (1994) believes that:

Certificate Programs

Changes are occurring around the United States. For example, the Wisconsin Educational Association Council's Professional Development Academy (PDA) is striving to develop a certificate program for that state's school support workers. Johanna Kaufmann, PDA director, is now working with higher level educators from Wisconsin state universities, technical colleges, and other facilities to "encourage them to seek Professional Development Academy approval for courses likely to be useful to school support employees in their jobs." Kaufmann states,

> *Education support workers will take 40 hours of specified courses, and the Academy will award them a certificate. The hope is that local Associations will negotiate higher salaries for employees who earn certificates.*
> *(NEA Today, September 1995)*

Paraprofessionsals in Vermont are also working to build a certificate process in their state, by collaborating with people from the University of Vermont and the Vermont NEA to develop training guidelines and decide job requirements. The instigating belief is that "if paraprofessionals were certified, they'd get appropriate training, have specific job descriptions, and get the respect they deserve" (NEA Today, September 1995). Keep your eyes and ears open for changes in your area!

> *The interstate commerce law is so broad that almost every employee of a child care center will be covered. If, on the job, an employee handles <u>any</u> goods that came from another state, such as toys, food or paper, then he or she meets the requirement. It doesn't matter whether the employer is a non-profit or for-profit organization.*

Nevertheless, one way that union law could be changed to benefit child care workers would be to include smaller schools and centers in the law.

A couple of particulars about union law are:

- Employers are forbidden by the National Labor Relations Board to spy on employee union activities. You have the right to check into and/or join a union without interference from your boss.

- Union organizers can petition for an election to be recognized as the exclusive bargaining representative of a group of employees. However, to call for an election the union must be able to prove that they have the support of at least 30 (thirty) percent of the employees in a bargaining unit" (Joel, 1993).

There is a broader discussion of union law discussed in Chapter 13.

The Special Education Employee Association (composed of para-professionals) in St. Louis County, Missouri was instrumental in saving over a third of the paraprofessional jobs in their district from being cut. They did this by banding together and voting as a block and also by proposing what led to a successful alternative financial plan (NEA Today Education Support Edition 1995–96).

PERSONAL PROFESSIONAL DEVELOPMENT

Sometimes the best thing you can do for yourself is to make a change, especially if you feel the job has become stale or if you and a coworker have serious difficulty working together. In the first case, it may be that you simply need to switch jobs with another paraeducator in your facility. If you have worked in kindergarten for years, maybe it is time for you to request to work in the media center or with visually impaired students. Unfortunately, the second case does occur and there are occasions when, try as you might, you have a personality or philosophy conflict with the lead teacher. Of course, first try again, try everything you can and give problems time to work out. You need to remember that it is not always the other person who is at fault. Be sure to evaluate your own conduct and responsibility for problems first. Next, try to learn how to cope with your adversary. Try reading books on different personality types. (*Coping With Difficult People* by Robert Bramson or *Positive Personality Profiles* by Robert A. Rohm) Implement wise suggestions but be very careful not to go seeking advice too freely from other coworkers. It really will be in your best interest and the best interest of others if you avoid gossip, no matter how tempting it is. If you sincerely feel that you have exhausted your own resources and the situation with a coworker is unmanageable, go to your administrator, but only if you think about this step long and hard. You never can be certain that a new position will be an improvement. Only take this final step if you know that you have to be switched or that one of you truly has to go! If you do go to an administrator with a request for change, do it privately, respectfully, and kindly. Hopefully, if there is really an unresolvable conflict, you will be moved to a different position (within the school or facility or within the school system). Then do your very best to make the next working relationship successful. As you start fresh, remember that your primary function is to help the teacher achieve goals as effectively and efficiently as possible. Go back and review information on

Check-up Time

You really know yourself how you are doing as a paraprofessional. It is good to do some honest self-evaluation occasionally. Ask yourself these questions:

1. Am I willing to accept suggestions for improvement or change?

2. How do I do with criticism? Do I get angry or upset? Do I take criticism seriously enough? Do I take criticism too seriously?

3. Do I have cooperative, friendly relationships with others? With other paraprofessionals? With the lead teacher? With the administration?

4. Do I refrain from criticizing the children, teachers, other staff members, and the school in general?

5. When I do have concerns or legitimate criticisms, do I express them through proper channels and in a constructive way?

6. Do I conduct myself in a professional manner? Do I open my mouth when I should keep it shut? Do I show respect to others? Do I hang around the office or the breakroom too much?

7. Do I pay enough attention to the children? Do I care about and have insights into their problems and needs?

8. Do I practice proficiency as a paraprofessional? Do I lend wholehearted support to the children, to the lead teacher, and the administration? Do I do everything I can to assist the teacher? Am I treating this job as simply a job or am I giving it my best?

(Developed from Cherokee Co. Substitute Workshop Material)

preparation in Chapter 3. Get to know the methods and style of your new lead teacher. Remember that your understanding of the methods the teacher applies to achieve goals is essential to the success of the entire class. To be the best possible paraeducator you must operate in a way that is congruent to the teacher. Sometimes it takes a new beginning to be able to do that.

One of the ways you can be a tremendous asset to your school or day care center is to voice your ideas. When you think of a new possibility don't be afraid to share it. Certainly you should respect those who are in authority over you, but don't let others intimidate you in ways that stifle your creativity and progress. Good ideas can come to anybody, not just those with college degrees. Many solutions to problems are just common sense and you probably have as many or more flashes of that as anyone else. You may be the very one to suggest the next successful program at your workplace.

Ideas for programs and changes come from being observant, looking around at how things flow and how people's needs are being met. Keep your eyes open. When you see a problem, think about what is needed to make it better. Brainstorm for possible solutions, without discounting any solutions at first, even ones that seem wild or impractical initially. Sometimes the crazy ideas turn out to offer the best solutions. However, think the whole thing through carefully before you speak. Once you have figured out that your idea could really work, or you work through it with a crony, talk to someone who is in charge about it. You never know!

The NEA Today (Sept. 1995 Special edition) says, "If you have an innovative idea to enhance student learning, go after it—instructional development grants and awards are not for teachers only." Your media specialist or an administrator may be able to help you find out more information about what grants are available.

If your school does not do any or one or some of the following, consider developing a program for your school or day care center:

- Publishing, making lasting books authored by the children

- Peer mediation

- Newsletter

- Schoolwide field days or "Olympics"

- Summer day camp

- Community service such as road beautification

- Recycling

- Educational garden

- Support and encouragement for local hospitals or retirement homes

- Thanksgiving dinner donations or kitchen for those in need

- Christmas giving program such as "Toys for Tots"

- Mentoring, a "buddy" system between volunteer adults and students who need extra encouragement

- Occasional training/support programs for parents dealing with such topics as drug abuse, latchkey kids, and homework helps

- End of the year special program for the highest grade students who will be leaving the school

Individuals and groups of paraeducators have won recognition for their special efforts. A group in Delaware (members of the Christina Paraprofessional Association) won an award for the program they started in an after-school program. The goal of the program is to encourage academic excellence among children in lower grades. The *instructional development* award was given to them by the Delaware State Education Association. Jody Neuman, a paraprofessional in Lansing, Michigan, encouraged her students to enter a contest sponsored by Continental Cablevision and the Discovery Channel. She helped the students design a space suit for a visit to Mercury. They won first place in the national science education contest and were awarded a free excursion to Space Camp in Huntsville, Alabama. (NEA Today Education Support Edition 1995–96).

Encourage your students to enter contests or submit their original artwork or writings, just as Neuman did. Local newspapers and children's magazines such as Cricket, Stone Soup, and Highlights are good opportunity sources (Oppenheim, 1989). When you encourage students to strive for success, you are successful yourself.

Take advantage of any further training opportunities in your area. If your school system offers workshops, check into them. Join associations and you will be notified of conventions and seminars that may interest you. Annual conferences are sponsored by preschool associations in some areas.

In 1996, the Fifteenth Annual Conference on the Training and Employment of the Paraprofessional Workforce in Education, Rehabilitation and Related Fields was held in Snowbird, Utah. This conference was sponsored by the National Resource Center for Paraprofessionals in Education and Related Services (NRC). Paraprofessionals, administrators, personnel planners, and others from all over the United States were invited to attend. Workshop topics included such subjects as training, changes in roles, inclusion, problem-solving, and classroom behavior. There was time built into this two-day conference for fun and interaction with other conference participants, including an opportunity to attend a mystery dinner theater. If you are interested in attending a future conference, contact:

> NRC for Paraprofessionals
> CASE/CUNY Graduate Center/ Room 620N
> 25 West 43rd Street
> New York, NY 10036
> (212) 642-2948

Some areas require paraeducators to attend training workshops in order to earn a license for working as a paraprofessional in that district. In Cherokee County, GA, the license must be renewed every five years by attending two workshop days. Your area may have similar requirements. If they do not, it would be in the highest interest of the paraeducator field in general for you to push for training standards for your area.

In today's world, one of the best ways you can upgrade your own personal position is to learn all you can about available technology. If you are not already, become computer literate. Believe me, the children will. Take computer courses and participate in in-services. It will help you to help the children as they learn about and on computers and it will help you learn skills that are mandatory in many areas of work in the current world.

In the book, *Smart Start: an Elementary Education for the 21st Century,* Patte Barth says that "computers will be so completely accepted in the classroom as to become part of the background." Barth says that computers will be used in the following ways:

- modeling in all subjects
- word processing
- networking so that all students may learn from input from and to one student
- communicating with other schools by modem
- researching, getting into the data bases at other libraries and information sources (1992)

Again, learn all that you can about these smart boxes.

The National Clearinghouse for Professions in Special Education has brochures and information sheets encouraging paraprofessionals to consider getting a degree. They remind paraeducators that the student population in special education is growing and so is the demand for special education teachers. Some advantages in pursuing a college degree are increased salary and broader authority in making decisions. The experience that special education paraprofessionals already have in the classroom works in their favor when they decide to become a special education teacher. If you should make such a decision, you would have a "leg up" on those without classroom experience. Suggested beginning steps are:

- Checking with the education department in your state to find out criteria for teaching in special education because the requirements for professional certification are determined by individual states.

- Asking the special education teachers with whom you currently work to tell you what they know about your area colleges' and universities' special education programs.

- Contacting special education departments in local colleges and universities to find out about being admitted and more about their programs.

- Applying to the college or university that seems to be the best fit for you and your goals.

- Going for it!

(Information from the National Clearinghouse for Professions in Special Education, fact sheet #20)

If you are interested in pursuing a college degree and money is a problem, don't give up before you start. You may be eligible for aid. A federal employment and training program came into existence in 1982 with the enactment of the *Job Training Partnership Act* (JTPA). States administer and direct JTPA programs. The goal of the act is to help economically disadvantaged individuals gain skills to enter either the work force or technical schools and colleges that will prepare the individuals for employment. Enrollees in JPTA programs may receive food, housing, medical services, counseling, and other supportive assistance. Your state Department of Labor or Department of Human Services can provide you with information about JPTA employment training opportunities.

Another possible way to find help is to contact your public school district office. They may be able to connect you with scholarship possibilities. Also ask the financial aid office of local colleges and universities.

Elizabeth Shafer, who became a district manager of the Massachusetts Department of Mental Health, began as a paraprofessional working with mentally retarded children. She continued to learn through the years through formal schooling (earning a bachelor's and a master's degree) and also through her experiences. In an article in *Social Policy,* she wrote that her experience as a paraprofessional was invaluable in paving the way toward her professional progress (1984).

There have been six women associated with one 1,000 student elementary school in Woodstock, Georgia who were paraeducators and then earned their degrees and became teachers. These teachers now teach in: first grade (2), third grade, fifth grade, sixth grade, and special education. One of these women was well over forty when she decided to go back to school. She raised her children, worked as a paraeducator, and then decided to "go for it" after her children were grown and established on their own.

Babe Ruth said, "Never let the fear of striking out keep you from swinging." So whether you decide to continue to work as a paraeducator or to further your career, always do your best and never let fear or intimidation keep you from reaching your full potential. When you reach your fullest potential, who knows how many children you can help to reach theirs?

CHAPTER 12

Policies and Procedures: Learning the Ways of Your Workplace

Now you are many steps closer to the daily world of a paraeducator. You have looked at what is involved in making a decision to become a paraeducator. Now it is time to reach closer to the specifics of your actual work site.

In this chapter many of the regulations and policies that affect your day-to-day work as a paraeducator will be touched on. Understanding your employer's regulations is essential to a good relationship between you and your administration. In turn, this good relationship is vital because the quality of the nitty-gritty classroom instruction is directly related to the health of this relationship.

Introductions, tours, oral and written instructions, and completing forms (tons!) are all part of paraeducator orientation. Since no one can remember everything, taking notes on names and information is recommended.

First impressions are important. Just as in your interview, how you dress in the first days sends an immediate communication to others about the respect you have for yourself and your new job. Your verbal responses and body language will also send many messages to others. So watch your step!

A desire to make a good first impression, as well as the newness of the people, setting, and information will likely cause temporary stress. Introductions and tours help new paraeducators to become familiar with people and places; that reduces the anxiety level. If you are not offered a general tour, politely ask for one. Finding another paraeducator who will be your buddy can help, too.

Be careful, though, about getting too tight with anyone initially. Guard your words. Avoid any commentary on people, procedures, or places. It will be best for you to keep fairly quiet, especially with criticism. Even if someone else "opens up" to you on her opinions about a situation, be careful that you do not respond too freely. Wait until you get a real sense of what is going on before you offer suggestions or criticism. If you are wise enough to get a "lay of the land," you will often avoid saying things that you may regret later. Remember that sometimes the people who are quickest to "tell you how it is" may be the ones who are dissatisfied and may not share the truest perspective.

Questions are vital; do not hesitate to ask them. Questions are smart, not stupid. It is better to courteously ask for a name to be repeated than to go for weeks avoiding calling someone by name.

An employee handbook is most likely one of the first things you will be given as a paraeducator; your handbook will answer many of your questions.

EMPLOYEE HANDBOOK: READ IT AND HEED IT

Employer printed handbooks acquaint workers with school rules and policies. They facilitate employees' and employers' understanding of what is expected (Joel, 1993). It is debatable whether handbook statements create contractual rights. Courts have ruled both yes and no on this issue. In Chapter 13, it mentions that handbooks are often considered to be implied contracts. Numerous lawsuits between employers and employees have hinged on handbook statements. Schools and centers are beginning to hire lawyers to scrutinize printed handbook statements. These days you may see a disclaimer at the beginning of your handbook. If a school's handbook states, "This handbook is not intended to be construed as a binding employment contract but only as a general source of information," the handbook can be changed at any time.

Employee handbooks may cover a wide gamut of topics. Your handbook may include policies ranging from scheduling the school stage, rules about using the laminator, to the procedure to follow during a tornado drill. There are subjects you would expect to be covered in any employee handbook; these include information on firing and performance standards, safety procedures, dress code standards, holidays, sick leave, and pay periods. There may also be topics that pertain specifically and uniquely to your facility, such as how to requisition supplies, rules about the nature trail behind the school, or information about your school's "Partners in Education" relationship with a local grocery store.

Take a look at the sample table of contents from an elementary school handbook (Table 12–1) to get an idea of what a wide range of topics may be covered in an employee handbook.

The following handbook sections are generally of particular interest to employees:

- Equal opportunity
- Firing and performance standards, firing "for cause"
- Promised training or orientation
- Disciplinary procedures (for employees), probationary periods
- Safety regulations, safety drills
- Grooming and dress requirements
- Overtime
- Pay periods and work hours

TABLE 12–1 Sample Table of Contents of a Teacher Handbook
Courtesy of Johnston Elementary, Woodstock, GA. Used with permission.

Child Abuse	Emergency Procedure
Report Cards	Emergency Lesson Plans
School Correspondence	Employee Data Sheet
Supervision of Students	Evaluations
Videos	Faculty Meetings
Weekly Newsletters	Field Trips
Accident Reports	Fire Drill
After School Program	Grade Level Meetings
Announcements	Honor Roll/Merit Roll
Attendance Sheets	Kroger Store
Bus Duty	Laminating
Cafeteria Guidelines	Lunches
Care of the Classroom	Math Management
Casual Conversation	Parent Conferences
Certification	Parties
Christmas Trees	Permanent Records
Computer Lab	Personnel
Corporal Punishment	Phone Calls
Counselor	Progress Reports
Curriculum Guides	PTA
Discipline	Purchase Orders
Discrimination	Reading Management
Doors	Requisitioning Textbooks
Dress Codes	Requisitioning Supplies

- Lunch and rest breaks
- Sick leave and holidays
- Performance appraisals and promotion policy

A close reading of your handbook is strongly suggested (Joel, 1993). Highlighting handbook passages and asking questions will help you gain a clear understanding of expectations. That basic understanding right from the outset will hopefully eliminate conflicts between you and your administration.

The topics that most likely will be covered in your orientation or in your handbook are lunch hour supervision, accident reports, break periods, and phone calls at work. We will consider these and a few other subjects in closer detail.

Lunch Hour Supervision

Federal labor law does not require employers to give breaks or meal periods, but most states have passed labor laws requiring them. Checking your state law is important. Make sure you understand whether or not you will receive pay for these periods.

Because licensed early childhood centers are required to provide constant child supervision and also have to maintain certain teacher-child ratios that are set by law, employers may not wish to hire additional staff for lunch/break periods. Doing so may cut profit. Consequently, this law, if your state has one, may be frequently broken. If your state law provides for lunch or other breaks and you do not get them, then you are donating your time. If you donate twenty or more minutes without pay each day, considerable pay is lost over a year's time.

When staff is off duty for lunch but must remain on the premises in order to maintain proper child-adult licensing ratios, the time must be *paid* time.

Some schools hire lunchroom monitors so that teachers and paraeducators can have "duty free" lunch. Some do this voluntarily even if state law does not demand it; others set up a cafeteria monitoring system so that they can fulfill the requirements of their state law.

If your school or center has a cafeteria, there probably will be a strict line-up procedure and time schedule in order to move the whole school in and out of the cafeteria in the most practical, logical order. This takes everybody working together and sticking to the regulations. See Figure 12–1 and Table 12–2. As a paraeducator, you will most likely

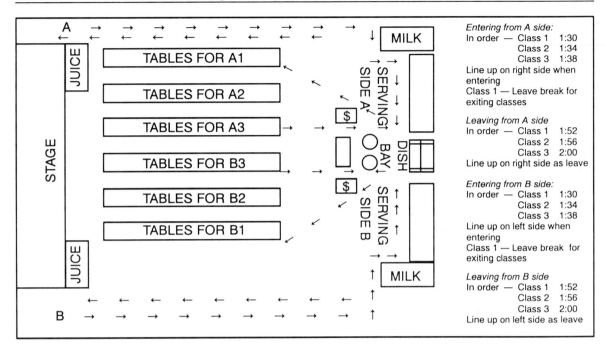

FIGURE 12–1 Sample Cafeteria Flow

TABLE 12–2 Sample Cafeteria Guidelines. Adapted from the ***Johnston Elementary Handbook,*** Woodstock, GA.

Cafeteria Guidelines:

1. Each teacher or paraeducator must stand with his or her students as they pass the cashier.

2. Students must make lunch choice decisions before coming to the cafeteria. They may not change their minds in the line.

3. Pick up blue laminated tickets from the cafeteria if you have students who want a *deli* lunch. Without a blue ticket students will not be allowed to get a deli lunch; they must get a hot lunch.

4. The teacher or the paraeducator must stay with the class until they are settled at the tables, then students may be left with the lunchroom monitors.

5. If a class is so noisy that they are put on silent lunch two times, then the teacher or paraeducator must sit with the class.

6. Each teacher or paraeducator will stand with his or her class as they empty their trays and dispose of their garbage. Dropped food and excessive numbers of trays being put into the dish bay at one time need to be supervised and remedied.

7. Each class is responsible for leaving the tables and floor clean for the class coming after them.

8. Each teacher or paraeducator needs to make sure that his or her class enters and leaves the cafeteria at the scheduled time.

have a lot of responsibility for helping children move efficiently through the lunchroom. No small task by any means! The best thing you can do is hold on to your sense of humor and follow the school procedures as well as you can.

Break Periods

Under the labor law in most break-giving states, a true break period is considered to be an off-duty period when the worker has no job duties and can leave the premises. Workers who smoke and are prohibited from smoking on child care center premises have a special interest in their state's labor law.

If your state law requires break periods for workers, the law usually specifies break time particulars, meaning a break may be considered a break if it occurs in the middle of a four- to five-hour work period. If your state does provide for break periods, these break periods are paid work periods.

If you are required to take unpaid break time, you need to clarify lawful break time rights with your state labor offices.

If your facility has a place set up for breaks, you will want to find out where that is pretty quickly!

Phone Calls at Work

Employers are entitled to limit and prohibit employee use of facility phones, and to monitor permitted calls. So if you are permitted to use the phone while at work, you can consider this a privilege and you should follow phone call policies strictly.

Often, teachers and paraeducators will not be called out of the classroom to take phone calls except in emergencies or special situations. You may be asked to inform family members or others that, in most cases, you will not be called away from your students and that they will need to leave a message for you.

Confidentiality

This topic was mentioned under professional conduct in Chapter 1; it is important enough to stress again. As previously discussed, as a paraeducator you represent a profession, you work alongside professionals, and as a paraeducator, you are obligated to abide by certain regulations, including an ethical conduct code. Confidentiality is an integral part of this code. There will most likely be some reference to this matter in your employee handbook.

Confidentiality protects children and families and should be maintained at all times. Paraeducators can become so involved with classroom happenings and individual children that they inadvertently discuss privileged information with another paraeducator, teacher, friend, or worse, within the earshot of a parent or student. You can easily see how this might happen and cause irreparable damage. You need to be aware of casual conversation in the school office, in the workroom, and in the halls. If you live in the same community as your workplace, you need to be especially careful of your conversations at the grocery store, at the ball field, or wherever you might be. It is not proper to talk about your "behavior problem" or your "space case" out in public, or in any way other than in a professional manner in an appropriate setting.

Imagine helping register children for summer day camp. As you hand enrollment cards to Barbara, one of the teachers, you give her a warning about little Kenny who will be in her class. You tell her that Kenny just about did you and the teacher in last year in kindergarten, that he was the first kindergartner that you had ever had who had to spend a whole day in ISS (in-school suspension), and that there were quite a few conflicts with the mother, too. You notice that Barbara's helper looks kind of funny, but she does not say anything. Later during the week you are appalled to see Kenny leave in the same car as Barbara's helper and to discover that she is Kenny's aunt! This type of situation is inexcusable. First of all, you need to always remember the old adage that, "if you can't say anything good about somebody, don't say anything at all." Secondly, you should never discuss a student's behavior, intelligence level, discipline problems, learning difficulties, family situation, and so forth, away from school or with anyone other than the student, the student's family, the teacher, or the administration.

Seen in a school clinic is a sign that says:

> *"What you see here,*
> *what you hear here,*
> *When you leave here,*
> *let it stay here."*

That is a good reminder about the things you see and hear at your school or center.

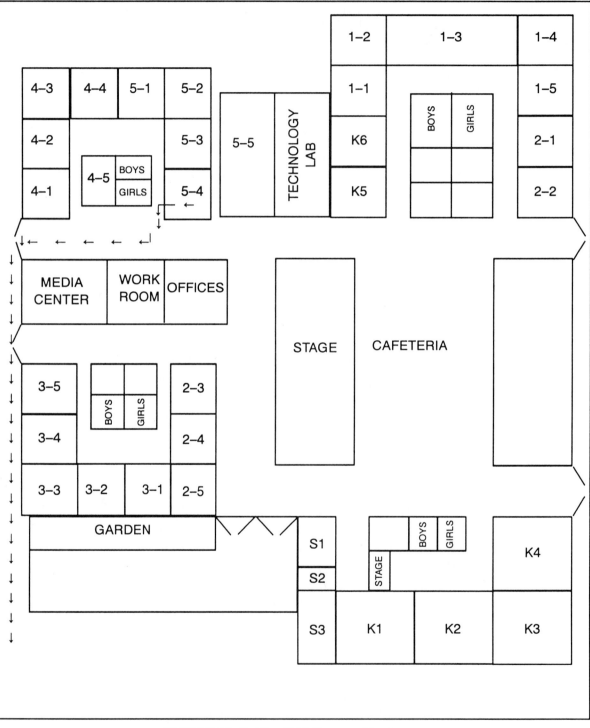

FIGURE 12–2 Fire Drill Escape Route

Emergency Procedures and Safety Drills

Each school or center has its own way of handling preparation for emergencies and conducting practices such as fire drills and tornado drills. You need to become familiar with procedures as soon as possible. You will need to know the fire drill exit route from your room, where to take your children during a tornado or other severe weather drill, and whether your main responsibility is to grab the class roll or to take care of the disabled child in your room, or both. Figure 12–2 indicates that it is necessary to exit by a prescribed route during a fire drill.

Many schools now sadly but wisely make provisions for announcing unwelcome and dangerous intruders. Your facility may have a coded message that would be announced over the public address system if someone entered the building with intent to do harm. In such a case you might be expected to keep all children in the classroom, lock the door, close curtains or blinds, prevent children from getting close to the door or windows, and do these things in a calm non-upsetting manner.

As a paraeducator, one of your duties may be to maintain emergency numbers for all your students. Schools must keep information about whom to notify in cases of emergency and illness and also about where the child should go if school is ever dismissed early due to severe weather. You need to make sure this type of information is up-to-date at all times.

Accident Reports

If one of your students or a coworker has an accident when you are on the scene, there are procedures you should follow. Of course, the first thing to do is to take care of the person who had the accident in the best way you can. Notify the appropriate person, usually the lead teacher, the director, or the principal. Most likely you will be required to fill out an accident report, possibly on a specific form and within a certain amount of time. Even if you are not required to do so, it is a good idea to write an account. Record when and where the accident occurred and what and how it happened. Also write down the names of anybody else who witnessed the accident (Maggs, 1980).

The following is a sample entry in an employee handbook regarding accident reports:

Students— All injuries to students must be reported to the principal's office immediately. There are accident report forms on file in the front office. An accident report must be completed by the staff member who witnesses the accident or the staff member who was in charge of the student at the time of the accident.

Personnel — All injuries to staff members must be reported to the principal's office as soon as possible. Workman's Compensation accident reports must be completed for any incident no matter how minor.

(Adapted from Johnston Elementary Handbook, Woodstock, GA)

Procedure for Dismissing Students

This ranks right along with an emergency code in terms of importance to children's safety. Very quickly, you will need to learn the policies for dismissal in your school or center. This is vital whether you work with middle-schoolers who ride home on the bus or infants who are given directly into their parents' care. You need to strictly adhere to guidelines in order to ensure that children go to the right place and with the right people when they leave your supervision. Enough horror stories have been seen through the media to alert us all to the need for the highest levels of care concerning this issue.

Copiers and Other Machines

Every workplace has its own particular guidelines about use of copiers and other machines. In fact, some places have a whole lot of rules about machines: who is allowed to use them; specified times to use them; and what to do when maintenance needs surface. Sometimes it can seem like the copier always and only breaks down when *you* use it. People can get kind of testy about office machinery, so watch your step! The laminator use policy in Table 12–3 indicates the kinds of rules that you may encounter concerning machines.

Copyright laws are discussed in Appendix G. As a paraeducator you may be called upon to make loads of photocopies. Remember that strict adherence to laws, codes, and regulations is a vital component of professional conduct.

TABLE 12–3 Entry in an Employee Handbook about Using the Laminator *Adapted from the Johnston Elementary Handbook, Woodstock, GA.*

> Only office staff and paraprofessionals will be allowed to operate the laminator. Be sure to put your name on each item to be laminated. Remove all staples, tape, or paper before you leave anything to be laminated. Items may be placed in the labelled box on the counter to the right of the mailboxes. Please be considerate and put your items on the bottom of the stack if there are other items already in the box. Your laminated items will be put in your mailbox when they are completed.
>
> Paraeducators, please leave the laminator on after you use it since it takes so long for it to warm up. Marigold will turn it off at the end of the day. Whenever you laminate something for your own room, try to laminate one other person's materials from the box as well. Thank you.

Getting a Substitute

You must find out right away what to do if you are unable to be there. Hopefully your need for substitutes will be rare or infrequent, but you never know when that need might arise. The policy in some facilities is that you have to find your own substitute from a list of willing people's names and numbers. Others request that you call one central source, possibly a secretary or even an administrator, to schedule substitutes. The key here is to be out from your job as little as possible, make necessary calls as soon as possible, and go through suggested channels whenever possible. (See Table 12–4).

Most employee handbooks cover a great portion of what you need to know about the way your facility operates. Study (Yes, study!) your handbook earlier rather than later. As stated before, it will help you understand some of your general responsibilities and will lessen chances for misunderstandings between you and the administration.

RECORD KEEPING AND PERSONNEL FILES

You know now that your employer is required to keep certain records about you and your work. In addition to entries listed in Appendix G, your employer may be required to keep signed statements indicating that you understand applicable responsibilities concerning child abuse and child discipline. In other words, your employer may need to main-

TABLE 12–4 Procedure for Obtaining a Substitute *Adapted from the Johnston Elementary Handbook, Woodstock, GA.*

1. Notify Penelope as soon as you know you will need to be out.

2. All personal leave days must be authorized by the principal at least five working days in advance.

3. Fill out a personal leave form (on file in Penelope's office) and return it to Penelope as soon as possible. Sick leave forms will be put in your mailbox to be completed the day you return. Please give your sick leave form back to Penelope as soon as possible.

4. If you find it necessary to call Penelope in the morning, please call her between 6:00 a.m. and 6:30 a.m. DO NOT CALL THE SCHOOL AT 7:20 a.m. EXCEPT IN <u>EXTREME</u> EMERGENCIES. This does not give Penelope enough time to get someone to cover your duties when the students arrive.

5. If you find it necessary to call Penelope at night, call BEFORE 9:00 p.m.

6. If you find it necessary to leave during the school day, see the principal before talking to Penelope about arranging for a substitute.

7. Penelope's home number is 000-0000. Please be considerate of her and let her know as soon as you can within the time frames given. You may leave messages on her answering machine if she is not home.

tain proof of informing all employees about legal obligations and school policies.

Remember that you may or may not have the right to inspect your own personnel file ("Legal Problem Solver", 1994). Research whether your state has established the right for you to look at your own file through recent record-access legislation. Also don't forget that some states give you the right to clarify information in your personnel file.

A good practice for you to follow is to keep your own records. It is suggested that you maintain a *personal personnel file* separate from your employer's personnel file (Joel, 1993). You need to keep copies of important papers concerning your job and you should document incidents that you may need to recall later. Here are items you should include in your records:

• Copies of performance reviews, job description

• Informal comments, oral statements and assurances

• Records of interactions with supervisors

• Faculty/staff meeting notes

- Tests taken for employment, information given at the interview
- records of any controversial occurrences with students or parents
- witnesses

Documentation facts should be specific and accurate. You should be careful to write down places, people, dates, times, and so forth. These facts will help to give credence to your recollections, and in the unhappy event of any conflicts, these facts will stand up under scrutiny. If you have detailed records, you can also help yourself tremendously should you ever need whistle blower protections.

ASKING FOR A REVIEW

Some centers rarely conduct employee job performance reviews. Some schools do evaluations on a routine basis, semi-annually or annually. Reviews will usually help you see how you can improve as a paraeducator. Reviews also document satisfactory job performance. On the other hand, if a review determines that you need to make improvements, and a time is set for you to make necessary improvements, it is good to have a follow-up meeting in order to note that progress has been made or skills have been accomplished. If not offered, you should ask for both written reviews and follow-up reviews. Again, remember that copies of these belong in your personal personnel file for your own protection.

Generally in a school district the principal will be the one who will conduct your review. In a center, the director will likely be the one who will sit down with you for a formal evaluation. In both cases, though, they will have likely sought input about your performance from the teacher with whom you work.

Evaluations will most likely include assessment or observations in the following areas:

- Prompt completion of tasks
- Clarity of instructions to students
- Correct reinforcement of the teacher's strategies
- Following instructions
- Cooperation as an instructional team member
- Appropriate initiative

TABLE 12–5 Instructions for Personnel Evaluations *Used with permission of the Cherokee County Board of Education*

The job descriptions of the Cherokee County Schools have been developed to also be used as evaluation instruments. Each job description includes a set of Performance Responsibilities that cover the tasks of each job.

Beside each task statement is a blank in which the evaluator will insert a number representing their assessment of the employee's performance on that particular task.

These numbers ranging from 1 to 5 are to be used according to the following scale:

1. Performance is unacceptable.
2. Performance is below average, needs improvement.
3. Performance meets expectations.
4. Performance is above average.
5. Performance is outstanding.

N/A   Used when task is not applicable.

Employee Name: _____

Job Title: _____Library Aide_____

Evaluated by: _____Media Specialist and Principal_____ Date: _____

Comments or Recommendations: ___*We are more caught up than we ever have been.*_____

_____

_____

_____

This form must be completed and attached to a completed copy of the evaluation form (job description form).

Employee's signature: _____ 6–1–93

Evaluator's signature: _____ Media Specialist

(Continued)

TABLE 12–5 Instructions for Personnel Evaluations (Continued) *Adapted from the Johnston Elementary Handbook, Woodstock, GA.*

POSITION TITLE: LIBRARY AIDE   Code: 3.31

Effective Date: March 8, 1988

Job Goal: To increase the efficiency of the library operation by performing various clerical duties and providing assistance to students and teachers

Reports To: Librarian and Principal

Performance Responsibilities:

_____5_____   1. Compiles, records, sorts and shelves books, periodicals, audio-visual and other materials.

_____5_____   2. Records information data and due date on cards (shelf list)

_____5_____   3. Inspects returned books for damage, verifies due date and computes overdue fines.

_____5_____   4. Compiles list of overdue books and issues notices.

_____5_____   5. Sorts books and materials and returns them to designated areas.

_____5_____   6. Locates books and materials for students and teachers.

_____5_____   7. Files cards in catalog drawers according to system.

_____5_____   8. Repairs books and periodicals.

_____5_____   9. Answers questions regarding library services and materials.

_____5_____   10. Assists librarian in typing, mailing and filing of correspondence.

_____5_____   11. Maintains bulletin board(s).

_____5_____   12. Operates various office machines.

_____5_____   13. Performs other tasks as may be assigned.

- Concern for respect and fair treatment of children
- Attention to safety and well-being of children

Tables 12–5, 12–6, and 12–7 are examples of evaluations for paraeducators in three different capacities.

The National Resource Center for Paraprofessionals in Education and Related Services has developed a sample performance review/evaluation for paraeducators. This is included in Table 12–8. The National Resource Center suggests that this "skill inventory" may be used by administrators to develop their own evaluation checklists; by teachers as "a guide for planning appropriate work assignments for paraeducators;" and for paraeducators to assess their own strong points and areas for improvement (Pickett, 1993).

ROTATED DUTIES

Most child care center and school staff members have some duties that everybody has to share. Some of these might include bus or car pool duty, stocking the break area, and cleaning the workroom. These types of shared general duties are often rotated among staff members. Be aware of schedules; don't overlook these schoolwide tasks while you are so busy with your own specific room tasks.

YOUR SURROUNDINGS

As you tour your new workplace and take those steps closer to your own work corner, pay attention to your environment and the interactions around you. Places and people have ways of their own; places can have atmospheres and people have personalities that may be very private or very open. Your director may welcome you to enter the office most any time, it may be perfectly acceptable to flag your principal down in the hall, or your administrator may prefer that you schedule appointments with the secretary. Likewise, it may be that you and other employees have free access to the entire building or there may be areas that are off-limits to other than designated individuals. Be a conscientious observer! This recommendation may seem trivial, but your careful observations could save you from unnecessary embarrassment.

TABLE 12–6 Adapted from "Staff Evaluation" by Kingsbury, Vogler & Benero, 1990. *The Everyday Guide to Opening and Operating a Child Care Center.* Vade Mecum Press.

STAFF EVALUATION

DATE
NAME OF EMPLOYEE
POSITION

1. Knowledge of Job: (Consider extent of person's knowledge of present job: knows what to do and why; increases his/her knowledge of the job)

    ___ Has an exceptionally thorough knowledge of job
    ___ Has good knowledge of work
    ___ Requires considerable coaching
    ___ Has inadequate knowledge of work

2. Quality of Work: (Consider ability to do high quality work: consistency; follow-through)

    ___ Highest quality
    ___ Well done
    ___ Passable
    ___ Poor

3. Quantity of Work: (Consider amount of work completed under normal conditions: produces expected number of projects and activities)

    ___ Large amount
    ___ Good amount
    ___ Slightly below average
    ___ Unsatisfactory

4. Attendance and Punctuality: (Consider frequency of absences as well as lateness)

    ___ Excellent record
    ___ Occasionally late or absent
    ___ Frequently absent or late
    ___ Undependable
    ___ Begins work promptly upon arriving
    ___ Unnecessary delays in starting work

5. Attitude: (Consider attitude toward work, school, associates, and willingness to work with others: pitches in when needed; works well with others; makes effort to understand policies; willing to do less desirable tasks)

    ___ Excellent cooperation
    ___ Good cooperation
    ___ Fair cooperation
    ___ Poor cooperation

6. Judgment: (Consider ability to make decisions and to utilize working time; plan logically; obtain facts before making decisions; knows when to seek advice; acts wisely in unusual situations)

    ___ Justifies utmost confidence
    ___ Needs little supervision
    ___ Needs frequent checking
    ___ Needs constant supervision

7. Reliability: (Consider ability to work under pressure and to complete job; retains composure under pressure; completes assignments satisfactorily and on time)

    ___ Very dependable
    ___ Generally dependable
    ___ Unpredictable

8. Personal Characteristics: (Consider manners, grooming and appearance, health, poise, patience, ambition)

    ___ Very satisfactory
    ___ Satisfactory
    ___ Needs improvement in certain areas; specify:

9. Miscellaneous

    Excessive misuse of breaks   ___ yes
                                        ___ no

    Excessive personal
    telephone calls   ___ yes
                                        ___ no

10. Suggestions for improvement:

    _____

    Signature of Employee

    _____

    Signature of Supervisor

TABLE 12–7 Paraprofessional Aide Job Evaluation *Courtesy of Cherokee County Board of Education*

POSITION TITLE: PARAPROFESSIONAL AIDE   Code: 3.13

                                                                    Effective Date: March 8, 1988

Job Goal: Serves as a support staff position working under the supervision of the
              classroom teacher — has some decision-making authority limited and regulated
              by the profession

Reports To: Classroom Teacher

Performance Responsibilities:

    1. Instructional:

_____   A. Conduct small group or individual classroom activities based on lesson plans
            developed by the teacher.

_____   B. Assist with supervision of students.

_____   C. Assist with student assessment, grading work and tests, and collecting data on
            student progress.

    2. Management:

_____   A. Assist with routine recordkeeping.

_____   B. Assist with preparation of materials for instruction (including the copying/
            duplicating of materials, construction of displays/bulletin boards, learning
            centers, and manipulatives).

_____   C. Locate, operate, and return needed equipment.

_____   D. Assist with classroom housekeeping.

_____   E. Assist in the ordering and inventory of classroom equipment and materials.

_____   F. Assist with schoolwide supervision such as loading/unloading buses.

_____   G. Perform other duties as assigned by the teacher

TABLE 12–8 A Performance/Skills Inventory for Paraeducators Revised and adapted from: *A Training Program for Paraprofessionals Working in Special Education and Related Services.* National Resource Center for Paraprofessionals in Education and Related Services, Center for Advanced Study in Education, City University of New York, 1988. Used with permission.

The first section of the Inventory contains tasks that are part of the instructional process. Part two centers on communication and problem solving skills. And part three is concerned with the ethical and legal duties of paraeducators. It is suggested that a numerical rating scale be used to assess the performance level for the individual items. In addition, space for written comments will enhance the results of the assessment.

I.   THE INSTRUCTIONAL PROCESS

A. Functional Assessment Activities

Does the paraeducator:

1. Describe a student's behavior in observable terms?

2. State a student's strengths and weaknesses in behavioral terms?

3. Use behavior checklists or other instruments for recording student behavior?

4. Administer assessment instruments using standardized procedures?

5. Accurately score informal/functional tests?

B. Instructional Strategies

Does the paraeducator:

1. Follow lesson plans developed by the teacher for the entire class or individual students?

2. Prepare materials prior to the lesson?

3. Isolate and teach one concept at a time?

4. Give clear concise directions to the class or student?

5. Provide appropriate prompts/cues or model the expected behavior?

6. Stay on task?

7. Use developmentally and age appropriate instructional and reinforcement strategies.

8. Provide reinforcement in a timely and consistent manner and use praise effectively?

9. Maintain control of the instructional process?

10. Use effective questioning techniques and allow adequate time for the student(s) to respond?

11. Use a varied portfolio of instructional strategies suggested by the teachers?

12. Report the results of the lesson to the teacher in objective/behavioral terms?

(Continued)

TABLE 12–8 A Performance/Skills Inventory for Paraeducators *(Continued)* Revised and adapted from: *A Training Program for Paraprofessionals Working in Special Education and Related Services.* National Resource Center for Paraprofessionals in Education and Related Services, Center for Advanced Study in Education, City University of New York, 1988. Used with permission.

II. COMMUNICATION AND TEAM PARTICIPATION

Does the paraeducator:

1. Follow the teaching strategies, disciplinary and behavior management techniques, and rules the teacher uses in the classroom?

2. Follow instructions/directions of the teacher and ask for assistance if s/he does not understand what is expected?

3. Follow the chain of command established by the district?

4. Let the teacher know about special interests, experiences, and talents s/he may have that will contribute to implementing instructional programs?

5. Make points or share ideas clearly and concisely using positive methods of communication?

6. Meet regularly with the teacher for the purpose of planning lessons, participating in on-the-job training activities and discussing problems in the classroom?

III. PROFESSIONAL, LEGAL AND ETHICAL RESPONSIBILITIES

Does the paraeducator:

1. Arrive on time or alert appropriate personnel in timely fashion if s/he will be absent?

2. Observe work rules and procedures established for district personnel?

3. Demonstrate an understanding of the differences in roles and responsibilities of professional practitioners and paraeducators.

4. Demonstrate a willingness to learn new skills?

5. Maintain confidentiality about all personal information, test results, medical history and other records concerning students and their families?

6. Respect the human and legal rights of children, youth and their parents?

7. Promote the safety and well being of students e.g. reporting cases of suspected abuse to the teacher or other designated personnel?

8. Demonstrate respect for cultural diversity and individuality of the students they work with.

Now you are more aware of the policies and procedures that will likely affect work as a paraeducator.

Remember to refer back to these from time to time in order to refresh your memory and enable you to most effectively interface with other members of the educational team.

CHAPTER 13

The Job Market for Paraprofessionals

So, you feel you are paraeducator material; you have the right qualities. Your choice of different types of jobs is wide. It is hoped that your choices will become even wider and more diverse as the demand for paraeducators outweighs the supply. This increased demand is predicted to happen; the shortage of pre-kindergarten staff is expected to continue into the next century.

Preschool enrollments are expected to rise in the years ahead. After years of decline in population growth, the number of young children has increased. The number increased from 19.6 million in 1980 to 21.2 million in 1988 (Kingsbury, Vogler, and Benero). That is a lot of children to educate and care for. Qualified helpers will be needed. The number of women in the work force has increased and probably will continue to increase along with pressure for child care provided by trained teachers and qualified paraeducators. According to Kingsbury, Vogler, and Benero, the percentage of working mothers with children under 18 years of age rose from 49 percent in 1976 to 68 percent by the mid-1980s, and, "By the year 2000, it is estimated that 82 percent of all women in the United States between the ages of 25 and 34 will be in the workforce" (1990).

There is also growing pressure for state support for preschool programs. Lottery money in some states has funded special pre-kindergarten programs within the public schools.

Special education enrollments have grown significantly in recent years. The United States Department of Education's annual reports to Congress have shown continued increases in the number of children being served since the enactment of the Education for All Handicapped Children Act of 1975 (Public Law 94–142). The 14th Annual Report to Congress indicates a jump of 130,000 students in 1990–1991. This 2.8 percent increase was the biggest jump for any year since 1980–1981. The 14th, 15th, 16th, and 17th Annual Reports indicate increases in the numbers of teacher aides working in special education and considerable number of paraeducators still needed to work in special education. (See Table 13–1.)

TABLE 13–1 Numbers of Special Education Teacher Aides Employed and Needed in the United States, Washington, D.C. and Puerto Rico. *Information courtesy of National Clearinghouse for Professions in Special Education.*

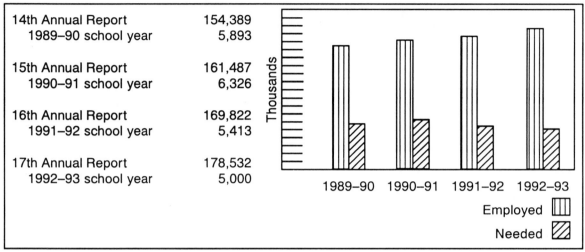

	Employed	Needed
14th Annual Report 1989–90 school year	154,389	5,893
15th Annual Report 1990–91 school year	161,487	6,326
16th Annual Report 1991–92 school year	169,822	5,413
17th Annual Report 1992–93 school year	178,532	5,000

Planning ahead to land the right job for you can be an exciting and rewarding task. The wide range of jobs for paraeducators and the huge number (1/2 million) of people who fit under the paraeducator umbrella have already been discussed. A job as a paraeducator may not be hard to find; however, a job that suits your talents and goals and offers satisfaction may take some planning. Something to consider is that many paraeducators are employed on a part-time basis, waiting to finish training and find a better-paying or a more rewarding position. This may be an option for you. You may decide to seek further training and career possibilities while you work as a paraeducator.

QUESTIONS TO RESEARCH

Depending on the competition and reasonableness of being selective, there are questions to research before deciding where you will apply. Following are some of the questions you need to answer before applying.

1. Is the school district growing? Does the district have growth in one geographical area but declining enrollment in another? Does it have growth at one level, for example, secondary, but declining numbers at the elementary level? Does the district have overall declining enrollment? What about transiency? What about political discord?

The answers to these questions relate directly to job security and satisfaction. Your best choice, if possible, is a district that has increasing enrollment at all levels, especially at the beginning grades—kindergarten, 1, and 2. Then you will know that if you do a good job, you will be back the next year. If you go on board with a district with declining enrollment, the usual policy is last on, first out, in which case you may get involved in an emotionally trying time. However, you may not really have much choice in your area, so just do the best you can.

Many school districts offer new employees a temporary position only. In the Parkhill School District of Kansas City, Missouri, for example, paraprofessionals are given a *letter of employment,* and are notified that if the student enrollments decrease, the employment decreases as well. This is true of paraeducator jobs in many places; you are given fair warning that if numbers go down, you may be out. A temporary position may automatically expire at the end of the school year. School administrators may wait until enrollment numbers are set for the next school year before they call you back again. Be sure to check. Procedures vary dramatically even in neighboring areas.

Problems can arise if you are hired at a school that is projected to have declining enrollment the following year. As mentioned, if you are the last hired, you will probably be the one to go if there are cuts. If the district has growth at other schools, you may take an involuntary transfer to one of them. This means you will have to start at a new school and probably a new grade, too, but at least you may have some job protection. You can see that it is best, whenever possible, not to seek employment with a school district with overall declining enrollment.

School transiency is another thing to consider before interviewing. Some schools have many students who are only there for a few months. If you are going to be interviewing at a school with a high turnover rate, will you still be satisfied with your year's work? If the answer is yes, go for it. If no, look for a more stable school enrollment.

Some school districts are in the midst of political turmoil. This can have a strong negative effect on staff morale. There may be turbulence on the school board or dissension between the district and the schools. It is important to be aware of this so that you are prepared for any skepticism or pessimism you may encounter after you begin the job.

How can you find out about all this? You can get information from district offices, teachers' associations, and local newspapers.

2. What is the district's financial state? If a district is in poor financial condition and has a history of money troubles compared with surrounding districts, give this some serious consideration. You can obtain this information from the county office.

3. What is the salary schedule for the district? Get a copy from the county office and compare it with other districts within easy-driving range. As mentioned earlier, there is a wide range of pay for paraeducators. It is not uncommon for paraeducators with identical amounts of education and service experience to be making vastly different salaries, even within five or ten miles of each other.

4. What about the benefit package? Will money be deducted from your monthly check to help pay for premiums? Is there a large deductible? Are HMOs and indemnity plans offered? Is there coverage in all areas of health, including physical and psychological therapy, vision care, and dental care? Is there any coverage for prescription costs? What about coverage for spouses or dependents? How are disability benefits handled?

Another consideration is the scope of the package. If the district has poor dental coverage, it will not do you much good if you are in generally good health except for massive dental problems. The cost of some prescription drugs is astronomical. If you or someone in your family is on expensive continuing drug therapy, then the provisions for prescriptions may be of supreme importance to you.

Consider your preference for an indemnity plan or an HMO. If you want the HMO, check to see whether the location is convenient. Talk to people who are already using the HMO.

Carefully evaluate the benefits in light of your needs.

JOB ADVERTISEMENTS

Job postings and advertisements for paraeducators may be listed under any of the titles listed in Chapter 1, so remember to check different categories. There are strict laws concerning wording of advertisements. An advertisement violates federal law if it indicates preference or limitation based on worker:

- Age. (An ad can pinpoint minimum age as long as this age is under forty and relates to some job task such as driving the day care bus.)

- Race, color.

- Sex. (An ad may specify male or female under certain conditions such as boys' school live-in house supervisor.)

- Religion.

- National origin or ancestry.

- Physical or mental disability.

- State laws may also add that employment advertisements cannot state a preference for a certain marital status.

- Suspect words and phrases that could be judged discriminatory include young, married, single, college student, and recent graduate.

There are penalties for employers who discriminate and thereby break federal Equal Opportunity Commission (EOC) laws. These penalties can include fines, stopping the ad, paying lost wages to a prospective job seeker, hiring a particular applicant, and giving compensation to former job applicants. As a worker, none of these penalties would be your responsibility, but you might want to know if the organization you work for now or in the future is in violation of the law.

The words *Equal Opportunity Employer* usually mean the program or center receives federal funds. Government contractors receiving $2,500 or more in public funds (both state and federal) are required to take *affirmative action* to hire minorities, women, the handicapped, and veterans. These laws are administered by the Office of Federal Contract Compliance Programs (OFCCP), a division of EOC.

It could help you to know that the United States Employment Service and state-operated employment services (Job Service in most states) form a national network of public employment offices that follow federal guidelines. Through these services you can gain access to job banks, computerized job listings, and referrals.

You might not know that an employer may be eligible to receive tax credit for employing you. The U.S. Department of Labor (1990) offers the following information on *target groups* and *target jobs tax credit*:

*An employer may take a targeted jobs tax credit for certain
wages incurred by or paid to members of targeted groups.......
Members of targeted groups are persons who are handicapped
individuals undergoing rehabilitation, economically disadvantaged youths from 18 to 24 years old, economically disadvantaged Vietnam era veterans, individuals receiving federal
welfare benefits or state and local general assistance, economically disadvantaged youths participating in a cooperative education program, ex-convicts, WIN registrants, involuntarily
terminated CETA employees, and qualified summer youth employees. The person must be certified as a member of a targeted
group by the designated local agency before he or she begins employment. ....The amount of targeted jobs tax credit allow-
able for a tax year is 40 percent of the first $6,000 of qualified
first-year wages. For summer youth employees, the credit is 85
percent of the first $3,000 of qualified wages. ("Employers and
Child Care," 1990)*

Whew! You probably did not know all this and more is involved
in job considerations and possibilities. Your decision may be as simple
as wanting to work in the same place where your own children go to
school. That may be the major consideration for you and you may not
care as much about the other factors. On the other hand, you may scrutinize all the factors mentioned here in your search through job possibilities. Whatever your decision is based on, you owe it to yourself to
be aware of laws, rules, and regulations before being hired. The general
job information in this chapter and other chapters will help you to approach employers and interviewers with more awareness of what can be
covered in discussions, what is lawful, and what is not. For example, by
now you realize that in most states paraeducators work under the direct
supervision of a teacher and are not asked to take a classroom of children alone.

RESUMÉ

Prepare a one-page summary of your background and your experience.
Your resume should include the following sections:

- Information about previous employment, beginning with most recent and going back no more than ten years.

- Responsibilities and duties.

- Education—diplomas, degrees, relevant courses.

- Any special achievements or recognitions.

- Groups or organizations you belong to, mentioning any leadership positions.

- Information about references—either a statement that you will be glad to supply them if requested or an actual list of names and numbers. (Koffel, 1994)

Remember not to sell yourself short. If you are fresh out of high school but you have worked as a lifeguard and a babysitter, be sure to mention the responsibility level you were given and list any courses, such as YMCA lifeguard training or Red Cross babysitter courses, that you have taken. If you helped organize a backyard Bible school on a youth mission trip, include that. If you have been a stay-at-home mom for the last ten years and you hardly remember where you went to college for two years much less what you learned there, don't forget to mention the organizational skills you have used to organize the neighborhood co-op and the trip you planned and supervised for twenty-three Cub Scouts. Your experience as a parent is valuable. Be sure you represent parenting skills as an asset.

You may not be asked to hand over your actual on-paper resume, but you will be asked the above-mentioned types of information. If you go ahead and prepare your resume, it will help set in your mind just what a valuable potential employee you are and will help you answer interview questions or fill out application forms more easily. Even if a resume is not requested, and there is an opportunity to submit it, do so as it will promote a professional and eager image.

APPLYING FOR POSITIONS

After you have looked into your options and made some decisions, make your application. This can be done by mail or in person. Consider the value of being in the right place at the right time and go in person if at all possible. Be sure you are dressed nicely and be friendly.

Paraeducator job opportunities are often posted on boards in centralized school district offices. This may be a good place for you to check if you want a job within the local school district. Job postings may not always be in newspaper ads. You may also want to notify local principals that you are interested in a paraeducator position in a local school and ask if they will keep your application on file.

INTERVIEWING

You may be in an area where plenty of jobs are available or you may be in an area where the job market is extremely competitive. In either case, the interview is extremely important and will strongly determine your chances for a job offer.

There are different types of interviews. Many districts do an initial screening interview at the district office prior to sending you to the school site. You may be interviewed by a panel of people or by an individual. (It is not necessarily considered better to be interviewed by a board versus an individual; it mainly relates to district size and policy.) You may be given either oral or written interview questions. In Massachusetts, paraeducators who work as *instructional aides* are hired by principals, and paraeducators who work as *special needs aides* are first screened by Special Education directors and then hired by principals.

Listen to the names and positions of the people interviewing you. Jot this information down so you will have access to it later. Study faces so that if you come across them in the future, you will be able to call people by name. You can then reintroduce yourself and remind them that you were interviewed around such and such a time. It is fine to then say that you are still very interested in a job in the district.

Somewhere along the interview line, you will most likely be interviewed by the principal of the school where the opening exists. Again, this may be conducted by the principal alone or a small team of teachers may be invited to sit in on the interview.

Make an attempt to be at your absolute best on the day of your interview. You, just like anyone else, are bound to feel nervous prior to an interview, so the more prepared you are, the more confident you will feel.

An interview is considered a formal experience. Come professionally dressed and impeccably groomed in every way, from hair to nails to shoes. Table 13–2 will give you some additional hints. Sit up straight, act alert, and show an eagerness for the job. (Remember all the traditional advice of moms about making a good impression.)

Interview questions should be directed at assessing your qualifications; they should be related to the job for which you are applying.

TABLE 13–2 The Do's for Interviews

Wear your hair in a neat, plain style. If you do dye your hair, make sure it is a natural color.

Avoid lots of make-up.

Make sure that your appearance is as clean and neat as possible. Shower or bathe that day.

Carefully pick out what you will wear. Look for tears or missing buttons ahead of time.

Make sure your nails look well-groomed. Avoid stains under your nails. Avoid long nails if you are applying for a position with children who are infants, toddlers or who need much hands-on care.

Wear a tie if you are a man.

Wear a dress, a skirt, or dress slacks if you are a woman.

Wear appropriate shoes (flats or low heels) that are shined if they are dress shoes.

Any questions that are irrelevant are probably illegal (Joel, 1993). Probes concerning who lives with you, whether you own or rent, when you left high school, your family or your intent to add to your family, child care arrangements, church attendance, if you smoke, or how you spend your time off the job fall into the irrelevant category. If you do not want to discuss something irrelevant, you can answer a questionable query by asking what relationship that question has to your ability to do the job. Illegal employer questions are listed in Table 13–3. Most employers exercise caution during interviews to avoid discrimination or invasion of privacy claims (Joel, 1993).

Of course, *how* you answer questions is very important. It is vital that you convey flexibility and a team player attitude. As a paraeducator you must be able to work cooperatively and be accommodating; your interviewer will be looking for that.

You may not know all the answers to your interview questions; that is okay. If you do not know a complete answer, speak of the part you

TABLE 13–3 A Sample of Questions You Cannot Be Asked During An Interview

"How old are you?"

"What year did you graduate from high school/college?"

"Are you married?"

"Are you pregnant?"

"Do you plan on having a family?"

"What are your day care arrangements for your child?"

"What religious holidays do you celebrate?"

"Are you willing to take a lie detector test?"

"In what country were you born?"

"Do you own or rent your residence?"

do know. If you do not know the answer at all, politely say you don't know but will be glad to try to find out. Remember, honesty is a key and when you are just beginning you are not expected to know everything.

It is important to act enthusiastic or you are not going to get many job offers. Once you do get an offer, be sure to think things through before accepting. A good policy concerning job offers is to take two days to make your decision whenever you are not absolutely sure you want to take it. Taking the time to step back can be important in making clear-headed evaluations away from the interview scene.

After you have had a good interview, do some follow up, especially if you are in a competitive area. This is where your notebook of names comes in handy. Write letters thanking the people who provided the opportunity for you to interview. You might write something like this:

I enjoyed meeting and interviewing with you on (whatever date). Thank you for giving me this worthwhile opportunity.

Your district seems dynamic and innovative. I hope to be a part of your team. I'm looking forward to hearing from you soon.

Sincerely, etc.

Make sure you have your complete name typed so that it is easy to read. If you go by a nickname and you used it during the interview, include it in the letter, too. Include your phone number so that people can call you without having to search through records.

Call individual principals or directors later and tell them of your continued interest. This will keep your name fresh in their minds. You might also check with the district office to see what progress is being made in the hiring process. You can always call and ask if they need another reference when you want to check on the status of a job opportunity. Be sensitive to the fact that you want to make yourself highly visible but you don't want to make a nuisance of yourself. Sometimes it is effective to be assertive and persistent because you can be forgotten otherwise; at the same time you must be careful not to become annoying.

There are several pieces of information an employer may want to know about you; there are laws that protect your rights concerning these bits of information. For example, if an employer asks a credit reporting agency to run a credit check on you, the law (Fair Credit Reporting Act) demands that you be informed in writing within three days. You have the right to find out about the nature and scope of the agency's investigation (Joel, 1993). You also have the right to know whether the credit report influenced your chances for the job.

Your potential employer may also ask for references from past employers. Your past employers can only give truthful, factual, job-related information. If you have ever been terminated for any reason, you can ask for both a reference and the opportunity to review your old personnel file. It is smart to request that false or negative information be deleted from the file. You may also ask that your own statements be added to explain or clarify. You have these rights under the Privacy/Access to Records Law (Joel, 1993).

Occasionally doctor's exams or fingerprinting are required for employment. Many states consider these to be the employer's financial responsibility. If there is any question, you can check with a local labor representative.

For your information, some states have legislation requiring criminal background checks on people working in child care. For example, criminal record checks are a regular part of preschool and day care hirings in Florida and Minnesota. Some states screen for felonies only. Table 13–4 is included for your information.

TABLE 13–4 State Legislation Requiring Criminal Background Check of Child Care Personnel

State	Criminal Record Check	State	Criminal Record Check
Alabama §38-7-4	I	Idaho §39-1105	I — State criminal identification bureau; FBI; criminal history check; National Crime Information Center
Alaska	Not stated		
Amer. Samoa	Not stated		
Arizona §36-883.02	I F A/S	Illinois §2214.1	I — In cooperation with state police
		Indiana §12-3-2-18	A/S
Arkansas §83-908	I	Iowa §237 A.5	I — Check the child abuse registry
California §1522.5	F	Kansas §65-516	I — With state Bureau of Investigation
Colorado §26-6-104; 107	I — By state Bureau of Investigations and by department agency F	Kentucky	Not stated
		Louisiana	Not stated
		Maine	Not stated
Connecticut	Not stated	Maryland §5-561	I — By any designated law enforcement agency, and both federal and state criminal background check
Delaware	Not stated		
District of Columbia	Not stated		
		Massachusetts	Not stated
Florida §402.305(1) §402.3055(2)	I — Screening and local, state, and federal (FBI) criminal record check F A/S	Michigan	Not stated
		Minnesota §245.783	I — Check, local, state, national criminal history record repositories with assistance from Bureau of Criminal Apprehension, County Attorney, County Sheriff and local Chief of Police
Georgia	Not stated		
Guam	Not stated		
Hawaii §346-154	I — Through Hawaii Criminal Justice Data Center F A/S		
		Mississippi	Not stated
		Missouri	Not stated

Key: I — Investigation by child care agency
  A/S — Affidavit or statement of clean record submitted by child care giver
  F — Fingerprint check
  O — Other

(Continued)

TABLE 13–4 State Legislation Requiring Criminal Background Check of Child Care Personnel *(Continued)*

State	Criminal Record Check	State	Criminal Record Check
Montana	Not stated	South Carolina §20-7-2720	I — Of applicant and staff, including references and other information about the character and quality of the personnel
Nebraska §71-192	I — Includes national criminal records check examination of state registry of abuse and neglect reports and central registry		
		South Dakota	Not stated
Nevada §432A.170	I — With law enforcement agencies F A/S	Tennessee §14-10-129	A/S, including social security number and disclosure of violations of the law I — in cooperation with State Bureau of Investigations
New Hampshire §170-E:4	I		
		Texas	Not stated
New Jersey	Not stated	Utah	Not stated
New Mexico	Not stated	Vermont	Not stated
New York §390-6	A/S	Virginia §63.1-198.1	A/S I — At request of department
North Carolina	Not stated	Virgin Islands §385	I — With police department, including search of nationwide criminal record
North Dakota §50-11.1-04	I		
Ohio §5104.09	A/S	Washington §74.15.030	I — In cooperation with criminal justice agencies
Oklahoma	Not stated		
Oregon §418.820	F I — Nationwide criminal record check	West Virginia §49-2B-8	I — And check both child abuse and neglect record and criminal conviction record
Pennsylvania	Not stated		
Puerto Rico	Not stated	Wisconsin	Not stated
Rhode Island	Not stated	Wyoming	Not stated

Key: I — Investigation by child care agency
A/S — Affidavit or statement of clean record submitted by child care giver
F — Fingerprint check
O — Other

Okay, now that we have gone through the whole job search process, we will give some attention to other aspects of employment that are necessary to consider on the front end. These aspects include part time/full time, wages, contracts, and unions.

PART TIME/FULL TIME

There are hour ranges associated with teacher aide jobs. Some paraeducators work part time, some do shift work, some are asked to be *on call,* and others work full time.

Part-time paraeducators work less than twenty hours per week. Of course they are legally paid less than full-time workers. If you do work part time, you may need to know whether state or federal minimum wage laws apply to your work, and whether any additional conditions or benefits apply. Worker's Compensation, coverage for job-related illness or injury, covers part-time workers, but unemployment compensation may not be available for fired part-time workers.

Occasionally early childhood workers are asked to work split shifts, that is, work three or four hours, leave, and return to work three or four hours later in the day. If you consider doing this kind of work, be sure to check your state labor laws concerning wages and hours constituting a work shift because extra pay for split shift work may be required by your state laws.

States often forbid the practice of employers asking workers reporting for scheduled work to go home because there isn't enough work that particular day. In preschools, that can happen if expected children don't arrive or for another reason such as a power failure. Many states require employees to be paid a certain number of minimum hours if they report to work.

Most paraeducators work full time. What constitutes full time and eligibility for benefits can vary among districts, centers, and states. In public schools, paraeducators are generally required to be at school from shortly before the bell rings until shortly after the bell rings. School day start and end times vary. One school may run from 7:45 A.M. to 2:15 P.M. for the children; while the paraeducators have to be there from 7:30 A.M. to 2:30 P.M. Yet another school may run from 9:00 A.M. to 4:00 P.M. Five seven-hour days per week constitutes full time in many school districts.

WAGES

The range of pay for paraeducators was discussed in Chapter 1 (from minimum wage up to $15 per hour). Federal minimum wage set by law in 1997 was $5.15 per hour. However, a number of states including Alaska, Iowa, and New Jersey have higher state minimum wage laws. A minimum wage that is *less* than federal or state minimum wage may be paid to apprentices, learners, and handicapped workers with the permission of that state's commissioner of labor (Joel, 1993).

If an employer provides housing, meals, transportation to work, and certain other items, the labor department considers this at a *reasonable cost* (actual cost) to the employer. It is deemed a partial payment of the employee's minimum wage. However, the employee must voluntarily agree to the arrangement.

Some child care employers may insist that employees sign statements concerning required unpaid additional hours for parent or staff meetings, fund raising events, conferences, lesson preparation, and so on. An employer cannot legally ask you to sign away your rights. You should be paid regular hourly pay or overtime hours for any employer job-related requirements. Also, under the law, any job errands that you do during off hours should also be paid time.

Any question you have about pay should first be directed to your employer, of course. Your state Department of Labor, wage and hour division offices can supply additional information to help you understand whether amounts have been correctly figured.

Paycheck Deductions

Most workers have taxes, social security, retirement contributions, union dues, and health insurance premiums deducted from their gross pay. Sometimes deductions are also made for debts and child and spousal support. A federal law limits how much can be deducted during any one pay period. Again, you can contact your state Department of Labor if you feel questionable amounts or items are withheld.

Employers may lawfully deduct wages from your check for the following reasons *only:*

- Legally required federal taxes, state taxes, social security, and state disability insurance (SDI)

- Court-ordered child or family support payments

- Payments for back taxes
- Payments the employee has the employer make for union dues, assessments or initiation fees, for bank deposits.
- Contributions the employee has asked the employer to make to charities, retirement plans, fringe-benefit plans, medical, or other insurance plans
- Legal, employee-requested wage assignments (Check with the Labor Commissioner.)
- Lateness (Employers do not have to pay for time not worked, regardless of the reason for lateness; if the time lost is less than 30 minutes, the employer can deduct a full 30 minutes pay.)
- Absences, even if caused by sickness or disability (unless the absence is covered by a benefit agreement)
- Infractions of safety rules enacted to prevent serious injury to other employees
- Breakage of equipment caused by a willful or grossly negligent act (NCECW, 1994)

Overtime Pay

In most states every hour an employee works over forty hours a week is paid at time and a half (one-and-a-half times the regular hourly pay). It's wise to check state laws because some states such as Montana, Alaska, Nevada, California, and Alabama require overtime pay for any hour worked over 8 hours in a work day. You may be offered compensatory (comp) time when you work overtime. Again, it is important to find out about your state laws; they can tell you whether you can request payment rather than time off. In some states, such as California, overtime pay may actually be more than time and a half ("Working For Quality Child Care," Unit II, 1994). Check your state laws!

There are also federal laws about comp time. The following are federal restrictions:

- The employee must request comp time in lieu of overtime payment in cash.
- If the employee is represented by a union, the union must agree to allow this option

- The time off accrues at the overtime premium rate applicable (e.g., one hour worked overtime earns one and one-half hours time off, etc.).

- Any overtime worked over a maximum of 240 hours must be paid in cash.

- The time off must be granted reasonably soon after the employee asks for it.

(NCECW, 1994)

When, where, how, how much, and how often employees are paid is also found in some states' labor laws. Not every state has such laws, but the majority of states do. Usually pay must be received in cash or in bankable legal tender at a place convenient to you, the worker. That is, you should not be paid with a check that can only be cashed in a bank on a coastal island that is accessible only by a seasonally operated ferry.

Since April 1, 1990 employers (under certain conditions) have been allowed to pay a training wage of at least 85 percent of the minimum wage (but not less than $3.25 an hour) for up to 90 days to employees under age 20. An employee who has been paid at the training wage for 90 days can be employed at the training wage for 90 more days if the work is under a different employer and if that employer also provides on-the-job training in accordance with regulations issued by the U.S. Department of Labor.

Health Insurance Coverage

Questions pertaining to health insurance have already been discussed for those of you whose employers sponsor health insurance as a job benefit. Many early childhood workers do not receive health insurance benefits. If you do receive these benefits, you need to know about the 1986 *Consolidated Omnibus Budget Reconciliation Act (COBRA)*. It requires employers to offer you the opportunity to continue in the group's health insurance plan no matter the reason (except gross misconduct) for your leaving. Besides continuation rights, you also have conversion rights should you choose a different health insurance carrier.

As you can see, there is more than meets the eye when you consider the wages involved with a position as a paraeducator. There are still more options concerning contracts, public versus private schools, and unions.

EMPLOYMENT CONTRACTS

Many public schools offer contracts to work as a paraeducator. A growing number of large preschools, large private corporations, and church affiliated preschools and centers offer employment contracts rather than hourly wages. A contract is a formal agreement between two parties defining mutual obligations and responsibilities for a specific period of time (Anthony & Roe, 1982). In signing a contract you agree to exchange certain services for compensation, which can include both salary and benefits.

Most public school personnel have negotiated contracts through a bargaining process between staff members and/or their representatives and the board of education. Often a bargaining agent or union negotiator represents the employees during contract discussions. Individual and group-negotiated contracts with both public and private school employees may include but are not limited to the following:

- Base salary

- Specific salary increments

- Fringe benefits

- Number of working days

- Policies regarding leaves for illness, emergencies, etc.

- Evaluation procedures

- Termination guidelines

- Renewability for both parties

Two basic types of contracts exist: comprehensive and supplemental. Comprehensive contracts list specific duties as well as extracurricular responsibilities when school is not in regular session (before, after, weekend, evening and summertime periods). A supplemental contract is sometimes called a special service contract; it lists specific duties and/or assignments covering extracurricular activities as a separate document.

Becoming a contract employee involves at least three phases:

(1) A contract is offered to you (verbal or written).

(2) You, the prospective employee, make a decision to accept or decline and you communicate your decision (verbally or in writing).

(3) You sign your contract and it is approved and signed by a school administrator and/or the owner-employer. Verbal acceptance only may also be legally binding. (Anthony & Roe, 1982)

As just mentioned, a contract can be either written or oral. The law usually views verbal agreements as contracts ("Legal Problem Solver," 1994). For future reference, you should know that proof may be a problem should you test this law. Witnesses or evidence would be necessary to settle a case if you had a dispute over a verbal contract. More will be discussed about keeping your own records later.

Any assurances made to you by your employer, either written or oral, can form the foundation of a so-called *implied contract* and could restrict your employer's right to fire you for anything short of just cause (Joel, 1993). Written teacher/staff handbooks, informal understandings, and school customs are considered implied contracts. Factors used in court cases to determine whether an implied contract exists include:

- Duration of worker employment

- Promotions

- Lack of criticism

- Acknowledged employer employment practices

- Circumstances surrounding your recruitment

Independent Contracts

Sometimes facilities attempt to make their associations with workers independent contractor relationships so they are *not* obligated to provide benefits or to withhold employee payroll taxes. The Internal Revenue Service has strict guidelines defining whether a worker is an employee or an independent contractor. When one or more of the following factors apply, the IRS could view the independent contract worker as an employee rather than an independent contractor:

When the worker:

- works only for one business;

- is paid hourly, weekly, or monthly wages;

- is controlled or significantly influenced by the business's working hours and/or work environment;

- uses tools and equipment furnished by the business;
- is not providing services that influence whether an at-risk business makes a profit or loss;
- works in a situation characterized by relationships similar to employee to employer relationships.

Lukaszewski (1991) notes one of the deciding questions whether a worker is or is not an independent contractor is whether the worker is under the employer's control (that is, the employer determines what is done and how it is done). In trying to avoid taxes and paperwork, some centers hiring *independent contract* teachers and paraeducators risk the collection of back payroll taxes, large fines, penalties, and interest. Again, just as with penalties for illegal hiring practices, you would not be responsible for these consequences, but you should know how your employment is legally classified.

On the other hand, *temporary employment agencies* can offer employment contracts to workers employed by the agency. The agency worker's contract might include length of employment, wages, salary, work hours, work location, paid workers insurance, Worker's Compensation coverage, free testing, employer contribution of FICA matching funds, vacation pay, and other benefits. Consequently, use of workers, substitutes, and temporaries provided by an agency may save a preschool employer payroll taxes and benefit money. It gets confusing!

As stated before, local state Labor Wage and Hour Division offices can help any of you who are paid by the hour to clarify your status under the state laws.

There are definite pros and cons to working as an independent contractor. Some positive aspects of independent contract paraeducator work include:

(1) Contracts clearly identify both employee and employer duties.

(2) Contracts provide job security.

(3) Pay for a specific time period is guaranteed.

(4) Employers cannot legally terminate except for gross misconduct.

(5) Employee job expenses may be deductible on federal taxes.

Drawbacks to working as an independent contract paraeducator include:

(1) Contracts are difficult to break necessitating a continued unhappy work situation.

(2) Employers may have had lawyer contract consultation while the employee is more likely to have less legal understanding of contract law.

(3) You are not covered under employer's Worker's Compensation insurance policies.

(4) The employer doesn't make matching social security contributions.

(5) Withholding taxes are not paid.

(6) You may feel private disability insurance is necessary.

(7) You are not covered under the National Labor Relations Act if you should be involved in unionizing activity.

Independent contractors have to pay their own Social Security and estimated income taxes. If business expenses are claimed on tax returns, complete records must be kept. In fact, clear, dated, and itemized records should be maintained concerning every aspect of independent contract work.

Lawsuits by employees against employers are increasing. Oral contracts and poor employer documentation promote this. Make sure that poor documentation problems are not on your part. Find out as much as you can about your own situation on the front end so that you can avoid serious misunderstandings and problems. Remember that employment laws vary from state to state, so before entering an employment contract, you should investigate your specific state laws.

PUBLIC VERSUS PRIVATE SCHOOLS

You may have the opportunity to decide between working as a private school paraeducator or a public school paraeducator. Your rights could differ depending on your choice, since normally private school teachers and staff cannot assert personal constitutional rights against private schools (Valente, 1989). Most employment disagreements and disputes between private school employers and their employees involve contract law. This includes previously mentioned implied contracts.

Courts have been reluctant to interfere with church-affiliated private schools due to the Constitution's First Amendment. Courts have routinely failed to rule against private church-affiliated school firings when employees have divorced or remarried against church doctrine or broken other religious precepts (Valente, 1989).

Be careful to consider the ramifications of your choice of employment in a private versus public school. There are probably personal advantages and disadvantages to each choice. No one but you can decide what situation is best for you.

UNION MEMBERSHIP

There is one more option associated with employment that needs to be discussed; that is union membership. About 15 to 18 percent of all workers in the United States are union members. Their unions represent them in negotiations covering most aspects of their jobs and job benefits.

Two large bodies of law affect workers involved in union activities: 1) *The Labor-Management Relations Act* (Taft-Hartley Act or LMRA); and 2) *National Labor Relations Act* (Wagner Act). Both laws are administered by the National Labor Relations Board (NLRB). Under Section 7 of the National Labor Relations Act, employees have the right to:

- Self-organize.

- Form, join, or assist labor organizations.

- Bargain collectively through representatives of their own choosing.

- Act together for the purpose of collective bargaining or other mutual aid or protection.

- Refuse to do any or all of these things.

In some states the agreements worked out between a union and an employer may force one to join a union to remain employed. In other instances, union and non-union workers work side by side. (Some states have union-security agreements between unions and employers that lawfully require employees to pay periodic dues and initiation fees. Nonmembers who inform the union that they object to the use of their payments going toward nonrepresentational purposes may be required to pay only their share of the cost of representational activities, such as collective bargaining, contract administration, and grievance adjustment.)

Before becoming involved in union activities it is wise for paraeducators to ascertain whether their work sites are covered by the two laws cited above. Smaller schools may not be covered. Church-affiliated private schools also may not be able to unionize and have NLRB protection because of First Amendment Rights. Jim Morin (1991) points out that paraeducators employed in a public school program, church-operated program or a multi-site child care company usually would not fall under NLRB jurisdiction. Preschools attached or administered by a school district, a state school system, or a state agency are by law excluded. Morin (1991) observes that exceptions do exist, particularly if the employer:

- Operates on a non-sectarian basis.
- Accepts state agency referrals.
- Receives government monies.
- Operates in the same way as a secular child care program.

As has been stated about other aspects of employment, it is important for you to look into the options available in your specific situation.

You may not feel equipped to negotiate a salary and benefits by yourself. If you feel this way, you are not alone. Many feel the efforts to upgrade their position suffer when group strength is nonexistent. Gaining nonwage benefits, such as health plan coverage, is often the top priority when groups are formed.

Unions are viewed by most workers as offering job security, insurance, and health plan access. Indeed, these pluses have been gained through unionization efforts. Union activity has improved worker salaries, benefits, and public awareness for child care employees in both Massachusetts and New York (NCECW, 1994). Look at the following results of union activity in other areas of the country:

- In West Virginia, the Wayne County Education Support Personnel Association won dental and optical coverage for all school employees in spring 1995.
- Education support workers in Hayward, California successfully bargained for increased pay, additional vacation time, and better benefits. Their pay was to be raised 11.5 percent over a period of four years.
- In Maryland, the Calvert Association of Education Support Personnel won the right to have representation on decision-making teams.

("NEA Today," 1995)

Access to a lobbying force that can apply pressure to change and improve existing laws and access to professional negotiators for contract mediation is another advantage to union membership.

Some factors have worked against unionization in many communities:

- Staff turn-over
- Employee fears
- Lack of worker leadership
- Unique and diverse nature of paraeducators and child care providers' jobs, roles, and responsibilities
- Wide diversity of facilities and programs

Although union membership is relatively small compared to other industries, early childhood worker membership is growing and may be something you will want to consider. More information about unions can be found in Chapter 11.

The information in this chapter has been included in order to broaden your vision of the options available to you as a paraeducator. Before choosing a job it is important to review as many of the possibilities as you can. The bottom line is that you will have to check out your own specific situation. Hopefully now you know more alternatives to investigate!

You will have many rights as a paraeducator. There are also many laws pertaining to your job. These will be explored in Appendix G. Paraeducators work under a myriad of regulations and policies; these were discussed in Chapter 12. Just as when you begin any job, there is often a lot of paperwork to get through, there are important issues for you to understand before you get to what your goal is, that is, to actually do the work of a paraeducator.

You are finally getting ready to push the paperwork away, leave the office, move through the halls, and go to your own place to begin your work as a paraeducator. It's about time, don't you think?

As a paraeducator you will have an opportunity to really impact young lives. Make a constant concentrated effort to impact them in positive ways. Remember that all these young lives are special; most have families who love them and want the best for them. Treat students like you would want your own children or yourself to be treated and do your job based on high standards of excellence and ethics. You'll do great!

APPENDIX A

End of Year Poem

At the end of the last day of your first year as a paraeducator:

You've made it through another year
    of see-it-all eyes and *selectively* attentive ears,
You've done your best to teach young minds
    and tried to make children sit on behinds.

You've listened to tattletales and left field excuses
    and taught that THINKING does indeed have uses,
You've provided the treasure of education
    as you've seen precious eyes light with expectation.

It's simply amazing all the people you've been—
    Counselor, instructor, role model, and friend,
Your job is so challenging—overwhelming at times—
    but always remember you've imprinted young lives.

No doubt you have dealt with major AT-TI-TUDES,
    What you probably want now is peaceful solitude,
So for all you have done for kids every day
    You deserve to have Calgon™ take you away!

—K. J. Skelton

APPENDIX
B   Abbreviations

Many abbreviations are used in the world of caring for and educating children. Some of the common ones are:

ADA—Americans with Disabilities Act

ADHD—attention-deficit hyperactivity disorder

ASP—after school program

BD—behavior disordered

DAP—developmentally appropriate practice

DEFACS—Department of Family and Children Services

ESL—English as a second language

FAPE—free appropriate public education

FAS—fetal alcohol syndrome

HOME—Home Observation for Measurement of the Environment

IEP—Individualized Education Program

IFSP—Individualized Family Service Plan

IHE—institutions of higher education

IQ—intelligence quotient

ISS—in-school suspension

LEA—local education agencies

LD—learning disability

SDE—State Department of Education

SDI—State disability insurance

SST—student support team

APPENDIX C

Paraeducator Competencies and Job Descriptions

PARAEDUCATOR COMPETENCIES

The following sections contain the competencies used to develop the curriculum and course content. Section one contains competencies required by all paraeducators no matter what program area they work in. Additional competencies for paraeducators employed in specific programs are presented in Sections II, III, and IV.

I. Core Competencies for All Paraeducators

To work in education and related services programs for children and youth with special needs paraeducators will demonstrate:

✓ an understanding of the value of serving children and youth with disabilities and other special needs in integrated settings;

✓ an understanding of differentiated staffing patterns and the distinctions among the roles and responsibilities of professional and paraprofessional personnel;

✓ an ability to communicate with colleagues, follow instructions, and use problem solving and other skills that will enable them to work as effective members of the instructional team;

✓ a knowledge of the legal and human rights of children and youth with special needs and their families;

✓ an ability to practice ethical and professional standards of conduct established by the agency where they are employed;

✓ a sensitivity to diversity in cultural heritages, life styles, and value systems among the children, youth, and families they serve;

✓ a knowledge of a) patterns of human development and milestones typically achieved at different ages; and b) risk factors that may prohibit or impede typical development;

✓ an ability to motivate and assist children and youth with special needs to a) build self-esteem; b) develop interpersonal skills that will help them avoid isolation in different learning and living environments; and c) strengthen skills to become more independent by monitoring and controlling their behavior;

✓ an ability to follow health, safety and emergency procedures developed by the agency where they are employed?

✓ an ability to use assistive technology and adaptive equipment, and provide special care or physical assistance infants, children/youth may require (e.g., positioning, transferring, and feeding).

II. Specific/Additional Competencies for Paraeducators in Early Intervention/Childhood or Home Visitor Programs

To work in home visitor programs paraeducators will demonstrate:

✓ an ability to participate as a member of the IFSP team responsible for developing service plans and education objectives for parents and their children;

✓ an ability to listen to and communicate with parents in order to gather information the service delivery team can build on to meet the needs of the child and family;

✓ a knowledge of: a) health care providers, social services, education agencies, and other support systems available in the community to assist parents and their child; and b) an ability to support parents and provide them with the skills and information they require to gain access to these services;

✓ an ability to enhance parent interactions with their child by using/demonstrating effective techniques and materials to stimulate cognitive, physical, social, and language development;

To work in center based programs for young children paraeducators will demonstrate:

✓ an ability to use developmentally appropriate instructional interventions for curriculum activities in the areas of cognitive, motor, self-help, social/play and language development for infants and young children ages 0–5;

✓ an ability to gather and share information about the performance of individual children with professional colleagues;

✓ an ability to prepare and use developmentally appropriate materials;

✓ an ability to communicate and work effectively with parents and other primary caregivers.

III. Specific/Additional Competencies for Paraeducators Working in Inclusive Classrooms and Programs for Students with Special Needs

To work in integrated settings paraeducators will demonstrate:

✓ an ability to tutor students in academic subjects and self-help skills using lesson plans and instructional strategies developed by teachers or other professional support staff;

✓ an ability to: a) gather and maintain data about the performance and behavior of individual students; and b) confer with special and general education practitioners about student schedules, instructional goals, progress, and performance;

✓ an ability to use developmentally and age appropriate instructional procedures and reinforcement techniques;

✓ an ability to operate computers, assistive technology, and adaptive equipment that will enable students with disabilities and other special needs to participate more fully in general education.

IV. Specific/Additional Competencies for Paraeducators Working in Vocational and Transitional Training Programs

To work in vocational and transitional programs paraeducators will demonstrate:

✓ an understanding of the distinctions among different employment models;

✓ an ability to participate as a member of the team responsible for transitional planning and vocational assessment for individual students;

✓ an ability to participate in pre-employment, vocational, or transitional training in classrooms or at off-campus sites;

✓ an ability to task analyze job requirements, sequence the day, observe and record data, and provide training at job sites using appropriate instructional interventions;

✓ an ability to motivate students to work;

✓ an ability to communicate effectively with employers and employees at work sites, and personnel or members of the public in other transitional learning environments;

✓ an ability to modify services based on school and worksite regulatory procedures; and

✓ a knowledge of a) social, rehabilitation and support systems that will enable youth to participate fully in the community; and b) an ability to provide students and parents with skills and information they can use to gain access to the services.

JOB DESCRIPTIONS

The examples of job descriptions presented here begin with an entry level position and move through two more advanced steps for: 1) instructional paraeducators who work in inclusive classrooms serving school age children and youth with special needs, and 2) paraeducators who work in: a) transition and vocational training programs, or b) early intervention/childhood programs. The steps demonstrate the range of tasks performed by paraeducators in positions where their duties become progressively more complex and where fewer restrictions are placed on their participation in program planning and decision making in consultation with professional practitioners.

In all of the descriptions it is assumed that teachers will have responsibility for directing the day to day work of paraeducators, although paraeducators working in levels II and III might also be supervised by occupational or speech therapists or transitional/vocational specialists. The ethical and legal responsibilities are the same for all paraeducators.

PARAEDUCATOR POSITION: LEVEL I (Entry Level)

Definition: In entry level positions, paraeducators work under the direct supervision of teachers. They do not act independently nor do they have any responsibility for making decisions about any aspect of a student's education program. Typical duties assigned to level I paraeducators fall into the following categories: monitoring and escorting students, record-keeping, material preparation, and reinforcing lessons for individual students.

Duties for LEVEL I paraeducators may include:

- Bus duty (e.g., assisting drivers and students with adaptive equipment and monitoring the physical welfare of students).

- Escorting students from classrooms to libraries, computer labs, resource rooms, and other programs.

- Supervising playground, lunchrooms, and study halls.

- Operating audio-visual and office equipment.

- Recording attendance, maintaining records, and other clerical tasks.

- Assisting students with personal and hygienic care.

- Preparing training materials and maintaining supplies.

- Setting up and maintaining classroom equipment and learning centers.

- Reinforcing lessons initiated by the teacher.

PARAEDUCATOR POSITION LEVEL II:
(Instructional Paraeducator)

Definition: Paraeducators in Level II positions work under the supervision of teachers or professional practitioners who provide related education/therapy services. The duties of Level II paraeducators are primarily instructional in nature. They also assist the teacher with administrative tasks. In addition to directing the day-to-day work of paraeducators, teachers provide feedback about the performance of a paraeducator and conduct on-the-job coaching. Depending on state laws or local administrative policies Level II paraeducators may have limited decision making authority with regard to non-instructional activities.

Duties for LEVEL II instructional paraeducators may include:

- Tutoring individual or small groups of students using instructional objectives and methods developed by teachers or other professional practitioners.

- Assisting with supplementary work for students and supervising independent study.

- Conducting prescribed/standardized reading and math programs.

- Administering standardized assessment instruments, scoring informal/objective tests, and keeping appropriate records for teachers.

- Observing and recording information about student performance and behavior.

- Implementing behavior management strategies using the same emphasis and techniques as the teacher.

- Assisting the teacher with crisis intervention and discipline.

- Preparing individualized instructional materials, bulletin boards, and maintaining learning centers.

- Attending staff or IEP meetings at the request of the teacher or administrative personnel.

- Recording attendance and performing other clerical tasks.

PARAEDUCATOR POSITION LEVEL III:
(Early Intervention/Childhood Teacher Assistant and/or Transition Trainer/Job Coach)

Definition: Level III paraeducators work in programs serving children and youth of different ages and/or their families. The programs may be administered by local school districts or other education agencies. Level III paraeducators may work in classrooms, homes, community learning environments or other education settings. Level III paraeducators work under the direction of teachers, occupational, speech, or physical therapists or transitional/vocational specialists. Depending on state and/or local policies governing the delivery of home and center based early intervention/childhood programs or transitional/vocational services, they may assist in the design of individualized programs, provide information and support services to parents and carry out tasks delegated by the professional staff member. While the duties of paraeducators working in early childhood education and transitional/vocational services are similar, we have developed separate lists of duties for the two programmatic areas in order to highlight the differences in the nature of the tasks they perform.

Duties for LEVEL III paraeducators working in home and center based early intervention/childhood programs may include:

- Consulting with teachers or other professional practitioners and participating in the design of: 1) developmentally and age appropriate programs for infants and young children with and without disabilities; and 2) services for parents and caregivers.

- Assisting teachers with functional assessment activities to gather information about children's developmental levels.

- Gathering information from parents about concerns connected with their child's development.

- Working with individual and small groups of children using developmentally appropriate curriculum activities.

- Supporting and encouraging (parents under the supervision of a professional practitioner) to use interactive techniques that will enhance the development of their child's communication and social skills.

- Providing parents with information and assistance they can use to gain access to community resources and support services for their child.

- Keeping records and performing other clerical duties.

- Attending IFSP/IEP and staff meetings.

Duties for LEVEL III paraeducators working in transitional/vocational programs may include:

- Consulting with teachers and/or vocational specialists to assist with the design of individual transitional programs.

- Preparing students to live and work independently or with support by training and supervising them in community centered learning environments.

- Developing instructional strategies (under the supervision of a professional practitioner) to teach students to perform a job as specified by an employer.

- Familiarizing employers and other members of the community with the special needs of students.

- Recording and sharing information about student performance and progress with professional practitioners.

- Maintaining records about student attendance and other information required by the district or employer.

- Providing information about resources and support services to students and their parents that will enhance transition to the adult world.

- Attending IEP/ITP and staff meetings.

* The material in Appendix C was developed by the National Resource Center for Paraprofessionals in Education and Related Services through a grant from the Division of Personnel Preparation, Office of Special Education Programs and Rehabilitative Services, United States Department of Education. Used with permission.

United States Civil Rights Offices

REGIONAL OFFICES

Region I: Connecticut, Maine, Massachusetts, New Hampshire, Rhode Island, Vermont

Office for Civil Rights, Region I
U.S. Department of Education
J. W. McCormack Post Office and Courthouse
Room 222, 01–0061
Boston, MA 02109–4557
617–223–9662 (Voice); 617–223–9695 (TDD)

Region II: New Jersey, New York, Puerto Rico, Virgin Islands

Office for Civil Rights, Region II
U.S. Department of Education
26 Federal Plaza, 33rd Floor
Room 33–130, 02–1010
New York, NY 10278–0082
212–264–4633 (Voice); 212–264–9464 (TDD)

Region III: Delaware, District of Columbia, Maryland, Pennsylvania, Virginia, West Virginia

Office for Civil Rights, Region III
U.S. Department of Education
3535 Market Street
Room 6300, 03–2010
Philadelphia, PA 19104–3326
215–596–6772 (Voice); 215–596–6794 (TDD)

Region IV: Alabama, Florida, Georgia, North Carolina, South Carolina, Tennessee

Office for Civil Rights, Region IV
U.S. Department of Education
P.O. Box 2048, 04–3010
Atlanta, GA 30301–2048
404–331–2954 (Voice); 404–331–7816 (TDD)

Region V: Illinois, Indiana, Minnesota, Michigan, Ohio, Wisconsin

Office for Civil Rights, Region V
U.S. Department of Education
401 South State Street
Room 700C, 05–4010
Chicago, IL 60605–1202
312–886–3456 (Voice); 312–353–2541 (TDD)

Region VI: Arkansas, Louisiana, Mississippi, Oklahoma, Texas

Office for Civil Rights, Region VI
U.S. Department of Education
1200 Main Tower Building
Suite 2260, 06–5010
Dallas, TX 75202–9998
214–767–3959 (Voice); 214–767–3639 (TDD)

Region VII: Iowa, Kansas, Kentucky, Missouri, Nebraska

Office for Civil Rights, Region VII
U.S. Department of Education
10220 North Executive Hill Boulevard
8th Floor, 07–6010
Kansas City, MO 64153–1367
816–891–8026 (Voice); 816–374–6461 (TDD)

Region VIII: Arizona, Colorado, Montana, New Mexico, North Dakota, South Dakota, Utah, Wyoming

Office for Civil Rights, Region VIII
U.S. Department of Education
Federal Building, Suite 310, 08-7010
1244 Speer Boulevard
Denver, CO 80204–3582
303–844–5695 (Voice); 303–844–3417 (TDD)

Region IX: California

Office for Civil Rights, Region IX
U.S. Department of Education
Old Federal Building
50 United Nations Plaza
Room 239, 09–8010
San Francisco, CA 94102–4102
415–556–7000 (Voice); 415–556–6806 (TDD)

Region X: Alaska, Hawaii, Idaho, Nevada, Oregon, Washington, American Samoa, Guam, Pacific Islands

Office for Civil Rights, Region X
U.S. Department of Education
915 Second Avenue
Room 3310, 10–9010
Seattle, WA 98174–1099
206–553–6811 (Voice); 206–553–4542 (TDD)

APPENDIX E

Forms that May Help in the Beginning Days

	Records Complete	Lunch $ or	Date Paid $10.00	Siblings and Other Notes	Transportation			
					First Day		Change After First Day	
					A.M.	P.M.	A.M.	P.M.

FIGURE E–1 First Days Information. *Courtesy of Jo Hogan and Mary Wofford.*

	Testing Skills	Projects Completed																	NOTES
Jon																			
Alanna																			

FIGURE E–2 Use a form such as this to record all sorts of information. *Courtesy of Jo Hogan and Mary Wofford.*

DIRECTIONS: Student writes the letter or number that the teacher says.

Name				
1	2	3	4	5
6	7	8	9	10
11	12	13	14	15
16	17	18	19	20
21	22	23	24	25
26	27	28	29	30
31	32	33	34	35
36	37	38	39	40
41	42	43	44	45
46	47	48	49	50
51	52	53	54	55
56	57	58	59	60

FIGURE E–3 *Courtesy of Jo Hogan and Mary Wofford.*

I can read these sight words:

_____ I		_____ can		_____ Go	
_____ go		_____ not		_____ A	
_____ to		_____ you		_____ We	
_____ a		_____ will		_____ Can	
_____ we		_____ help		_____ You	

Student marks the word that the teacher says.

1. to	we	help	2. can	go	you
3. a	we	I	4. not	A	will
5. you	Will	We	6. Help	to	Can
7. not	can	go	8. We	You	I
9. Will	We	You	10. to	help	not
11. you	can	will	12. not	help	we

FIGURE E–4 *Courtesy of Jo Hogan and Mary Wofford.*

_____ recognizes these body parts!

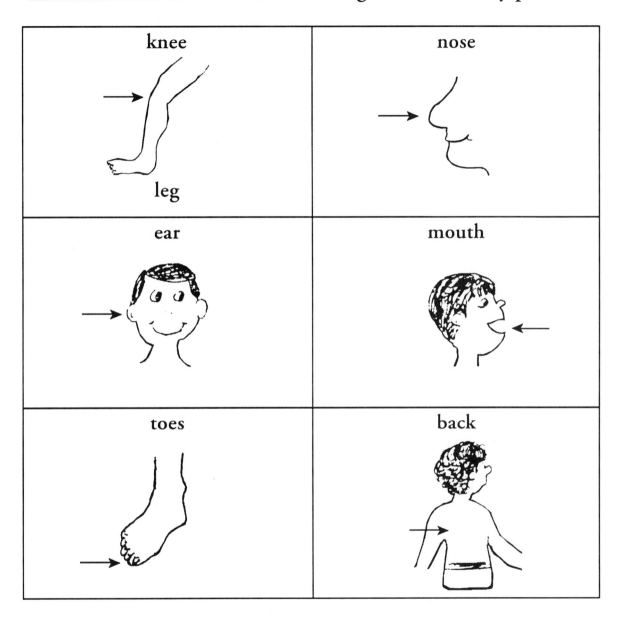

FIGURE E–5 *Courtesy of Jo Hogan and Mary Wofford.* (Continued)

_____ recognizes these body parts!

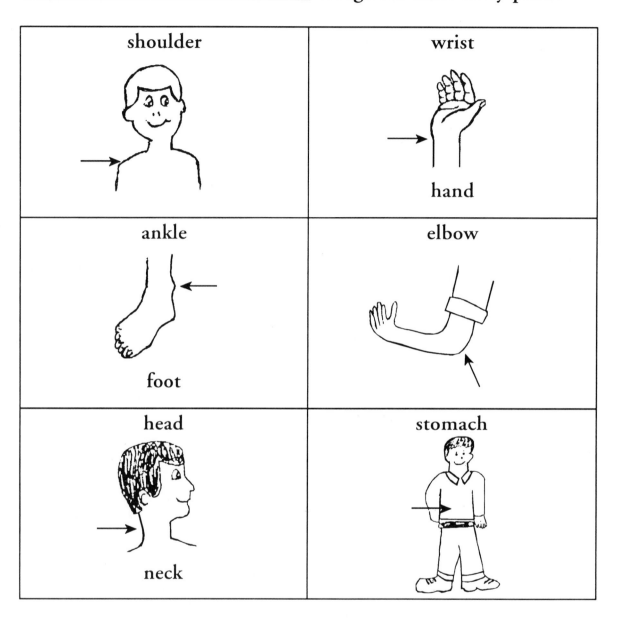

FIGURE E–5 *Courtesy of Jo Hogan and Mary Wofford.*

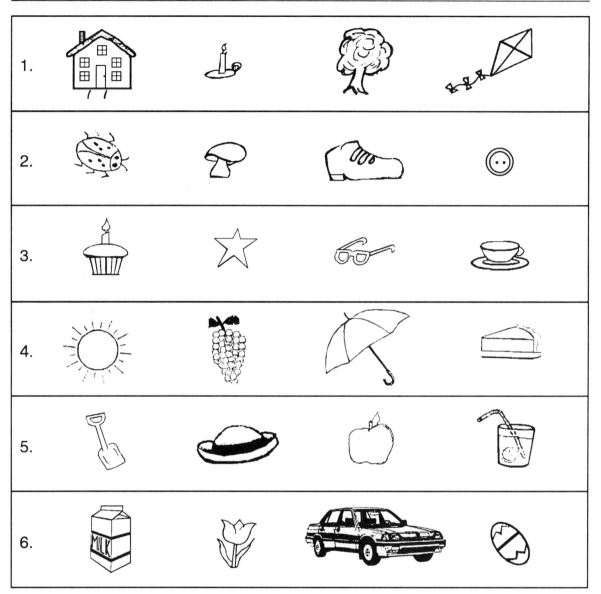

1. Underline the object to the right of the candle; Circle the object to the left of the tree.
2. Circle — left of the mushroom; put an X on the object to the right of the shoe.
3. Underline — right of glasses; circle — left of glasses.
4. Circle — right of grapes; X — left of umbrella.
5. Underline — right of hat; circle — left of apple.
6. Circle — right of car; underline — left of flower.

FIGURE E–6 *Courtesy of Jo Hogan and Mary Wofford.*

NAME _____

Correctly writes number called out by teacher.

FIGURE E–6 *Courtesy of Jo Hogan and Mary Wofford.* (Continued)

FIGURE F–1   Sample Bingo Cards A and B. *Courtesy of Nick Hobbs.* (Continued)

FIGURE F–1 Sample Bingo Cards A and B. *Courtesy of Nick Hobbs.*

OCTOBER

Monday	Tuesday	Wednesday	Thursday	Friday
2 Review Week: letters: s, m, t, f, h, n shapes: ▲, ●, ■, ▬, ◆, ⬬, color words: red, yellow, blue, green, brown math: sorting & classifying Theme: Fire Prevention	**3**	**—HOMEWORK—4** Bring one object that begins with each of the following letters: s, m, t, f, h, n. We're reviewing our beginning sounds. —Library Day— —Send book—	**5** Bring a snack that begins with either S, M, T, F, H, N to eat at snack time	**—DRESS UP— 6** Choose a letter: S, M, T, F, H, or N! Be creative and wear things that begin with that letter. We'll do some fun activities. Deadline for Chaperone Notes
9 **NO SCHOOL**	**10** letter — A a (Vowel) color — purple math — sorting & classifying Theme: Good Nutrition	**—HOMEWORK—11** Find capital & lower-case Aa's in magazines, etc. Find 5 animals in magazines. Glue all Aa's & the 5 animals on a paper & bring to school —Library Day— —Send book—	**12**	**—DRESS UP— 13** Wear an apron or anything that begins with a long a or short a sound. Bring a snack that begins with an a. Deadline for permission form & money for field trip.
16 letter — E e (Vowel) color — orange math — same, more, fewer Theme: 4 Food Groups	**17**	**—HOMEWORK—18** Bring a hard boiled egg from home. They need to be hard-boiled so we can make egg babies at school. Pack them safely so they won't break on the way to school —Library Day— —Send book—	**19** *We'll make "Egg Babies" today!!*	**—DRESS UP— 20** Wear exercise clothes (sweats, leotards, tights, sweat bands)
23 letter — I i (Vowel) color — black math — same, more, fewer Theme: Spiders	**24**	**—HOMEWORK—25** Bring an instrument from home (toy guitar, toy flute, toy drum, harmonica, etc.) —Library Day— —Send book—	**26**	**—DRESS UP— 27** Wear clothes inside out!
30 letter — O o (Vowel) color — review of all 8 basic colors math — review categorizing same, more, fewer	**31**	**—HOMEWORK—1** If you have anything from the ocean that you would like to show, bring it today (shells, pictures, art projects, etc.) —Library Day— —Send book—	**2**	**—DRESS UP— 3** Wear overalls or old clothes for the letter O.

FIGURE F–2 Sample Calendars. *Courtesy of Jo Hogan and Mary Wofford.*

FEBRUARY

Monday	Tuesday	Wednesday	Thursday	Friday
5 letter — V v math — Geometry 100 activities 100 Days of School Send a small "v" item that begins with v for the floral tree. Theme: Valentine's Day	**6** PARENTING CONFERENCE 6:45–8:30 P.M.	**7** —HOMEWORK— Bring something that begins with the v sound. —Library Day— —Return books—	**8** —DRESS UP— Wear something that begins with v. Be creative.	**9** *SEND YOUR CHILD'S VALENTINES*
12 letter — D d math — patterns & left & right Send a small item for the floral tree that begins with d. Theme: Fairy Tales	**13**	**14** Teddy Bear Tea Valentine Party 11–11:45 All parents invited! Your child may go home with you. —HMWK—Bring a picture of your dad or dog or draw a picture of either one of them. —Library Day— —Return books—	**15** —DRESS UP— Wear something that begins with d. Be creative. *Doughnuts for Dads* 8:30 A.M. – 9:00 A.M. All dads are invited to attend!	**16**
19 **HOLIDAY NO SCHOOL**	**20** letter — Review Week language — rhyming math — patterns & left & right Theme: Nursery Rhymes	**21** —HOMEWORK— Bring 2 things that rhyme! —Library Day— —Return books—	**22** —DRESS UP— Choose a letter that we've had. Wear something that begins with that letter. We'll play the guessing game.	**23**
26 letter — X x language — rhyming math — money, recognition & value of coins & bills Send a small item for the floral tree that begins with x, or that ends with x. Theme: Nursery Rhymes	**27**	**28** —HOMEWORK— Bring something that begins with the x sound. (or ends) / e.g. – box – —Library Day— —Send book—	**29** —DRESS UP— Wear mixed up clothes for the letter x! Ex: backwards, inside/out, wrong feet, wrong size, etc. LAST DAY FOR PIZZAS!!	**1**
	FEBRUARY IS THE FINAL MONTH FOR THE PIZZA HUT BOOK-IT PROGRAM. MAKE SURE YOUR FEBRUARY VERIFICATION PAPERS ARE IN TO ME BY FEB. 28. THANKS FOR YOUR PARTICIPATION!			

FIGURE F–2 Sample Calendars. *Courtesy of Jo Hogan and Mary Wofford.* (Continued)

APRIL

Monday	Tuesday	Wednesday	Thursday	Friday
1 Letter — Review & sequencing math — addition & subtraction language — describing words science — water activities & experiments Theme: Spring	**2** Send NO snack! April birthdays celebration!!	**3** —HOMEWORK— Bring one thing that will sink in water. Bring one thing that will float in water. —LIBRARY DAY—	**4** SHOW N' TELL FOR EVERYONE!	**5** Easter Egg Hunt 11:00–11:45 *Everyone* is invited!! Lots of parents are needed to help hide eggs. Be here at 10:30 if you can help.
8	**9**	**10**	**11**	**12**
— — SPRING HOLIDAYS — SPRING HOLIDAYS — —				
15 letters — Review & sequencing math — Addition/Subtraction language — Action words Theme: Plants/Seeds	**16**	**17** —HOMEWORK— Collect & bring to class a variety of seeds. Label the seeds in a plastic baggies. Color and draw a picture of where the seed or seeds came from. —LIBRARY DAY—	**18** SHOW N' TELL FOR EVERYONE!	**19** Letter People Day 11:30 A.M. Everyone is invited!!
22 math — addition/subtraction & geometry language — naming words Theme: Insects	**23**	**24** —HOMEWORK— Bring an insect to school. Examples: stuffed animal, picture, book or drawing. —LIBRARY DAY—	**25**	**26** SHOW N' TELL FOR EVERYONE!
29 math — graphing language — telling & asking sentences Theme: Circus	**30** —HOMEWORK— Bring something to share that you have related to the circus.	**1** MAY FIELD TRIP TO YELLOW RIVER GAME RANCH	**2** SHOW N' TELL FOR EVERYONE!	**3** RAIN DATE FOR FIELD TRIP TO YELLOW RIVER GAME RANCH

FIGURE F–2 Sample Calendars. *Courtesy of Jo Hogan and Mary Wofford.*

Alphabet Inventory The 4 corners in each box represent the four grading periods. They will be color coded for each grading period.
Code: ✓ = mastered (color coded for each grading period); ✓– = knew name of letter but couldn't distinguish between
          capital and lowercase   blank = not mastered

M	q	x	T	u	F	H
j	N	A	r	B	y	w
k	Z	o	i	P	c	g
S	d	l	V	e	E	v
L	s	D	p	G	C	I
O	z	K	b	W	Y	a
n	R	h	f	J	t	U
X	m	Q				

Number Recognition   ✓ = mastered   blank = not mastered

7	13	5	12	19	1	10
8	17	3	15	0	2	11
18	16	6	14	9	20	4

FIGURE Appendix F–3   Alphabet Inventory *Courtesy of Jo Hogan and Mary Wofford.*

APPENDIX G

Legal Issues for Paraeducators: Your Rights and Your Obligations

Professionalism was stressed in Chapter 1 of this book. You need to constantly remember that as an instructional paraeducator you represent the professionals whom you assist. Do you remember what Katz said about the relationship between the educator/caretaker's need for ethics and the vulnerability of the students? Because of the nature of your role, it is very important that you maintain high standards of conduct in your dealings with children and their parents. Strict adherence to all laws, codes, and regulations is essential.

In your job as a paraeducator you will be protected under the law in many ways. You will also have legal obligations as a paraeducator. First we will look at some of the rights you have as an employee.

YOUR RIGHTS

Civil Rights

As an employee you have the right to be treated fairly, without any prejudice or differential treatment because of certain facts about you. Human rights law is the body of legislation that regulates discrimination because of race, color, sex, or national origin. As an employee, you will be covered under some form of human rights protection. You need to check if your employment is covered by Title VII of the Civil Rights Act of 1964 or by state human rights laws. State laws may apply to employers of smaller groups when federal law omits these work sites. In 1991 an additional civil rights law was passed by Congress. The new law retained much of the old provision and also increased worker protection.

An example of possible discrimination is when an employer refuses to hire a married or pregnant woman, or a woman with children, but instead hires a childless applicant with the same qualifications. Another example is when an employer refuses to hire a male applicant as a paraeducator when he has the same or better credentials than the female candidates. If you are a male, you have the right to work in an early childhood position. Civil rights law is violated if an employer refuses to hire a male just because he is male. None of the following are valid reasons for not hiring males as paraeducators or early childhood workers:

Stereotyped view of males

Preference of the coworkers

Preference of the administration

Preference of parents or customers

The sex of the worker is not a bona-fide occupational qualification in early childhood work. If you are a female, your sex should not mean that you have an *edge,* and if you are a male, your sex should not be a drawback to being hired as a paraeducator.

The subject of national origin discrimination generates both a right and an obligation. You have the right to work in an environment that is free from discrimination against your national origin. There is also an obligation to avoid such discrimination yourself. We have all heard jokes about ethnic groups. Ethnic slurs that denigrate a worker's national origin create a hostile working environment and can be considered harassment. Make it a practice never to be part of any action that could be construed as discriminatory.

Sexual harassment has received considerable attention in the press. The law considers whether a "hostile working environment" exists in a sexual harassment complaint, and whether the acts of others at the workplace are part of a general pattern. If you have questions concerning sexual harassment, it will be necessary to do some reading and research since the debate continues as to what is and what is not harassment. The Equal Employment Opportunity Commission (EEOC) is a proper source of information. Again, do your part in keeping your workplace clean and free from anything that even remotely smacks of sexual harassment.

Standing up against civil rights violations can be very difficult and serious. If you feel that you have been discriminated against, you have the option to sue for damages, but intentional employment discrimination must be proved.

Age Discrimination

The Age Discrimination in Employment Act protects workers over age 40 who are employed by employers who have at least 20 workers. Age discrimination might involve lower pay, refusal to hire, and/or unequal job benefits. Court cases have been won when *age-related* derogatory remarks were a common work site practice.

A number of stereotypes about older workers are considered erroneous. Note Johnson's (1986) remarks in the following:

> ......*there appear to be many benefits when child care program administrators employ older adults. Staff turnover, a perennial and difficult problem for many administrators, can be reduced by the employment and proper assignments of older adults. Not only are older employees more committed to and satisfied with their work, they are generally more committed and loyal to the organization for which they work. In paraprofessional job assignments, older employees will likely outperform younger employees. Finally, older employees are likely to have fewer avoidable absences than do their younger counterparts.*

Johnson (1986) describes the provisions of legislation affecting older workers:

> *The Age Discrimination in Employment Act as amended in 1978 provides specific protection against discrimination in employment decisions for employees and job applicants between the ages of 40 and 70. The effect of this act is to require administrators to make job assignments, promotions, pay raises, training opportunities, and all other personnel decisions without regard to employee's age.*

As mentioned earlier, civil rights legislation makes discriminatory hiring of either married or unmarried workers, childless workers, or mothers illegal. A center or school may prefer young childless or married female workers for any number of reasons. One reason may be that the administration feels that the young, childless or married female workers project the kind of "teacher image" that could attract more parent clients, but acting on this preference in hiring is an illegal practice.

Pregnancy, Family, and Medical Leave

The Civil Rights Act of 1964 was amended to include the Pregnancy Discrimination Act. This act forbids employers to discriminate against pregnant workers. It applies to employers of fifteen or more workers and requires all workers to be treated the same—whether pregnant or experiencing medical conditions related to pregnancy. Consequently, employers may not:

- require you to take a maternity leave with a duration of *their* choosing.
- refuse to reinstate you after a maternity leave to the same or an equivalent job, with equivalent benefits and seniority.
- refuse to offer leaves of absence for pregnancy and childbirth-related disabilities under *different terms* than what they offer workers with other disabilities.

Civil rights regional office locations are listed in the appendix.

Handicapped Workers

If you are handicapped, there are two large bodies of law that affect your employment: 1) the Americans with Disabilities Act (ADA), and 2) the Vocational Rehabilitation Act of 1973. You are perceived as handicapped if you have:

- a physical or mental impairment that limits one or more major life activities.
- a record of an impairment but have recovered.
- a condition that is perceived as an impairment (i.e., AIDS, HIV).

The ADA requires employers to make reasonable accommodations for handicapped individuals who can perform the essential functions of a job. Reasonable accommodations are considered accommodations that do not create undue hardship for the employer.

There are considerations about your physical strength related to paraeducator positions. For some positions you must be able to lift disabled children or restrain angry children. If you think there is a question if you are physically capable of performing the tasks in the job you are offered, you need to speak up. Remember that you want to guard the safety of both yourself and the children.

Privacy

Appropriate interview questions were discussed in Chapter 13. There *are* some questions you are not required to answer. Refer back to

Table 13–3. You may also need to know that medical exams cannot be ordered until a job is offered. You are not required to answer questions about your medical history before you actually get an offer for employment.

You may work in a facility where your employer uses cameras for any number of reasons. Only work areas may be photographed or videotaped. Areas where employee privacy is necessary may not be photographed or videotaped. Your employer also may not single you or any other employee out for surveillance ("Legal Problem Solver," 1994).

Generally, employers have the right to search employees' lockers, workstations, briefcases, purses, lunchboxes, and additional items ("Legal Problem Solver," 1994). But you need to know that just as with surveillance, in the unlikely event this kind of search is ever done, you should not be *singled out*; all employees would have to be searched.

Wages and Benefits

Some of your rights related to wages and benefits were discussed in Chapter 13. There are a few more angles to examine.

Most states have adopted laws concerning wages for men and women performing the same level of work. Idaho's Human Rights law deals with the issue in the following way, which is similar to laws in all other states:

> *44–1702.* **Discriminatory payment of wages based upon sex prohibited.** *(1) No employer shall discriminate between or among employees in the same establishment on the basis of sex, by paying wages to any employee in any occupation in this state at a rate less than the rate at which he pays any employee of the opposite sex for comparable work on jobs which have comparable requirements relating to skill, effort, and responsibility. Differentials which are paid pursuant to established seniority systems or merit increase systems, which do not discriminate on the basis of sex, are not within this prohibition.*

Under the Federal Equal Pay Act, an employer may not pay you less than a coworker simply on the basis of your sex. For the work to be considered equal, *all* of the following conditions must apply:

- the work to be done is approximately equal.

- The work requires approximately the same effort, training, experience, and education.

- The work has approximately the same degree of responsibility.

- The work requires approximately the same intellectual or physical effort.

- The work is to be done under approximately the same working conditions.

(NCECW, 1994)

Not all paraeducators receive benefits such as health insurance, retirement plans, free child care, tuition grants, and so on. In fact, it is rare for early childhood workers to receive a large number of benefits. Considerations about benefits were given in Chapter 13 in the event they are offered. If benefits are offered to your coworkers, you have the right to receive them, too. If benefits are offered to some employees and not to others, that may warrant an investigation. Something else to remember about benefits are the rights you have under COBRA. Your COBRA benefit continuation and conversion rights were mentioned in Chapter 13.

Union Activity

Your rights to participate in union activities have already been introduced. If you fall under the jurisdiction of the National Labor Relations Board (NLRB), you have the right to join a union, and to recruit other members and distribute union literature during off-duty hours in nonworking areas. Again, if applicable under the NLRB, you have strike privileges and the right to picket peacefully under certain conditions. If you are a union member, you are free to be involved in union activities without the fear of employer scrutiny; employers are forbidden by the NLRB to spy on employee union activities.

Protection Against Unfair Firing

Most early childhood workers are *at-will* employees. If you are an *at-will* employee, you can be fired or decide to leave on your own accord. You are protected under the law against wrongful discharge. Wrongful discharge occurs when an employer fires a worker:

1. On the basis of race, sex, religion, handicap, age, marital status, color, ancestry, or national origin (Civil Rights Act of 1964, Title VII).

2. Because the worker attempts to organize a union (National Labor Relations Act).

3. If the worker asks for lawful wage and hour consideration (Fair Labor Standards Act).

4. If the worker complains about the worker's safety and employer requirements (Occupational Safety and Health Act).

5. Because a worker needs to serve on a jury or answer a summons.

6. Because a worker refuses to break a public law.

7. The worker refuses to commit perjury on the employer's behalf.

Wrongful firing may also involve breaking an implied employer-employee contract. If your employer's actions lead to changed working conditions that make it virtually impossible to continue on the job and you are fired, this may be wrongful discharge as well.

Some of the above situations deal with *whistle blower* protection in the law. The U.S. Department of Labor's Small Business Handbook (1993) explains the protection the law offers employees who call their employers to task regarding the following:

> **Employee Protection** provisions are built into most labor and public safety statutes, e.g., the FLSA, the OSHA Act, ERISA, many environmental protection statutes, etc. These provisions protect employees who exercise their rights under these acts to complain about employers, ask for information, etc. (remedies can include back wages and reinstatement). They are normally enforced by the Department of Labor (DOL) agency most concerned, e.g., OSHA enforces those arising under the OSHA Act.

Before considering whistle blowing actions, Joel (1993) suggests making sure you are right and that you have given the employer time to correct problems. He also suggests that you run the complaint by an attorney who specializes in labor law. In any situation when illegal firing is an issue, legal advice is highly recommended.

It *is* lawful to fire an employee for good and valid reasons. These good, valid, legal reasons include:

- Insubordination
- Violation of program rules, policies, or handbook
- Lying or misrepresentation on job applications
- Excessive absence or lateness
- Poor quality work
- Negligence
- Stealing
- A job classification is omitted
- Lack of child enrollment
- A physical or mental factor that prevents adequate worker performance of duties, and the employer cannot make a reasonable accommodation to rectify the situation
- Breaking employer dress codes.

In many cases if you are discharged (fired), you can apply for unemployment compensation benefits. Voluntary resigning, on the other hand, disqualifies you from unemployment benefits. If you are forced to resign, you are not disqualified from unemployment compensation benefits, but you must prove your case. There is a stipulation that you must have earned sufficient wages to qualify for unemployment compensation. There are some other conditions that impact your eligibility for these benefits. If you are fired for repeated willful misconduct or a single act of willful misconduct that seriously endangers the life, safety, or property of your employer, a fellow employee, or the general public, you are ineligible for unemployment benefits.

Your File

You also have legal rights concerning your personnel file. First of all, you need to know that your employer is required by law to keep the following records concerning you and your work:

- Full name, home address, sex, and occupation (job title)
- Social security number
- Hours: regular time of work day and when work week begins
- Total additions to or deductions from wages for each pay period
- Day of pay and the pay period covered by payment

- Payroll, time sheets

- Tax information

- Safety records and worker's compensation records

- Application forms

- Hiring, promotion, demotion, transfer, and termination records

Record entries should be strictly job-related (Joel, 1993). Information should be tied to the operation of a successful organization.

Some states give you the right to inspect your own personnel file; others do not. As of 1993, private businesses and corporations in the following states were ordered to give employee record access:

> Alaska, California, Connecticut, Delaware, Illinois, Maine, Massachusetts, Michigan, Minnesota, Nevada, New Hampshire, Oregon, Pennsylvania, Rhode Island, Washington, and Wisconsin ("Legal Problem Solver", 1994).

Only certain documents in these states may be reviewed and the law may or may not permit you, the employee, from inserting a rebuttal to the reviewed information. In some states you may be allowed to add clarifying statements to your file; in other states removal of records or parts of records that you, the employee, deem erroneous or outdated is permitted.

Specific rules about what will be viewed, when this is possible, and who will be present are found in existing state law. It is wise for employers to keep personnel files confidential and locked away; that is best for you and everybody else concerned.

You need to know your rights concerning your medical records. The Americans with Disabilities Act (ADA) protects medical file confidentiality for workers whose employers have at least 25 workers. Medical records must be stored separately and only certain individuals (supervisors), medical personnel, and government representatives have a right to access the material under the ADA rules.

Voting

States vary widely in labor laws covering time off and/or pay or no pay when voting. Again, check your state's policies. You just need to be aware that some states do make provisions for this.

Contracts

There are rights and responsibilities associated with contracts. Since a completed contract is a legal instrument, it may be difficult to find a legitimate reason for granting/obtaining release from a contract. Common reasons to request a contract release are:

- Work transfer of spouse

- Health

- Family responsibilities

- Personal reasons including extreme job dissatisfaction, personality conflicts, and employment misconceptions

- Career changes or other offers of employment

Valente (1987) notes:

Teachers as well as employers are protected from unlawful breach by contract law. When a private school in breach of its contract terminates a teacher before the end of the contract period, the teacher may recover the salary for the full term. If the teacher breaches his or her contract, that breach justifies immediate termination by the school.

Contract release is not automatic, and seeking legal assistance and counsel is sensible. Most employers who would offer you contract employment have already had the benefit of legal counsel. If you find that you need to get out of a contract, get some legal help.

Enforcement

Who has the responsibility to enforce all these laws? Who can help you protect your rights as a paraeducator? It may seem complicated. The line of responsibility has been alluded to previously in this chapter. Whichever department is most concerned with the specific law in question is the one most equipped to give you assistance. For example, the Wage and Hour Division of the U.S. Department of Labor enforces the Fair Labor Standards Act (FLSA); they can help you concerning questions of rights related to your paycheck. Claims can be processed by local offices or state offices. These local offices (or agencies) conduct investigations into your problem, and if necessary they conduct informal hearings.

If you ever need to make a claim concerning your legal employment rights, there are several things you need to take into consideration. You need to know that employers can appeal decisions, but it is illegal for them to fire you because you make a claim. You need to be reminded to collect as much evidence supporting the claim as possible. Evidence includes written or oral policies of the employer, specific details such as meeting notes, employee diaries, job reviews, other employees' testimonies and observations, and other reliable documentation. There will be more information about employee files and the records you need to keep as a paraeducator in succeeding chapters.

Most states require employers to post state labor laws in a conspicuous place at the work site. In many states an employer may be fined or face legal consequences when laws are not posted. A federal labor poster is also required and outlines your rights under FLSA.

By now you have the idea that many aspects of your job as a paraeducator have numerous protections under the law. You also have many legal obligations as a paraeducator. Now we will begin to look at some of the laws that apply to your job.

Some workplaces are controlled by state law only, others by federal law only, and yet others by both state *and* federal law. As Joel (1993) points out, "In cases where an issue is addressed by conflicting state and federal laws, you, the employee, are covered by the law that affords you the most rights or protections."

On the reverse side, when laws are concerned with your obligations rather than your rights, if there is a discrepancy between state and federal laws, the law setting the more stringent standard must be observed.

YOUR OBLIGATIONS

Underage Workers

Workers under eighteen are covered by FLSA Child Labor Laws. Under FLSA, sixteen- and seventeen-year-olds may work for unlimited hours in nonhazardous jobs. Fourteen- and fifteen-year-olds are limited to no more than three hours on a school day and a limit of eighteen hours in a school week. During school vacations and breaks, a limit of forty hours per week exists. Work hours are limited to 7 a.m. to 7 p.m. except for June 1 through Labor Day when evening hours are extended to 9 p.m. ("Fact sheet ESA 91-3," 1994).

In addition to these federal stipulations, most states also have laws relating to working minors. If your state has laws related to working minors, the information will be available through your state Department of Labor.

If you are underage, you and your employer are obligated to follow the legal working age standards.

Speaking "English Only" Rule

You may be interested to know that you may be obligated to speak English while you are on the job. Under Title VII of the Civil Rights Act of 1964, an employer may require employees to speak only English at all times on the job, but the employer must show that this is necessary for conducting business. If this rule is invoked at your place of work, your employer must inform employees when you may use English-only speech and what the consequences are for violating the rule.

Privacy for Students

One of your obligations is to protect the privacy of your students. Part of this is a general protection of students' files. Public schools have to comply with the Family Educational Rights and Privacy Act (FERPA). Under this act, only authorized school personnel are allowed access to student records, and parents have the right to forbid the release of their children's file information to anyone other than school personnel. Parents also have the right to review their child's file and to challenge anything they feel is inappropriate or incorrect (Oppenheim, 1989). You need to know this in case you have any responsibility for student records, whether you work in a public school or another facility. Be careful that children's records are viewed only by appropriate people and contain only appropriate entries if you have any input into the matter.

Copyright Law

As a paraeducator, you may be asked to make reams of photocopies. Since you will probably become very well acquainted with the copier, you must be aware of the law that governs some aspects of the copier's use. Copyright law is *federal law* and its history goes way back.

The *New Book of Knowledge* (Grolier, 1982) says copyright is a "term that means that the creator of an artistic work such as a book, article, play, poem, or musical composition owns the right to copy and sell it and that no one else may do so without permission." In other words, copyrights and copyright law exist to protect the people who take creative ideas and put them in some tangible form such as books and songs and computer games. An idea itself cannot be copyrighted but once that idea is framed out into something concrete, then it certainly is protected under the law.

The first U.S. copyright laws were state laws formed back in the 1700s. The first federal copyright law was passed by Congress in 1790. Since that time the law has changed and been updated to include advancements like records, movies, and computer programs. The copyright law that we are currently under went into effect in 1978.

Under the 1978 law, if the work was done from 1978 on, copyrights cover materials for 50 years after the creator's death, whether the work was published or not. If the work was done before 1978, then the copyright protects for 28 years and can be renewed for 47 years.

There have even been efforts to bring other countries under a common copyright law, beginning with the Berne Convention as far back as 1886, and up to the present through the United Nations.

You should be getting the idea that this is a serious subject. Consequences for breaking copyright laws can be stiff, ranging from fines of $500 to $250,000, and imprisonment from one to five years, depending on the extent and willfulness of the violation.

In addition to protecting authors, etc., the 1978 copyright law (Title 17, U.S. Code, Section 106, Section 107) also attempts to see to the needs of society in general. First of all, after the specified time, material enters the *public domain* and may be used freely. Next, Section 107 defines the concept of *Fair Use.* Under this section, special considerations are given to uses related to 1) criticism, comment, and news reporting, and 2) teaching, scholarship, and research.

Four criteria are examined in order to determine Fair Use:

- The intentions for the use (Is it for commercial or nonprofit reasons?)

- The type of copyrighted material

- How much is used

- Any monetary effect

So what does this mean for you, the paraeducator standing next to the copier and ready to press *start?* There are guidelines for you to follow. The latest guidelines come from a congressional subcommittee made up of authors, publishers, and educators.

These guidelines say it is okay to make single copies of:

- A chapter of a book.
- An article from a periodical or newspaper.
- A short story, essay or short poem, whether or not from a collective work.
- A chart, graph, diagram, cartoon or picture from a book, periodical, or newspaper.

These guidelines say it is okay for you to reproduce multiple copies of:

- A complete poem (less than 250 words, less than 2 pages).

- An excerpt from a long poem, but no more than 250 words.

- A complete article, story, or essay (less than 2,500 words) or an excerpt (1000 words or less, no more than 10 percent of the whole) from a larger work.

- One chart, graph, diagram, or picture per book or periodical.

There are limits to the guidelines above. Some other considerations include:

1. It is illegal to copy copyrighted, syndicated cartoon characters.

2. Fax copies are treated the same as photocopies under the law.

3. Copyright law applies to music you might want to use as background for slide shows, skits, etc., that will be taped, and to music lyrics you might want to revamp. For example, you need permission to write new words to a well-known tune for a school program.

4. It is a violation to record copyrighted stories onto cassette tapes except when done for legally blind students.

5. There are strict guidelines about videos. If a program is taped off of broadcast TV, it can be kept and used for educational purposes for no longer than 45 days, then it is supposed to be erased. It is wise to be cautious about children bringing programs taped from home to school to be shown to a class. It is also best for your facility to make sure about correct licensing since there are stipulations about using videos for instructional purposes versus entertainment.

6. It is permissable to print pages or articles from an encyclopedia on CD-ROM, but it is a violation to copy large portions.

This is all very complicated and much is open to interpretation in the courts. It takes volumes to fully explain copyright law and Fair Use applications. We haven't even gotten to computer software and laser discs! The ramifications go on and on.

In some places it may be common practice to pass around black line master books so that each classroom can have its own photocopied version, but this is wrong unless express permission has been given for more than one teacher to make copies. Whenever this kind of grade-level or schoolwide copying is done without authorization, the author is shortchanged royalties, which is a percentage of the sales price.

Do not be afraid to write for permission. Be specific in your request; tell what you want to do and why. Often the response is favorable, and the worst you can hear is no. Sometimes you may be asked to pay a small fee.

Most schools and public libraries place warnings about copyright laws in the vicinity of copiers. Your school board or center probably has directions concerning copyright law. If not, still be cautious; you do not want to be the defendant in a court case that prompts them to develop guidelines!

When you get down to particular questions, this can all be confusing. A good source for clear, practical guidelines is Gary Becker's © *Copyright: A Guide to Information and Resources* (1992). You may also ask your school's media specialist or local public librarians. The main thing is for you to be aware of copyright law and to use prudence with any copyrighted material. If you have any doubts, check before you copy.

Corporal Punishment

Knowledge of legal bounds for punishment in your state is vital. Corporal punishment *is* illegal in the majority of states. Some state law and state licensing law do not forbid corporal punishment. Your state may allow spanking or paddling to be administered in schools or centers. However, most states at least place restrictions on the practice, including the admonishment that punishment must be reasonable, and not out of proportion to the offense and the child's age. Some states describe exactly how much force can be used and caution that parents must have prior notification and that approval be obtained.

The practice of corporal punishment has persisted in some religious-affiliated centers and schools. You just need to be very careful about compliance with your state laws. If your state law forbids corporal punishment, parents cannot give you permission to break the law, even if they sign an authorization form giving you permission to spank, etc.

It can be noted that early childhood experts and professionals urge all workers to use positive guidance techniques and suggest that corporal punishment is inappropriate for young children in group care. Of course, differences in philosophies of discipline are controversial. The important thing for you to do is to be aware of the philosophies and laws that apply to *your* work. Any paraeducator who oversteps legal boundaries may face lawsuits, criminal charges, job discipline, and firing ("Legal Problem Solver," 1994).

Child Abuse or Neglect

This is probably the area in which the bulk of your legal responsibility lies as a paraeducator. Conservative estimates put physical child abuse at 500,000 cases per year or 1,365 cases per day (Toelle, 1993). Note the statistics in Table G–1. You can see why this subject is of prime importance and why increasing numbers of laws are concerned with child abuse and/or neglect.

The Child Abuse Prevention and Treatment Act as amended by the Child Abuse Prevention, Adoption, and Family Services Act of 1988 (Public Law 100–294) defines both abuse and neglect as "physical or mental injury, sexual abuse or exploitation, negligent treatment, or maltreatment" (Koralek, 1992).

The heartbreaking truth is that if you work in a daycare center or in a school, chances are there will be times when either abuse or neglect

TABLE G–1 National Incidence Study (1988) estimates on numbers of children abused, neglected, and sexually abused. N = 1,424,400.

Physical Abuse #	Sexual Abuse #	Emotional Abuse #	Neglect #
311,500	133,600	188,100	917,200

Please note that some children suffered multiple forms of maltreatment.

will be suspected. There is an agency in every state that is mandated by state law to receive and investigate reports of suspected child abuse and neglect. Reporting is a means of getting help for a child or family.

You are under a legal as well as moral obligation to report if you suspect child abuse or neglect. Signs of abuse and neglect are listed in Tables G–2, G–3, G–4, and G–5.) If you suspect abuse or neglect and fail to report, legal penalties are considerable. The state laws determining *failure to report* penalties are diverse; consequences for child care employees range from fines, imprisonment, damage settlements, misdemeanor prosecution, and firing.

TABLE G–2 Signs of Abuse *(Information used courtesy of the Department of Family and Children Services, Cherokee County, GA.)*

Some of the more common indicators of physical abuse are:

Bruises — that occur on the posterior side of the body
that are found in unusual patterns or clusters
that are found on an infant, especially on a baby's face
that show different stages of healing
Bruises are the most common sign of physical abuse. Bruises generally change from blue or purple to yellow over time.

Burns — that appear to be from cigarettes, ropes, irons, or scalding water on the palms of the hands, soles of the feet, or genitals

Lacerations and Abrasions — *cuts and scrapes*
on lips or eyes
on any part of an infant's face
on genitals
on gum tissue (from forced feeding)

Missing or Loosened Teeth

Head Injuries — indicated by absence of hair
hemorrhaging beneath the scalp (from hair being pulled)
subdural hematomas (from hitting or shaking)
retinal hemorrhages or detachment (from shaking)
broken nose or jaw

Skeletal Injuries — broken bones, especially fractures caused by twisting and pulling
stiff, swollen, enlarged joints

Internal Injuries — deep bruises on the abdomen (caused by hitting or kicking)
rupture of major blood vessels
infection in the abdominal cavity (caused by hitting or kicking)

Injuries such as the ones above can also be from accidents. Consider the child's age and developmental stage, the location of the injury, whether there are multiple injuries, the size and shape of the injury, and the explanation for the injury. For example, if an injury is in the exact shape of a belt buckle or bruises all over a child's body are said to have come from a fall on the head, you should be suspicious.

TABLE G–3 Behavioral Characteristics of an Abused Child *(Information used courtesy of the Department of Family and Children Services, Cherokee County, GA.)*

Child who is abused at an early age, frequently and severely:

- unusually neat in eating habits
- overly compliant, avoids confrontation
- lacks curiosity
- seems afraid of physical contact
- cries little
- does not seem to enjoy much of anything
- slow in development (because of all the energy going toward self-protection)
- excessive self-control

Child who is less severely abused, less often, and is a little older when abuse starts:

- timid, easily frightened
- psychosomatic complaints
- seems to crave affection
- persists in declaring love for the abusing parent
- delayed in language development
- occasional temper tantrums
- problems in school even though seems to have normal ability
- either seems to take on the parent role or is very immature in interactions with parent
- becomes attached to strangers

Child who is mildly, infrequently, or inconsistently abused at an older age:

- hurts other children
- controlling
- extremely aggressive
- rages
- hyperactive, short attention span
- demanding
- lags in development
- seems accident-prone or clumsy

Other indicators of abuse:

- embarrassed by abuse
- fearful of discovery
- wears inappropriate clothing, such as long sleeves when it is hot
- refuses to change clothes for gym

Contributing factors:

- family crisis such as bankruptcy, unemployment, death, divorce, illness
- severe personal problems such as drug abuse, alcoholism, mental illness
- child seen as being different, or child who actually is different
- ignorance of normal child development
- abuse of the parent as a child

TABLE G–4 Indications of Neglect *(Information used courtesy of the Department of Family and Children Services, Cherokee County, GA.)*

- a baby shows "failure to thrive"
- falls asleep in school
- learns poorly
- poor attendance or chronic tardiness
- chronically hungry or tired
- begs or collects leftovers or steals from other children's lunches
- comes to school early and stays late
- appears dull, apathetic
- squints
- uses drugs or alcohol
- vandalizes
- participates in sexual misconduct

TABLE G–5 Signs of Emotional Maltreatment *(Information used courtesy of the Department of Family and Children Services, Cherokee County, GA.)*

- when an older child bites, rocks, bangs his head, or sucks his thumb
- feeding disorders
- anxiety during the day and unrealistic fears
- nightmares and sleep disorders
- when an older child continues to wet the bed
- speech disorders, such as stammering or stuttering
- defiance
- withdrawn and antisocial behavior
- distrust and inordinate fear of strangers
- poor relationships with peers
- hypochondriac tendencies
- low self-esteem
- unreasonable fears, anxieties, and hatred
- lack of creativity or ability to play
- apathy, lack of, or low amount of emotion
- apparent unawareness of dangers and risks
- destructive behavior
- obsessive or compulsive behavior
- extremes in behavior
- frequent daydreaming or fantasies
- academic failure
- sadomasochistic behavior
- self-destructive behavior

The amount of time allowed before reporting suspected child abuse is delineated in state reporting statutes; in most states a report must be made within 24 or 48 hours (Berliner, 1993).

Should reporting be necessary, you need the following information on hand:

- Child's name, address, and phone number
- Day neglect or abuse was first noticed
- Marks and location of marks on child
- Pertinent information on child and/or family

To report a suspected case of child abuse, you should notify the mandated agency in the state *where the child lives.* The correct agency is listed in the telephone directory, usually in the Government Blue Pages under the state's Rehabilitative Services, under Children and Family Services, or the Yellow Pages. Often a hotline number will be given inside the front cover of your phone book. If you have difficulty finding the agency in your community, call your local police department or call the Childhelp USA/IOF Foresters National Child Abuse Hotline (800) 442–4453. Childhelp USA/IOF Foresters has listings of protective service agencies across the country (National Committee for Prevention of Child Abuse, 1992).

What are other legal implications of reporting suspected abuse? You are protected under the law in most states when you make a report of suspected child abuse or neglect. Most state law codes provide for reporter immunity from civil or criminal liability and from termination of employment. You do not have to *prove* that child abuse has occurred; that is up to the investigator (National Committee for Prevention of Child Abuse, 1992). In most states you may even be able to make a report anonymously.

However, bad faith reporters (false reports) are *not* protected in most states; many states are considering or have passed legislation as a reaction to unfounded reporting that has damaged individuals and families. In these states, unless a caller gives a name, the report will not be investigated. Stiff legal penalties such as fines, misdemeanor prosecution, etc., may exist for malicious reporting.

Berliner also suggests that the cultural values and ethnic differences of parents should be considered before making a child abuse report. Recent parent émigres may be unaware of U.S. laws. Berliner (1993) notes that informing the parents when a child abuse report is about to be undertaken is preferable in most cases.

Unfortunately, abuse and neglect can happen in early childhood facilities. Koralek (1992) points out:

Recently, media attention has focused on incidents of sexual abuse that have occurred in child care centers and family child care homes. Individuals who sexually abuse young children in child care settings might be family child care providers, caregivers, directors, support staff, bus drivers, or volunteers: in short, anyone who has access to the children. Abuse occurs most frequently in bathrooms while children are being assisted with toileting. For this reason, many centers have removed the walls from toilet stalls in bathrooms used by children aged 5 and under. A recent study defined the risk to children as 5.5 sexually abused children per 10,000 enrolled, which is lower than the risk that children might be sexually abused in their own households, 8.9 per 10,000 children under 6 years of age.

In Finkelhor's (1988) study of reported perpetrators of child abuse in child care settings the following are listed:

- Owners or directors
- Teachers or other child-care professionals
- Nonprofessionals (aides, assistants, volunteers, parents, teenagers)
- Janitors and bus drivers
- Family members of the staff (husbands, adolescent sons, daughters, etc.)
- Multiple perpetrators (a group of people)

As you can see, it is generally agreed that an abuser in a child care facility can be anyone with access to the children. Both men and women are perpetrators. Commonly, men are considered the prime perpetrators of sexual abuse, but Finkelhor (1988) states that "women were significantly involved in the sexual abuse of both boys and girls in day-care settings."

Finkelhor (1988) emphasizes the diversity in child abuse cases involving early childhood personnel:

These cases have been extremely varied. A small proportion resembled the McMartin situation, with its large number of victims and perpetrators and the complexity of its legal proceedings. Other cases involved only a single abusing teacher. Some took place in small family-based operations where the husband of the operator molested one or two children. Others involved trusted centers where bus drivers or janitors were implicated and were quickly dismissed from their jobs.

Places with excellent reputations, centers with interlocking doors, federal grant programs, and church-operated facilities have all had incidents of child abuse.

As a paraeducator, it is essential that you listen to the children, observe closely, and think critically when suspicions are aroused.

Few researchers have tried to compare the risk of child abuse young children encounter at day care facilities versus their own families, but Finkelhor (1988) offers estimates in Table G–6. As you recall, Koralek cited a study that seemed to indicate a higher chance of abuse in homes than in child care facilities.

About half of all states require criminal record checks of new employees. This was mentioned in Chapter 13 as being of interest to you as you go through the job search process. Table 13–4 shows information concerning state requirements to investigate backgrounds of child care personnel in licensed facilities. The screening of people, though debated, may alert job applicants with past histories of violence and abuse that criminal background checks *do* take place by law in a number of states and will hopefully deter them from contact with children.

Many states specify that licensing agencies must establish standards involving child/staff ratios, health and safety, discipline and use of corporal punishment. Check the specifics of your state.

This subject of child abuse is very difficult to face. One of the hardest aspects for honest, caring paraeducators is dealing with an at-

TABLE G–6 Summary of Risk of Reported Abuse in Day-Care Centers and Families From D. Finkelhor, L. M. Williams, & N. Burns, *Nursery Crimes: Sexual Abuse in Day Care,* © 1988. Reprinted by permission of Sage Publications.

Conclusions

I

30.7 of every 10,000 *centers* have cases of reported child sexual abuse

15.3 of every 10,000 *families* have cases of reported child sexual abuse

II

5.5 children out of every 10,000 enrolled in day-care *centers* are reported to be sexually abused

8.9 children out of every 10,000 ($\leq$6 years old) children in *families* are reported to be sexually abused

III

Although a day-care center is more likely to be reported for child sexual abuse than is a family, a given child has a lower risk of being abused in a day-care center than in his or her own home. (This is because there are more children in each day-care center, thus spreading out the risk.)

mosphere of distrust. It is certainly not pleasant to suspect a parent or a coworker of anything as awful as abuse. Likewise, it is very uncomfortable to think that you yourself could be the object of others' suspicions. Through communication with your employer and by using caution you can protect yourself from the unfounded suspicions of others. Phyfe-Perkins (1989) recommends the following preventive actions:

- Staff in-service for all new hires.
- Copies of the state reporting law given to all staff.
- Training in recognizing symptoms.
- Training in documenting suspicions and concerns.
- Written school policies and written child toileting and diapering procedures.
- Recognition of employee at-risk situations including nap time, lighting, cot placement, staff lying down, lunch times, playground supervision, field trips, and emergencies (see Table G–7).
- Offering a personal safety curriculum for the children.

What might cause child care workers to commit child abuse? That is a difficult question to answer because no one factor accounts for child maltreatment, but it is a question Koralek (1992) has attempted to answer. Koralek supplies the following possible explanations:

- Inadequate training and supervision
- Insufficient knowledge of child development
- Difficulty in guiding behavior in appropriate ways
- Angry, punitive reactions to child behaviors

TABLE G–7 Principal Time When Abuse Occurred: In-Depth Sample (in percentages) From D. Finkelhor, L. M. Williams, & N. Burns, *Nursery Crimes: Sexual Abuse in Day Care,* © 1988. Reprinted by permission of Sage Publications.

Time	Cases (N = 43)
Naptime	31
Bathrooming	21
Beginning/end of day	17
Outdoor play	14
Field trip	3
Overnight	3
Other	10

- Stress and depression
- Unrealistic expectations
- Substance abuse
- Working with a child or children described as hyperactive, health problem-prone, learning disabled, psychologically impaired
- Individual worker personality and view of the world
- A history of family violence
- Poverty and severe emotional pressure
- Abused in childhood
- A belief in harsh punishment
- Isolation

Some states are moving in legislative directions that will benefit the children, the parents, and the workers. North Carolina and New York licensing laws mandate that centers provide information to parents and guardians regarding 1) the detection of child abuse and maltreatment, 2) procedures for reporting abuse and neglect, and 3) how to seek legal remedies (Bulkley & Jackson, 1989). Idaho and some other states grant parents the right to enter a child facility at all times while their children are in attendance.

Emergency Care and Good Samaritan Laws

The next discussion deals with both obligations and protections. Of course parents are the ones who have the legal right and responsibility to provide medical care for their minor children. By law in most states early childhood centers obtain emergency information and authorization signatures from parents when they enroll their children. The information alerts the center about specific emergency care for the children; authorization signatures may give the parents' consent to emergency treatment if they are unreachable. When parents cannot be reached or emergency forms are lost or destroyed in a disaster, it becomes your lawful obligation to obtain medical care for a child when that child's life or health is in danger.

Although state Good Samaritan Laws vary, they usually offer immunity from responsibility if the rescuer exercises *ordinary or reasonable care* ("Legal Problem Solver," 1994). These laws protect you from liability for acts you commit while providing assistance to someone in distress.

The Child Care Law Center explains Good Samaritan law this way:

If the situation is a life-threatening emergency requiring you to immediately render some form of first aid (e.g., mouth-to-mouth resuscitation), you should give only what aid you are capable of. According to California's 'Good Samaritan' law (Health and Safety Code Section 1999.102), a person render-

ing emergency care at the scene of an emergency cannot be held liable for damages resulting from any act or failure to act. However, the person rendering aid is only protected as long as 1) professional medical care was unavailable, and 2) she/he acted in good faith without expecting to be paid for his/her efforts.

(CCLC, 1992)

You are under at least a moral obligation to give help to a child who needs it. In addition to difficulty living with yourself, you could also face legal consequences if you do not help. An article in the New York Times (November 4, 1995) reported a million dollar lawsuit involving a teacher aide and others who did not give assistance to a girl who was choking on a hot dog. The thirteen-year-old girl died. The lawsuit was filed by the girl's mother against both the Board of Education and New York City. According to testimony, a whole string of events led to the girl's death. First of all, lunch was so delayed that students only had two minutes to eat, so teachers allowed them to take their food to their next class. The seventh grade girl was called on while she had food in her mouth, and she choked. The teacher sent her to the bathroom, an aide unlocked the bathroom door for her, then told her to drink some water. The girl collapsed and then the aide found a teacher who had had first-aid training. The teacher got to the girl but did not do anything. The jury found that the school staff was negligent and awarded just over a million dollars to the mother.

Many times early childhood workers are forced to make decisions that might open them to lawsuits. When children are injured, trapped in equipment, bitten by animals, insects or reptiles, emergency actions may need to be undertaken *on the spot* and the results are not always what you would desire or expect. Nevertheless, when a child needs help, the caretaking adults must, in good faith, do what they can to help. Although schools and centers are going to great lengths to prevent unauthorized release, a staff member could be fooled and release a child to an adult with forged credentials who comes to take a child to a "dying" parent or grandparent, etc. A paraeducator may attempt to usher children from a burning or collapsing building and in the process a child could be injured by a car. You could be faced with any number of possibilities when you are in a forced position of being a Good Samaritan.

Protect Yourself and Others

How can you best be prepared for future possibilities? What should you do about your own liability as a paraeducator? It is imperative that you heed the following suggestions:

- Know what licensing law requires.
- Know what child abuse law requires.

- Report dangerous situations, room and yard areas, furniture and equipment.
- Question your employer about liability coverage.
- Act prudently in emergencies.
- Practice disaster drills.
- Obtain early childhood association insurance, or self-insurance for liability if your employer's business coverage is faulty.

Learn as much as you can about all kinds of different situations so that you can be as prepared as possible. Take the American Red Cross Infant and Child Care First Aid Course and get certified in CPR even if you are not required to do so. (Some places and states do require these for anyone working with infants or young children.) These courses give you some protection if you use what you have learned in the instructed manner.

In order to guard yourself from any suspicion or false claim of abuse, avoid unmonitored situations. For example, if you are left in the classroom with a child while the teacher and the other students go out on the playground, be sure that you leave the door wide open. Ideally, you should be within vision or sound range of a teacher or another paraeducator whenever you are working alone with a child. In fact, your school or center should also be taking measures to guard against suspicion or possibilities for abuse. For example, toilet facilities should be constructed in such a way that they will decrease risks of undetected activity. Kingsbury, Vogler, and Benero suggest that:

> *Toilet facilities in a toddler program should be as open to view as possible. Since toilet training activities can sometimes be viewed as an opportunity for abuse or improper handling of a situation, the more open to view the toilet facility is, the lower the risk involved can be. (1990)*

Well, there has been a lot of material to take in within this section. Information concerning laws that protect children with special needs was introduced in Chapter 7. The purpose of this appendix has been to at least familiarize you with some of the laws that affect your job as a paraeducator. You may have even wondered whether the information is necessary for you. Yes, it is. Laws and regulations affect almost every aspect of a paraeducator's working day, including working conditions, wages, job benefits, personal liability, and professional status. Your awareness of legal standards protects the children, their families, and, ultimately, *you.*

Where to Find Answers to Common Questions

Bibliography

Allen, K. E., & Marotz, L. (1994). *Developmental profiles: Pre-birth through eight.* (2nd ed.). Albany, NY: Delmar Publishers.

Allen, K.E., & Schwartz, I.S. (1996). *The exceptional child: Inclusion in early childhood education.* Albany, NY: Delmar Publishers.

American Academy of Pediatrics and Gerber Products Co. (1981). *A handbook of child safety.* Fremont, MI: Gerber Products Co.

Armstrong, T. (1996, February). ADD: Does it really exist? *Phi Delta Kappan,* (Vol.77, No.6, pp. 424–428).

Ayers, G. E. (1994, January). Statistical profile of special education in the United States. *Teaching exceptional children* supplement (Vol. 26, No.3, pp. 1–4).

Barth, P. (1992). *Smart start: Elementary education for the 21st century.* Golden, CO: North American Press.

Bauer, A.M., & Shea, T.M. (1990). *Teaching exceptional students in your classroom.* Boston: Allyn & Bacon.

Becker, G. (1992). © *Copyright: A guide to information and resources.* Lake Mary, FL.

Bell, I. W., & Wieckert, J. E. (1980). *Basic classroom skills through games.* Littleton, CO: Libraries Unlimited, Inc.

Bennett, D.I., Meyer C., Meyer, D.E. (1994). *Elementary Field Experiences.* Albany, NY: Delmar Publishers.

Bennett, N. (1976). *Teaching styles and pupil progress.* Cambridge, MA: Harvard University Press.

Bennetts, L. (1996, July). Why are today's parents such wimps? *Ladies Home Journal* (Vol.113, No.7, p.84, 86–88).

Berns, R. M., (1994). *Topical child development.* Albany, NY: Delmar Publishers.

Brown, J., & Kritsonis, W. A. (1992, December). 13 ways not to be part of the discipline problem. *The Education Digest.* (Vol. 58, pp. 51–55). Article condensed from *School discipline: The art of survival.*

Bruns, J. H. (1992). *They can but they don't.* New York: Penguin Group.

Bullock, J. (1993). Supporting the development of shy children. *Day Care and Early Education,* 20 (4), 8–10.

Carl B. & Richard, N. (no date). *One piece of the puzzle: A practical guide for schools interested in implementing a school readiness program.* Lumberville, PA: Modern Learning Press.

Charles, C.M. (1989). *Building classroom discipline.* White Plains, NY: Longman, Inc.

Charlesworth, R. (1996). *Understanding child development.* (4th ed.) Albany, NY: Delmar Publishers.

Cherokee County Board of Education, uncopyrighted materials and information, especially the workshop for paraprofessionals led by Jean Jackson.

Cherokee County Department of Family and Children Services.

Chinn, P.C., Winn, J. & Walters, R.H. (1985). *Two-way talking with parents of special children: A process of positive communication.* St. Louis: C.V. Mosby.

Clearinghouse on Handicapped and Gifted Children. (1990). Being at ease with handicapped children. *The Council for Exceptional Children* ERIC document #E366. Reston, VA.

Cruickshank, W.M. (1977). *Learning disabilities in home, school, and community.* Syracuse, NY: Syracuse University Press.

Daugherty, J. (1996, February). Taming temper tantrums. *Atlanta Parent* (Vol.15, No. 2, p.20).

Department of Family and Children Services, Cherokee County, GA. Information about abuse and neglect and prevention.

DeSpelder, L.A., & Prettyman, N. (1980). *A guidebook for teaching family living.* Boston: Allyn and Bacon, Inc.

di Paolo, T. (1990). *Oral presentation.* GA Preschool Association — 1990 Annual Study Conference.

Division for the Visually Handicapped. (1992, August). Visual impairments. *The Council for Exceptional Children* ERIC document #E511, EDO EC 92–1. Reston, VA.

Division of Innovation and Development. (1994). To assure the free appropriate public education of all children with disabilities." *Sixteenth Annual Report to Congress on the Implementation of The Individuals with Disabilities Education Act.* Washington, DC: U.S. Department of Education.

Division of Innovation and Development. (1993). To assure the free appropriate public education of all children with disabilities. *Fifteenth Annual Report to Congress on the Implementation of The Individuals with Disabilities Education Act.* Washington, DC: U.S. Department of Education.

Division of Innovation and Development. (1992). To assure the free appropriate public education of all children with disabilities. *Fourteenth Annual Report to Congress on the Implementation of The Individuals with Disabilities Education Act.* Washington, DC: U.S. Department of Education.

Dobson, J. (1992). *The new dare to discipline.* Wheaton, IL: Tyndale House.

Feingold, B.F. (1975). *Why your child is hyperactive.* New York: Random House.

Fernandez, J. A. (1993). *Tales out of school: Joseph Fernandez's crusade to rescue American education.* Boston: Little, Brown, and Company.

Finkelhor, D., Meyer, L., & Burns, N. (1988). *Nursery crimes: Sexual abuse in day care.* California: Sage Publications.

Finn, C. E., Jr., & Rebarber, T., (1992). (Ed. for Educational Excellence Network, Vanderbilt University). *Education reform in the 90s.* New York: Macmillan Publishing Company.

Flating, S. (1991). *Child care: A parent's guide.* New York: Facts On File, Inc.

Florine Dial Johnston Elementary School handbook. Principal- Jane Elliott. Woodstock, GA.

Fraiberg, S.H. (1959). *The magic years.* New York: Charles Scribner & Sons.

Freed, M. (1989). *The educator's desk reference: A sourcebook of educational information & research* (EDR). New York: American Council on Education & Macmillan Publishing Company.

Garber, S. W., Ph.D., Garber, M. D., Ph.D., & Spizman, R. F. (1992). *Good behavior made easy.* Fallbrook, CA: Family Life Productions.

Georgia Preschool Association. (1990). Annual Study Conference, Feb. 23 & 24, College Park, GA.

Gerber, M. (1971). *Resources for infant educators.* Los Angeles: Resources for Infant Educators.

Gerlach, K. Ph.D. Pacific Lutheran University, Tacoma, WA. (phone conversation).

Gibson, R. (1993). *You and your child number games.* Saffron Hill, London, England: Usborne Publishing Ltd.

Gibson, R. (1993). *You and your child reading games.* Saffron Hill, London, England: Usborne Publishing Ltd.

Good, T. & Brophy, J.E. (1984). *Looking in classrooms (3rd ed.)* New York: Harper & Row.

Gordon, T. (1989). *Teaching children self-discipline.* New York: Time Books.

Gorden, T. (1974). *Parent effectiveness training.* New York: Peter Wyden, Inc.

Harter, S. (1989). *Manual for the self-perception profile for adolescents.* Denver, CO: University of Denver.

Harter, S. (1983). Developmental perspectives on the self-system. In P.H. Mussen (Ed), *Handbook of child psychology (4th ed.),* (Vol. 4). New York: Wiley.

Hawkins, D. (1995, October 30). Johnny can read for cash and freebies. *U.S. News & World Report* (Vol. 119, No.17, p.72–73).

Hendricks, C. M. (1993, March). Safer playgrounds for young children. *ERIC Clearinghouse on Teacher Education.* (EDO-SP 92/5).

Herr, J. & Libby, Y. (1995). *Creative resources for young children.* (Albany, NY: Delmar Publishers.

Holt, J. (1986). *How children fail.* Washington, DC: National Association for the Education of Young Children.

Honig, A.S. (1988). Humor development in young children. *Young Children, 43,* (4) 60–73.

Hyson, M.C. (1979). Lobster on the side walk. In. L. Adams & B. Garlick (Eds.), *Ideas that work with young children* (Vol. 2. pp. 183–185). Washington, DC: National Association for the Education of Young Children.

Jerkins, L. (1996, February). News you can use. *Atlanta Parent* (Vol. 15, No. 2, p. 4).

Jerkins, L. (1996, February). Teaching kids to value differences. *Atlanta Parent.* (Vol.15, No. 2, pp. 5, 37).

Joel, I.G. (1993). *Every employee's guide to the law.* New York: Pantheon Books.

Johnson, H. M. (1996, July). Defensive play. *Ladies Home Journal* (Vol. 113, No. 7, p. 70).

Johnston, S. D., et al. (1995, Fall). A new partner in the IEP process: The laptop computer. *Teaching exceptional children.* (Vol. 28, No. 1, pp. 46–48).

Jones, E. (1986). *Teaching Adults.* Washington, DC: National Association for the Education of Young Children.

Katz, L. & Ward, E. (1978). *Ethical behavior in early childhood education.* Washington, DC: National Association for the Education of Young Children.

Kaye, P. (1991). *Games for learning: Ten minutes a day to help your child do well in school—from kindergarten to third grade.* New York: Harper Collins.

Kephart, N.C. (1967). Teaching the child with a perceptual handicap. In M. Bartner (Ed.). *Evaluation and education of children with brain damage.* Springfield, IL: Charles C. Thomas Publisher, pp. 147–192.

Kingsbury, D. F.; Vogler, S. K., & Benero, C. (1990). *The everyday guide to opening and operating a child care center.* Lakewood, CO: Vade Mecum Press.

Kirk, S.A. (1972). *Educating exceptional children.* Boston: Houghton Mifflin.

Kohlberg, L. (1968). The child as a moral philosopher. *Psychology Today, 2,* 25–30.

Koffel, L. (1994). *Teaching workplace skills: creative ways to teach students the skills employees want.* Houston, TX: Gulf Publishing Company.

Kurkjiian, J. *Music for the young child.* California Music Educators Association Conference, March 17, 1990. Oakland, California.

Lickona, R. (1983). *Raising good children.* New York: Bantam.

Lovitt, T. C. (1978). Managing inappropriate behaviors in the classroom. *The Council for Exceptional Children* (ERIC No. ED 157 255). Reston VA.

Machado, J.M. & Botnarescue, H.M. (1997). *Student teaching: Early childhood practicum guide.* Albany, NY: Delmar Publishers.

Maggs, M. M. (1980). *The classroom survival book: A practical manual for teachers.* New York: New Viewpoints.

Martinez Unified School District. (1996, Winter). Correspondence with Richard B. McLaughlin, Director of Administrative Services. Martinez, CA.

Meigs, B. (1996, Winter). Special education teacher in Kansas City, MO. Correspondence and phone conversations.

Meisels, S.J. (1987). Uses and abuses of developmental screening and school readiness testing. *Young Children, 42* (2), 4–6, 68–73.

Meyen, E.L. (Ed.). (1978). *Exceptional children and youth:* An introduction. Denver: Love.

Morisi, T. L. (1994, July). Employment in public schools and the student-to-employee ratio. *Monthly Labor Review* (Vol. 117, pp. 40–44).

Mt. Diablo Unified School District. (1996, Winter). Correspondence with Anne Burk, Personnel Specialist. Concord, CA.

Mulac, M. (1971). *Educational games for fun.* New York: Harper & Row, Publishers, Inc.

National Clearinghouse for Professions in Special Education. Paraprofessionals have the advantage to advance to a professional career, Fact sheet #20. *The Council for Exceptional Children.*

Nechas, E., & Foley, D. (1995, December). Children's health matters, *Atlanta Parent* (Vol.14, No. 12, pp. 20–21).

Office of Special Education Programs. (1995). *Seventeenth annual report to Congress on the Implementation of The Individuals with Disabilities Education Act,* excerpts. Washington, DC: U.S. Department of Education. (Courtesy of the National Clearinghouse for Professions in Special Education).

Office of Special Education Programs. (1992, Fall). Section 504 of The Rehabilitation Act of 1973 and The Americans with Disabilities

Act of 1990. *Legal Foundations,* Number 1. Washington, DC: U.S. Department of Education. (ERIC document, courtesy of the Clearinghouse on Handicapped and Gifted Children).

Office of Special Education Programs. (1992, Winter). The Individuals with Disabilities Education Act, *Legal Foundations,* Number 2. Washington, DC: U.S. Department of Education. (ERIC document E537, courtesy of the Clearinghouse on Handicapped and Gifted Children).

Oppenheim, J. (1989). *The elementary school handbook.* A bank street college of education book. New York: Random House, Inc.

Paraeducators from various locales who graciously discussed many subjects and offered information and materials, especially Jo Hogan, Cherokee County, GA.

Pepalis, B. (1996, March 1). Volunteers plan march for healthy babies. *Lakeside Ledger* community newspaper, p. 7.

Perrone, V. (1993). *101 educational conversations with your kindergartener-first grader.* New York: Chelsea House Publishers.

Piaget, J. (1950). *Introduction to genetic epistemology.* Paris: University Press.

Piaget, J. (1965). *The moral judgment of the child.* New York: Free Press.

Pickett, A. L. (1993). *Improving the performance of paraeducators in the workforce: A technical assistance manual for administrators and staff developers.* New York: Center for Advanced Study in Education, The Graduate School and University Center, City University of New York, grant through the U.S. Department of Education.

Pinkerton, D. (1991, November). Substance exposed infants and children. Clearinghouse on Handicapped and Gifted Children. *The Council for Exceptional Children.* ERIC Digest #E 505, EDO-EC-91-10. Reston, VA.

Reich, P.A. (1986). *Language development.* Englewood Cliffs, NJ: Prentice Hall.

Rimm, S. B. (1995). *Why bright kids get poor grades: And what you can do about it.* New York: Crown Publishers, Inc.

Rogers, C.R. (1961). *On becoming a person.* Boston: Houghton Mifflin Company.

Rogovin, A. (1980). *Let me do it!* New York: Thomas Y. Crowell.

Roopnarine, J.L., & Honig, A.S. (1985). The unpopular child. *Young Children, 40* (6), 59–64.

Rubin, K.H. (1982). Social and social-cognitive developmental characteristics of young isolate, normal, and socialable children. In K.H. Rubin & H.S. Ross (Eds.) *Peer relationships and social skills in childhood* (pp. 353–374). New York: Springer–Verlag.

Sanders, B. (1992). *School daze.* Tarrytown, NY: Fleming H. Revell Company.

Schickedanz, J. Chay, S., Gopin, P., Sheng, L., Song, S., and Wild, N. (1990) *Preschoolers and academics: Some thoughts.* Young Children, 46(1), 4–13.

Sciarra, D.J. & Dorsey, A.G. (1995). *Developing and administering a child care center.* Albany, NY: Delmar Publishers.

Selye, H. (1974). *Stress without distress.* New York: The New American Library, Inc.

Shafer, E. (1984, Winter). My experience as a paraprofessional. *Social Policy* (Vol. 14, No. 3, pp. 47–49).

Smelter, R., et al. (1996, February). Is attention deficit disorder becoming a desired diagnosis? *Phi Delta Kappan* (Vol. 77, No. 6, pp. 429–432).

Stout, D. (1995, November 4). Jury awards girl's mother $1 million in choking death. *New York Times.*

Strauss, A.A. & Lehtinen, L.E. (1947). *Psychopathology of the brain-injured child.* New York: Grane & Stratton.

The Teacher's Almanack. West Nyack, New York: The Center for Applied Research in Education, Inc.

Thompson, A. M. (1996, February). Attention deficit hyperactivity disorder—A parent's perspective. *Phi Delta Kappan* (Vol. 77, No. 6, pp. 433–436).

Thonis, E.W. (February/March 1990). *Teaching English as a second language.* Reading Today, IRA, 7 (4), p. 8.

Trademarks and copyrights. (1982). Reviewed by Wechsler, N. F. *The new book of knowledge.* Danbury, CT: Grolier Incorporated.

Wallace, D. & McMurray, S. (1995, October 30). How to disagree (without being disagreeable). *U.S. News & World Report* (Vol. 119, No. 17, special supplement).

Weiss, S., (Ed.). (1995, September). *NEA Today* (special ed., education support personnel) (Vol. 14, No.1, pp. 1–64).

White, L. (1996, February; 1995, December issues). *Atlanta Parent.* Atlanta, GA: Atlanta Parent, Inc.

White, R. (1994, Winter). Paraprofessionals in special education. *Social Policy* (Vol. 14, No. 3, pp. 44–46).

Index

Note: Page numbers in **bold type** reference non-text material. Entries in **bold type** reference titles.

Printed in Canada